TALKIN' TAR HEEL

Talkin' Tar Heel

HOW OUR VOICES TELL

THE STORY OF NORTH CAROLINA

Walt Wolfram & Jeffrey Reaser

The University of North Carolina Press | Chapel Hill

This book was published with the assistance of the
Blythe Family Fund of the University of North Carolina Press.

Designed and set in Quadraat types by Sally Scruggs. The paper in this book meets
the guidelines for permanence and durability of the Committee on Production
Guidelines for Book Longevity of the Council on Library Resources. The University
of North Carolina Press has been a member of the Green Press Initiative since 2003.

Library of Congress Cataloging-in-Publication Data
Wolfram, Walt, 1941–
Talkin' tar heel : how our voices tell the story of North Carolina /
Walt Wolfram, Jeffrey Reaser.
pages cm
The book is enhanced by maps and illustrations and augmented by more than
100 audio and video recordings, which can be found online at talkintarheel.com.
Includes bibliographical references and index.
ISBN 978-1-4696-1436-6 (hardback)
ISBN 978-1-4696-2999-5 (pbk.)
ISBN 978-1-4696-1437-3 (ebook)
1. English language—Dialects—North Carolina. 2. English language—Dialects—
North Carolina—Electronic information resources. 3. English language—North
Carolina. 4. Americanisms—North Carolina. 5. North Carolina—Languages.
I. Reaser, Jeffrey Leo, 1976–II. Title.

PE3101.N76W65 2014
427'.9756—dc23
2013041124

CONTENTS

PREFACE

Linguists usually write books about particular languages or dialects, not about language diversity within a political state. But there are also few states that showcase regional, ethnic, and social diversity of language more stylishly than the Tar Heel State. In many respects, North Carolina is a microcosm of the vast range of language differences that have developed over time and space in the United States. After more than two decades of interviewing and recording thousands of residents and shooting hundreds of hours of video footage, we feel that we would be remiss if we did not share the rich assortment of North Carolina voices with a broader audience.

Under the rubric of the North Carolina Language and Life Project (NCLLP), we have undertaken the challenge of describing the dialects and languages of North Carolina. The NCLLP is a unique, language-based program at North Carolina State University that focuses on research and outreach programs related to language in North Carolina. Its goals are: (1) to gather basic research information about language varieties in order to understand the nature of language variation and change; (2) to document language varieties in North Carolina and beyond as they reflect the varied cultural traditions of their residents; (3) to provide information about language differences for public and educational interests; and (4) to use research material for the improvement of educational programs about language and culture.

Since the NCLLP's inception in 1993, its staff has been conducting sociolinguistic interviews with residents in North Carolina that connect language, culture, and history. Discussions typically cover a wide range of topics, from history and remembrances to current livelihood and lifestyle changes. All of the interviews are archived on a website hosted by the library at North Carolina State University, the Sociolinguistic Archive and Analysis Project (http://ncslaap.lib.ncsu.edu). This interactive, Web-based archive of sociolinguistic recordings integrates with annotation features and technical analysis tools. It is an ongoing, constantly growing archive that contains (as of September 2013) over 6,000 audio files, 3,200 hours of audio, 100 hours of transcribed audio, and more than 1 million words accurately linked to the audio. We are serious about preserving the voices of Tar Heel speech in the digital age.

The NCLLP is a major research program, but it is more than that. Following the adage "if knowledge is worth having, then it is worth sharing," we have been engaged in a number of community-based language and dialect projects that focus on regional, social, and ethnic varieties of southern English, attempting to represent the major dialect areas of North Carolina as well as the urban-rural dimension of dialect patterning. Extensive, community-based studies have taken place in more than twenty-five different community sites spanning literally from Murphy to Manteo. We initially focused on more remote, rural areas, but our colleagues have more recently undertaken studies of urban areas so that we can understand the current rapidly expanding metropolitan context of North Carolina. We have studied ethnic and social dimensions of language differences that include African American varieties of English, American Indian languages and varieties of American Indian English, and emerging ethnic varieties of English spoken by Latinos in rural and metropolitan areas.

In addition to its sociolinguistic research commitment, the NCLLP engages in a full array of public-outreach programs related to language diversity. These activities have led to the production of a series of television documentaries that range from a general profile of language variation throughout North Carolina (Voices of North Carolina, 2005) to documentaries on particular dialects, such as Outer Banks English (The Ocracoke Brogue, 1996; The Carolina Brogue, 2009), Southern Highland speech in western North Carolina (Mountain Talk, 2004), Lumbee English (Indian by Birth: The Lumbee Dialect, 2001), and languages (Spanish Voices, 2011), with more in progress. The staff of the NCLLP has further produced a number of oral history CD collections and published trade books on particular varieties of English, such as Lumbee English and Outer Banks English. They have also constructed exhibits on dialects at museums and cultural centers in partnership with local communities as well as at the State Fair in Raleigh. A dialect-awareness curriculum for middle school students has been developed throughout the state (Voices of North Carolina: From the Atlantic to Appalachia, 2007), and staff members routinely give presentations and conduct workshops on language diversity in the public schools and at local civic organizations, including preservation and historical societies.

The simple goal of this book is to share knowledge and respect for the heritage of languages and dialects in North Carolina in a readable, audible, and visual format accessible to the general reader. We try to avoid linguistic jargon, but when it is necessary to use technical terms, we define them in a way that our nonlinguist friends and family can understand. We also employ a convention used in our field where dialect words and structures are written in italics to separate them from the rest of the sentence. Most of the time, these are followed immediately by definitions or translations, which appear in parentheses and quotation marks to keep them separate. We also include more than 125 audio and video enhancements from our rich archive of audio and video footage as well as other resources to allow the voices and people to speak for themselves. Though the extensive integration of audio and visual enhancements throughout the text is somewhat novel in the field of linguistics, the inclusion of the clips seems as natural as language diversity itself. We want the general reader to experience language and dialect rather than imagine it, and experiencing the enhancements is easy. Each enhancement has a brief description so that the reader knows what he or she might hear or see. All the reader has to do is navigate any Web browser to the provided URL or use a smartphone or any device with a QR reader to snap a picture of the QR code to access the media directly. In the enhanced e-reader version of the book, these enhancements are embedded in the text itself.

From the onset of this project, Walt Wolfram's goal was "to have my wife, Marge, read this book, listen to the audios, and see the people for herself." Marge, an avid reader, is a nonlinguist who finds linguistic books boring. At the same time, Marge, like most people, finds language differences curious and captivating in her everyday interactions with people. Our challenge, then, has been to capture and present the inherent language intrigue that language differences hold for the general public. We hope that our appreciation of and respect for the language traditions of the Tar Heel State will resonate distinctively in the voices of the North Carolinians represented here.

WALT WOLFRAM AND JEFFREY REASER

ACKNOWLEDGMENTS

No project of this magnitude is possible without a community. In fact, one of the greatest attributes of the staff of North Carolina Language and Life Project is the collaborative spirit and teamwork. For a couple of decades, we have had an outstanding collective of faculty, students, and other professional partners. We complement and support each other, work hard, and have lots of fun in the process. We even eat well—if not healthfully—from the limitless snacks that fill one of the cabinets in the Linguistics Lab. We hope that the presentation of language in this book is representative of our joyful spirit and the pride we take in portraying the language legacy of the Tar Heel State.

The description of language in *Talkin' Tar Heel* comes from the efforts of our linguistic colleagues, our student researchers, and, perhaps most of all, the many community participants who shared their lives and language with us over the years. North Carolina State University faculty colleagues Drs. Erik R. Thomas, Robin M. Dodsworth, Agnes Bolonyai, and Jeff Mielke have conducted many research projects that we rely on in our descriptions, and colleagues such as Dr. Connie C. Eble from the University of North Carolina at Chapel Hill and Drs. Boyd Davis and Rebecca Roeder from the University of North Carolina at Charlotte contributed greatly to our understanding of North Carolina speech. Professors Eble and Davis read an earlier draft of the manuscript and provided invaluable comments and guidance. Dr. Jeffrey (Jeff) Crow, the former deputy secretary of Archives and History for the North Carolina Department of Cultural Resources and a respected historian of North Carolina, graciously read the chapter on history and made helpful suggestions about the historical context of North Carolina language and dialect development; Dr. Kirk Hazen of West Virginia University read and made useful comments on an early version of chapter 4 on urban and rural dialect differences; Dr. Bridget Anderson of Old Dominion University made useful suggestions on chapter 6 on Mountain Talk and graciously provided photographs for that chapter as well; Dr. Hartwell Francis, director of the Western Carolina University Cherokee Language Program and Dr. Ives Goddard, curator emeritus in the Department of Anthropology of the Natural History of the Smithsonian Institution, offered useful feedback on chapter 8 regarding American Indian languages in North Carolina; and Dr. Phillip Carter of Florida International University and Dr. Mary E. Kohn of Kansas State University provided beneficial comments and feedback on chapter 10 related to Spanish and Hispanicized English. Despite the generous amount of help from so many colleagues, we are certain there remain shortcomings in the text, for which we take full responsibility.

Graduate-student contributors to our research and engagement over the years are too numerous to name, but a dedicated group of students worked directly and extensively on the project. Jaclyn Daugherty and Martha Summerlin spent a couple of semesters extracting and compiling audio and video materials for the book's enhancements. Joel Schneier became our skilled in-house cartographer, Web master, and counsel on many technical and substantive aspects of presentation, and Meghan Deanna Cooper took the lead in copyright permissions, proofing, formatting, and related editing tasks as intern editor on the project. Caroline Myrick completed the audio and visual collections, recording additional samples and integrating them into the text. She also read and commented on the entire text and provided many of the captions for our enhancements and figures. Furthermore, she was instrumental in organizing and selecting many of the photographs. Instead of listing her additional contributions, we simply note that we can't recall any part of the process that she didn't work on. Without the commitment of these remarkable student colleagues who dedicated their summer to our mission, we would not have completed the book and audio and video enhancements on schedule. As usual, our students were the best!

Videographers Danica Cullinan and Neal Hutcheson, whose documentary productions have greatly enriched the understanding of language and life in North Carolina, helped organize and compile the audios and videos selected for the enhancements and produced some clips just for the book. They also are responsible for collecting the vast majority of the original video footage that we have used from archives of the North Carolina Language and Life Project. Without the collection of this footage over the last fifteen years, this project would have been limited to the traditional parameters of a book. Neal and Danica's creative vision and tireless work have demonstrated that culture is best understood when presented by local voices and framed by indigenous vistas, fauna, music, and sounds.

It has been a privilege to work with the staff at the University of North Carolina Press, extending from early conversations about the book's feasibility with former editorial director David Perry to the completion of the project under current editorial director Mark Simpson-Vos. Manuscript editor Jay Mazzocchi was accessible and helpful as we finalized the manuscript, and our consultations with Dino Battista, Caitlin Bell-Butterfield, Tom Elrod, and Elaine Maisner were always productive and instructive. We thank them for their attentiveness to our goals and for all they have done to transform our vision into a final product that eclipsed the one we imagined.

Throughout our professional lives, our spouses, Marge and Emily, respectively, and our families have demonstrated unwavering yet patient support for our preoccupation with the research and projects resulting in this book. Authors are routinely expected to thank patient partners in their books, but our indebtedness goes far beyond formulaic gratitude. Coming home at the end of the day to our families has always been the most important and meaningful part of our lives.

Finally, we would like to dedicate this effort to the late Dr. William C. (Bill) Friday, one of the most remarkable North Carolinians in the history of the state. Few people will be remembered with such universal respect and fondness. From the initial meeting in his office more than two decades ago—when Walt Wolfram inadvertently gave him a book he had inscribed for Marge with the greeting "Dear Sweetie"—to the last conversation on the telephone about the value of preserving languages and dialects in North Carolina as we were completing this manuscript, we experienced Dr. Friday's gracious encouragement and support. His principled loyalty to and love for things North Carolinian, including its language heritage, is without parallel, and he will be treasured forever.

TALKIN' TAR HEEL

Tar Heels in North Cackalacky 1

I think North Carolina has a level of cultural and historical resources that are unsurpassed nationally. We are known and envied across the country. —LINDA CARLISLE, secretary of the North Carolina Department of Cultural Resources, quoted in the *Raleigh News and Observer*, December 9, 2011

"From Manteo to Murphy" (or "from Murphy to Manteo") is a common expression used throughout North Carolina. The idiom spans 475 miles (544 driving miles)—from the Intracoastal Waterway community of Manteo (population 1,500) on Roanoke Island, located at the site of the first English settlement in North America, to the southwestern border town of Murphy (population 1,700), nestled in the Smoky Mountains. The physical geography extends from the most expansive coastal estuary on the East Coast of the United States to the lush, rock-garden vegetation of the Smoky Mountains. But "Manteo to Murphy" refers to much more than distance and topography. History, tradition, arts, food, and sports also define the cultural landscape.

North Carolinians like their state a lot, and so do the 50 million yearly visitors. We are surprised by how many people we encounter who decided to move to North Carolina without any previous connection to the state—and even without a destination job—simply because it seemed like a good place to live. North Carolina is not shy about marketing its resources as one of the top states for both living and vacationing. There is, however, one notable characteristic that rarely makes it into advertisements about its cultural and historical resources: its language and dialect heritage. Language reflects where people come from, how they have developed, and how they identify themselves regionally and socially. In some respects, language is simply another artifact of history and culture, but language variation is unlike other cultural and historical landmarks. We don't need to visit a historical monument, go to an exhibit, view an artist's gallery, or attend an athletic event to witness it firsthand; language resonates in the sounds of ordinary speakers in everyday conversation. Other landmarks recount the past; language simultaneously indexes the past, present, and future of the state and its residents. The voices of North Carolinians reflect the diversity of its people. They came to this region in different eras from different places under varied conditions and established diverse communities based on the natural resources of the land and waterways. The range of settlers extends from the first American Indians who arrived here at least a couple of thousand years ago from other regions in North America to the most recent Latino immigrants from Central and South America in the late twentieth century. The diverse origins and the migratory routes that brought people to North Carolina have led to a diffuse, multilayered cultural and linguistic panorama that continues to evolve along with the ever-changing profiles of its people.

Dialects and Legacy

When Walt Wolfram first moved to North Carolina in 1992, he often described his midlife passage as "dying and going to dialect heaven." Since then, he and the staff of the North Carolina Language and Life Project (NCLLP) have conducted several thousand interviews with residents of the state—literally from Manteo to Murphy—which have only reaffirmed his observation (though his colleagues may have tired of hearing his heavenly proclamation). So why is North Carolina so linguistically intriguing? And why has this richness not been celebrated in the same way as other cultural and historical treasures of the Tar Heel State?

The conditions for dialect and language diversity are tied closely to physical geography and the human ecology of the region that eventually became known as North Carolina. From the eastern estuaries along the Atlantic Ocean, the terrain transitions into the Coastal Plain, the Piedmont, and the mountains of southern Appalachia—from sand to rich loam, to red clay, to mixed rock and dirt. The varied soils and climates contribute to diverse vegetation, wildlife, natural resources, and cultural economies. Waves of migration at different periods originating from different locations here and abroad have helped establish communities in both convenient and out-of-the-way areas that still reveal a distinct "founder effect" in language even centuries after settlement. (Founder effect is the term linguists use for a lasting influence from the language variety of the first dominant group of speakers to occupy an area.) So, the western mountains of North Carolina still bear the imprint of Scots-Irish English, brought by the many settlers who came from their homeland to Philadelphia before traveling west and south on the Great Wagon Road in the early 1800s.[1] For example, the use of *anymore* in affirmative sentences such as "We watch a lot of videos anymore," the use of *you'uns* for plural *you* in "You'uns can tell some Jack Tales," and the use of *whenever* to refer to "at the time that" as in "Whenever I was young I would do that" can all be attributed to the lasting influence of linguistic traits originally brought by the Scots-Irish. In fact, the current use of *anymore* in positive sentences follows the migration route from Philadelphia through western Pennsylvania and down the Great Wagon Road, diffusing outward from this path as travelers set up communities along the way.

Similarly, the coastal region and the Outer Banks still echo the dialect influence of those who journeyed south by water from the coastal areas of Virginia. Dialect features like the use of *weren't* in "I weren't there," the pronunciation of *high tide* as *hoi toid*, and the pronunciation of *brown* more like *brane* or *brain* are shared along this and adjoining estuaries. The interconnected waterways and the settlement history help explain why speakers from North Carolina Outer Banks communities, such as Ocracoke and Harkers Island, sound much more like the speakers of Virginia's Tangier Island and Maryland's Smith Island in the Chesapeake Bay than they do the speakers of inland North Carolina. Mix in the contributions of American Indian languages; the remnants of African languages; and Europeans speaking Gaelic, German, French, and other languages, and the result is a regional and ethnic language ecology as varied as North Carolina's physical topography and climate—the most varied of any state east of the Mississippi River.

Tar Heels in North Cackalacky

States commonly bear nicknames that highlight some attribute of the state, ranging from shape (for example, *Keystone State* for Pennsylvania) and location (*Bay State* for Massachusetts; *Ocean State* for Rhode Island) to its natural resources (*Granite State* for New Hampshire; *Peach State* for Georgia) or even presumed character attributes of the people (*Show-Me State* for Missouri; *Equality State* for Wyoming). There is always a story behind the nickname. *Carolina*, derived from *Carolus*, the Latin word for *Charles*, was originally named after King Charles I in 1629. The land from Albemarle Sound in the north to St. Johns River in present-day South Carolina was appropri-

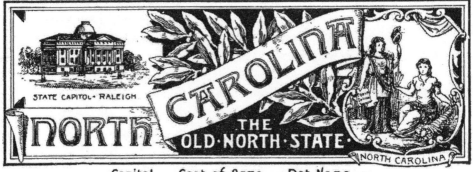

FIGURE 1.1. The state banner of North Carolina, 1893.
(Florida Center for Instructional Technology)

ated in the original territorial designation. When Carolina was divided into North Carolina and South Carolina officially in 1729, the older settlement in North Carolina was referred to as the *Old North State*, a nickname commonly used for a variety of purposes, including a state banner from 1893 (Figure 1.1). The official song of North Carolina, "The Old North State," was adopted by the State Assembly in 1927. Though less common today, the nickname is still used on occasion.

North Carolina, however, is much more frequently called the *Tar Heel State*, most likely alluding to major products of the colonial era—tar pitch and turpentine made from the longleaf and loblolly pine trees so prominent in the state. Earlier legends attribute the name to the laborers who walked out of the woods with the sticky black substance on their shoes or to stories of incidents during wars. One legend comes from the Revolutionary War, when North Carolina soldiers continued marching after wading through a river coated with liquid tar, but the most popular stories involve the Civil War, when the tar and turpentine industries were flourishing. One story, preserved in the *Creecy Family Papers*, reports that a regiment from Virginia supporting the North Carolina troops was driven from the field, leaving the North Carolina troops to fight alone. After the battle was won by the North Carolinians, they were greeted by the deserting soldiers from Virginia with the question, "Any more tar down in the Old North State, boys?" The North Carolinians responded, "No; not a bit, old Jeff's bought it all up," referring to Jefferson Davis, president of the Confederate States of America at the time. When asked by the abandoning regiment what old Jeff was going to do with

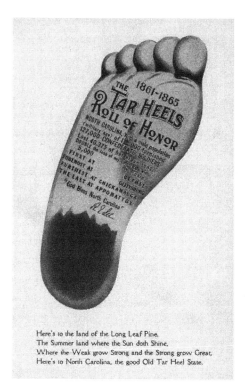

it, they were told: "He's going to put it on you'ns heels to make you stick better in the next fight." The legend continues that General Robert E. Lee was told about this incident, to which he responded, "God bless the Tar Heel boys"—and the name stuck.[2]

A less-flattering story of the origin of *Tar Heel* was recorded in John S. Farmer's *Americanisms, Old and New*, published in 1889.[3] He recounts a battle involving Mississippi and North Carolina soldiers in which the brigade of North Carolinians performed poorly. According to Farmer, the Mississippians taunted the North Carolinians about their failure to tar their heels in the morning, leaving them unable to hold their position.

People from North Carolina have also been referred to as *Tar Boilers* in reference to the distillation process used for producing tar and pitch. Pine logs were stacked and covered with dirt and burned, the tar running through channels on the low side of the pile—a messy and smelly process. In fact, poet Walt Whitman derisively referred to North Carolinians as Tar Boilers in 1888.[4] This term faded, however, while Tar Heel has remained.

For a period after the Civil War, Tar Heel was viewed as a derogatory reference to North Carolinians, but it was rehabilitated by the turn of the twentieth century. Once a state nickname becomes associated with a university sports program, it sticks—much to the chagrin of rival athletic programs. The fact that Tar Heels as a nickname has been appropriated by the University of North Carolina at Chapel Hill has certainly promoted its visibility and popularity. But those from rival state universities, such as North Carolina State University and East Carolina University, would prefer not to talk about the *Tar Heel Nation* as if it were synonymous with the state where they have competing athletic programs. The popularity of the nickname, however, is clear, and a book titled *Talkin' Tar Heel* might just as readily be interpreted as a description of speech by students and staff on the UNC–Chapel Hill campus as a book about the speech of North Carolinians.

Tar Heel and Old North State are not the only nicknames for North Carolina, though competing monikers like *Land of the Sky*, *Turpentine State*, or *Good Roads State* have little popular currency. One of the popular and spreading nicknames for the state and its neighbor to the south, however, is the term *Cackalacky*. *North Cackalacky* and *South Cackalacky*, or their abbreviated forms, *North Cack* and *South Cack*, have both increased in popularity in recent years. The term's currency is strong enough that it has been appropriated by commercial products that wish to reflect their regional heritage. Original Cackalacky Spice Sauce, a zesty, sweet potato–based sauce, was trademarked in 2001 and is now distributed in twenty-six states.[5] The term Cackalacky for a sweet potato–based sauce is fitting since North Carolina produces approximately 40 percent of all the sweet potatoes consumed in the United States. In 1995 the tuber was designated as the state vegetable of North Carolina following a two-year campaign initiated by a group of fourth graders from Elvie Street School in Wilson.[6] While the origin of Cackalacky is still uncertain, its history began long before the sauce was created. At the very least, we can definitively trace the term to 1937, when it was used in a popular song. It is likely that Cackalacky's etymology runs much deeper than this song, however, and there remains much popular speculation and discussion about its possible origins.

The term may have arisen from a kind of sound-play utterance used to refer to the rural ways of people from Carolina—a play on the pronunciation of the state. Another hypothesis is that Cackalacky was derived from the Cherokee term *tsalaki*, pronounced as "cha-lak-ee," the Cherokee pronunciation of *Cherokee*. Yet another hypothesis traces it to a cappella gospel groups in the American South in the 1930s, who used the rhythmic (but ap-

FIGURE 1.3. Cackalacky becomes a commercial product. (Reprinted with permission from Cackalacky, Inc.)

parently meaningless) chant *clanka lanka* in their songs. Derivations related to the German word for cockroach (*kakerlake*) and a Scottish soup (*cocklaleekie*) have also been suggested, but no one really knows the origin. Certainly, the popularity of Cackalacky has risen in the last decade, and it has now become a positive term of solidarity used throughout the state. We favor the sound-play etymology for Cackalacky, but we are honestly just venturing our best guess. Support for the sound-play interpretation comes not only from earlier songs and references but also from a more recent song written by North Carolina folksinger Jonathan Byrd titled "Cackalack" (2011).[7]

> 95 South, 95 South, but that is the way to my baby's house,
> Cackalack cackalack, cackalack cackalack, cackalack cackalack;
> I'm on 95 South and I ain't goin' back.

In this refrain, notice how *cackalack* is used in repetitive, rhythmic sequence at the same time it is linked with its Tar Heel State meaning. Unfortunately, the word Cackalacky also demonstrates how elusive tracking down word origins can sometimes be, even for professional linguists. Or maybe it simply speaks to an unwitting conspiracy of outsiders, insiders, the sweet potato industry, and the barbecue-sauce industry to highlight the significance of native status. For sure, it shows how a word can become strongly associated with identity, regardless of origin.

While we cannot be certain of the origin, the development of Cackalacky demonstrates how terms of reference can change over their life spans. Evidence from the 1940s suggests the term was used in a somewhat derogatory way by outsiders; for example, servicemen assigned to one of the rural bases in the state in the 1940s referred to their environs as "Cackalacky," perhaps deriding the rural ways of native North Carolinians. Though it may have been intended as an insult by outsiders, it has now been embraced affectionately by native and adoptive residents.

The positive use of North Cackalacky is spreading, and the button that reads "I speak North Cackalacky" is one of the most popular items given away at our annual exhibit on languages and dialects at the North Carolina State Fair in Raleigh. But occasionally, we do get older North Carolinians who wonder why we are promoting a derogatory term. Their stories of how this term was used by outsiders to insult North Carolinians "back in the day" tend to support our contention that it was once used as a word-play insult by outsiders that has since reversed its meaning for residents of the state.

Tar Heel Words

Some dialect words, pronunciations, and sayings are heavily concentrated in North Carolina, but dialects don't pay much attention to state boundaries. The lack of extensive natural boundaries separating North Carolina from South Carolina to the south and from Virginia to the north allow the dialects to spill over the state line, and the mountains in the western part of North Carolina are shared by eastern Tennessee so that the state line arbitrarily cuts across the mountain range. The dialect map given below—based on our community studies and other dialect surveys of the region for North Carolina and South Carolina—depicts how the major dialect areas disregard the state boundary. The lines separating dialect areas, technically called *isoglosses*, are idealized rather than absolute boundaries. Linguistic transitions tend to be gradual rather than abrupt. Even where natural boundaries of water may appear to set off one dialect region from another, there is often a transitional zone. For example, the Outer Banks islands are discretely separated from the mainland by the sounds but still show a transition area.

The map reflects the influence of early migration and European settlement on the major dialects of North Carolina, mostly southward through

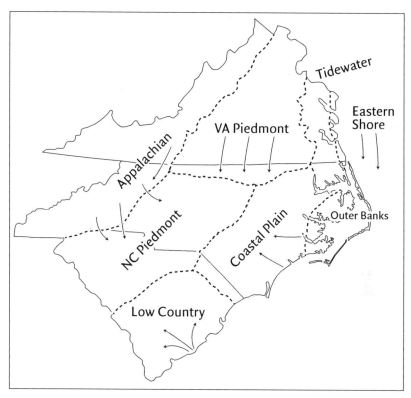

MAP 1.1. Dialects and Settlement in North Carolina

Virginia and inland from the coastal area. It also captures how North Carolina dialects have spread into South Carolina. At the same time, dialects diffused inland from Charleston, a major port of entry for some of the early population of the Palmetto State. It also illustrates the relative insignificance of the state boundary in the development of dialects.

The comprehensive, six-volume *Dictionary of American Regional English*, over a half century in the making, lists fewer than 100 words that are "North Carolinian," and many of these, even those labeled "chiefly" or "especially" North Carolinian, extend beyond the state's borders.[8] Terms like *Banker* for a "person from the Outer Banks" and *pocosin* for "a nontidal inland marsh or swamp that contains some ocean salts" can be heard into Virginia and even Maryland, though their use may be more concentrated in North Carolina. Similarly, *boomer* ("a type of red squirrel") and *devil's shoestring* ("hobblebush, branches spread upon the ground") are listed as North Carolinian though they extend into the mountains of eastern Tennessee.

At the same time, studies of North Carolina communities have turned up hundreds of dialect words that are restricted to particular regions within North Carolina. Outer Banks words like *dingbatter*, *dit-dot*, and *woodser* for "outsiders" have not been observed in any other state to our knowledge. Similarly, words like *Russian rat* ("nutria"), *meehonkey* ("a cross between hide and seek and Marco Polo"), *buck* ("good friend"), and *slick cam* ("calm water in the sound") have not been found elsewhere. But they are also unknown by most native mainland North Carolinians and just about everyone who hasn't grown up around these communities. Hundreds of community-restricted terms have eluded even the dialect word mavens of the *Dictionary of American Regional English* because they are so localized within the communities of North Carolina.

As mentioned, the NCLLP hosts an exhibit on the dialects and languages of North Carolina at the State Fair in Raleigh. As part of the exhibit, we offer free buttons featuring words from different dialects of North Carolina. Buttons with localized words like *sigogglin* ("crooked, not straight or square"), *juvember* ("slingshot"), *dingbatter* ("outsider"), and *buddyrow* ("good friend") accompany our more-inclusive statewide buttons, such as "I speak North Cackalacky" and "Bless your heart." The dialect words on the buttons represent just a few of the dialect communities of the state, but they also illustrate the different parameters that define a dialect word in North Carolina. The term *juvember* for "sling shot" is used mostly by the Lumbee Indians who live in the southeastern part of the state, but it is also known by some white and African American residents of that region. This word thus represents both a regional and ethnic dimension of North Carolina speech. *Sigogglin* (pronounced as "SIGH-gog-lin" or sometimes as "SIGH-gog-ly"), a label for something "crooked or not straight or square," is used by speakers only in the mountains of the western part of the state, mostly in the Smoky Mountains. Other dialects of North Carolina use other words for describing objects that are not straight, such as *cattywampus*, *catterwampus*, *whopperjawed*, and *antigogglin*. *Dingbatter*, a term used on the Outer Banks for "outsiders or nonnatives," is also a regionalized word within the state and limited to the Outer Banks; it is most concentrated in Ocracoke. The etymology of this word demonstrates how dialects are constantly changing and some of the peculiar reasons for their changes. On the 1970s sitcom television show *All in the Family*, the term *dingbat* was used by Archie Bunker (actor Carroll O'Connor) to refer to his wife, Edith (actor Jean Stapleton). It was appropriated and extended by residents of Ocracoke when islanders first received access to regular television during that period, including this popular sitcom. It seemed like a perfect way to describe the lack of common sense sometimes exhibited by tourists, replacing earlier terms for outsiders such as *foreigner* and *stranger*. While it is still in use today, it is losing ground to the blended term *touron*, which results from a combination of *tourist* and *moron*, demonstrating how dynamic and creative words can be.

At the other end of the insider-outsider dichotomy is the word *buddyrow*, a term for "a good friend." Its use is scattered throughout North Carolina but extensively among the Lumbee Indians. Symbolically, it distinguishes a community insider, as do terms like *cuz*, *buck*, *Lum*, *daddy*, and so forth. Terms for insiders and outsiders indicate how important such designations are, even in our increasingly globalized world.

Make no mistake: there is a clear divide between outsiders who were born elsewhere and natives born and bred in the Old North State. Status as an authentic Tar Heel is a birthright, and the state offers no adoption papers for outsiders. Words are not just words—they index region, status, and identity, and some of these words are strongly connected to being North Carolinian. The University of North Carolina at Chapel Hill's fight song captures how important words can be for identity, as it notes: "I'm a Tar Heel born and a Tar Heel bred / And when I die I'm a Tar Heel dead." To no one's surprise, it also adds (unofficially): "Go to Hell, Duke!"

Sounding Tar Heel

As pronunciation would have it, the names of counties, towns, rivers, and other landmarks in North Carolina can serve effectively to distinguish locals from outsiders. The following is a list of some place names in North Carolina. Try pronouncing them and see how many match the pronunciations of lifetime residents of North Carolina who are familiar with these locations.

Manteo, Buies Creek, Ahoskie, Pasquotank, Tuckasegee, Corolla, Bodie Lighthouse, Conetoe, Fuquay-Varina, Robeson County, Bertie, Rowan, Kerr Lake, Chowan, Tyrrell County, Rodanthe, Lake Waccamaw, Hatteras, Rhodhiss, Ocracoke, Nantahala, Albemarle, Duraleigh, Sauratown, Bethabara, Chicamacomico, Cabarrus, Cashie River, Iredell, Uwharrie, Saxapahaw.

More than 200 people volunteered to read and record these words for us at the 2012 State Fair, but very few people read all of the words like native

speakers from these respective areas. Naturally, people from out of state were the most challenged by this task, but even lifetime residents of North Carolina had trouble with place names for distant locations. Some of the mispronunciations based on spelling were fairly predictable, but others were quite imaginative.

To hear local pronunciations of North Carolina place names, visit http://www.talkintarheel .com/chapter/1/audio1-1.php

To hear common mispronunciations of North Carolina place names, visit http://www.talkintarheel .com/chapter/1/audio1-2.php

Some of the mispronunciations can be traced to the different languages that have contributed to the state's cultural and linguistic diversity. A number of place names derive from American Indian inhabitants of the region.[9] Towns and counties like *Chicamacomico* (chick-uh-muh-KAHM-ih-ko), *Ahoskie* (uh-HAHS-kee), *Pasquotank* (PAS-qua-tank), and *Tuckasegee* (tuck-a-SEE-gee) may be tricky for outsiders because of their obvious non-English origin, though reliance on traditional symbol-sound correspondences can get a reader close to the native pronunciation.

A number of vowel differences in local pronunciations can be painfully indicative of nonnative status. For example, the pronunciation of the town *Corolla* the same as the car (kuh-ROW-luh) instead of kuh-RAH-la is a significant phonetic transgression, and the pronunciation of the *Bodie* lighthouse as BOW-dee instead of BAH-dee usually can be traced to a driver bearing a license plate from another state. Drivers traveling through Edgecombe County on Route 64 may read the sign for the small town *Conetoe*, but based simply on its spelling they have practically no chance of pronouncing it as a local. A person might render it as KOWN-tow or KAHN-uh-tow, but we have never heard anybody pronounce it as kuh-NEE-tuh unless they have had it pronounced for them by someone familiar with the local pronunciation. And we have witnessed more than one recent transplant in *Fuquay-Varina* (outside of Raleigh) pause and then uncomfortably say FUHK-way-var-ih-na when they should have said FEW-kway-vuh-REE-nuh. When a new newscaster on TV in Charlotte, Greensboro, or Raleigh pronounces *Robeson County* as ROW-bih-sun instead of RAH-bih-sun, viewers cringe at his or her ignorance about the counties in the state—and, in response to viewers' complaints, executive producers quickly correct the pronunciation before the next newscast.

Some differences in syllable accent or stress are among the most prominent icons of in-state and out-of-state status. *Bertie*, *Rowan*, and *Chowan* counties all have their accent on the second syllable (ber-TEE, row-AN, cho-WAHN, respectively), while *Tyrell County* (TER-il) and the town of *Etowah* (EH-tuh-wuh) have their stress on the first syllable for reasons that are certainly not obvious to those who haven't learned how to pronounce these names growing up in North Carolina. And then there is *Rodanthe*, featured in the book, *Nights in Rodanthe*, written by the popular North Carolina author Nicholas Sparks and featuring Richard Gere and Diane Lane in the film version in 2008.[10] Locals and those in the know pronounce it as row-DAN-thee.

In other cases, local pronunciations differ in the number of syllables in a word. Outsiders often pronounce the Outer Banks town of *Hatteras* as HAD-er-uhs with three syllables, but the few remaining families raised there typically pronounce it as HAT-rihs, much like the British pronunciation that only has two syllables and the t fully pronounced. Given the many differences in native and outsider pronunciations, a lot of items can separate the dialect chafe from the wheat. With 100 counties and hundreds of small towns, the pronunciation challenge of place names in North Carolina is the equal of any state. In some cases, you simply have to know someone from the community or region in order to know how to pronounce the name.

To hear a more complete list of the pronunciation of North Carolina counties and place names by Bland Simpson and Michael McFee, visit http://www.talkintarheel.com/chapter/1/audio1-3.php

A more complete list of North Carolina counties and place names pronounced by well–Tar Heeled speakers Bland Simpson and Michael McFee is found in "Talk Like a Tar Heel: North Carolina Place Names."[11]

Developing Language Differences

Perhaps North Carolina has never touted its language and dialect heritage as one of its cultural commodities because many North Carolinians have grown up ashamed of their dialect rather than proud of it, viewing their dialect as a cultural liability to be overcome rather than a cultural resource to embrace. We have interviewed numerous people who report that they were told—by teachers, parents, and others—that their southern-based dialect needed to be replaced by a less regional, more neutral one if they ever wanted to "succeed" in life.

Attitudes about language can be complex and nuanced, but ultimately they are tied to attitudes about people. The attitudes of the language spoken by politically and/or socially subordinate groups will naturally take on the descriptors of that group. Since at least the Civil War, southern dialect has been viewed as "inferior" speech. If the outcome of the war had been different, of course, the dialect would have been considered "Standard English" and other Englishes considered inferior. Southern speech was already somewhat different from northern speech before the Civil War, but it started diverging much more substantially after the war.[12] The rate and direction of language change is often connected to major historical and cultural events, so change following the Civil War is not unusual. The post–Civil War cultural divide, the regional entrenchment, and the oppositional feelings toward the North offered a fertile environment for the independent development of southern speech. Many of the icons of current southern speech—including the use of y'all for plural subjects, as in "Y'all have lots of kinfolk"; the pronunciation of time as tahm; and the identical pronunciations of pin and pen (usually pin)—spread like kudzu during the post–Civil War era. Coincidently, the boundary of kudzu neatly matches the boundaries for these iconic southern dialect features, though no one is suggesting kudzu wrapped around the tongues of North Carolinians in cultivating their dialect. As southern speech diverged from northern speech, it became more symbolically regional and strongly associated with southern cultural lifestyles. This may have been good for southern regional identity, but the speech of the South was not highly valued outside of the region—except perhaps to the ears of listeners from the British Isles, where southern speech still is considered preferable to northern speech. As southern speech became more regionally delimited and socially stigmatized, it was subjugated to what linguists call the "principle of linguistic subordination."[13] Simply put, this means that the speech of a socially subordinate group will be interpreted as linguistically inferior and socially unworthy by comparison to the language of a dominant social group. The politically and socially dominant North, then, simply ascribed attributes associated with their stereotypes of the South to its speech—rural, slow, and ignorant. Over a century and a half after the Civil War, this ideology still lingers, and educated parents in the South still attempt to eliminate the "southern drawl" in their children so that they won't sound like country bumpkins, yokels, or hicks, derogatory terms that evoke The Beverly Hillbillies stereotypes of uneducated, impoverished rural people. The South itself has not always been able to fully resist these language attitudes, since socially dominant beliefs about language became ingrained in our institutions, particularly in schools and government agencies. Political and social power is linguistic power, and the social valuation of language variation in society simply follows the lines of this social and political power. In this context, the southern dialect has often been viewed from within as an undesirable or unfortunate aspect of being southern rather than a reflection of a distinct cultural and linguistic legacy.

A closer examination of how southern speech is viewed in different situations suggests that the story is more complicated than the simple categorization of good and bad speech.[14] In reality, both southern and non-southern listeners show a somewhat schizoid reaction to southern speech. At the same time that this speech can be viewed as inferior, it is also perceived as genteel and charming. North Carolinians, especially women, are told that their speech is attractive, sweet, and sexy—part of gendered southern charm. People "just love to hear you talk!" Further, southern speech is viewed as more polite than northern talk, which is often interpreted as direct and rude by comparison. The collection of stereotypes results in an odd image of what a southerner must be: rustic, slow, and ignorant, yet genteel, kind, and pleasant.

Southern dialect may also serve to indicate sincerity and authenticity. Every night, the late-night news in North Carolina is sponsored by auto dealerships whose sales representatives—often the owner—use a local southern dialect to offer the best deal for the latest model car. Owners appear with their families and even their family pets to convey genuineness and trustworthiness—a "neighborly" person who is worthy of the viewer's trust (and money) on a major purchase. The character is transformed from stereotype to authentic through the use of dialect—because local speakers are considered by their viewers to be trustworthy, friendly, and honest. Marketing specialists rely on this speech as part of their presentation of sincerity and authenticity. The same listeners may rate northern dialects more highly on language qualities associated with professional competence and standardness, but southern dialects clearly get the nod on personal character and social solidarity. To put it another way, viewers might consider the northern-speaking salesperson as competent, but they are more likely to trust the southern speaker to take care of them if the car turns out to be a lemon. Understanding some of the more subtle, positive attributes of sounding southern is a start to understanding the legacy of regional dialects of the South.

In some situations, speaking southern is clearly an advantage rather than a liability—and of course in other situations, the opposite is true. One of the great linguistic ironies aired on national television during public political investigations presided over by the late U.S. senator Samuel James Ervin Jr. from Morganton, North Carolina. Known simply as "Sam Ervin," the long-serving senator (1954–74) liked to call himself a "country lawyer," and he

FIGURE 1.4. Senator Sam Ervin during the Watergate hearings.

often told stories in a rich southern Mountain dialect. His public persona could beguile his colleagues into underestimating him, but he was an erudite constitutional lawyer who first came to prominence in 1954 for his work in bringing down so-called McCarthyism, the political movement that pursued alleged communist subversion plots among well-known Americans without substantiating facts. Senator Sam Ervin later assumed leadership of

To view a speech by
Samuel Ervin, U.S. senator,
visit http://www.talkintarheel
.com/chapter/1/video1-1.php

the Senate committee investigating the Watergate scandal that led to the resignation of President Richard Nixon in 1974. The Watergate committee is, in fact, still referred to as the "Ervin Committee" because of his powerful leadership, persuasive rhetoric, and personal character. He was the television favorite for viewers during the Watergate hearings, not simply for his penetrating queries and intelligence but also for the voice in which he crafted his persuasive arguments.

The description of Ervin as a "simple country lawyer" has become part of the caricature of the self-deprecating personality who is actually a shrewd, effective professional. Andy Griffith's character on the television show *Matlock* was also an unpretentious country lawyer who always won his cases. Part of Griffith's depiction was rooted in his impoverished childhood background in rural Mount Airy, North Carolina. His southern dialect was a natural part of his socialization as a child, but he learned to use it to his advantage in portraying a character who could outwit an antagonist who prejudged the intelligence of the southern-talking protagonist. That kind of behavior is not unlike the "trickster" archetype found in the mythology of many cultures, particularly oppressed groups, where the trickster hero uses rhetorical ability to outwit or overcome a character of superior physical power or social dominance. The language and rhetoric of a trickster lulls the oppressor into complacency, only to overcome the socially powerful through shrewd rhetoric, usually using a vernacular voice. The trickster is well established in southern literature; the fictional character Sut Lovingood was a southern trickster—a "Nat'ral Born Durn'd Fool"—in the work of author George Washington Harris, who was widely popular in the 1850s and 1860s.[15] It is also popularized by author Joel Chandler Harris in the mid-1800s depiction of the Brer Rabbit character.

Linguists who study social attitudes about language make a distinction between what they refer to as *overt* and *covert* prestige. Overt prestige refers to the positive value ascribed to language forms based on the values of mainstream, institutional norms of the society. Covert prestige, on the other hand, is based on local or regional value rather than the norms of the larger, mainstream society. From this perspective, using one of the different regional or social dialects of southern speech certainly carries some covert prestige even though the Standard English of mainstream institutions carries overt prestige. In fact, one of the reasons that southern speech has been so resilient is due to covert regional language pride—despite the fact that this regional variety has been overtly stigmatized. The seeds for recognizing the cultural resource of language differences in the South have been germinating for an extended period now, mostly in the form of covert prestige. We hope that we are now entering a season of public growth in the recognition of language and dialect overtly as an authentic part of cultural legacy.

Embracing Language Legacy

Changing attitudes about language does not happen overnight. In this respect, attitudes about language are like other foundational belief systems, such as religion, politics, and morality. Americans have long been socialized to think that southern speech, including the dialects of North Carolina, is not proper, notwithstanding some positive associations of these language varieties related to personal character and regional identity. On a rational level, we may understand that language varieties are strongly connected to culture and history, but we still maintain a "not-in-my-backyard" stance when it comes to the tolerance of southern language differences. In fact, we have found that language attitudes are so strong that they often transcend political persuasions and cross ethnic and social lines. When the so-called Ebonics controversy erupted in Oakland, California, in 1996, both conservative and liberal commentators seemed to unite in their stance against the Oakland School Board's program to help teachers understand the home dialect of their African American students in order to more effectively teach them Standard English. On what other topic might we expect the conservative media icon Rush Limbaugh and the lifelong social activist Jessie Jackson to agree? But both initially were united—independently, of course—in their condemnation of the Oakland School Board for their stance on Ebonics.[16] If nothing else, the controversy and the media blitz surrounding the resolution revealed (1) the intensity of people's beliefs and opinions about language diversity; (2) the widespread level of misunderstanding about language diversity; and (3) the need for informed knowledge and its role in public life and education. The same can be said for the legacy of southern dialects.

The South in general and North Carolina in particular have an emergent sense of regional pride in their history and culture, but language heritage has been noticeably absent from this celebration. North Carolina public-school students in fourth grade and eighth grade study the settlement, history, and culture of the state, including the contributions of various ethnic and social groups, but the texts include only a few oblique references to different languages. Until the introduction of our eighth-grade dialect curriculum a few years back, there was no mention of English dialects. How can history and culture be studied adequately without noting the linguistic contributions of different groups of settlers and migrants? How can we understand the development of Mountain culture in the western part of the state without recognizing that region's distinctive dialect, with its enduring influence from the Scots-Irish of Ulster via the Great Wagon Road? How can we understand the unique maritime culture of the Outer Banks without considering the traditional and changing associations of the so-called brogue? And how can we understand the role of African Americans and Lumbee Indians in North Carolina without reference to the unique dialects of English that have arisen from the remnants of their ancestral languages?

Language is slowly edging its way into the known legacy of North Carolina. As native Tar Heel author Nicholas Sparks noted in an interview in the *Raleigh News and Observer*: "North Carolina is a novelist's dream. Every town is

FIGURE 1.5. William C. (Bill) Friday, North Carolina statesman. (Courtesy of the *Raleigh News and Observer*)

different. We even talk with different accents."[17] Part of the heritage of small-town North Carolina is the dialect. But we will also see that dialect is a part of the traditional and developing culture of urban areas like Raleigh, Greensboro, Winston-Salem, and Charlotte as well. Citizens of the state and outsiders find the varieties of the English language intriguing, even more so once they are exposed to sociocultural context and their symbolic status.

The late Dr. William C. (Bill) Friday, one of North Carolina's greatest statesmen and respected citizens, served twenty-six years as the University of North Carolina system's first president and hosted UNC-TV's longest running program, *North Carolina People*, for more than thirty years. During this period, he interviewed more than 1,500 guests from all walks of life, documenting the vast personal resources and traditions of the state. His lifetime of work in North Carolina and with its peo-

To view a vignette featuring Bill Friday, visit http://www.talkintarheel.com/chapter/1/video1-2.php

ple situates him as the ideal person to evaluate the markers of North Carolina culture. He notes: "We've gone through our period of adolescence as a country. We now know the value of history. We now know why we should preserve history, we now know why we should preserve buildings and languages and people and traditions, because they've become a part of what you really are."[18] We agree with Bill Friday that the linguistic heritage of the state is as important and iconic as other cultural and physical markers, including the Lost Colony Historical Landmark, the Hatteras Lighthouse, back-porch music, and barbecue.

Nothing is more intrinsic to culture, identity, and community than language. At the same time, language is also among our most indispensable tools. We use language to teach, learn, console, love, harm, and create. Despite the incredible utility of our words, sometimes what we say is less revealing than how we say it. Southern-bred linguist Dr. Boyd Davis—currently at the University of North Carolina–Charlotte—talks about a game that she sometimes plays with her students. She has them lower their eyes and pretend they can't see her as she talks. She reports:

To view the video of this quote from Boyd Davis, visit http://www.talkintarheel.com/chapter/1/video1-3.php

As they hear me talk, they can hear me use a number of southern features that they associated with upper- or middle-class speech with the "R's," the "ahs" and "G's." They'll hear that it's southern but I talk too fast to be deep southern. You can hear that I'm over eighteen—I've lost that beautiful breathless quality. And we hope that I'm not yet eighty because it's not thoroughly cracked. You can hear that I probably like the situation. I have some education. And if you listen to me for another minute, you can hear me smile at you. You give away all of that every time you say anything. That's what an accent does.[19]

Our voice offers a glimpse into our inherited past—who we are—but even more so, a glimpse of our imagined future—who we wish to be. It is this unique intersection of past, present, and future that makes language so interesting to study.

North Carolina has a remarkable, living history that lingers on the tongues of its citizenry. In this book, we examine these voices to discover where they came from and how they came to be. Our aim is to preserve a cultural past while simultaneously looking toward the future. We concentrate more on dialects of English than other languages, in part because the vast majority of the population still speaks only English in the home. But growing populations now speak other languages. Most visible are Spanish speakers, whose recent immigration to North Carolina has made it one of the top states in the United States over the past two decades in the growth of Spanish speakers—with the highest percentage of monolingual Spanish speakers. There are also communities of Hmong (7,500) and Vietnamese (about 16,000), including subgroups such as the Montagnards (5,000) from the central mountains of Vietnam for whom Vietnamese is not their first language (Bahnar, Koho, Mnong, etc.) and who first started coming to the state about three decades ago. These complement more dispersed communities of Hungarian (1,000) and Polish (2,000) speakers. Speakers of Arabic varieties such as Lebanese Arabic (15,000) have been present in North Carolina for more than a century, and of course German speakers (28,000) have resided in North Carolina since before it was officially a state. In addition to its dialect varieties, over twenty-five different languages are part of the language legacy of North Carolina.[20]

Following an overview of the history that has given rise to different cultural and linguistic groups, this book examines, in separate chapters, some of the distinctive dialects and languages to see how the dialects and languages of North Carolina shape its regional and ethnic culture. In the process, we hope to convince readers that language diversity is one of the state's greatest regional, cultural, and historical legacies.

2 The Origins of Language Diversity in North Carolina

That's who we are. Our language is who we are. Once you start learning the language, it branches out to all other areas—history, culture, traditions. So, when they're learning the language they're learning, you know, everything about the Cherokee people as well. —**MYRTLE DRIVER,** Eastern Band of the Cherokee, quoted in *Voices of North Carolina*, produced by Neal Hutcheson (Raleigh: North Carolina Language and Life Project, 2005)

Historical settlement patterns and migrations provided the blueprint for modern language diversity, and culture and society are the agencies for managing it. Language variation is so tightly woven into the state's cultural fabric that it is not realistically possible to study the history of North Carolina without considering language. Voiceprints from the many groups who arrived at different times and under different circumstances are still heard in the diverse regional and ethnic languages and dialects used throughout the state. But the shifting sounds, words, and grammar are not simply a legacy of the past; they are part of a dynamic, ongoing narrative.

Language is not bound by the political boundaries of the state, and the history of the land is, of course, much deeper than the documented record. The land now parceled into the 100 counties of North Carolina has been continuously inhabited for at least 12,000 years. Before it was a state, it was a territory and then a colony of England. More precisely, it was a series of quite different colonies with different names and shapes. At one point, the colony's borders extended south to current-day Florida (see Figure 2.1), while at another time, it spread westward to the Pacific.

This brief historical overview of North Carolina highlights some of the

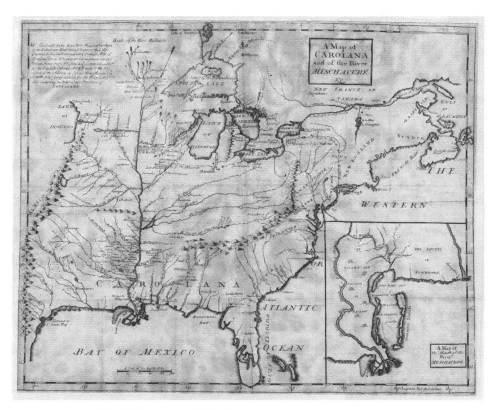

FIGURE 2.1. Daniel Coxe's map of Carolana, 1722,
from *A Description of the English Province of Carolana.*

groups that have shaped the linguistic landscape of the modern state, but it
is not meant to be an alternative to the many excellent accounts of the state's
history.[1] And while the focus is on North Carolina, some mention of the Virginia Tidewater and Charleston, South Carolina (the latter once being a part
of one colony before it was split into North and South Carolina), is necessary since these adjacent areas are important to the historical development
of North Carolina. It is worth remembering that the present-day state did not
take shape until relatively recently. As much as possible, the discussion in
this chapter focuses on the area now known as North Carolina even though
many of the events took place well before these state borders existed.

We view the state as having four areas—Outer Banks, Coastal Plain, Piedmont, and highlands—but these boundaries are as much political and cultural as they are geographical. It seems that these boundaries were important
even before modern populations recognized their existence. In this regard,

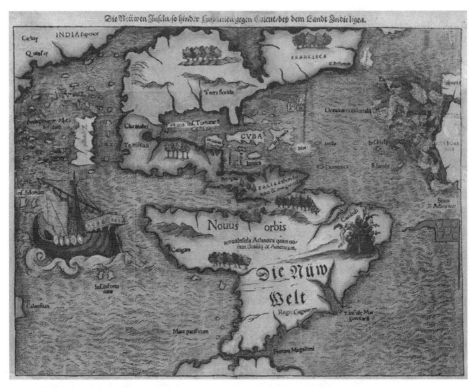

FIGURE 2.2. Woodcut map of North and South America by Sebastian Munster, ca. 1540, repeating Giovanni da Verrazzano's erroneous interpretation of the Outer Banks as an isthmus separating the Atlantic Ocean from an arm of the Pacific Ocean (seen directly above the flag).

the native peoples certainly had a better understanding of the region than did the first Europeans. In 1524 Italian explorer Giovanni da Verrazzano, sailing under the French crown, charted the Eastern Seaboard of North America. Arriving at the North Carolina Outer Banks, he made a rather remarkable cartographic error, thinking the islands were a narrow isthmus connecting two large land masses (one containing Florida, Georgia, and South Carolina and the other containing the land between Virginia and Newfoundland). Verrazzano believed the body of water on the western side of the Outer Banks—the Pamlico Sound—was the Pacific Ocean. For the next 100 years, much of Europe reproduced this error in maps (see Figure 2.2). Verrazzano was not the last person to err in his geographical interpretation of North Carolina; later Europeans were mistaken not only in their perceptions of the geography but also in those of the native populations.

Prehistoric Residents and Language

In North Carolina, the archaeological evidence—consisting of over 250 spearheads from sixty-five counties in the Coastal Plain and eastern Piedmont—suggests that there were small and highly nomadic bands of hunters in the area during the Late Pleistocene era, or about to 12,000 years ago, when the final Ice Age gripped much of the northern part of North America.[2] These Paleo-Indians hunted ground sloth, giant bison, mastodon, mammoth, moose, elk, and caribou, and they supplemented their diets with local plants, fish, and shellfish.[3] Though there is no evidence of semipermanent Paleo-Indian settlements in North Carolina, two rhyolite "quarries"—in present-day Stanly and Montgomery Counties—were likely places of encounters among speakers of the at least six major language families of southeastern Paleo-Indians.[4] We don't know much about the language of these groups, though they remain intriguing to historical linguists, but we can say with certainty that language diversity in North Carolina existed as far back as we can possibly trace.

American Indians

The Paleo-Indians gradually gave way to less nomadic and more technologically advanced societies that relied on nascent agriculture as a means of sustenance. The shift was slow, but it occurred between 3000 and 1000 B.C.E. Without historical records, it is unclear whether the Paleo-Indian families in North Carolina eventually became the American Indian groups or whether they left with the big game, allowing other groups to resettle the area. American Indian culture is separated from the Paleo-Indian culture by three technological developments: pottery, the bow and arrow, and agriculture, all of which developed in the Woodland period (from about 1000 B.C.E. to 1000 C.E.). Development of pottery and the bow and arrow allowed for a less nomadic life, leading to improved leatherwork, complex shelter construction, and textiles. Agriculture was the last of the three to develop, spreading circa 1000 C.E. from the Mississippian culture located south and west of present-day North Carolina to the state's three Woodland groups, Siouan, Iroquoian, and Algonquian, each with distinctive languages and cultures that existed well beyond the area that became North Carolina. It was likely these Woodland groups that Giovanni da Verrazzano encountered in 1524 near the Cape Fear River.

They go completely naked except that around their loins they wear skins of small animals like martens, with a narrow belt of grass around the body, to which they tie various tails of other animals which hang down to the knees; the rest of the body is bare, and so is the head. Some of them wear garlands of birds' feathers. They are dark in color, not unlike the Ethiopians, with thick black hair, not very long, tied back behind the head like a small tail. As for the physique of these men, they are well proportioned, of medium height, a little taller than we are. They have broad chests, strong arms, and the legs and other parts of the body are well composed. There is nothing else, except that they tend to be rather broad in the face: but not all, for we saw many with angular faces. They have big black eyes, and an attentive and open look. They are not very strong, but they have a sharp cunning, and are agile and swift runners. From what we could tell from observation, in the last two respects they resemble the Orientals, particularly those from the farthest Sinarian regions.[5]

Verrazzano's account reveals little of the culture of the natives, noting: "We could not learn the details of the life and customs of these people because of the short time we spent on land, due to the fact that there were few men, and the ship was anchored on the high seas."[6]

More well-known accounts of American Indians come from Spanish conquistador Hernando de Soto, who most likely encountered Mississippian Indians to the south and west of North Carolina; and from Philip Amadas and Arthur Barlowe's expedition in 1584, which was commissioned by Sir Walter Raleigh and brought Manteo and Wanchese, two Roanoke Indians, back to England.[7] To this day, the names of these two natives are commemorated by towns on Roanoke Island. Though the two men were in England for less than a year, this exposure likely led Manteo and Wanchese to be the first American Indians to learn English. Thomas Harriot was charged with deciphering their language, and his linguistic skill made him an indispensable member of the subsequent 1585 voyage sponsored by Raleigh. Despite this relatively intense contact, European explorers were more concerned with documenting details of the land and its resources than they were the language and culture of American Indian populations in North Carolina.

The linguistic legacy of the American Indian groups is most prominent in North Carolina place names, including many counties (for example, Alamance, Alleghany, Catawba, Cherokee, Chowan, Currituck, Pamlico, Pasquotank,

Perquimans, Watauga, Yadkin), bodies of water (*Pee Dee River, Eno River, Neuse River, Yadkin River, Lake Mattamuskeet, Pamlico Sound*), and place names (*Hatteras, Manteo, Ocracoke, Saxapahaw, Swannanoa, Wanchese, Waxhaw, Roanoke Island, Sauratown Mountains*). Place names far outnumber the relatively restricted list of American Indian words for material objects such as plants (*tobacco, tomato, maize*), foods (*hominy, chili, succotash*), animals (*raccoon, chipmunk, coyote*), equipment (*canoe, hammock, toboggan*), and topographical features (*pocosin, muskeg, bayou*). Some of these have become regional words in American English, including dialect areas of North Carolina. In the western part of North Carolina, a toboggan is a type of hat that is worn in cold weather, whereas in other regions, it refers exclusively to a type of wooden sled that was used by Indians in Canada for transporting goods over snow and ice. Most likely, the need for a head cover while using this sled, a toboggan cap, was simply shortened and generalized to refer to the stocking or knitted cap. More will be said of these American Indian groups in chapter 8.

The First Imposition of English

Raleigh's second commissioned expedition, led by Richard Grenville in 1585, returned Manteo and Wanchese to North Carolina. It also brought to Roanoke Island John White, an artist whose watercolors remain historical treasures (see Figure 2.3), and Thomas Harriot, who had studied the language of Manteo and Wanchese while in England, learning enough Algonquian to communicate with the local tribe. In fact, this experience allowed him to write some of the most extensive descriptions of American Indians' culture, including religion, war practices, and language. He noted that each settlement seemed to have its own government and variety of language: "The language of every government is different from any other, and the further they are distant the greater is the difference."[8] Harriot, despite viewing his own culture and religion as superior and "true," clearly admired the American Indians he encountered, describing them as "very ingenious" and having an "excellencie of wit."[9]

Gaining a toehold in the New World was by no means an easy task. Sir Walter Raleigh sponsored a number of expeditions with the goal of establishing a permanent colony that would be profitable to England. Though North Carolinians know of the Lost Colony, there remain many unanswered questions today, most notably: what happened to the settlers? One theory suggests the settlers assimilated with American Indian groups, while another posits that

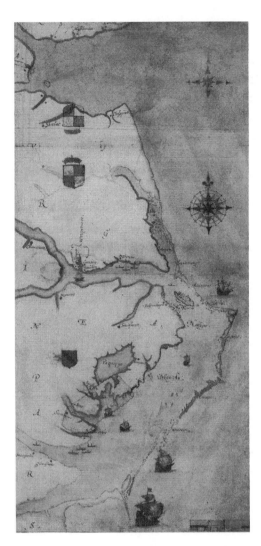

American Indians slaughtered the colonists. A third theory posits that it was hardship or illness that did in the settlers. A fourth attributes the disappearance to a Spanish raid. A fifth possibility is that the colonists simply moved south to Hatteras Island, north toward present-day Jamestown, or westward to a more-sheltered inland location near present-day Edenton.[10] One of the most famous clues is linguistic in nature—the letters "CRO" carved into a tree and "CROATOAN" carved into a post on the fort—although linguists don't have much to add to the conversations about the significance of these clues. The Lost Colony contributed little to the current linguistic landscape of the state, preserved only in place names such as *Dare* County and the name of the capital city, *Raleigh*, which was established more than 200 years after the Lost Colony. Though North Carolina was the location of the earliest arrival of the English language, it wasn't until the founding of Jamestown, Virginia, in 1607 that English gained a permanent place in the New World. By then, other languages, including Spanish, Portuguese, and French, were being spoken in established, permanent colonies in North America.

Shaping North Carolina

Following the Lost Colony period, English settlement attempts stopped until King James, in 1606, authorized a private corporation called the Virginia Company to colonize the area between present-day Bangor, Maine, and the Cape Fear River. In 1607, 104 men on three ships led by Christopher Newport landed at Jamestown, Virginia, the site that Raleigh had intended to settle during his 1587 expedition. Many were from aristocratic backgrounds, but they hailed from different areas of (mostly) eastern England. John Smith was from Wiloughby, Lincolnshire, while John Rolfe, known for cultivating tobacco in the New World and marrying Pocahontas, was from Heacham, Norfolk, a town farther south. Christopher Newport was from Limehouse (near London), which was even farther south along the eastern coast.[11] These areas of England had—and still have—distinct dialects, which would have mixed in the colony. Working-class settlers, who made up nearly half of the initial group of English-speaking settlers, would have spoken a dialect quite different from those in the upper classes, so regional and class language distinctions were present in the earliest English spoken in the earliest settlements. In 1608 two British women arrived, along with a number of Dutch, German, and Polish settlers.[12] Africans were first brought in 1619.[13] Thus, there was remarkable linguistic diversity from the outset. With the development of tobacco, the fortunes of the colony were shifted, bringing wealth and more European interest to the area, enticing more settlers, mainly from southeastern England. It is these English dialects that began to diffuse into what is now northeastern North Carolina.

The first documented forays from the Virginia settlements into North Carolina were led by John Pory, an English administrator considered by many to be the first news correspondent, who explored the Chowan River area in the early 1620s.[14] Shortly thereafter, in 1629, King James's successor and son, Charles I, granted the land between 31° north (near present-day Brunswick,

Georgia) and 36° north latitudes (near present-day Kill Devil Hills, North Carolina) to Sir Robert Heath. The new Carolana colony—after *Carolus*, the Latin version of *Charles*—included a provision allowing Heath to rule as a king in Charles's absence, including granting him the right to raise an army, collect taxes, and create towns. Heath made no attempts to settle or govern the region, and in 1638 he transferred the grant to Henry Frederick Howard. Through the beheading of Charles I in 1649 and the subsequent eleven-year interregnum, Carolana remained a place of little law and even less oversight. Following the reestablishment of the monarchy in 1660, Charles II used the land of the Carolana grant to repay some his allies. It is in this same year that the first-known official transfer of land in the colony took place, when Nathaniel Batts, in 1660, purchased land from "Kiscutanewh Kinge of Yausapin."[15] By the time of this purchase, there were doubtlessly many English-speaking homesteaders in what is now North Carolina.

Charles II turned the land of the Carolana grant over to the "true and absolute Lords and Proprietaries" in 1663, and eventually, in 1665, the king negotiated an extension to include valuable resources and settlements one-half degree north (to the current North Carolina–Virginia border) and two degrees south (to about Cape Canaveral, Florida). At this time, the name was also changed to the present-day spelling, *Carolina*. The eight Lords Proprietors have left an onomastic imprint since they included Edward Hyde, William Craven, and Sir George Carteret, all of whom are the namesakes for modern counties in the eastern coastal region of the state. The Lords Proprietors set up a functioning government overseen by Sir William Berkeley that successfully drew settlers from New England and Barbados, increasing yet again the linguistic diversity of the budding colony.

One of the most successful early settlements in the colony was Charleston, established in 1670 and already the fifth-largest town in North America by 1690. At that point, of course, Charleston was still a part of the unitary state of Carolina. While initially populated by English settlers, the port attracted settlers from all over Europe, including France, Scotland, Ireland, and Germany, as well as from the Caribbean, resulting in a diverse mix of religions, politics, and languages that would eventually disperse into North Carolina. Even later, the port became the termination point of the Middle Passage and received more African slaves than any other port in North America, providing a rich assortment of African languages along with pidgin and creole English.

The relative sparseness of the population, the wild and sometimes treacherous coastlines and sounds, and the lawlessness of the colony made it a haven for pirates during the early eighteenth century, including, of course, the infamous Edward Teach (ca. 1680–1718), more widely known as Blackbeard, and Major Stede Bonnet, "the gentleman pirate."[16] Meandering coastal waterways, topographical barriers, and sparse populations are also good for developing and sustaining language diversity. This lawlessness attracted other diverse groups as well. French Huguenots, for example, left Manakin Town (near present-day Richmond, Virginia) for Carolina to escape religious persecution from encroaching English settlers in Virginia. German-speaking Palatines from southwestern Germany and Switzerland arrived shortly thereafter, beginning in about 1710. They established New Bern, North Carolina, which became the colony's and then the state's capital during the American Revolutionary War. The seeds of language diversity were sown in the physical, human, and political ecology of this early settlement period.

During the eighteenth century, major sociohistorical events deeply affected the developing colony and its linguistic composition. African slaves first arrived, mostly via Tidewater Virginia and Charleston, South Carolina. It is estimated that by 1730, about 30,000 whites and 6,000 slaves lived in what is now North Carolina, with this population restricted almost exclusively to the Coastal Plain. Second, in a defining moment for the state, the Lords Proprietors succumbed to heavy pressure and sold South Carolina to the Crown.

Under Governor Gabriel Johnston (1734–52), the population of North Carolina began to increase substantially, and the frontier steadily extended westward to the foot of the Blue Ridge Mountains. The population grew from the estimated 36,000 residents (free and slave) in 1730 to more than 265,000 spread from the coast to the mountains by the American Revolutionary War.[18] While much of the original English population spread westward, often along rivers, other arrivals—Germans, Swiss, Scots-Irish, Highland Scots, Welsh, and French Huguenots—came directly from other parts of Europe and settled in enclaves across the colony. Other settlers arrived in the western Piedmont via the Great Wagon Road (discussed in more detail below).

From this early settlement history, we can explain the major dialect regions depicted in the map of the previous chapter. The spillover from the Virginia Piedmont and Tidewater is still heard today; the Coastal Plain reflects the diverse Englishes that marched westward, while the Highland areas were populated most predominately by the Scots-Irish and Highland Scots, who also spilled into the Piedmont. The Outer Banks dialect is shaped after the influence of the earliest English speakers and has ties to the Eastern Shore region of Maryland. Today's concentrations of vernacular regional dialects in the coastal estuaries in the east and in the mountains in the west and their diluted presence in the Piedmont area reflect the historical settlement and dispersion trends of the English-speaking population.

Smaller Immigrant Groups

While the English influx from Virginia was initially the most influential source of new settlers, they were not the only early arrivers. Lowland Scots were one of the earliest groups, arriving in the Cape Fear region before 1700. The aforementioned German-speaking Palatines began arriving in about 1710, establishing New Bern, North Carolina, at the confluence of the Neuse and Trent Rivers. Welsh settlers came to North Carolina via Pennsylvania between 1730 and 1734 and settled in what is now Pender County at the lower Cape Fear River. Highland Scots arrived a little later, in 1740, with a group of about 360 immigrants who came after Governor Johnston exempted foreign Protestants from local taxes for ten years. The British defeat of the Highland Scots in the 1746 Battle of Culloden increased the flow of Scots into the Wilmington area, from which they moved up the Cape Fear River to near where Fayetteville is located today in Cumberland County. From there, the group expanded southward into what is now Scotland, Robeson, and Hoke Counties. Several of the distinct dialect traits of these areas were molded during this era, exemplifying the founder effect.

In the western part of the state, two other groups were arriving: Ulster Scots (or Scots-Irish) and Germans came via the more than 450-mile long Great Wagon Road. These settlers—often the children or grandchildren of those who had first emigrated, many as indentured servants, from Ulster Plantation to Pennsylvania—were finding land scarce in Pennsylvania and were drawn to the newly opened North Carolina frontier after the colony was reclaimed by the Crown in 1729. Though there were a handful of early arrivers, the European presence in the western part of North Carolina didn't start in earnest until a little before the midpoint of the eighteenth century. Once the migration gained some momentum, it grew vigorously right up until 1775.[19] Later, newly arriving Ulster Scots left Philadelphia directly for the North Carolina mountains and western Piedmont. The Scots-Irish were independent, industrious, and highly literate. They quickly developed a network of sawmills, flour mills, and tanneries. They even set up trading-post

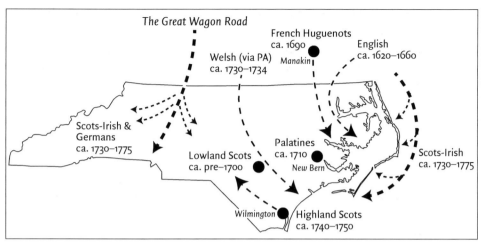

The Great Wagon Road

French Huguenots
ca. 1690

English
ca. 1620–1660

Welsh (via PA)   Manakin
ca. 1730–1734

Scots-Irish &
Germans
ca. 1730–1775

Palatines
ca. 1710

Lowland Scots
ca. pre-1700

New Bern

Scots-Irish
ca. 1730–1775

Wilmington   Highland Scots
ca. 1740–1750

MAP 2.1. North Carolina Settlement Overview

stores along the Great Wagon Road. Perhaps most important for our perspective, they left a linguistic legacy in the western part of the state that is still heard in the dialects of the mountains and flows into the Piedmont.

THE SCOTS-IRISH

The Scots-Irish were one of the largest and most influential groups of immigrants in North Carolina. The name of this group—discussed in more detail momentarily—suggests, perhaps, a more homogenous culture and language background than was actually the case. The Scots-Irish were a diverse group that was mostly composed of people originally of Presbyterian Scottish and Anglican English heritage but also included members of other persecuted populations, such as political dissenters from Northern England, Wales, and the London area, and even peoples of non-British origin, including Calvinists from Flanders, German Palatines, and French Huguenots. These diverse religions, cultures, and languages mixed on the Ulster Plantation in present-day Northern Ireland, which was created as the culmination of nearly a century of British attempts to conquer Ireland during the reigns of King Henry VIII (1509–47) and Elizabeth I (1558–1603).[20] Ulster Plantation began in earnest in 1606, spurred initially by wealthy, private landowners. Adding to the local language diversity were the Gaelic chieftains and clans and the Spanish mercenaries they enlisted in an unsuccessful rebellion in 1609. Although groups of many cultural and linguistic backgrounds came to Ulster Plantation, they were required to learn English and affirm allegiance to Protestantism upon their settlement. The colonization and subsequent language and religious stipulations were intended to quash any further rebellion, offering just one example of how language can be used as a means of controlling populations. A second case, examined in chapter 7, occurred when linguistic conformity was used as a means of preventing African slave rebellions. In Ulster, as with African slaves, diverse ethnicities and languages came together and forged a language first out of necessity; later, it would serve as glue for the community as they again left their homelands, this time for America.

The terms *Scots-Irish* and *Scotch-Irish* are used somewhat synonymously today in the United States, though the latter tends to be disfavored in the United Kingdom, dismissed by the quip: "Scotch is a drink, Scots are a people." Somewhat surprisingly, perhaps, the disfavored form seems to be older, with the earliest attestation in 1573, when Queen Elizabeth I used it to distinguish Gaelic speakers in the Highland region of Scotland from the "mere Irish" who lived in Ireland: "We are given to understand that a nobleman named 'Sorley Boy' and others, who be of the Scotch-Irish race, . . . at this time are content to acknowledge our true and mere right to the countrie of Ulster and the crowne of Ireland. . . . [Therefore, they] shall be reputed and taken for denizens, and not for 'mere Irish."[21] This name would continue to be used for over a century in England to refer to these Gaelic-speaking groups. The term Scots-Irish is first attested in 1645, also designating Gaelic-speaking groups. According to the *Oxford English Dictionary*, the first attestation of either spelling used to refer to emigrants from Ulster Plantation is Scots-Irish, which appears in a text written in Scotland by Andrew Fletcher in 1698; however, linguist Dr. Michael Montgomery has discovered a Maryland affidavit from 1689/1690 where "you Scotch-Irish dogg it was you" is used to identify an English-speaking emigrant from Ulster Plantation.[22] This suggests that the shift of reference from Gaelic-speaking groups to those from Ulster Plantation happened roughly concurrently in both the United Kingdom and America.

However, British and American usage soon diverged. In the United Kingdom, Scotch-Irish gave way to Scots-Irish as the preferred term where it could refer to either Gaelic speakers in Scotland or Ulster Presbyterians. In the United States, Scotch-Irish remained the predominant label, where it became used almost exclusively for reference to Ulster Presbyterians, along with the synonyms *Irish*, *Ulster-Irish*, *Northern Irish*, or *Irish Presbyterians*. In America, the Scots-Irish were most commonly called simply *Irish* until the Irish migration caused by the Great Irish Famine in the 1840s introduced a group that needed to be differentiated from the earlier immigrants. Michael Montgomery has scoured seventeenth- and eighteenth-century American colonial records for these competing terms, finding twenty-four uses of Scotch-Irish and only three of Scots-Irish.[23] Even today, while the use of Scotch-Irish is virtually nonexistent in the United Kingdom, it remains the more common variant in America. The Library of Congress contains more than six times the number of books containing Scotch-Irish in the title than Scots-Irish. As with any ethnic label, some attestations capture derogatory characterizations of the group they describe, and there is some suggestion that the term Scots-Irish was preferred among early immigrants. However, in the present-day United States, there is no clear pattern to show that one form or the other is more commonly used in a negative fashion. We adopt the more modern term in this book because it appears to be generally more neutral in its connotations.

All told, from 1717 to 1775, somewhere between 150,000 and 300,000 Scots-Irish came to America (or an average of 2,500 to 5,000 per year). Significant ebbs and flows to this movement led to concentrated waves of emigrants, including one from 1725 to 1729 that was so large that the English Parliament commissioned a study to evaluate whether Ulster Plantation was in danger of being lost entirely. A number of forces converged to entice the Scots-Irish to leave their adopted homeland for North America, including religious tension between the Protestant and Catholic populations, trade restrictions and tariffs, rent extortion, a series of droughts (1714–19), a bovine disease epidemic called rot (1716), and an outbreak of smallpox (1718). Afraid they would face persecution if they returned to England or Scotland, many Scots-Irish elected to seek out a new life in America.[24]

The Scots-Irish arrived in North Carolina later than they had in the northern colonies, as rumors had reached Ulster that the southern plantations viewed indentured servants as short-term investments to be maximally exploited. The earliest Scots-Irish emigrants were welcomed to New England by Cotton Mather for their religious dogma and their perceived physical prowess; however, they received such chilly welcomes in Boston that their letters home encouraged others to instead emigrate to the Quaker Colony set up by William Penn. Thus, most Scots-Irish settlers arrived in Philadelphia and nearby towns along the Delaware River and, following their period of indentured servitude, spilled into the Great Valley—the fertile plains along the Susquehanna River that stretch for over 100 miles westward, converge with the Potomac River, turn southwest to join the Shenandoah Valley, and end in the Valley of Virginia (the area that connects the sources of the James, Roanoke, and New Rivers). The Valley of Virginia terminates to the west at the Appalachian Mountains and to the south in the Carolina Piedmont.

The Pennsylvania colony was particularly attractive to Scots-Irish indentured servants, who were estimated to make up between 50 and 66 percent of the Scots-Irish immigrants, as the local agricultural economy was similar to that of Northern Ireland.[25] Even more attractive to the former tenant farmers was the promise of owning land. The Pennsylvania legislature stipulated that in exchange for a four- to seven-year term of service either on a ship, at a trade, or on a farm, servants were to be given fifty acres of land, as well as "two complete sets of apparel," a new axe, one "Grubbing Hoe," and "one Weeding Hoe."[26]

The Great Wagon Road, also called the Great Philadelphia Wagon Road, crossed into North Carolina near the borders of present-day Stokes and Rockingham Counties before continuing southward past Pilot Mountain and eventually joining what is now the Interstate 85 corridor between Greensboro and Charlotte. A map of the Great Wagon Road (Figure 2.4), created in 1751 by Joshua Fry and Peter Jefferson (the father of Thomas Jefferson), traces in detail the 455-mile route from Philadelphia to Wachau-die-Aue (the Moravian tract also known as *Wachovia*), including river crossings and landmarks. However, the southernmost portion of the road developed slowly. It took twenty-three years from the initial arrival of the Scots-Irish in 1717 before the Great Wagon Road brought enough settlers to western Piedmont North Carolina to establish small towns, which often grew out of trading posts set up along the road. The trickle of settlers gradually grew into a stream, but the lack of natural barriers in the western Piedmont led primarily to the creation of isolated farmsteads rather than towns. This isolation likely is at the root of the microdialect differences that can still be heard among many descendants of the Scots-Irish today. Not until 1755 was a population concentrated enough to support the first inland Presbyterian church, established at the Mill Bridge Community near what is now Salisbury.

By this time, North Carolina was attracting nonindentured servant immigrants who, arriving late, found land in Pennsylvania and Virginia either too densely populated or too expensive to purchase. The English government saw the settlers as a means of controlling the American Indian populations in the western part of the territory and offered land grants as a means of pushing the American Indian populations west. Some of these settlers, including the legendary Daniel Boone, were spurred by the 1750 English dis-

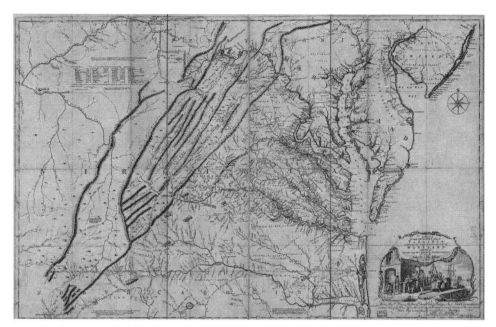

FIGURE 2.4. The Great Wagon Road, as drawn by Joshua Fry and Peter Jefferson, 1751.

covery of the Cumberland Gap and the promise of the adventure of the frontier that lay beyond it.

The immigration of the Scots-Irish into the western part of North Carolina nearly doubled the population from 50,000 to 90,000 during Gabriel Johnston's term as governor (1734–52).[27] It should be no surprise, then, that the language of this group has been the most important influence on the dialects heard today in the western Piedmont and Appalachian Mountains.

While the Scots-Irish migration along the Great Wagon Road is relatively well-known, there was a lesser-known, ship-based migration of Scots-Irish from Wilmington, North Carolina, and Charleston, South Carolina. From these towns, settlers moved up the coast to the Pamlico Sound region, sometimes integrating into established communities and sometimes establishing their own, adding to the cultural—and linguistic—diversity of the coast. It is this two-pronged migration—along the Great Wagon Road and along the coast—that has led to the sharing of many grammatical, pronunciation, and vocabulary features by speakers in the farthest eastern and western portions of the state. In chapter 6, we will discuss more of the specific influences from the Scots-Irish founder effect, but a brief sampling demonstrates just how influential this dialect has been in shaping the linguistic landscape

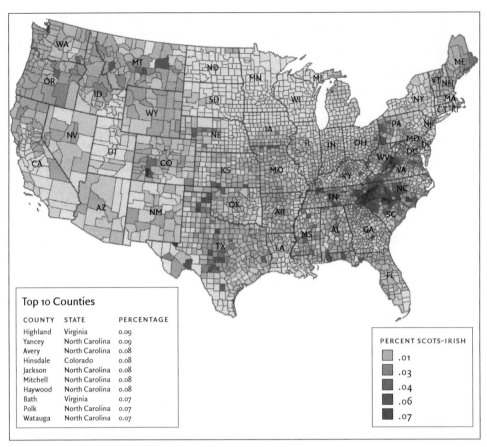

Top 10 Counties

COUNTY	STATE	PERCENTAGE
Highland	Virginia	0.09
Yancey	North Carolina	0.09
Avery	North Carolina	0.08
Hinsdale	Colorado	0.08
Jackson	North Carolina	0.08
Mitchell	North Carolina	0.08
Haywood	North Carolina	0.08
Bath	Virginia	0.07
Polk	North Carolina	0.07
Watauga	North Carolina	0.07

PERCENT SCOTS-IRISH

.01
.03
.04
.06
.07

MAP 2.2. Concentration of the Scots-Irish Population in the Present-Day United States by County (Courtesy of AncestryMaps.com)

of North Carolina. A few relatively iconic language forms are traceable directly to the Scots-Irish, including grammatical features such as the *a*-prefix ("he's a-hunting"); the *-s* on the verb in "The women goes to the store"; plural *you'uns*, as in "You'uns should come with us"; *needs* plus past participle verbs like *washed* or *fixed*, as in "The car needs washed"; and vocabulary items such as *piece* ("short distance"), *poke* ("bag"), *vittles* ("food"), and *till* (as in "It's quarter till five").

The American Revolutionary War effectively ended the Scots-Irish immigration. Within a decade, the inhabitants of the young United States began to look westward more strongly than ever before. The Cumberland Gap provided one such passage, opening a new chapter of American history. In these narrow channels of the Appalachians, people from diverse backgrounds came together to challenge the frontier, shedding labels such as *English*, *Scots-Irish*, *German*, *Welsh*, or *Scot* and instead taking on a new moniker: *American*. Beyond the mountains, the languages, like the groups, began to merge. Even on the western slopes of the mountains, the languages and groups came to lack the distinctiveness found a few ridgelines to the east. The Scots-Irish represent one of the most influential groups of settlers in America, both culturally and linguistically. In fact, their arrival and dispersion from the Pennsylvania colony can still be seen in modern demographic statistics, as is clear in Map 2.2, which captures the percentage of Scots-Irish in each county of the United States. The particularly strong and lasting impact of the Scots-Irish in North Carolina—home to seven of the ten counties with the highest percentage of Scots-Irish—is clearly visible and audible.

GERMAN IMMIGRANTS

The largest group of Germans settled in the western Piedmont of North Carolina concurrently with the Scots-Irish. The first Germans in the western part of the colony—associated with Lutheranism and the German Reformed Church, a Calvinist denomination—arrived around 1747 near Salisbury in what is now Rowan County. These early arrivals established German-speaking settlements stretching as far east as present-day Orange County. They built schools that doubled as churches and developed a series of towns and farms. Many of these German settlers owned slaves who learned German, often catching outsiders by surprise.

The Moravians, perhaps the group that is most well-known today, arrived shortly after this first wave. Unlike the German Palatines in the east and the earliest arriving Germans in the western Piedmont, the Moravians lived in an enclave community and, consequently, maintained their German longer. Bishop August Gottlieb Spangenberg led a party that explored the northern part of the colony, searching for a swath of land to purchase. They purchased a tract of nearly 100,000 acres from Earl Granville in 1753 and officially settled *Wachovia* or *Wachau-die-Aue* on November 17 of that year in current-day Forsyth County.[28] The name was selected for the land's resemblance to *die Wachau* valley along the Danube River in Austria; Wachovia is a Latinate rendering of the original German word. Many English speakers struggle to pronounce the German sound *ach* of *Bach* and *ach*, which is not a k sound but a continuous sound produced at the same position as the stop k sound in English. Since English does not have this sound, early speakers simply used the English k sound instead of the German sound *ach*, and the pronunciation stuck. Salem became a Moravian cultural center, hosting medical and dental care and a tavern that catered both to locals and visitors. Surrounding Salem were the agricultural towns of Bethabara, Bethania, Friedberg, Friedland, and Hope.

To hear the German pronunciations of *Bach*, *Ach*, and *Wachovia*, visit http://www.talkintarheel.com/chapter/2/audio2-1.php

In many ways, the Moravians displayed more-progressive views than were common at the time in North Carolina. Education was compulsory for children, and in 1772 Moravians established the first school for women in North Carolina, the Salem Female Academy (now Salem Academy and College), one of the longest-enduring women's institutions in the country. While the Moravians did hold slaves, their slaves seem to have held a slightly elevated position compared to slaves in other parts of the South. One slave, Johann Samuel, even served as superintendent of the Bethabara farm from 1788 until he was freed in 1801, after which he remained and rented farmland from the church.[29] In 1839, while the practice was illegal in many parts of the country, Moravians mandated that all slave children were to receive free education, including instruction in German.

As pacifists, the group remained neutral during the American Revolutionary War, selling supplies to both the revolutionaries and the British, but the Germans in Salem were the first to hold a public celebration of independence in what may have been the very first Fourth of July celebration in the newly formed United States. They even hosted and entertained President George Washington at the Salem Tavern in 1791, who was likely served by German-speaking slaves. The Germans represented the second-largest European immigrant group during this period of North Carolina's history (trailing only the Scots-Irish), and their cultural and linguistic heritage is still on display in the preserved Moravian community of Bethabara and in Old Salem, which became present-day Winston-Salem in 1913.

SLAVES AND FREED BLACKS

Like other groups, African slaves in North Carolina cannot be described in a single history; similarly, their language cannot be described in a unilateral way. Slaves were not evenly distributed across the colony, and the experiences of slaves and freed blacks in the colony were not at all homogeneous, as discussed in chapter 7. Instead of detailing the individual histories of groups throughout the colony, this overview weaves these narratives into

FIGURE 2.5. Werner Willis, *Washington's Southern Tour,*
May 31, 1791, Old Salem, North Carolina.

a more general history, presenting it as more unified than was actually the case. Of course, African Americans in the western part of the state, where some were taught German, had a very different history from those in the plantation region of the Coastal Plain, where many were punished for literacy, and slaves on the estuaries of the coast had their own unique history in comparison to these two groups.

Slavery as an institution in North Carolina took shape first in the 1665 Concessions and Agreement and was defined legally in the 1669 Fundamental Constitutions. It is not until 1694 that the slaves in the colony are noted in legal documents, when five whites petitioned the colony for extra land because of the eight slaves they possessed. Sixteen years later, there were estimated to be about 900 slaves living in the colony—all in coastal communities—with 211 in Pasquotank Precinct and ninety-seven in Currituck.[30] Even early on, there were a few free blacks living in the colony, though it is only through indirect means—such as the identification in court documents—that we know about these free blacks, who ranged from family farmers to artisans and slave owners.

The population of blacks in North Carolina increased slowly at first, taking over twenty years (1717) before there were more than 1,000 slaves in the colony. The number then began to grow more quickly, reaching 3,000 in 1720, 6,000 in 1730, and 30,000 in 1765.[31] North Carolina's slave demographics differed substantially from other southern states, as there were relatively few large plantations. The largest plantation in North Carolina reached 50,000 acres, but the large plantations did not have the same numbers of slaves as equivalently sized plantations to the north and south. Governor Gabriel Johnston, for example, one of the wealthiest men in the colony, owned about 24,000 acres but only about 100 slaves.[32] Compare this to the situation on George Washington's plantation, Mount Vernon, which in the mid-eighteenth century had over fifty-five slaves working on less than 500 acres—a concentration of slaves that was twenty-five times that of the Johnston plantation. In the years prior to independence, 53 percent of North Carolina slave owners held five or fewer slaves, and less than 3 percent of slaves lived on plantations with more than fifty slaves.[33] The slave holdings per family, the relative density of the slave population in a particular region, and the interaction between blacks and whites are important for assessing the kind of language used by the earliest black population in North Carolina. Linguistic evidence points to the conclusion that slaves in different conditions spoke quite differently from each other, and this difference is still evident today.

With tensions mounting between the colonies and England, American colonists began to fear that the British would help free slaves and enlist their help in defeating the American revolutionaries. In response to this fear, in 1774 the North Carolina Provincial Congress banned the importation of slaves, which was not lifted until 1790. Following the lifting of this ban, the slave population in North Carolina began to increase more rapidly than it ever had previously.

The first official U.S. census in 1790 reported 100,572 slaves and 4,975 free blacks living in North Carolina, making up a little over 25 percent of the reported population of the state. The number of slaves would double to just over 200,000 by the 1820 census and more than triple by the outbreak of the Civil War, reaching 331,059 slaves and 30,463 free blacks in the 1860 census. The largest increases coincided with the looming abolition of slavery in the British colonies, which eventually came to pass in 1833. The slave population of North Carolina stagnated in the 1830s as many Tar Heels moved to the newly opened lands of the Old Southwest—Alabama, Mississippi, and Texas. They took their slaves with them; in fact, there was a mass migration of slaves from the older eastern slave states such as Virginia and North Carolina to the new states on the Gulf and lower Mississippi River in the years before the Civil War. During the decade before abolition, widespread antislavery sentiment led to a series of revolts, and landowners throughout the Caribbean eventually thought it wise to sell their slaves to the United States before the British government could strip them of their property without compensation. These slaves brought from Caribbean locales may have arrived speaking a very different variety of English—creole—than the slaves in the United States. To this day, Afro-Caribbean populations have remarkable variation in their varieties of English.

As in most other places in America, there is a paucity of detailed records regarding the slaves brought to North Carolina; however, few slaves arrived directly to the colony via Wilmington, North Carolina. Most slaves arrived from Africa, Barbados, or the West Indies to markets in Jamestown and Charleston, where North Carolina planters went to purchase slaves. By 1800, blacks in North Carolina outnumbered whites by a ratio of two to one. As noted, North Carolina generally did not have the sheer numbers or concentration of slaves as other southern states. This difference led to important social and linguistic differences among slaves in North Carolina when compared to elsewhere in the South. Socially, the smaller number of slaves per farm meant less specialization of labor. It is possible that slaves in North Carolina often worked in both the fields and the home as opposed to one or the other. It is also possible that North Carolina slaves were more likely to be involved in trades other than farming, including carpentry, masonry, maintenance, fishing, and boat piloting along the Outer Banks. Furthermore, the smaller size of farms in North Carolina made it easier for slaves on different farms to interact. It was common for slaves to walk between properties during their free time, and many did so with the goal of finding a spouse. No doubt, the differential occupations and the interactional patterns with slave owners and other locals had an effect on the diversity of African American speech still evident today in North Carolina. Our research reported in chapter 7 reveals variation among different African American groups that aligns with the rich diversity of language variation for other groups in North Carolina.

North Carolina's agrarian slaves would have worked alongside vernacular-speaking white indentured speakers and, at least initially, learned their versions of English. These slaves would likely have learned the stigmatized dialects of indentured servants, while slaves in other trades learned more-standardized English and others perhaps spoke a creole variety that arose out of the slave trade and/or the Low Country of South Carolina. Many slaves likely picked up the regional varieties of English spoken in their locale, so that those on the coast and Outer Banks picked up that distinctive dialect while those in the western part of the state picked up a variety of Mountain speech. Probably nowhere in the South was the speech of different groups of African Americans more diverse from each other than in North Carolina.

While slavery, along with North Carolina's cultural ecology and geography, provided the conditions for the early development of African American Englishes, a few events of the abolition movement and from the early emancipation era shaped the dialects in significant ways. Antislavery sentiment began to grow in the newly formed United States, spreading most strongly from Pennsylvania, where the Quakers resolutely opposed slavery. Pennsylvania became a haven for escaped slaves, and Underground Railroads emerged by which sympathetic whites would help runaway slaves find their way to freedom. Although a few routes cut through North Carolina, the most noteworthy development was a robust, marine-based Underground Railroad. One of these routes through the Coastal Plain led slaves to a gathering place in the Great Dismal Swamp in the northeastern part of the state, a stopover point for so many slaves that the North Carolina government eventually targeted it with continuous patrols. A route through what is now Guilford County created by Quaker leader Levi Coffin saw so much traffic that Coffin was nicknamed "President of the Underground Railroad."[34] Due to the clandestine nature of the Underground Railroad, no official records exist detailing its popularity or the success rate of slave escape attempts, but some historians suggest that as many as 100,000 slaves attempted to escape during the nineteenth century. The number of routes through the state, including the waterways of Edenton, New Bern, and Wilmington, certainly brought slaves into contact with other slaves and various dialects of English. At the same time, it is possible that from this intermixing of slave Englishes arose some core features of modern African American English.

Eventually, black schools and churches began to spring up around the state. In 1865 a group of freed slaves formed a community along the Tar River in Edgecombe County known as Freedom Hill, making it the oldest town established by African Americans in the United States. In 1885 Freedom Hill was incorporated as Princeville, North Carolina. Eighteen African Americans were elected to the state's House of Representatives in 1868 and proposed legislation that would begin the long fight for equal rights, giving African Americans a voice in the politics of their state that grew from a whisper to a shout over the next century.

Conclusion

The known history of North Carolina is expansive and the unknown history even more so. This chapter merely has offered a rough sketch rather than a detailed picture of that rich history, focusing mostly on the people and events that were most important for the remarkable linguistic diversity in North Carolina today. In doing so, many details—including some that have had dramatic effects on the development of the state—have been minimized or omitted. The Yadkin River, for example, absent entirely from this discussion, figured prominently in the settlement of the western Piedmont and was important to Scots-Irish, German, and African American groups. Also omitted are the histories of the second and third waves of settlers to these areas. We have focused on the earliest settlers of each region because of the founder effect, the profound impact of the earliest settlers' speech patterns described in chapter 1.

The settlement history of North Carolina can be summarized succinctly: many different groups have come to the region for many different reasons. Some came for isolation, while others came for a sense of community. Each group has left a little trail of linguistic clues that reveal who they were and where they were from. Place names tell not only the origins of groups but, in many cases, also what they hoped to find in North Carolina. Sometimes the names hearkened back to the homeland, as New Bern did for the Swiss and Fayetteville for the French. Sometimes they pointed forward, as Hope did for the Moravians and Freedom Hill for the freed slaves. The indelible marks of these groups on the state are not, however, limited to geographical names. The various art, music, food, and cultural traditions throughout North Carolina today are the living histories of these groups, each told in a language variety a little bit different from the others.

The diversity represented in the settlement history is partially what gave birth to the rich dialect variation in the state. Though the history presented here ends shortly after the Civil War, it is important to note that new groups continue to arrive through the present day. Different periods during the twentieth century saw sizable groups of Lebanese, Vietnamese, Hmong, Indian, Polish, and Japanese immigrants. More recently, North Carolina has become home for many people of diverse Latino backgrounds, as will be examined in chapter 10. Further, the increased mobility of Americans, along with economic shifts, have resulted in Americans from all over moving into the urban centers of North Carolina, sharpening the divide between rural and urban voices, as will be seen in chapter 4. While some individual dialects may be threatened by this encroachment, the linguistic diversity of the state continues even in the face of mass media and pop culture that highlights homogenous modernity above traditional diversity.

Just as the history of the state is still being written, an old topic has recently come back around. Debates over the borders of the colony started even before the first Europeans settled here. The borders were renegotiated and redrawn many times throughout the years for various reasons, and even today, with improved mapping technology, the borders are once again being fine-tuned. In 2012 the border between North Carolina and South Carolina was reexamined for the first time since about 1740, and the previous line was found to be off by up to 150 feet. Ninety-three homes near Charlotte were suddenly declared to be in a different state. The anecdote is a reminder of just how alive the past remains in the Old North State, a state with a long history that spans many centuries, cultures, and tongues.

Landscaping Dialect   3

From Manteo to Murphy

I quickly saw the enormous variety of landscapes that would be encountered if I had
the courage and fortitude to try to paint a portrait of North Carolina from the westernmost border to the coast. I was transformed by a great pride in the pictorial possibili-
ties of the North Carolina scenic landscape. —J. CHRIS WILSON, North Carolina artist, from "Artist Statement for Murphy to Manteo—An Artist's Scenic Journey," http://
www.jchriswilson.com/about/detail/murphy-to-manteo-artist-statement/

Driving the 544-mile trek from the coast to the mountains—from Manteo to
Murphy—can now be done in one very long day thanks to highways such as
Route 64 and Interstate 40. But every year, scores of people choose, instead,
to bike, run, and even walk across the state. For their effort, they experience
in a unique way changes in North Carolina's physical terrain and cultural and
linguistic landscape that cannot be envisioned or perceived from a speeding automobile. Speed, mobility, and accessibility may have contracted the
world, but the historical and social forces we described in the last chapter
have not yet leveled the linguistic diversity in the Tar Heel State.

For those not up to the challenge of walking or biking their way across
North Carolina, there is an alternative: drive the highways and interstates
and choose some strategic exits that lead to small towns, historic communities, and the expanding urban areas of the state. Eat at local restaurants, go
to local shops, visit some of the historical landmarks, and attend local cel-
ebrations, especially local church services. But above all, engage local residents in conversation to get a feel for the diverse voices of different regions
and communities. The freeway system may be highly efficient for getting
from point A to point B, but the drive numbs the senses and drowns out

FIGURE 3.1. Roanoke Marshes Lighthouse and boardwalk on the Manteo waterfront. (Photograph by Joel Schneier)

the sounds of vibrant culture and language situated just beyond the iterative green exit signs on the thoroughfares. One artist, J. Chris Wilson, has taken this trip from Murphy to Manteo more than twenty times, stopping to paint 100 scenes along the way. He notes, "My principal objective is to paint the scenes that cannot be photographed descriptively, or at all . . . even more than the human eye could see."[1] Similarly, it is impossible to experience the dialect landscape of North Carolina without leaving the roads most traveled and listening to the variety of community voices along the way. An audio journey from the mountains to the coast—or in this case, from the coast to the mountains—is every bit as fascinating as a visual portrait.

An Audio Trip from Manteo to Murphy

We start our trip on Route 64 in Manteo on the coast, surrounded by luxury boating and lavish marinas that complement the extravagant commemoration of the Lost Colony on Roanoke Island. It is easy to overlook a small but important African American community on the "other side of the highway." Many of the approximately 150 residents of this community are descendants of the Freedmen's Colony established on Roanoke Island during the Civil War. When the Union army took over the island in 1862, slaves from eastern North Carolina flocked there for freedom, establishing a colony of several thousand ex-slaves in 1863 as part of the U.S. government's developing policy for the future independence of blacks. Roanoke Island became an autonomous community with a productive sawmill, a school, and churches. After the war, property in the colony was returned to its former owners, but a few black families remained, eventually buying small parcels of land and establishing a small, stable African American community that has persisted to the present. The dialect of this community, which we have studied in detail, merges regional and ethnic heritages, combining the distinct regional Outer Banks features described in chapter 5 with some distinctive African American English traits that developed in the rural South, which are described in chapter 7. The significant role of African Americans in the early life of North Carolina's coastal estuaries, including the establishment of a maritime version of the Underground Railroad, is one of the stories recently coming to light in North Carolina.[2] Everyone knows the story of the Lost Colony, and most people are well aware that Andy Griffith called Roanoke Island his home for four decades, but few visitors to Manteo reported that they had heard of the Freedmen's Colony before they visited the exhibit on the "Other Lost Colony."

To hear an excerpt from a speech about the Freedman's Colony, visit http://www.talkintarheel.com/chapter/3/audio3-1.php

To view a clip from the Freedman's Colony documentary If They Could Cross the Creek, visit http://www.talkintarheel.com/chapter/3/video3-1.php

With the Virginia Dare Memorial Bridge fading in the rearview mirror, we travel west on Route 64, crossing swampy land made suitable for farming though the construction of deep drainage ditches. The brackish swamps and pocosins, along with the "Watch out for bears" signs, serve as a reminder of how the physical geography served to isolate earlier communities. After almost fifty miles of mostly two-lane roads bordered by ditches filled with black water, turtles, and snakes, we exit for Edenton about ten miles north of Route 64 and just across a finger of the Albemarle Sound.

Founded at the mouth of the Roanoke River in 1712, Edenton was incorporated in 1722 and served as the capital of North Carolina from then until 1743. Among the notable events that took place there was the involvement of a group of women who signed a petition in 1774 to boycott British tea (the "Edenton Tea Party"), the first known political action by women in the colonies.[3] As far as we know, this was the first group of North Carolina women who was described in the press as "uncontrollable." It was also the home of Harriet Jacobs, an escaped slave, abolitionist, and writer who hid there for seven years as a fugitive.

Recently, some archaeologists have conjectured that the Lost Colony may have traveled to a site near Edenton that is now home to a golf course com-

FIGURE 3.2. Harriet Jacobs, author of *Incidents in the Life of a Slave Girl*, photographed in 1894.

munity. As a local news reporter observed: "Turns out the settlers of the Lost Colony were like many other North Carolinians. They hung out on the Outer Banks and retired to a golf course."[4]

We emerge in a port town where the residents sound decidedly different than the speakers who exemplify the Pamlico Sound dialect region to the east. Edenton exemplifies the second prominent geographical and dialect region of North Carolina—the Coastal Plain, an area much more in tune with broad-based southern pronunciation, grammar, and words than the Outer Banks where we started our trek. The speech of Edenton sounds more like the dialect associated historically with the Plantation South—good southern vowels, historic *r*-less pronunciations of words like *farm* as *fahm* and *fear* as *feauh*, and classic southern grammatical constructions like double modals in "She might could go," *fixin' to* in "She's fixin' to go now," or *liketa* in "He liketa died he was so scared."

To hear the speech of a life-long Edenton resident, visit http://www.talkintarheel .com/chapter/3/audio3-2.php

As we merge back onto Route 64 West, the flat terrain gradually becomes less swampy and larger farms growing cotton, tobacco, peanuts, and soybeans dominate the roadscape. Another sixty miles west on Route 64 in Edgecombe County lie a couple of intriguing communities, but no traveler would ever recognize them speeding along the elevated blacktop of the high-

FIGURE 3.3. The town of Princeville under water after Hurricane Floyd. (Photograph from the U.S. Army Corps of Engineers)

way with its endless repetition of exit signs. Approaching Exit 487, we see a small sign announcing Princeville. Two miles later, Exit 485 presents another modest green, rectangular sign that says Tarboro. The two signs in no way hint at the magnitude of difference that two miles can make. On the north side of the highway stands a nondescript, low-lying field with abandoned utility poles that mark the field once used by the Federal Emergency Management Agency (FEMA) following Hurricane Floyd in 1999. The trailers that once filled this field housed some of the 2,000 residents of Princeville who had to evacuate their homes during the ensuing flood. Every home in Princeville was lost during that devastating flood, which received national attention and visits from prominent politicians, including President Bill Clinton. This history of loss and rebirth cannot be envisioned from the windows of cars as they speed by.

The much larger adjacent town of Tarboro, across the Tar River from Princeville, was chartered in 1760 and served as a thriving port at the bend of the river. It also was once a central location for slave trading in North Carolina. When the slaves were freed after the Civil War, many of them went to Freedom Hill, a low-lying flood plain on the southeastern side of the Tar River that was useless to the Tarboro landowners. In 1885 that low-lying town became Princeville, the first town incorporated by blacks in the United

States. When the 1999 hurricane floods came, there was government pressure to abandon the area and relocate its residents, but the community remained resolute and the town was rebuilt. Today, within an ever-changing southern black identity, the people of Princeville demonstrate communal support through religious, political, and economic self-determination that makes the town more alive than ever. Along with the historical and cultural traditions of Princeville, the voices of its residents still resonate with the marked structures of some earlier rural African American English forms, and the "people of words" in Princeville—preachers, town leaders, and community activists—still effectively rely on their dialect tradition to persuade, cajole, and reassure community members that the first town established by blacks will survive.[5]

To view scenes from the documentary *Princeville Remembers the Flood*, visit http://www.talkintarheel.com/chapter/3/video3-2.php

The journey west from Princeville is accompanied by an increase in urban sights. Billboards for chain restaurants and hotels replace signs for local establishments. At Rocky Mount, Highway 64 crosses one of the most heavily traveled routes in the United States, Interstate 95. Fields of wheat now wave in the breeze alongside the shorter crops familiar in eastern North Carolina. The soil here shifts from black to a distinctly reddish color from the iron-rich clay. The amount of visible pavement expands as we continue westward, leaving the Coastal Plain for the rolling hills of the Piedmont. As we pass through major cities of North Carolina's Piedmont, the modest skyscrapers of Raleigh symbolize the expanding metropolitan areas of the state. That's a major story in its own right with important implications for dialect that we will take up in detail in the next chapter, but there are also intermediate zones in suburban towns like Zebulon to the east and Garner to the south of Raleigh where the lifestyle and the dialect reflect a mix of the urban and rural—and the old and the new.

To view an excerpt from the documentary *This Side of the River*, visit http://www.talkintarheel.com/chapter/3/video3-3.php

Route 64 now passes directly through towns in the Piedmont, offering a slower, closer view than that of Interstate 40, which in this part of the state follows a near-parallel arc about twenty-five miles to the north. The slower speed makes the residential settlements more transparent, both in historical perspective and dynamic transition. And if you don't obey the speed limit that abruptly drops to thirty-five miles an hour as you enter the city limits, you will surely contribute to the small-town economy. There are lots of churches along the highway as we enter Siler City, and many now have mar-

FIGURE 3.4. Roadside church in Siler City with marquee in Spanish. (Photograph by Caroline Myrick)

quees with announcements in Spanish. These are a testament to the flow of the Latino population into a community that was once stably black and white. The Siler City Latino population in 1990 was virtually nonexistent, but today they constitute nearly half the town's residents. Teaching English as a second language, once irrelevant, is now a critical program in the educational system. Furthermore, the robust southern dialect spoken by whites and blacks in this rural Piedmont town has influenced the English of the emerging Hispanic population. One of our students conducting interviews with schoolchildren in Siler City was patiently waiting for a parking spot in the city square when a young Latino gentleman rolled down the window of his pickup truck and politely informed her, "I'm feexin' to move in a meenute," wrapping his newly acquired southern phrase *fixin' to* in a layer of heavily Spanish-accented pronunciation.

To hear a Hispanic speaker from Siler City, visit http://www.talkintarheel.com/chapter/3/audio3-3.php

As we travel westward near Statesville, we leave Route 64 for Interstate 40, a four-lane highway that offers a faster, more direct route to the west. The heavy vegetation along the sleek contours of I-40 camouflages the small communities that sit beyond the billboards and sound walls. But again, each town has a substantive community legacy that contributes to the historical, cultural, and dialect landscape of the state. The farther west we drive, the more the road undulates, anticipating the mountains. The "foothills,"

FIGURE 3.5. Rhodhiss cotton mill, ca. 1900. (Photograph courtesy of the William Lynch Postcard Collection, Spartanburg County, S.C., Public Libraries)

though typically classified as part of the Piedmont region, represent the transition between it and the Appalachian Mountain region. These labels are linguistically quirky since the word "piedmont" is a combination of the French words *pied* ("foot") and *mont* ("mountain"), or literally, "foothills." So while Raleigh, Durham, Greensboro, and Charlotte are commonly identified as being in the Piedmont ("foothills"), they are actually east of the region we call the foothills. The distinction between the Appalachian Mountain region and the Piedmont region is also geographically quirky, as both zones are classified by the U.S. Geological Survey as being part of the Appalachian Mountain range.[6]

An impulsive exit off of I-40 to the small town of Rhodhiss (population 390) by the outskirts of Hickory in the foothills of the Appalachian Mountains exposes yet another of those small North Carolina towns so easy to overlook. Rhodhiss was once a textile town straddling the Catawba River between Caldwell and Burke Counties, proudly bearing the distinction of weaving the material used for the U.S. flag that astronauts Neil Armstrong and Buzz Aldrin raised on the first visit to the moon in 1967.[7] It was woven at the Burlington Mills plant, now closed along with most other textile factories. The furniture and textile industries once thrived in this region due to their proximity to expansive forests and accessible transportation routes via intersecting railroads, but these are largely gone now, leaving many lifetime residents with the prospect of living out their lives in search of "alternative economic opportunities." The economic times have changed, but the speech of locals in Rhodhiss still resounds with a dialect welcome to Mountain Talk. The dialect of Rhodhiss natives has remained relatively strong with distinct traces of Scots-Irish.

Few travelers choose to stop in Rhodhiss, but Asheville, about seventy-five miles west on I-40, is the largest city in the western part of the state and a popular destination for tourists, artisans, and transplants. As one person put it, "If you want to know where all of the hippies went in North Carolina, go to Asheville." It was once located within the boundaries of the Eastern Band of the Cherokee and served as an open hunting ground until the middle of the nineteenth century. It is squarely embedded in the Appalachian Mountains, but its connection to Mountain culture seems to be a bit tenuous. Some of the elegant edifices—for example, the Biltmore Estates and the Grove Park Inn—are sophisticated symbols of opulence that seem somewhat out of place alongside the modest farmhouses in the surrounding rural communities. The Biltmore Mansion was built by George Washington Vanderbilt II between 1889 and 1895 while he was still in his twenties, and it remains the largest privately owned home in the United States—175,000 square feet and 250 rooms. The Grove Park Inn across town has been an elegant resort site for a century, catering to affluent visitors from near and far.[8]

The population of Asheville as a whole is known for its liberal, progressive politics and its active artisan community, but these folks are mostly transplants. Those who grew up modestly and lived in the small, often overlooked homes are still readily identified by their distinct Appalachian voices. In the early 1970s, Duke linguist Dr. Ron Butters conducted interviews with white and black lifetime residents of Asheville that tell a story of the community in a voice that has become much more difficult to find now in the city even though it is the common voice elsewhere in the region. The dialect mix of outsiders and locals in Asheville is not unlike the larger cities of North Carolina, somewhat drowning out the traditional local speech that was once its dominant voice.

To hear a white Asheville speaker from Butters's study, visit http://www.talkintarheel.com/chapter/3/audio3-4.php

To hear an African American Asheville speaker from Butters's study, visit http://www.talkintarheel.com/chapter/3/audio3-5.php

The last leg of the trip to Murphy requires the traveler to leave I-40 for almost a hundred miles of winding, mountainous roads south through the Smoky Mountains. It is not a drive to be taken in poor visibility or at night, even by those who have driven it many times. The highway offers breathtaking views of valleys and mountains. The terrain also offers glimpses into the fortitude of the area's settlers and the ingenuity

FIGURE 3.6. Early twentieth-century Cherokee County Courthouse, located in downtown Murphy, North Carolina. (Photograph by Alfred Morgan)

of those who laid the agricultural heritage of the state. Hay and corn grow in fields that seem impossibly steep, and livestock seem to move about the hilly country easier than people. Christmas-tree farms dot the landscape, representing another major agricultural industry of the state; in fact, North Carolina produces some 7.5 million Christmas trees a year, trailing only Oregon in production.

Our drop-by destination along the main highway is Texana, a mile outside of Murphy. It is a small community of about 150 African Americans located high on a mountain that bears the name of a black woman, Texana McClelland, who moved with her family to the area in the 1850s.[9] To give an idea of the sparse population and rugged terrain in "them thar hills," the community stands in the area where the notorious Olympic Park bomber, Eric Rudolph, hid for up to five years before he was inadvertently captured while eating from a dumpster behind a local store. Along with hundreds of FBI agents and other law-enforcement officers—*the law*—our team of researchers never even heard any rumors about his imminent whereabouts as they interviewed residents. In many respects, the speech of this small black community in the Smoky Mountains is ironically analogous to the small black community where we started our trek in Manteo, visibly out of the mainstream but significant in terms of the historical diversity of the state. The speech of Texana residents is a mixture of things Appalachian and things African American, so much so that outside listeners have trouble identifying locals' ethnicity when presented with speech samples of whites and blacks from the region.

Our trip from Manteo to Murphy, sketched in Map 3.1, illustrates a couple of important lessons for our description of the dialect regions of North Carolina. It demonstrates how fluid shifts between dialects can be and the importance of social and cultural factors in understanding them.

In this chapter, we consider regional dialects, and in the next we will consider the strong influence of the rural-urban dimension. In other chapters, we see the role of ethnic affiliation in describing regional dialects, including the influence of other languages historically and currently.

To hear a speaker from Texana, visit http://www.talkintarheel.com/chapter/3/audio3-6.php

To hear a second speaker from Texana, visit http://www.talkintarheel.com/chapter/3/audio3-7.php

Regional Dialects of North Carolina

"So professor, how many dialects are there in North Carolina?"
"It's difficult to say, to be honest."
"But haven't you done all of this research on dialects throughout the state?"
"Um, yeah, but . . ."
"So how many dialects are there?"
"Um, somewhere between two and 200"
"What? I thought you were a dialect expert!"

While the study of language can be precise and scientific in describing dialect structures, the determination of precise dialect boundaries is another matter. It is often difficult to tell exactly where one dialect ends and the next one begins. Further, the delimitation of a dialect area depends on the particular structure being examined. Perhaps an appropriate response by a dialectologist to the question about the number of dialects in North Carolina would be to answer the question with a question: "How many pieces can you cut a pie into?" We've actually tried that response—and have mostly gotten quizzical looks. But that doesn't stop us from thinking it's an appropriate metaphor. The number of dialects depends on how thinly one chooses to cut the language pie and how solid the dialect ingredients within the pie are.

On one level, North Carolina may be viewed as part of a unitary South—

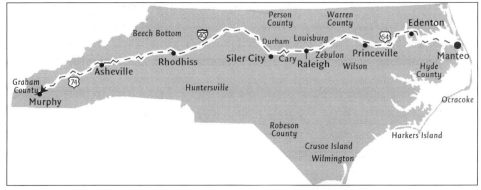

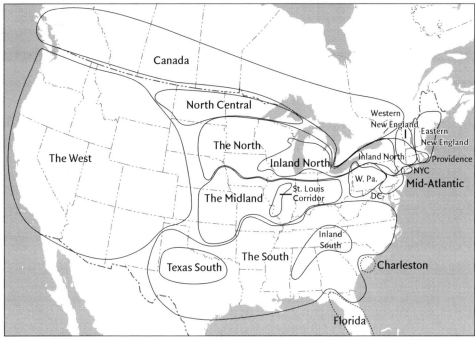

(top) MAP 3.1. An Audio Trip from Manteo to Murphy;
(bottom) MAP 3.2. Map of Dialects of North America (From William Labov,
Sharon Ash, and Charles Boberg, *The Atlas of North American English*
[Berlin: Mouton de Gruyter, 2006])

a perception of lots of northerners and even some linguists who have conducted dialect surveys of American English. Defining the South linguistically, geographically, and culturally is still fair game. Fortunately, North Carolina is located in the regional core of the southern dialect area, so it is excused from most discussions about whether or not it is a southern state.

In 2006 *The Atlas of North American English*, one of the most important dialect surveys of the United States ever conducted, was published by a team of researchers led by the world's leading sociolinguist, Dr. William Labov.[10] Above is a dialect map from that book depicting an overarching South with a couple of subareas. One of these areas is the highland area that encompasses the western part of North Carolina. Other dialect maps based on different linguistic criteria vary, but all of them place North Carolina comfortably and exclusively within the South. *The Atlas of North American English*'s map also demonstrates the different approaches that can be used in determining major dialect areas of a region. The map is based solely on the examination of vowels collected during telephone interviews with two native speakers of all cities in the United States of 50,000 or more residents. This criterion greatly restricts representation in eastern North Carolina, where only Wilmington, Greenville, Rocky Mount, and Jacksonville qualify, and in the western part of the state, where only the city of Asheville qualifies. But the map still shows how thoroughly southern the vowels of North Carolina can be.

Perhaps the vowel trait that most defines the South is the weakening, or "ungliding," of the long i in words like *time* and *side* so that they sound more like *tahm* and *sahd*. The boundary of this trait coincides neatly with the boundaries of other southern pronunciations. A similar range is found for where folks pronounce *pin* and *pen* the same way—usually pronounced as *pin*. As it turns out, vowel traits like these serve to define the boundaries of the South as well as any other historical, social, or cultural definition.

To hear the pronunciation of unglided *time* and *side*, visit http://www.talkintarheel.com/chapter/3/audio3-8.php

To hear examples of the *pin-pen* merger, visit http://www.talkintarheel.com/chapter/3/audio3-9.php

We note that the boundary for the growth of kudzu, a climbing vine concentrated in the South, closely matches the general southern dialect boundary and widespread dialect features that include the ungliding of the long i of *time* or *tide* and the identical pronunciation of *pin* and *pen*. The growth of kudzu, selected to represent a natural ecological boundary of the South, seems as adequate as cultural or historical traits in defining the region. Ironically, kudzu was actually introduced in Philadelphia by the Japanese at their

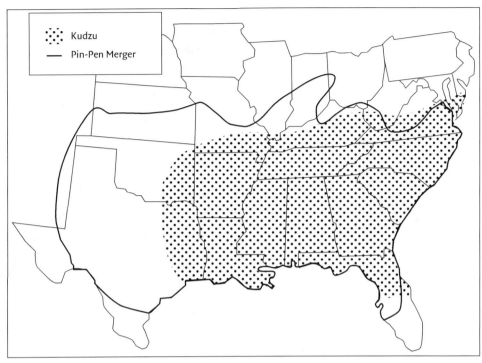

MAP 3.3. The Growth of Kudzu and the Merging of Vowels in *Pin* and *Pen*

pavilion in the 1876 Centennial Exposition, but like a few linguistic features introduced originally in Philadelphia by the Scots-Irish, it flourished in the South. In Map 3.3, the boundaries for southern ungliding from *The Atlas of North American English* are superimposed on the map of Kudzu growth simply for the sake of comparing two independent factors considered to be "southern born and bred." The line indicates the dialect area and the shaded area indicates the growth of kudzu. The factors conflated in Map 3.3 could not be more unrelated, yet there is an impressive alignment that illustrates the range of physical, cultural, political, and linguistic factors that have come to define the South. Any discussion of dialects in North Carolina starts with recognition that it is encompassed by the overarching South.

Tar Heel Dialects

When people find out we study dialects for a living, they often ask, "So can you tell me where I'm from by the way I talk?" That's a loaded question, and

we sometimes respond glibly with an equally loaded answer: "Yep, all you have to do is pronounce one word—the name of your home town." On a more serious level, we can often pinpoint the general region within North Carolina that a person is from by asking about a few key pronunciations, lexical choices, or grammatical patterns. In some cases, we can make a fairly specific identification—if we know about iconic dialect features from a particular community or region. For example, if a North Carolinian refers to the trunk of a car as a *boot*, we would say that he or she was from one of the Coastal Plain counties such as Bertie, Martin, or Lenoir since these are the locations where we have heard this term in North Carolina. Of course, this is the common term in British English and has been found in some other southern regions, but it is used most commonly in North Carolina in the strip of Coastal Plain counties. Similarly, if a person refers to "hide and seek" as *meehonkey*, we know immediately that they are from Ocracoke; or if a person calls a "slingshot" a *juvember*, they are from southeastern North Carolina, probably from Robeson County. The long-term study of most communities often turns up a few of these indexical dialect forms, but of course it is not possible to do that for every community in North Carolina. We therefore have to depend on a dialect version of the well-known parlor game of Twenty Questions, in which key questions and deductive reasoning help narrow down the possible options for identifying a regional dialect.

Just a few questions about pronunciation can often provide a clue about the regional identity of a speaker in North Carolina. Except for the Outer Banks, most of traditional North Carolina speech unglides the long i of *time* and *side*, so that it sounds more like *tahm* or *sahd* than *taheem* or *saheed*. But not all inland North Carolinians follow the same patterns of ungliding. While the entire mainland of North Carolina is prone to unglide i when the word is time or side, only speakers from particular parts of the state unglide i in words like *white* and *rice*. If a person says *whaht rahs*, he or she is either from the western mountains or the Coastal Plain but not from the Piedmont.

In the mountains and the Coastal Plain, ungliding can take place anytime a long i occurs, so we call this *general i ungliding*. In the Piedmont, ungliding can ONLY take place before a voiced sound like *d, b, v, z, m, n*—or at the end of a word like *bah* for *bye* or *lah* for *lie*. In the Piedmont, speakers do not typically unglide the vowel when it is followed by an *s, f, p, t*, or *k*—technically, a *voiceless sound*. Because the ungliding pattern is limited by the following sound, we refer to this as *restricted i un-*

To hear the pronunciation of unglided *white rice*, visit http://www.talkintarheel.com/chapter/3/audio3-10.php

TABLE 3.1. Examples of General and Restricted i Ungliding

General Ungliding	Word	Restricted Ungliding
tahm	time	tahm
tahd	tide	tahd
bah	bye	bah
rahs	rice	rahees
lahf	life	laheef
braht	bright	braheet

gliding. The ungliding of the long i in the list of words in Table 3.1 illustrates the different patterns.

Another vowel pronunciation that comes up in our attempt to regionally locate a North Carolinian is the pronunciation of the vowel of *out, about, brown, town*, etc. Though this pronunciation doesn't differ much from the Coastal Plain region in the east to the mountains in western North Carolina, it is quite distinctive in some counties that border Virginia—from Gates, Hertford, and Northampton along the northeastern border to the north-central counties of the state, such as Person, Caswell, and Rockingham. This is where the *out* and *about* pronunciation sounds more like *oat* and *aboat*. This pronunciation is most often associated with Canadian English and Tidewater Virginia. In fact, its occurrence spills over from Virginia to the northernmost counties of North Carolina. In chapter 5, we will discuss a distinct Outer Banks pronunciation of the "ou" vowel where words like *sound* are more like *saind* and *brown* more like *brane* or *brain*. In fact, we have speakers who recall incidents in which people thought that they were talking about a "brain" pocketbook when they were actually talking about a "brown" pocketbook. If only we could carry our brains in a "pocketbook"—or a "purse," for the current generation. The pronunciation of brown close to brain is a common trait that extends from the Outer Banks of North Carolina north into the Eastern Shore of Maryland and Virginia as well as on islands in the Chesapeake Bay, such as Tangier Island in Virginia and Smith Island in Maryland. However, this is the only region of the United States where we have ever found this distinctive pronunciation of the "ou" vowel.

Not all of the differences in pronunciation are found in the vowels. The loss of r after a vowel in *fahm* for *farm* or *feauh* for *fear* is another indicator of regional place in North Carolina, though its changing status as an index of southern speech makes it less reliable than it once was. The Outer Banks region and western mountain range have, however, always pronounced their r's in words like farm and fear. The north-central and northeastern areas near the Virginia border are historically r-less—the effect of Virginia piedmont and Tidewater diffusion—as is the Coastal Plain region, especially the areas where there was more of a plantation culture historically. The Plantation South was once quite r-less; the Piedmont region of North Carolina was historically r-less, but this trait is receding so rapidly that it is only found among older people today.

Grammar can also pinpoint people's regional identity. If speakers use *weren't* for negative sentences with *be*, as in "I weren't there or she weren't there," for sure they come from the Outer Banks—unless they're a Lumbee Indian living about fifty miles inland. The fact that the Lumbee Indians in Robeson County use this form is intriguing, and some have suggested that it might show an earlier linguistic affinity with the Outer Banks. The historical dialect facts, however, show that the Outer Banks variety was once more widely distributed in the eastern, mainland part of the state but has since receded to the coastal area.[11]

To hear an example of the Lumbee use of *weren't*, visit http://www.talkintarheel.com/chapter/3/audio3-11.php

Other grammatical forms show a similar kind of regional distribution, such as the use of the preposition *to* where other dialects use *at* in sentences like "She's to the dock now" or "She's to Melinda's house for dinner." In this case, the preposition *to* is used for "static location"—that is, location at a particular place rather than movement to a place. In other dialects, the preposition *to* is used only for directional location, as in, for example, "going to the store" or "going to the house."

One of the patterns used most frequently in the mountains and on the Outer Banks is the attachment of an *-s* to a verb following a plural noun, as in "People thinks this is the right way" or "The friends that we just met gives us lots of support." Grammar can sometimes provide excellent clues about regional differences in North Carolina speech, although grammatical markers are not usually as bountiful as pronunciation or vocabulary.

The use or meaning of particular words can also help locate the region where people come from, and if we know what to look for, we can sometimes cut quickly to the dialect chase. Lexical geography has been very helpful in demarcating regional dialects in the United States for more than a century, and some surveys rely exclusively on words to mark regional boundaries. Sometimes, the same word has different meanings depending on its regional context, and sometimes there are different words for the same thing.

Take a word like *barbecue*. To begin with, barbecue means pork in the Old North State. Hogs were introduced to the Southeast by the Spanish in the 1500s, and they thrived much better than cattle did—so much so that each year, roughly two hogs are marketed for every person in the state. In the eastern part of the state, barbecue is made with salty vinegar and red pepper, and in the western part of the state, so-called Lexington-style adds a red sauce. In the east, they use the whole hog, both white and dark meat, while in the west, they cook only the pork shoulder—the dark meat that some think is fatty and juicier. In the southern Piedmont, a mustard-based sauce, sometimes called "Carolina Gold," has persisted, though it is much more common in South Carolina than in North Carolina.[12] And when a person invites you for a barbecue, it's not for hot dogs and hamburgers—unless they're a Yankee and don't know the difference between "barbecuing" and "grilling" or "cooking out."

Many dialect words characterize the Outer Banks and the mountains, but fewer words are unique to the intervening regions. Lots of distinct vocabulary involves local geography and economy; for example, the maritime culture of the Outer Banks and the Mountain culture of the highlands each have dozens of words that set these regions apart from others. There are many words used only by those on the Outer Banks, from terms related to the water and terrain—for example, *creek* ("inlet between ocean and sound"), *camelback* ("mound in the sand"), *hammock* ("grove of trees"), *ways* ("track for pulling a boat out of water"), *lightering* ("removing cargo to make a boat lighter"), *guano* ("fertilizer from fowl or coastal birds"), *hard blow* ("strong wind"), *fatback* ("menhaden"), *Russian rat* ("nutria"), *up the beach* ("off the island to another island"), *scud* ("a ride around the island, usually in a car or boat"), *slick cam* ("calm water, usually with reference to the sound"), and *water fire* ("light that occurs in water [on the sound] from decaying plant matter")—to terms for insiders and outsiders, such as *dingbatter*, *dit-dot*, *yonker*, *touron*, *woodser*, *foreigner*.[13] Similarly, there are scores of terms used only in the mountains, including *bald* ("small area on a summit that has no trees"), *scald* ("an area on a mountain having little vegetation"), *sag* ("a low area along a ridge connecting mountain peaks"), *holler* ("gap between ridges of a mountain"), *boomer* ("red squirrel"), *toboggan* ("knitted hat"), *vittle* ("food for a meal"), and *sigogglin* ("crooked, not perpendicular"), as well as other terms for different types of outsiders, such as *jasper* ("a contemptible person"), *peckerwood* ("a contemptuous person"), and *halfback* ("a northern transplant to Florida who vacations in the mountains during the summer").[14]

When we start drawing boundary lines, or isoglosses, between regional dialect features, we notice that there are slight differences in the lines for different words, but many tend to converge. Places where isoglosses converge form the basis for demarcating the major dialect boundaries of North Carolina, but establishing the precise boundaries is still not often as clear-cut as it might seem at first glance. To begin with, most boundaries are not discrete; there are transitional zones where one feature fades out and another picks up. In this transitional zone, both variants of a dialect feature may be in use. Even the Outer Banks, set apart by a large body of water, is not clear-cut as a dialect area, as there are parts of mainland Dare, Hyde, Pamlico, and Carteret Counties that use the traits described for the Outer Banks. As one goes from east to west in the coastal mainland, these traits gradually recede, but they don't abruptly stop. One study of Bertie County by Angus Bowers, a native of the county, found that the transitional zone between the Outer Banks and Coastal Plain dialects was still in effect several counties removed from the islands themselves.[15]

Another complication in setting dialect boundaries is the fact that not all dialect markers are equally important. For example, one dialect feature, the pronunciation of *out* and *about* more like *oat* and *aboat*, seems to be sufficient to demarcate the dialect zone along the northern Piedmont and coastal area of North Carolina. And the pronunciation of *hoi toid* for *high tide* is enough to judge a person from the Outer Banks. Meanwhile, our linguistic analysis of different dialect traits shows that the use of *weren't* in "I weren't there" and the pronunciation of *sound* and *brown* more like *saind* and *brain* are probably more indexical of the unique Outer Banks dialect than the *hoi toid* vowel. Should the dialect truth be known, the *hoi toid* vowel is not as peculiar to the Outer Banks as residents and others think it is, and a similar vowel has been documented in other dialects of American English, including—of all places—traditional New York City speech.

Yet another complication to clearly defined boundaries emerges from the small-town history of North Carolina. Within the broader regional zones, some towns carve out a unique character that may be indexed by their dialect. For example, Crusoe Island is a small, out-of the way settlement of about 100 people that is bounded on three sides by the Waccamaw River and on the fourth side by the Green Swamp. It is not an island, but its residents tend to be isolated as though it were. They survived for generations by hunting, fishing, subsistence farming, shingle making, basket weaving, and occasionally trading furs in the nearby town. They are also known for their skill in carving homemade canoes.[16] As one resident characterized Crusoe Island, "It being a dead-end road back in and one road back out, you know everybody." It has a colorful reputation—the stuff of legends—and the settlement tends to be viewed somewhat mysteriously by outsiders. Some of this hype is embraced by residents who observe: "If they didn't like you, you didn't go into Crusoe"; or "They was some good people down there and they was some mean ones, too. And about as mean as I could hope, they'd fight you in a minute, shoot you in a minute, and it didn't matter; if you say one word out of the way, it was history."[17] By the same token, there are residents who think "it's just more far-fetched, they just make it something drastic, but it's not."[18] Though it is speculation, the most commonly accepted theory is that the original inhabitants were white residents from French Haiti who migrated there in the late 1700s and early 1800s. Because of its historical isolation and history, Crusoe Island was of great interest to the dialect studies of the North Carolina Language and Life Project. We found a few distinctive dialect features used by older, lifetime residents—for example, the use of a nasalized vowel instead of a nasal segment *n* like the French nasalization of a vowel in *pain* ("bread") or *bon* ("good") and the extensive reduction of consonant blends such as the pronunciation of *roas'* for "roast" or *wil'* for "wild." But for the most part, the community shares most of its features with other

 small towns found in the Coastal Plain—like the ungliding of *i* in *right* and *nice* and other traditional southern vowel traits. Mostly, it is distinguished by the permeation of southern rural vernacular features of the type discussed in the next chapter.

To view video excerpts from Crusoe Island, visit http://www.talkintarheel.com/chapter/3/video3-4.php

Small towns that have a distinct dialect quality are sometimes overlooked in general regional surveys, and North Carolina probably has more than its share of these situations because of the role played by small towns in its historical development.

In Map 3.4, we repeat the dialect map of the major dialect regions of North Carolina according to our current information without showing the settlement patterns included in the map introduced in chapter 1. The map combines dialect surveys of the Southeast done under long-term dialect survey projects, particularly *The Linguistic Atlas of the United States and Canada*, an ongoing survey that began in the late 1920s, as well as some of the more recent research from *The Atlas of North American English* in the 1990s.[19] But these large-scale surveys do not adequately capture the linguistic diversity in North Carolina that are revealed by community-based research efforts, so we have relied most heavily on our own community-based studies in creating the map. We exclude the dialects of adjoining states to the north and south despite the general transmission of dialect from Virginia into North Carolina and from North Carolina into South Carolina. Running counter to this trend is minor dialect seepage north from South Carolina dialects among particular populations in the southeastern part of the state. For example, the use of be(s) in sentences like "that's how it bes" seems to have spread north from Horry County in South Carolina to Robeson and Columbus Counties in North Carolina.[20] Some evidence suggests a second influence from the south, as the Geechee-Gullah culture-language corridor of the South Carolina coastal islands may have extended into Brunswick and New Hanover Counties in North Carolina.[21] It is not necessary to include contiguous states to the west since there was no significant dialect diffusion from the west into North Carolina from Tennessee. One important conclusion drawn from the map is the relative insignificance of state borders in the development of dialects. That is to be expected: throughout the United States, the only state boundaries that align with dialect boundaries are those that coincide with natural boundaries like rivers, such as the Ohio River or the Mississippi River.

Levels of Dialect

In our discussion of regional dialects, we presented *pronunciation* differences, *vocabulary* or *lexical* differences, and *grammar* differences. We might also have included different conventions of *language use*, such as routines for greeting and leave-taking, performing politeness, address forms, and so forth. Language is structured simultaneously on all of these levels, and they can all participate in differentiating dialects. But they don't always work in the same way.

Pronunciation is probably the most significant indicator of dialect differences; as we have noted, the most recent survey of American English dialects, *The Atlas of North American English*, is based exclusively on the pronunciation of vowels.[22] Some of the information about vowels can get quite technical, including specific details of articulation or acoustics. Linguists often describe vowels according to where the tongue is located in the mouth during production, so they talk about back vowels, front vowels, high vowels, and low vowels. For example, the vowel in words like *beet* and *feet* are produced much higher and more fronted in the mouth than the vowel of *father* and *top*, which are produced lower and more backed in the mouth. We sometimes need to refer to these relative positions of vowel production in the mouth because

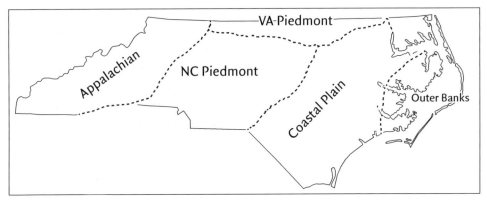

MAP 3.4. Dialect Map of North Carolina

they are critical in describing dialect differences, but we avoid referring to the precise, technical details that are now available. Phonetics has become a highly specialized and technically sophisticated science, allowing us to explore the nature of microscopic phonetic detail that differentiates dialects. Though we do not refer to these technical details, such precise analyses offer a firm analytical basis for our discussion of vowels.

Vocabulary, or lexical differences, can also be diagnostic of regional dialects, starting from the inclusive definition of the South to highly localized subregions within the region.[23] One word can sometimes give away regional, social, and ethnic identity, including insider-outsider status. Over the years, we have collected many stories about the way that words are used to identify how people fit in or don't fit in with local communities.

During the first field trip to Ocracoke with students in the winter of 1993, Walt Wolfram, his wife, and a new graduate student named Chris were set up to have dessert in the home of a family in order to meet a couple of the men of the community. The only problem was that the conspiring spouses "forgot" to tell the men that we were there on a dialect mission. The men were not happy about being set up as dialect bait, and the conversation started out awkwardly. As we reported in the book *Hoi Toide on the Outer Banks*, one of the older gentlemen in the family, Wallace Spencer, suddenly turned to the student, Chris, and said, "I bet you never heard of the word *meehonkey* before; I bet you can't find out what it means."[24] Wallace continued teasing Chris for an hour about the meaning of the word until, near the end of the visit, he called him aside and explained that meehonkey was a local word for a game combining elements of Marco Polo and hide-and-seek that islanders played some years ago. It also signified a breakthrough and the start of a cross-generational friendship between a salty seventy-six-year-old lifelong resident of Ocracoke and a wide-eyed twenty-three-year-old graduate student from the Piedmont. Wallace cooked dinner for Chris a couple of nights later, gave him some fresh seafood to take home, and even bequeathed him a new pair of shoes that Chris proudly wore for years afterward. In telling Chris the meaning of a unique, rather obscure island word that we—and no other dialectologist for that matter—had ever heard of, Wallace opened the door to his dialect world and began an enduring friendship. Words can sometimes do that. They can also be powerful indicators of regional dialects, and some surveys of regional dialects of English rely solely on words to define dialect regions. We have offered examples of regional lexical differences, but there are many more. Some older surveys rely on foods (for example, *batter bread* for "spoonbread" and *press peach* for "clingstone peach"), traditional farm implements (*swingletree*, *whiffletree*, and *whippletree* for "crossbar in a horse's harness to which the ends of the traces are attached"), and rural traditions that are not always current, but some more-recent surveys focus on fast foods (*soda*, *pop*, *cola*, *dope*, etc., for "soft drink" and *hoagie*, *submarine*, *grinder*, *torpedo*, *hero*, etc., for "a long Italian roll filled with of a variety of meats, cheeses, vegetables, and seasonings") and modern equipment (ATM, *cash machine*, *bank machine*, *cash point*, etc.).

Grammatical differences aren't as abundant as regional vocabulary, but they can sometimes readily mark regional or sociocultural dialects. Earlier in this chapter, we introduced the restricted uses of *bes* in "That's how it bes," the use of *weren't* in "She weren't there," and the use of the preposition *to* for "at" in "She's to the dock" as examples of regional grammatical use.

To view a clip about the Lumbee use of *bes* and *weren't*, visit http://www.talkintarheel.com/chapter/3/video3-5.php

A limited sample of the distribution of dialect traits for major regions of North Carolina on three levels of differentiation is given in Table 3.2, organized by pronunciation, lexicon, and grammatical traits. A check mark indicates that the trait is found in the area. The table offers representative features of major regional varieties, but a more complete list would show that some areas have many more distinguishing traits than others. The Outer Banks and Appalachia have an abundance of dialect traits that set them apart from other regions, making their status as regional dialects quite transparent. The examples from the western mountains (*bald*, *scald*, *boomer*, etc.) are just the beginning of a long list of dialect words that are used in this region. Drs. Michael B. Montgomery and Joseph S. Hall's 700-page

TABLE 3.2 Regional Dialect Features in North Carolina:
Pronunciation, Lexicon, and Grammar

	Outer Banks	Coastal Plain	Piedmont	Va. Border	Appalachian
PRONUNCIATION					
ou of *sound, brown, out, about*	*sound/brown* as *saind/brain*			*out/about* as *oat/aboat*	
long i of *tide, high, right, nice*	*high tide* as *hoi toid*	*side/right* as *sahd/raht* (unrestricted i ungliding)	*side/time* as *sahd/ tahm* (restricted i ungliding)	restricted i ungliding	unrestricted i ungliding
r-loss following a vowel; *fear/short* as *feauh/sho't*		✓		✓	
ou sound of *bought, caught*	unglided *oh* like British *boht*	*bought* as *bawt*	*bought* as *bawt*		*bought* as *bawt*
LEXICON					
slick cam ("smooth water")	✓				
creek ("inlet")	✓				
hammock ("grove of trees")	✓				
shivering owl		✓			
tow bag/sack		✓	✓	✓	✓
cow house				✓	
batter bread ("cornbread")				✓	
bald ("summit without trees")					✓
toboggan ("[knitted] hat")					✓
boomer ("red squirrel")					✓
mommuck ("harass, bother, mess up")	✓ ("harass, bother")	✓ ("mess up")			✓ ("mess up")

	Outer Banks	Coastal Plain	Piedmont	Va. Border	Appalachian
LEXICON (cont.)					
pizer/piazza	✓	✓			
cattywampus/ whopperjawed/antigoglin/ sigogglin ("crooked, not straight")	✓	✓	✓ *antigoglin/ cattywampus*		✓ *sigogglin*
GRAMMAR					
It weren't me. (past *be* negative regularization)	✓	✓			
He's to the dock. (locational *to*)	✓				
People likes the weather. (Plural noun -s)	✓				✓
That's how it bes. (inflectional be[s])		✓			
She likes DVDs anymore. (positive *anymore*)	✓		✓		✓
It's hisn. (possessive 'n)	✓				
Whenever I was 8 years old . . . (single event *whenever*)					✓
ten pound of fish (plural absence with measure nouns)	✓	✓		✓	✓

Dictionary of Smoky Mountain English includes more than 6,000 names, usages, meanings, and folk expressions.[25] Not all of the words are unique to the region, but there are enough to eliminate any question about its status as a regional dialect. By contrast, we had to dig deep in the records of different dialect surveys to come up with just a few distinctive words for the Tidewater and Coastal Plain regions. And the Piedmont region seems to be defined more by what is *not* found there compared to the easternmost and westernmost areas of the state than by its distinctive traits. Lots of southern traits are found in the central parts of the state, but most of them are shared throughout a large portion of the South and not just the Piedmont of North Carolina. Not all dialect regions are highly marked and easy to identify on the basis of just a few words. We further see that defining a dialect region is not so much a matter of identifying unique dialect traits as it is identifying the combination of traits that typify the region. Since we have a difficult time defining dialect traits unique to the Coastal Plain region, we rely on combinations of traits like the loss of r following vowels; the nonrestricted ungliding of long i in *time, side,* and *nice*; and a bunch of lexical items that are, for the most part, shared with other southern dialects (*cut on/off the lights, mash the button, fixin' to go,* etc.). Few unique dialect traits are found there, but the combination of traits makes it a dialect area set apart from other regions of North Carolina.

At the outset of the chapter, we noted that identifying different dialect regions was not a precise science, and dialectologists have still not come up with a consensus for establishing dialect regions. Debate about the delimitation of dialect regions has been ongoing since the inception of the American Dialect Society in 1889, and we suspect that it will continue long after this book is out of print or virtually inaccessible. Despite highly scientific measurements, large amounts of data, and objective marking of boundaries for particular words and pronunciations, a lot of interpretation goes into the process. We weren't being overly modest when we said that nobody really knows with certainty how many dialects there are in the South or in North Carolina. Our map features a Coastal Plain dialect area that runs the length of the state, but some earlier maps divide this area into a southern and northern region bounded by the Cape Fear valley. That's an option that aligns with some of the earlier settlement and migration patterns indicated by the arrows shown in Map 1.1 in the first chapter. It would also coincide with the isoglosses for some dialects traits we have found—for example, the use of inflectional *be(s)* in "That's how it bes" or the restriction of dialect words like *juvember* for "slingshot" and *fatback* for "bacon" to the sandhills region south of the Cape Fear valley in North Carolina. If we cut the dialect pie into thinner slices, we would have recognized the southeastern region of the state. At this stage, we prefer slightly bigger pieces of regional dialect pie and a focus on the ingredients found in the different dialect pieces in particular communities. The pattern that we present here matches the history and culture of the state and reinforces our point that language is the equal of any other cultural artifact in marking regional and cultural groups.

To take a North Carolina dialect identification quiz, visit http://www.talkintarheel .com/chapter/3/video3-6.php

4 Talkin' Country and City

The older folks, you know, they speak kind of the old country type, but the new people are—like next door—he's from Albemarle and she's from New York, so you get a bit of a mix of the speech. But my parents, they speak the old North Carolina country. —**MICHAEL PHILMON,** Charlotte, born in 1950s, quoted in *Voices of North Carolina*, produced by Neal Hutcheson (Raleigh: North Carolina Language and Life Project 2005)

I don't want us to lose all of our southern charm, but it's okay to lose some of it. And I think it's okay for us not to sound so country. —**SALLIE GRIFFIN,** Winston-Salem, born in 1960s, quoted in *Voices of North Carolina*, produced by Neal Hutcheson

To view the video of the Philmon quote above, visit http://www.talkintarheel.com/chapter/4/video4-1.php

Some of the regional differences in North Carolina can be quite striking, but we don't have to travel very far to hear distinctive dialects. Lots of differences can be explained by appealing to a couple of distinctions: rural and urban and young and old. To hear the contrast, residents of metropolitan centers like Charlotte, Raleigh, or Greensboro only need to go to a farmers market where an older farmer is selling fresh produce from his family farm, putting your *snaps*, *taters*, and *butter beans* in a *poke* for you to *carry* home. Or go to a local country barbecue pit and learn about the intricacies of eastern and western style *'cue*. Rural folks are known for maintaining more traditional ways of southern speaking to complement a range of other lifestyle differences, and city folks may shift their ways of speaking and acting to sound more cosmopolitan.

A worker in the Bank of America Corporate Center in Charlotte who asks you to "mash the button" for the elevator or to "he'p him tote the computer right yonder" would get a quizzical look or a patronizing chuckle for "talking country" in the towering edifice representing the second-largest financial center in the United States. But those who react in condescension may not realize that this way of speaking was the dialect norm in the city just a couple of generations ago—and probably in the residential home that once stood on this site. As one elderly Charlotte resident, born in 1919, recalled: "I remember when Discovery Place was just a little neighborhood store."[1] Discovery Place, of course, is the modern science and technology museum built in the uptown area of Charlotte in the 1980s.

The label *country* in "they speak country" is more than a synonym for rural. It embeds a set of personal and social traits that index assumptions about a lack of cultural sophistication, a limited education, and a rustic lifestyle. A recent study of students from the North Carolina mountains attending a southern urban university found that they had diverse reactions to "country speech" ranging from mild amusement to anger about the linguistic profile of an imagined country persona and nonstandard southern speech.[2] When combined with the noun *bumpkin*, as in "We don't want to sound like country bumpkins," it takes on a highly pejorative connotation.

The term bumpkin has a long history in the English language, and some derivatives such *pumpkin bumpkin*, or even *bumpkin lumpkin pumpkin*, have been used as terms of endearment. But more traditionally, *country bumpkin* suggests an inability to adjust to the pace of the modern world associated with city life. Bumpkin has been used in English far longer than English has been spoken in what is now North Carolina.[3] The term comes up quite regularly in interviews with residents in Charlotte when they talk about the transformation of the city. As one business and political leader, sitting in his Charlotte office on the top floor of a skyscraper, put it: "Communication today is so important, not only in the words you say but in the way you say them. The image that we project is in large measure determined by the way we say it. If we aren't very careful, we might be characterized as a country bumpkin."[4]

To view the video of this quote, visit http://www.talkintarheel.com/chapter/4/video4-2.php

The label *country* reflects underlying ideologies about American lifestyle and values, and it is open to varying interpretations. The popular country song popularized by Barbara Mandrell, Reba McEntire, and George Jones, "I was Country When Country Wasn't Cool," points to the value conflict resulting from the mixing of "urban" and "rural":

They call us country bumpkins
For stickin' to our roots.
I'm just glad we're in a country
Where we're all free to choose
I was Country, when Country wasn't cool.[5]

Language change takes place everywhere, but the speed and direction of change in remote areas is different from urban environments. Wherever these changes take place, they carry social meaning. In the South, the cities have been the focal point of some rapid and socially significant changes in dialect, making them highly intriguing research sites. One of our linguistic colleagues, Dr. Robin Dodsworth, has spent over a half dozen years interviewing more than 250 native-born Raleighites of all ages to study the intricate and changing dialect patterns in the shifting social milieu of the metropolitan South.[6] In Raleigh, as in most other big cities of the South, the population now mixes longtime southern urban residents, rural residents who moved to the city from outlying regions, and, of course, the Yankee transplants who have helped change the face—and the voices—of southern cities over the past couple of generations. Also contributing to the linguistic mix are voices from other countries, as the southeastern United States experienced the largest proportional increase of immigrants of any region of the United States over the last few decades.

The cities mix people from different places, but they don't always match them well, and a natural tension can exist between those whose kinfolk have lived there for generations and newer residents. As one transplant sees it, "So many of us are coming to the South now, and the whole nature of the South will change because of it." But then she alludes to the potential clash: "So we will be North Carolinians—*whether the locals like it or not.*"[7]

Some southerners see urbanization as a positive, progressive change, while others think it is the worst thing that ever happened to the South. Most have mixed emotions. As Sallie Griffin puts it, "I don't want us to lose all of our southern charm, but it's okay to lose some of it."[8] How much is enough—in language and in custom? How much linguistic accommodation can happen before compromising identity in language and lifestyle? There are no quotas for Yankee transplants and no regulations governing interregional unions, though we've met people who would prefer that there were some.

The Urbanization of North Carolina

After years of giving lectures about dialects to all kinds of groups throughout North Carolina, we are generally prepared for questions that seem to come out of left field. Questions range from the relationship of dialects to physical attributes to the influence of the southern climate on dialect. In fact, questions about the effect of the climate on speech are not that uncommon, and we are used to framing responses that diplomatically reject the purported link between the warm, humid climate of the South and the slow southern "drawl." After one lecture to a group of businesspeople and educators in Hickory, North Carolina, a leading car dealer from the area asked a different version of the role of the southern climate on dialect: "Professor, what has been the effect of air-conditioning on Southern dialect?" Walt Wolfram offered an evasive two-minute "courtesy response" that ended up politely saying, "None!" But the question may have deserved a more thoughtful response if air-conditioning was intended to be a proxy for a deeper social and economic issue brought about by industrial changes in the South, many of which coincided with the widespread availability of residential and industrial air-conditioning in the second half of the twentieth century. These industrial and commercial changes set off the avalanche of Yankee transplants that has reconfigured the demography of the South. Aside from air-conditioning's effects on demography, it is also possible that it changed some social interactional patterns of North Carolinians, who could remain comfortable and isolated in their homes watching television instead of sitting on their front porch chatting with neighbors.[9]

Historically, North Carolina was by design a predominantly rural state, dominated by small incorporated towns rather than cities. In fact, it still has more than 200 towns with populations totaling fewer than 1,000 residents and about 500 towns with fewer than 6,000 residents, and these towns are a significant part of its sociohistorical heritage. However, the clear trend in North Carolina has been toward urbanization. Defining urban as any town with more than 2,500 residents, less than 15 percent of the population of North Carolina was urban a century ago. Defining urban as any town or city with more than 50,000 residents, over 60 percent of North Carolinians now live in urban areas. However, even with the steady increase of the urban population over the century, North Carolina still ranks as the tenth most rural state in the United States, and its rural population remains quite traditional in many ways, both culturally and linguistically.

FIGURE 4.1. Front-porch conversation before air-conditioning. (Lafayette Studios Photographs Collection, University of Kentucky Special Collections)

The different urban areas in North Carolina—the Triangle (Raleigh, Durham, Chapel Hill), the Triad (Greensboro, Winston-Salem, High Point), and the Charlotte metropolitan area—grew at different times, for different reasons, and in different ways. The dramatic growth of Charlotte's population in the 1950s coincided with the growing presence of bank headquarters and continued through the 1970s and 1980s as Charlotte rose to prominence as the second-largest banking center in the United States. As the banking industry grew, high-rise buildings replaced residential units and small stores, making Charlotte an economically attractive city for relocation both from within North Carolina and from other states, as well as from outside the United States. Other areas of the state urbanized later than Charlotte, as can be seen in Figure 4.2, which captures Greenville in 1967 before it began its urbanization.

The Raleigh-Durham area saw rapid expansion beginning in the 1960s and 1970s after the establishment of Research Triangle Park in 1959, which drew technology, research, and development enterprises to the area defined by several nationally renowned universities. This growth hasn't slowed since then, as the metro areas in the Research Triangle area grew 40 percent from 2000 to 2010, the highest percentage of any metropolitan area in the

FIGURE 4.2. Rural Greenville, North Carolina, in 1967.
(*Daily Reflector* Image Collection, East Carolina University Digital Collections)

United States during this period. And it is predicted that it will be the fastest-growing metro area through 2025.

The Piedmont Triad area of Greensboro, Winston-Salem, and High Point held onto its traditional southern identity longer than the other metropolitan areas. The Triad was notable for large textile, tobacco, and furniture industries, but as these industries diminished, the area has increasingly turned into an attractive area for technological companies. It now has 1.6 million residents and is projected to have more than 2 million people by 2025. Today, more than 5.8 million of the roughly 9 million residents of North Carolina live in the Research Triangle, the Piedmont Triad, and the Charlotte metropolitan areas.

The story isn't simply that rural folks have moved to the cities. Fifty years ago, only 15 percent of the residents in Wake County, where Raleigh is located, were born outside of the state, approximately the same percentage as the state as a whole. By 2010, the number of North Carolinians born in a different state increased to about one-third of the population, but in urban counties such as those encompassing the Research Triangle and Charlotte, out-of-staters now account for more than 55 percent of the population.[10]

The Yankee invasion started a little earlier in Charlotte, but the Research

FIGURE 4.3. Charlotte's skyline boasts the tallest building in North Carolina, the Bank of America Corporate Center. (Photograph by Neal Hutcheson)

Triangle has now caught up with the infusion. The reinterpretation of the Raleigh suburb of *Cary* as a tongue-in-cheek acronym for "Containment Area for Relocated Yankees" or "Congested Area of Relocated Yankees" speaks to the cohabitation. Indeed, while the overall North Carolina population has increased steadily, the population increase of the three major metropolitan regions has been dramatic, thanks in a large part to residents from elsewhere. No wonder Tar Heels sometimes feel like they're experiencing another invasion of Yankee forces.

North Carolina joins a growing list of southern cities experiencing similar demographic transformation—Atlanta; Houston; Austin; Jacksonville, Florida; and Memphis, among others. The urban sprawl, the metropolitan population growth, and the influx of outsiders create a crucible for rapid and dramatic language change. In fact, some linguists think that the urban and rural dialect divide in the South now may equal the split between northern and southern dialects in its significance. Some current Charlotte and Raleigh residents, for example, live in such enclave transplant communities that they barely recognize what a speaker of the traditional regional dialect sounds like. As one bilingual immigrant from Venezuela now living in Charlotte observes: "Most of the people here are from someplace else. You know the typical Charlottean doesn't exist very much. So when you actually hear it, when somebody says this is a typical Charlottean accent, you go, 'Oh, that's what a Charlottean sounds like.' But it needs to be pointed out."[11] Another transplant from the North notes: "It's very hard to hear a pure southern dialect, which suggests to me that it's changed a lot. In fact, I'm always struck by hearing it. Ah, this is someone probably from Charlotte, not from some other place coming to Charlotte."[12] The urbanization of the South seems to be an irreversible social and demographic reality. The cities conveniently, if not always comfortably, accommodate a core of native residents, in-state migrants who have moved there from rural areas for economic or social reasons, and transplant residents who "will be North Carolinians whether the locals like it or not."

To view a video of these quotes, visit http://www.talkintarheel .com/chapter/4/video4-3.php

Southern voices from metropolitan areas now compete with the sounds of the outlying rural areas. But change is not extinction. As Parks Helms, a well-known Charlotte lawyer and long-term chair of the County Commissioners in Mecklenburg County, puts it: "This community, I think, has always been willing to change. At the same time, I think we've had the feeling that we needed to preserve some of those important qualities that set us apart from other large urban areas."[13] In the next section, we explore some of the details of dialect change and preservation that define rural and urban areas of North Carolina. The voices may sound different from those of the past, but they are still distinguishably southern.

To view the video of this quote, visit http://www.talkintarheel .com/chapter/4/video4-4.php

Dialect Traits

The urban-rural and young-old divide is apparent on all levels of language, from the minute phonetic details of vowel production in words like *boot* or *boat* to broad-based, obvious meet-and-greet routines. A simple greeting of *hey* instead of *hi* or the use of *y'all* instead of *you guys* or *youse* may index southern identity before any real conversation can even take place.

No cultural trait more clearly captures the cultural transformation of the South than the term *Yankee*. The term means different things depending on where you live. Those from other nations often use it to refer to any American, regardless of their region. In the northern United States, the term typically refers to someone from New England, so a person from Boston would undoubtedly be a Yankee while a person from Minnesota or Illinois would not be. And in New England itself, the term is often reserved for those who are descendants of English or Dutch settlers in the region. But in the South, following the Civil War, it was appropriated for anyone who was not from the South, so a person from Minnesota, Illinois, or Massachusetts would all be subsumed under Yankee—usually "damned Yankee." Today, in fact, people from south Florida are often considered Yankees.

In the following sections, we highlight some of the vocabulary, pronunciation, and grammatical differences that help to delimit rural from urban speech in North Carolina. In the process, we see that the social and regional meaning of language is certainly a lot more complex than these basic categories; the urban-rural dimension intersects with age, generation, social status, and identity, among other social and psychological factors.

VOCABULARY

Though words may have unique origins and histories, they do not just appear randomly. Thus, the term *meehonkey* presented in the last chapter was probably created on the island of Ocracoke to imitate the sound of a goose so that the seeker in hide-and-seek would have a rough idea of where hiders might be located. Meanwhile, the island word *token* referring to a sign or presage of death in the same community can be traced back to Old English, though its meaning has shifted over the centuries. Words provide clues about local culture and community. Part of the North Carolina language narrative is told through its lexicon. In this context, the distinction between urban and rural communities is important, but the reduction to this exclusive dimension would be a bit like saying that only two sizes are needed for clothing the entire population. Nonetheless, lots of words carry strong associations of rural and urban status, so it is a convenient starting point. The list ranges from stereotypes to locally diagnostic words that may not even be recognized as being regional by a particular community.

Nothing is more iconic of southern speech than the plural form of *y'all*, and its use transcends urban and rural areas of North Carolina, except in the mountains, where *you'uns* or *yins* competes with it. Notwithstanding the reaction of Yankees who prefer plural forms like *youse* or *you guys* to address more than one person, the use of y'all remains productive and pervasive. Furthermore, it has been embraced throughout the South as an overarching symbol. The city of Atlanta closed the 1996 Summer Olympics by proudly displaying a banner that read "Y'all Come Back," reminding the world that it was the first southern city to host the world's greatest multisport event. No word in the American English vocabulary probably carries as much regional capital. Some Yankee transplants vow never to use y'all, but others appreciate its usefulness, adopting it along with terms like *barbecue*, *hushpuppies*, and *sweet tea*. Yankees should be cautious about the vows they make, because y'all has a way of making its way into the unwitting mouths of transplants. It is, for example, one of the earliest southern entries to be found in the vocabulary of immigrants from Latin America who speak English as a second language. Besides that, it has a highly functional role when there is a need to address more than one person directly, a convenient distinction that makes the singular-plural paradigm regular for all personal pronouns: *I/we*, *you/y'all*, and *he-she-it/they*. Within linguistics, there are at least half a dozen articles and a couple hundred pages written on whether y'all can ever be used to refer to a single person or whether it is exclusively reserved for more than one person. Our conclusion is that it is traditionally plural but sometimes can be used in a formulaic way to address a single person. This interpretation was confirmed during a 6:00 A.M. visit to a convenience store by Walt Wolfram in a small town in North Carolina. Alone in the store, the clerk told him: "Y'all come back now." Less discussed but equally important may be the pragmatic function of y'all to soften the directness of a statement. Telling a group of people "Y'all need to quiet down now!" seems more polite than telling them "You need to quiet down now!"

At the other end of the lexical spectrum are items that we may not even realize are regional, rural, or even southern until someone points it out to us. *Butter beans* and *biscuits* are southern terms that span the urban-rural divide, but most of us don't even realize their regionality until some occasion raises a question. We've now had multiple discussions with people and vendors at farmers markets over the difference between a *lima bean* and a *butter bean*. For some, there is no difference, and butter bean is just a southern version of lima bean; but for others, it is a small lima bean—or a big one. The comprehensive *Dictionary of American Regional English* reference work coyly defines butter bean as a "lima bean, especially a small one," though our students still sometimes insist it is larger one.

People throughout North Carolina don't need to be told that you can't order *iced tea* without specifying whether you want it *sweet* or *unsweet(ened)*. It doesn't make any difference if you order tea in Robbinsville (Graham County), Charlotte (Mecklenburg), Calabash (Brunswick County), or anywhere in between; the failure to specify the kind of tea is a dead giveaway to a server that a person has not been in North Carolina very long. There are plenty of southern dialect words that are shared by urban and rural areas alike. Conversely, a *Coke* or *Co-cola*, a specific type of beverage for the majority of Americans and for urban North Carolinians, is used for any carbonated beverage in lots of rural contexts.

As we have noted, age and social status often intersect with the rural-urban distinction. Words like *favor* to refer to one's resemblance of related person, as in "She favors her momma," *recollect* ("remember") in "I recollect when the Bank of America was a little store," or *meddlin'* ("interfere") in "They're always meddlin' in my business" might still be used by older speakers in the urban areas of North Carolina, but they are falling out of use among younger speakers. For sure, younger speakers know what they mean, but they have a kind of quaint, older-person connotation in a metropolitan area. Everyone knows what *kinfolk* and *young 'uns* mean regardless of where a person has lived in North Carolina, but in urban areas, these are more likely to be used in conversation by older people. In lots of rural areas, these words are in active use regardless of age. And in some rural contexts, a question like "Who are your kin?" is a significant question about family heritage and social status.

Some southern lexical items were once widespread in North Carolina and the South but have now narrowed in their regional identity and taken on the connotations of "country." Words like *mash* ("push") *cut off* or *cut on* ("turn off/ on"), *chunk* ("throw"), *swanny* ("swear," as in "I swanny you will pay for what you've done"), or *airish* ("breezy") were once in widespread use throughout North Carolina, but they are now mainly restricted to rural areas of the state. Traditional lexical items are also receding in some rural areas, like *plumb* as an intensifying adverb meaning "completely" or "very," as in "He was plumb wore out." The term *slam* (for example, "He was slam wore out") seems to be taking over for *plumb* in some rural communities, while *right* ("That pie was right good") has persisted more in the urban areas. We recently heard a North Carolina legislator use the term *flat* or *flat-out* in a similar way as he testified on the senate floor that "the legislation is flat wrong." There are at least three options for intensifying a condition: country, rural, and urban, though there is a lot of overlap in the distribution.

Rurality is also associated with region. We found at least four different dialect words—each with various pronunciations—to describe things that are "crooked" or "not quite straight." The term *sigogglin* is fairly restricted to the rural mountains, while *cattywampus* is more concentrated toward the coast and *whopperjawed* and *antigoglin* seem less regionally restricted.

In Table 4.1, we give a sample of some of the words that help define the urban-rural dialect continuum in North Carolina. We subdivide the categories of rural and urban into older and younger speakers since age often intersects with this dimension. A check mark indicates that it is typical of the population of speakers. Given our focus on more traditional southern words, we don't include a designation for words used only by younger speakers, though there are certainly words that fit this designation. For example, younger speakers may use *like* to introduce a quotation (as in "She was, like, 'What are you doing?'") or *sketchy*, as in "He was acting sketchy" (that is, "questionably" or "up to no good"). If we included slang terms used by the younger generation, there would be countless words that only younger people knew and used. Table 4.1 is not intended to be comprehensive; in fact, that would require a separate dictionary. It is simply an illustrative list of lexical items that seem to be distributed along the rural-urban scale and by age.

PRONUNCIATION

Pronunciation is often the most reliable indicator of the intricate changes that have been shaping the dialect landscape of North Carolina and the South since the earliest English-speaking settlements. These pronunciation patterns also reveal some rather complex shifts in the social meaning of dialects that coincide with the urbanization of the South. Some of the patterns that govern pronunciation can get pretty complicated, but we will try to keep our description accessible to those who have not chosen to major in linguistics.

R-loss, or r-lessness, is the phenomenon in which the r sound after a vowel is not pronounced, so that a word like *fear* is pronounced like *feauh* or *North Carolina* is pronounced as *No'th Carolina*. Typically, the loss of the r can only take place after a vowel, so the loss of the r would not occur at the beginning of a word like *reckon* or *run*; it also does not usually occur between vowels in a word, as in *periscope*, *very*, or *ferry*.

R-lessness is still used in caricatures of southern speech in movies and popular media; Scarlett O'Hara's southern speech in *Gone with the Wind* is a typical Hollywood portrayal of the southern r-less trait. During the period portrayed in this film, r-lessness was quite common in the Plantation South, but not all regions of North Carolina have actively participated in r-lessness. Thanks to the formative influence of the founder dialects—particularly the Scots-Irish, the Irish, and settlers from regions of England who brought r-ful dialects of English with them—speakers in the Outer Banks and the western mountain range of North Carolina have always

To hear examples of r-less word pronunciations, visit http://www.talkintarheel.com/chapter/4/audio4-1.php

TABLE 4.1 A Sampler of Lexical Differences: Rural and Urban, Old and Young

Word	Example	RURAL		URBAN	
		Old	Young	Old	Young
y'all (pron., "you plural")	Y'all have been around a long time.	✓	✓	✓	✓
biscuit (n., "heavy bread made from wheat flour")	I love biscuits and gravy.	✓	✓	✓	✓
snaps/snap beans ("green beans")	I'll take a pound of snaps.	✓	✓	✓	✓
butter bean (n., "lima bean")	They have the best butter beans at the State Fair.	✓	✓	✓	✓
sweet/unsweetened tea (n., "tea with/without sugar")	I'll have sweet tea with my meal.	✓	✓	✓	✓
cornpone (n., "cornmeal bread"; adj., "cake")	I love me some cornpone with my meal.	✓	✓	✓	✓
kin(folk) (n., "relative")	We have lots of kin in the area.	✓	✓	✓	
favor (v., "resemble, look like")	She favors her momma.	✓	✓	✓	
young 'uns (n., "children")	They have lots of young 'uns.	✓	✓	✓	
recollect (v., "remember, recall")	I recollect them sitting around the fire at night.	✓	✓	✓	
carry (v., "accompany, take")	I'll carry you to the movies tomorrow.	✓	✓	✓	
fixin' to (v., "plan to, intend")	I'm fixin' to go to the show now.	✓	✓	✓	
cut off/on (v., "turn on/off")	Could you cut off the light so we can see the movie?	✓	✓	✓	
stay (v., "currently live")	Do you stay out in Kinston?	✓	✓		
hey (exclamation, "casual greeting")	Hey! Good to see you.	✓	✓		
chunk (v., "throw")	If it gets close, just chunk a rock at him.	✓			
reckon (v., "guess, suppose")	I reckon it'll be airish tonight.	✓			
swanny (v., "swear")	I swanny they won't do that.	✓			
poke (n., "bag, sack")	Put that soda in a poke.	✓			
plumb ("completely")	He was plumb tuckered out from working so hard.	✓			
addle(d) (adj., v., "confused, dazed")	James Barrie was addled by the new regulations.	✓			
airish (adj., "cool, breezy")	It's airish out tonight.	✓			
cattywampus, sigogglin, antigoglin, whopperjawed (adj., "crooked, not straight")	That fence sure was cattywampus/sigogglin, antigoglin/ whopperjawed.	✓			

pronounced their r's in *fear, north, farm,* and so forth. In the Coastal Plain and the Piedmont—the so-called Plantation South—r-lessness pronunciation was the norm at one point.

The r-loss pattern flourished in the Plantation South due to a paradoxical social juxtaposition of southern aristocracy and slavery. Prior to the eighteenth and early nineteenth centuries, standard British dialects pronounced their r's. In fact, English-language historians have concluded that William Shakespeare most likely spoke an r-ful dialect of English rather than the r-less one that actors now use when staging his plays. During the late eighteenth and early nineteenth centuries, the r-less pattern emerged as the British English standard norm. During this period, the children of many southern aristocrats were educated in England and brought this language innovation back with them to the Coastal Plain and Piedmont.

At the same time, Africans who came to the South via the Middle Passage spoke a variety of English that was r-less. Most English-based creoles in West Africa and in the Caribbean are r-less, as are other varieties of English spoken in the African diaspora. So the r-less speech of the slaves reinforced the speech of aristocrats in a kind of phonetic irony. It may seem strange that the socially elite and the enslaved would converge on the same phonetic pattern, but such paradoxes are not uncommon in the social life of language. It also shows how arbitrary the social meaning of particular language traits can be. One generation's socially prestigious pronunciation may turn into the next generation's stigmatized production.

R-loss is changing fairly rapidly in the South and in North Carolina, but the way in which it is shifting tells an important story about language change and social meaning. When Walt Wolfram first moved to North Carolina in 1992, he and his wife would spend their weekends visiting small towns in the state, including many located in the Coastal Plain and the Piedmont. He was impressed with how r-less some of the residents of these small towns were, particularly those involved in farming and agriculture. In many of these same rural regions, educators and businesspeople were r-ful, so that there seemed to be a class dichotomy between the r-ful upper class and the r-less lower class. This, of course, is different from the historical picture painted above in which r-lessness was associated with the aristocracy.

Meanwhile, back in the city, Walt's first social interactions with residents in Raleigh and Charlotte led him to believe that the residents of these cities were now completely r-ful. Eventually, he was deemed worthy to be invited to a couple of social events hosted by elderly, socially privileged Raleighites.

The norm for these speakers was the older r-less pattern, a kind of holdover of the aristocratic pattern. So the elderly, metropolitan upper crust would now ironically share r-lessness with working-class, rural residents, revealing a quite different social meaning for this pattern in these varying regional contexts for different generations of speakers.

To hear an older r-less Raleigh speaker compared to a younger r-ful Raleigh speaker, visit http://www.talkintarheel .com/chapter/4/audio4-2.php

Cases like r-lessness illustrate how fluid and arbitrary the social meaning of dialect items can be. The shift from positive to negative social meaning can take place within a couple of generations. A parallel shift happened in New York City, where r-lessness was the prestigious pronunciation before World War II and then became stigmatized and associated with working-class speech in generations of speakers following the war.[14]

To hear older and younger r-less working-class rural speakers, visit http:// www.talkintarheel.com/ chapter/4/audio4-3.php

Overall, urban areas are certainly leading the way in the recession of r-lessness, and North Carolina, like other areas of the South, is becoming r-ful. This change has been taking place for some time now. One of the earliest sociolinguistic studies in the 1960s focused on the generational change of r-lessness in Hillsborough, North Carolina, which at that time was still a fairly rural area rather than the literary community it has become today.[15] That study found that younger speakers in Hillsborough were becoming r-ful, and current research indicates this trend has continued. Though caricatures of the modern-day South in film and the theater still seize on iconic r-lessness to depict its regional speech, these are mostly nostalgic portrayals of an older South. The urban norm of the South is now r-ful, and rural areas are following the lead, though often at a slower rate and with different social meaning.

A number of other patterns of consonant pronunciation also reveal a rural-urban dimension. One fairly well-known pattern, commonly referred to as *g-dropping*, is alternation of the final -in' and -ing in unstressed syllables. In words like *swimming*, *ringing*, or *dropping*, -ing is pronounced as -in', as in *swimmin'*, *ringin'*, and *droppin'*, respectively. The -in' pronunciation is much more common when the word is a verb rather than a noun, so it would be more common to use -in' in "They were swimmin' every day" than in "Swimmin' is so much fun," although it can occur in both. This pronunciation is hardly unique to southern dialects; in fact, it correlates with social status in practically all dialects of English. But in the South, it carries social significance in relation to the urban-rural dichotomy, age, and identity. The -in' is more common in rural dialects than urban dialects, and among older speakers in urban areas, following other patterns that mark southerners. But it also can be used to index rurality, so that higher frequencies of -in' are associated with country speech. That is why some younger speakers who live in urban areas but want to identify with a more country persona or lifestyle use -in' at higher levels. It's also one of the phonetic features that American Idol winner and country singer Scotty McCreery, from the Raleigh suburb of Garner, manipulates in projecting his country persona. This pattern is not that unusual for a young person from the suburban community adjacent to Raleigh where southern rural identity is embraced by some youth.

The use of -in' versus -ing can also be used to project folksiness by politicians and other leaders. An article in the *Raleigh News and Observer* by noted columnist Barry Saunders refers to the use of this trait by Governor Pat McCrory in a television advertisement during his political campaign.[16] He comments that "McCrory ends the ad by saying, in his most folksy, aw-shucks manner, 'I'm Pat McCrory, and I'm ruuunnin' for governor.'" Saunders refers to this move as Political Linguistic Slumming (PLS) and interprets it as "politicians who are well-educated, though, cynically try to strike a populist, folksy tone by playing down their intellect. They seek to convey, as near as I can tell, that 'Hey, y'all. I'm just like you.'" Our interpretation would be a little more generous—we might see it as a politician attempting to relate to his audience through linguistic affinity. The column evoked strong reactions from readers, from congratulations to condemnation, showing how contentious simple issues of language differences can play out in public life. It also underscored how language variation naturally enters into personal presentation and everyday interaction.

Those consonantal features with the strongest southern rural associations are largely absent from urban speech today. So the loss of l in *help* and *wolf*, making them sound like *hep* and *woof*, respectively, are now found almost exclusively among elderly and especially rural speakers. It may be mere coincidence, but it is worth noting that the mascots of North Carolina State University, Mr. and Ms. Wolf, are usually spelled as *Wuf*, like the rural pronunciation of wolf without the l. In fact, the officially trademarked names for the mascots are Wuf, not Wolf. This pronunciation harkens back to the agrarian roots of North Carolina. It is possible that it arose from the agricultural focus of N.C. State and has been preserved even as the pronunciations of the students shifted. While commemorating this university's history, it may simultaneously encourage continued negative derision by some fans of their competitive rival, the University of North Carolina at Chapel

Hill, who refer to N.C. State as "Cow College" or "Moo U." As with most linguistic features, the social meanings of terms and pronunciations are seldom straightforward.

A number of traditional southern pronunciations are fading throughout the state, with urban areas changing about a generation faster than rural areas. These include the pronunciation of a z sound before an n as a d, as in *bidness* for *business*, *wadn't* for *wasn't*, or *idn't* for *isn't*; the pronunciation of th in *mouth* or *bath* as *mouf* and *baf*; and the pronunciations of *chimbly* for *chimney*, *postes* for *post*, *oncet* for *once*, *hit* for *it*, and so forth.

Perhaps the best-known pronunciation of southern speech is the ungliding or weakening of the long-i glide of words like *side* and *time* introduced in chapter 3. This trait permeates the South, but its distribution in North Carolina is different from that of some other southern states. As we noted in the previous chapter, the Piedmont has a restricted pattern where the vowel is unglided only before voiced consonants and at the ends of words, while in the western mountains and the Coastal Plain, ungliding happens regardless of linguistic environment. Folks from the mountains and coast can say *raht*, *lahk*, and *rahs* for *right*, *like*, and *rice*, respectively, while those in the Piedmont would pronounce these with a glide as something like *raheet*, *laheek*, and *rahees*. To people in the Piedmont, pronunciations like *raht*, *lahk*, and *rahs* carry a strong rural association, while the same feature in pronunciations like *sahd* or *tahm* go unnoticed. In the bigger cities, restricted ungliding is still quite robust among older and middle-aged speakers, but it is now receding among younger speakers.

Other southern vowel differences, such as the merger of the vowels in *steel* and *still* (usually *steeuhl*) and *feel* and *fill* (usually *feeuhl*) are still quite common in rural areas but rapidly receding in metropolitan areas, if not gone completely. The merger in the vowels of *sell* and *sale* (usually *sale*) or *well* and *whale* (usually *whale*) is also fading rapidly in the urban centers. A recent study of older and younger speakers in Winston-Salem clearly demonstrates the loss of the mergers before l even while speakers maintain and are aware of the vowel merger involving words like *pin* and *pen*, which is a characteristic feature of general southern speech.[17] In rural areas, both the merger before l and n are alive and well.

While giving up on one vowel merger, city folks may be gaining another. Urban areas of North Carolina such as Raleigh are starting to participate in a merger of the vowels in *cot* and *caught* that is spreading across the United States. Older speakers in these cities would pronounce these two vowels differently, and both younger and older rural speakers still pronounce the vowel of *caught* and *bought* with a glided vowel or diphthong, something like *cawt* and *bawt*, respectively.

Other southern vowel distinctions may be even more subtle than those described above. The short front vowels of words like *bed* and *bid* have traditionally been pronounced a little higher in the mouths of southerners than other Americans, sounding more like *beyd* or *biyd*. At the same time, the vowels of *bead* and *raid* drop a little bit and are accompanied by tongue movement so that they sound more like *bih-ud* and *ruh-eed*. The phonetic nuances of this shift are difficult to describe, but they can be perceived in careful listening to their production. Though subtle differences, these pronunciations are becoming increasingly uncommon in the urban areas of the state.

Meanwhile, southerners move the back vowels of *boot* and *boat* forward so that they sound more like *biwt* and *bewt*. This vowel pronunciation, unlike the previous ones, is spreading beyond the South, though it remains strongly associated with southern speech. Distinctly southern pronunciations in the vowel system are certainly more subtle than they were just a couple of generations ago, but one can hardly say that southern vowels are no longer found in the cities of the South. Southern metropolitan speakers are sometimes surprised when northerners readily identify them as southern from their vowel productions.

To view and listen to an interactive image of the southern vowel shift, visit http://www.talkintarheel.com/chapter/4/other4-1.php

GRAMMAR

Asked to describe the kind of North Carolinian who might use sentences such as "James Barrie was a-buildin' a new house," "I done finished my new house," or "She liketa died when she saw the price of the new house," people will no doubt assume the speaker to be rural and probably uneducated. This is not surprising, given the fact that Americans are more judgmental of grammatical differences than pronunciation. Furthermore, these kinds of features are used to construct caricatures of rural southern residents. The late Andy Griffith, North Carolina's treasured actor and comedian, used such features to create the country persona in his famous monologue originally performed in 1953 about a country person's introduction to football. The following passage from "What It Was, Was Football" liberally diffuses these rural structures throughout his routine. Some of the nonstandard structures employed by Griffith are italicized to help identify the kinds of features we have in mind.[18]

And somebody *had took* and *drawed* white lines all over it and drove *postes* in it, and I don't know what all, and I looked down there and I *seen* five or six convicts *a-running* up and down and *a-blowing* whistles. *They was!* And then I looked down there and I *seen* these pretty girls *a-wearin'* these little bitty short dresses and *a-dancin'* around, and so I *sit* down and thought I'd see what it was that was *a-gonna* happen. I did. About the time I got *set* down good I looked down there and I *seen* thirty or forty men come runnin' out of one end of a great big outhouse down there. They did! And everybody where I was *a-settin'* got up and hollered!

Through these grammatical traits, in conjunction with distinctive southern vowel pronunciations, Griffith creates a stereotypical southern country bumpkin caricature. The reality, however, is that the grammatical structures in these sentences and in Griffith's monologue are all well-documented, systematic patterns in the history of English. For the record, Andy Griffith used the *a*-prefixing structure and other grammatical structures in quite patterned and appropriate ways that are in keeping with his poor country roots in Mount Airy, North Carolina—unlike most actors who make southerners and dialectologists cringe with their poor imitations of southern speech.

To hear Andy Griffith's routine "What It Was, Was Football," visit http://www.talkintarheel .com/chapter/4/audio4-4.php

Historically, many of the traits used in rural areas were considered be perfectly standard and used by highly respected people. Linguistically, some of these structures even serve to mark distinctive meanings. For example, the use of *done* as a helping verb in "I done finished the house" conveys a completive aspect that can extend to emphasis. A builder who has *done finished the house* has totally and completely finished the job—or told a boldfaced lie.

The form *liketa*, derived historically from the phrase *like to have*, serves as a special kind of single helping verb that marks an "avertive" or "counterfactual" construction—that is, a fate narrowly avoided in the mind of the person experiencing it. It is often used figuratively rather than literally to underscore the perceived severity of the situation. People who say that they were so cold that they *liketa froze to death* may be very cold, but they usually aren't literally in danger of freezing to death. Students in linguistics commiserating after an exam may utter "that test was so hard I liketa died," but we have yet to see a student die from a linguistics exam. The historical precedent for this construction is well attested in the history of the English language, including its use in the plays of the Bard himself. Thus, in *Much Ado about Noth-*

ing (1599), Claudio says, "We had *liket to have* had our two noses snapt off with two old men without teeth"; and Touchstone in *As You Like It* (1600) says, "I have had foure quarrels and *like to have fought* one." And no one thought they were country bumpkins for saying this.

The attachment of an *a*-prefix (pronounced as *uh*) to a verb in *He was a-buildin'* or *She went a-fishin'* was once widespread in the English language and considered quite standard. Over time, it was lost in some dialects, and it just so happened that this change took hold more rapidly among some socially favored groups in cities, leaving behind those in outlying areas.

Though many southern grammatical constructions have become socially stigmatized, making them rare among educated metropolitan residents, all is not lost for southern grammar in urban areas. Three recent governors of North Carolina—James B. Hunt Jr., Mike Easley, and Beverly Perdue, all well-educated and middle-class native southerners—used combinations of helping verbs such as "I might could do it" or "She might oughta do it." These so-called double modals are combinations of two verbs expressing "moods" such as certainty, possibility, obligation, or permission. Possible combinations include *might could*, *useta could*, *might should*, *might oughta*, and so forth. Sentences such as "I might could go there" or "You might oughta take it" are exclusively southern in the United States. They serve a special intentional purpose, lessening the force of the obligation conveyed by a single modal. A sentence like "She might could do it" is less forceful than single modals such as "She may do it" or "She can do it." So a person who responds to an invitation to come to a party with "I might could come" is not obligated to attend. They may or may not show up, but don't expect them. We can see how this mitigated obligation might come in handy for a politician. To Yankees, these kinds of constructions are quite obtrusive, but we have also found outsiders who consciously end up using them because they serve to signify a convenient, elusive intention.

The use of different kinds of irregular verbs—like *growed* for *grew* in "He growed a nice garden," or the use of *give* or *come* in the past tense of "He give her a present last year" or "He come to class yesterday"—doesn't survive urbanization and formal education. Neither does the regularization of the past tense of *be* in "We was home last night." By the same token, distinctly southern constructions that do not draw corrective attention as being "bad English" have a better chance of survival.

A few years ago, Jackson Wolfram, the seven-year-old grandson of Walt Wolfram, traveled south from Connecticut to participate in a regional wrestling tournament in the Raleigh area. Unfortunately, he had a freak accident in which he suffered a broken arm that required a trip to Wake Med Hospital in an emergency vehicle. As the medics emerged from the door with the stretcher carrying Jackson, one of them good-naturedly announced, "We got us a Yankee this time." The use of *we got us* instead of "We got a Yankee" expresses a special kind of personal relationship to the subject of the sentence. The subtle meaning of a sentence like "I got me a new car" is different from the more impersonal "I got a new car" or even "I got myself a new car." This construction, which is used in general southern speech, can still be heard wherever one meets native North Carolinians, though it may be receding somewhat in younger urban speakers. When a southern medic "gets him a Yankee," he has him something special.

Some grammatical traits of southern dialects are more camouflaged in everyday conversation. These may sound a bit strange to those from outside the South, but they are not particularly marked socially, and language purists don't pay much attention to them. There's also a good chance that teachers use them in their own speech without noticing. For example, in the North, so-called stative verbs—verbs that are used for actions that have undefined duration, like *want*, *like*, and *know*—are not usually used with the progressive verb form with -*ing*. A northern transplant in the South would say, "I wanted an A in your class" or "She likes dialects a whole lot." But a native North Carolinian might say, "I was wanting an A in your class" or "She is liking dialects a whole lot." Though these constructions sound somewhat odd to outsiders, they do not sound "country," and most southerners are unaware that this is a dialectal grammatical construction—until we point it out to them. In fact, some of our most educated southern colleagues with doctoral degrees have been known to use them routinely in speech and writing even while maintaining that they don't speak southern.

Some constructions are even more nuanced and go unrecognized. In English, negative sentences with *be* or *have* can contract with *not* in a couple of different ways. One option is to contract the subject and *be* ("He's not here") while the other option is to contract *be* and *not* ("He isn't here"). The same is true of *have* and *not* in "He's not been here for a while" and "He hasn't been here for a while." Most dialects of English, including southern dialects, can use both kinds of contractions, but southern dialect speakers use more contractions with *be* or *have* ("I've not been there" and "He's not at home") than their northern counterparts, who are more prone to contract the negation as in *I haven't* or *He isn't*. In this choice, the South is more like British dialects than other American English dialects.[19] This pattern might go unnoticed by most people, but careful studies show that the higher frequency of *be* and *have* contraction correlates with southern dialects in both urban and rural settings.

Language Use Conventions

The camouflaged grammatical differences, the distribution of certain southern pronunciations, and the persistence of some southern vocabulary combine with particular kinds of language use conventions that include politeness, address forms, and uniquely southern expressions to paint a picture of a vibrant and sustainable southern dialect. Southerners in cities as well as rural areas address a wide range of adults with the respect labels *Sir* and *Ma'am*, including parents, whereas in the North, only a few adults with special status are addressed by these titles. Southern speakers may also use *Mr.* or *Miss* with a first name to indicate special familiarity not found in the North. These address forms suggest a kind of extended kinship relationship, so that children of Jeff and Emily's close friends may address Jeff and Emily Reaser as *Mr. Jeff* and *Miss Emily*. Usually, this ceases when the children reach adulthood, but the conventions have also been used traditionally by domestics in the South, as captured in the popular film *Driving Miss Daisy* (1989), in which the older African American chauffer and other domestics addressed their employer with this title and first name. There is a similar extension of the kinship terms *aunt* or *auntie* (pronounced *ahntee*) and *uncle* to nonrelatives who are close friends of the family. It's common for southern-born students to pause while explaining why they missed class to add, "Well, she's not my real auntie," which underscores both the importance of the relationship and the prevalence of the convention.

Of course, there are also a host of well-worn southern expressions that do not stop at the borders of the cities: *gettin' above your raisin'*, *tighter than a fiddle string*, *good ole boy*, *bless your heart*, and so forth. These expressions are not only rural and urban southern, but they also express some traditional southern values. The cultural value expressed in *gettin' above your raisin'* is expressed in the lyrics of the Flatt and Scruggs country song with the same title:

Now I got a gal that's sweet to me,
But she just ain't what she used to be
Just a little high headed; That's plain to see
Don't get above your raisin'; stay down to earth with me.[20]

Most people have an idea of what *good ole boys* are, and it can have a positive or negative reading. A humble and respected person can be a good ole boy, but in an urban context it is more likely to be used to refer to someone who engages in cronyism, especially with people who share values and have known one another for a long period of time. Socially, the "good ole boy network" usually excludes women and minorities.

Bless your heart, introduced in chapter 1, is an explicit expression of sympathy or pity. A beloved elderly relative or friend, or an act of kindness, can be tagged with this phrase. But it is often—and more commonly now—used to veil a negative judgment of a person's character or behavior: a polite excuse for making a rude remark. So a student who says, "He's an awful teacher, bless his heart" mitigates the negative judgment about the teacher's capability with an expression of superficial sympathy. It gives license to criticize a person, not unlike the comment "I don't mean to criticize you, but . . ." Once people hear the expression, they can brace themselves for the criticism. Or, in the case of outsiders, they may not realize they're being criticized at all!

To view a discussion of "Bless your heart," visit http://www.talkintarheel.com/chapter/4/video4-5.php

The *Daily Reflector* newspaper in Greenville, North Carolina, even has a daily "Bless Your Heart" section in which, keeping with the spirit of the phrase, readers are allowed to "pick a bone" or "share thanks" under this phrase.[21] The range of possible positive and negative uses makes it one of those southern expressions that readily evokes lots of opinions and stories about its use, meaning, and social function.

When all levels and uses of language are considered, there seems to be plenty of southern speech that has survived and continues to thrive in urban areas. It may be different from a couple of generations ago, and it is certainly more subtle and camouflaged than it was even a generation ago, but there is no immediate danger that southern speech has been silenced in the urban centers of North Carolina.

Yankee Speech in the South

Some areas of North Carolina, like other regions in the South, have become inundated by new residents from the North, altering the demographic, political, and cultural landscape of the state. These changes in population are well recognized by North Carolinians and outsiders alike, leading to a convenient but not always comfortable coexistence. As Martha Pearl Villas, author of cookbooks and a mainstay of Charlotte society, puts it in her highly marked

FIGURE 4.4. Author Martha Pearl Villas discusses the rapid changes she has seen in Charlotte. (Photograph by Neal Hutcheson)

southern dialect: "And these No'thuhnuhs come down heuh, and we take 'em in. And befo' you know it, it ain't the same. It's really not. They don't think and ac' like we do. Well they shu' don't tawk like us. They have a shahpness to theuh speech, don't you think so? Most South-uhnuhs and all, ah mean ah feel like we have kahna a soft, me-lodious voice. Of cou'se, whah shouldn't ah think it; ah don't know any different."[22] Notice that her speech, as an elderly, upper-class resident of the city born in 1916, is characterized by r-lessness and i ungliding. And the content is permeated with the undercurrent of tension between the old and the new.

To view the video of this quote, visit http://www.talkintarheel .com/chapter/4/video04-6.php

No matter how long they live in the South, transplants usu-ally remain recognizable as outsiders to native southerners. But they often do, in fact, adopt some subtle southernisms that they may not even be aware of. Just ask a transplant who has lived here for a few years how they are perceived when they re-turn home to their nonsouthern community for a visit. Trans-plants often report that when they return home for a visit, their family and friends back home now think that their speech sounds southern.

To view a clip about "sounding southern," visit http://www.talkintarheel.com/ chapter/4/video04-7.php

Is it their friends' and family's imaginations, or is there really something linguistically to this perception? We've heard this report too many times sim-ply to dismiss it, though it's difficult to pin down the specific dialect traits that might lead to this assessment. Sometimes, it might be a single emblematic southern word, most notably *y'all*, that triggers the reaction from family and friends in the North. Or it might be the use of an address term like *Hey* used for a casual greeting when meeting an acquaintance—or even a double modal like *might could* that helps mitigate a commitment. Words or expressions that seemed so exceptional and conspicuous when outsiders first moved to North Carolina have a way of becoming useful and natural after living here a while.

Nonnatives may eventually find themselves buying *butter beans* at a farmers market, *grilling* their hamburgers and hot dogs, and drinking *sweet tea*—without noticing that these are regional expressions of the South that they've accommodated.

The most conspicuous and indexical features of southern vowels, like the ungliding of the long i in *tahm* for *time* or *bah* for *bye* or the merger of vowels in *pin* and *pen*, are not assimilated by northerners, but the more nuanced fronting of back vowels in *boot* and *boat* as *biwt* or *bewt* might be accommodated over time, making nonnatives sound a little more southern—at least to those back home.

Regardless of how long they have lived in the state, transplants are assigned outsider dialect status by Tar Heel natives. Though they can never be natives, they may, however, lose some of their back-home dialect credibility. Furthermore, this kind of indeterminate dialect status is often transmitted to the children of transplants, even if they are born in North Carolina. Few children of Yankee transplants end up speaking robust versions of southern dialect because that dialect is now in the minority in urban environments, and, unfortunately, many transplant parents maintain prejudices against southern speech so that they correct their children when they use the most salient southernisms. We have regrettably talked to transplants who admit that one of their greatest fears for their children is that they might grow up speaking southern— "not that there's anything wrong with southern speech." A version of the not-in-my-back-yard syndrome—or, more accurately, the "not-in-my-family" syndrome—applies to speech as much as it does to any other behavior. Such is the Yankee dialect resettlement in the South.

The Outer Banks Brogue

We're losing our heritage basically. I mean . . . we're going from a fishing community to more like a tourism community. . . . And you don't realize it, but you slowly
adapt to a new way of life. And it ain't nothing negative, but it ain't nothing positive.
—**BUBBY BOOS,** age thirty-one, Ocracoke Island, from *Ocracoke Still Speaks: Reflec-
tions Past and Present,* oral history CD compiled by Jeffrey Reaser, Paula Dickerson
Boddie, and Walt Wolfram (North Carolina Language and Life Project) and DeAnna
Locke, Chester Lynn, Phillip Howard (Ocracoke Preservation Society) (Raleigh: North
Carolina Language and Life Project, 2011)

Islands make for considerable linguistic intrigue—from the
lore of splendid seclusion, where a language can exist without
interference from the outside world, to the eruptive linguistic
mixture taking place when incomprehensible languages col-
lide in an isolated setting. Linguists are highly curious about
these situations since they offer natural laboratories for observing the dynamics of language change and maintenance. Researchers
don't have the luxury of capturing speakers and placing them on an island to
see what happens to their language, though one linguistic researcher actually proposed a study to the National Science Foundation that would take a
group of volunteers speaking different languages to an uninhabited island to
see how a common language developed. Federal guidelines for the treatment
of human research participants don't allow for such unusual treatment, so
we are on hold until a major television network bankrolls a reality television
version of "Linguistic Survivor." Unfortunately, only a few linguists would
probably watch that show.

Barring the unlikely reality show, linguists turn to island communities
where natural geographic barriers may affect languages and dialects in pro-

To hear the quote above, visit
http://www.talkintarheel.com/
chapter/5/audio5-1.php

found ways. The Outer Banks of North Carolina is one of those special cases of long-term isolation that enabled the development of a distinctive dialect of English. It is also a place where dramatic social and linguistic changes have taken place over the last half-century thanks to the boon of tourism that has transformed the chain of barrier islands from a modest, vulnerable, marine-based economy to a sustainable, robust, tourist-based economy.

The myths about Outer Banks language and life start with one of the most frequent questions about Outer Banks English: is it Elizabethan or Shakespearean English? In fact, at one point in our research, a television crew from the British Broadcasting Company (BBC) showed up on Ocracoke with the plays of William Shakespeare for the residents to read, assuming that the island's residents still speak in the same way as the Bard did 400 years ago. The BBC crew seemed disappointed but undeterred by our insistence that the notion that the residents spoke Elizabethan English was a romantic myth and that Outer Banks speech is dynamic and constantly shifting—like any natural language. Several weeks later, we started receiving messages from friends and colleagues around the world informing us that the BBC and CNN International News had aired a story claiming that Shakespearean English had been located on Ocracoke Island in North Carolina. We had obviously not convinced the producers of one of the most foundational truths about language change: no dialect is an island unto itself. In the process, we also learned a lesson about the strength of preconceived language notions and dialect mythmaking.

Like the dialects in the western mountains, Outer Banks English has undeniably retained some older forms of English; at the same time, it has combined them with innovative items. A sentence like "Dingbatters sure do mommuck us during the summer" juxtaposes the relic form *mommuck*—the earliest attestation of this particular usage is, in fact, attributed to Shakespeare—with the innovative term *dingbatters*, which, as mentioned in chapter 1, arose in conjunction with a modern-day television series, *All in the Family*.[1] The combination of something old with something new perfectly describes the natural and ordinary life of everyday language, but that does not seem to deter the perpetuation of the Elizabethan English myth by intelligent, well-meaning people. One of the first English professors Walt Wolfram encountered when he arrived on the campus of N.C. State took him aside and advised him to go to Ocracoke because they spoke Elizabethan English there. The advice about a research destination was helpful, but the rationale was unfortunately misguided.

The Outer Banks

Despite its ecological vulnerability, the 200-mile stretch of sandy barrier islands off the coast of North Carolina, fashionably abbreviated as OBX on signs and decals, is one of the most geographically, historically, and culturally distinct areas along the Atlantic Seaboard. The Outer Banks islands extend about half the length of the state, stretching from Corolla near the Virginia border in the north to Harkers Island by the Core Sound and Back Sound in the south. These islands separate the lagoon-like areas, or *sounds*, of the Atlantic Ocean from the mainland by as little as a few hundred yards to as much as thirty miles. Technically, a sound, derived from the Old English word for "swimming" (*sund* or *sunde*), is a stretch of water between the mainland and the ocean, but the technical distinctions between a sound, bay, strait, cove, inlet, and so forth are not preserved in the arbitrary naming conventions on our maps. Along the coast of North Carolina, the larger bodies of water standing between islands and the Atlantic Ocean are called sounds and the term *bay* is reserved for smaller, local indentations of water such as Cedar Bay in Manteo, Kitty Hawk Bay, or Onslow Bay between Cape Lookout and Cape Fear.

The Outer Banks is replete with history, including its status as the site of the first English settlement, the birth of the first person of English descent (Virginia Dare, born August 18, 1587), the infamous Lost Colony, the base and death of the fabled pirate William Teach (better known as Blackbeard), the Wright brothers' first flight, and a fleet of offshore shipwrecks in the Atlantic Gulf Stream that have led it to be labeled "The Graveyard of the Atlantic."[2]

Lesser known, but just as significant, these estuaries provided a maritime route of the Underground Railroad for escaping slaves, the site of the Freedmen's Colony on Roanoke Island, and the location of the first all-black lifesaving station on Pea Island that served from 1880 until 1947.[3] That's a lot of history for a small set of barrier islands that was the domicile for only a few thousand residents until its emergence as a prime tourist attraction in the latter half of the twentieth century. Even today, the permanent population on the Outer Banks is only about 30,000 people, well under a half percent of North Carolina's population.

Notwithstanding the Outer Banks' impressive history, the current economy and culture is driven by the extensive and pristine beaches and surf, recreational activities on the sounds, and deep-sea fishing. The recognition of

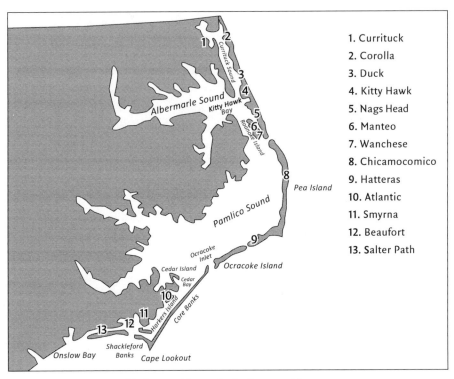

1. Currituck
2. Corolla
3. Duck
4. Kitty Hawk
5. Nags Head
6. Manteo
7. Wanchese
8. Chicamocomico
9. Hatteras
10. Atlantic
11. Smyrna
12. Beaufort
13. Salter Path

MAP 5.1. Map of Referenced Outer Banks Communities

the beach on Ocracoke Island as the "Best Beach in the United States" on June 8, 2007, by "Dr. Beach"—Florida International University professor Dr. Stephen Leatherman—marked a symbolic landmark of recognition for this narrow barrier island, completing its transformation from a once-obscure village site based on a marine-subsistence economy into one of the Atlantic coast's most popular tourist sites.[4] As the national television crews descended on Ocracoke to broadcast the announcement of this prestigious award, they claimed that they "didn't know where to find it on the map," and Dr. Beach himself proclaimed that "it's not the end of the world, but you can see it from here."[5]

That romantic exaggeration of isolation is also found in Outer Banks lore, captured in the observation of a Coast Guard enlistee some years ago. The serviceman was taken in the back of a pickup truck from Beaufort to Harkers Island and to other Core Sound regions, bumping over the rough mounds of sand on the beaches called *camelbacks*. As Ocracoke fisherman James Barrie Gaskill tells it: "He [the Coast Guard enlistee] picked up a postage stamp

FIGURE 5.1. The Outer Banks, the "Graveyard of the Atlantic."
(Courtesy of the Ocracoke Preservation Society)

and they said he put one sentence on it and sent it to his momma in Geor-gia. Said, 'They have sent me to the end of the world.' So the next day, they decided—you know, the Coast Guard, you know, to break these guys in—to go to Cedar Island and check for life preservers and stuff. And they went over there and he said that 'he couldn't understand a damn word they were say-ing.' So they come back and picked up the mail to Atlantic, he picked up and he got another postcard, said, 'Dear Momma, yesterday I lied to you. Today they sent me ten miles further.'"[6]

It is difficult to imagine current-day tourists gazing at the end of the world as they stand in line for a meal at a fashion-able restaurant on the Outer Banks or anxiously search for a "vacancy" sign in one of the numerous motels serving tourists during the height of a tourist season, but that's all part of the lore of the Outer Banks that uniquely mixes ecology, history, and culture with tourism.

To hear the full story told by James Barrie Gaskill, visit http://www.talkintarheel.com/chapter/5/audio5-2.php

The Outer Banks Brogue

For a couple of centuries, the small villages dotting the barrier islands of North Carolina and the adjacent coastal mainland have harbored one of the most distinctive varieties of English in the United States, the so-called Outer Banks *Brogue*, a word borrowed from the Irish word *barroq*, meaning "twisted tongue." A number of dialect situations may be described by this label, but it seems that only on the Outer Banks is it becoming a proper noun referred to simply as the brogue. Mainland North Carolinians and other visitors have recognized this distinctive variety, and islanders themselves have become accustomed to its unique status thanks to regular comments about their speech by outsiders. As one native Outer Banks resident experienced: "This man and woman walked in and I was like, 'Hi, how are y'all,' you know, and they walked around and stuff and everything, and the lady come up and she said, 'Speak!' And I said, 'Excuse me?' She's like, 'Speak!' And I said, 'What do you mean, speak? I'm talking to you right now.' 'No! You have this way that y'all are supposed to talk down here. Speak!' And I'm like, 'Ma'am, this is the way I talk. I've lived here thirty some years,' I said, 'and I've always talked like this.' So that was basically about the story: she wanted me to speak and I got ready to say, 'Well, you gonna give me a biscuit and I'll be glad to speak.'"[7] If enough people keep telling you that you have a distinctive way of talking, eventually you will start believing it and accept it as part of your character and community.

To hear this quote and others about the Ocracoke Brogue, visit http://www.talkintarheel.com/chapter/5/audio5-3.php

Various terms have been used to describe the dialect of the Outer Banks, including "Banker speech" and "Hoi Toider speech," though the most common term used by native islanders is the brogue. We've been studying these dialects in different communities along the Outer Banks coast for a couple of decades now, including Ocracoke, Harkers Island, Roanoke Island, and a few other locations along the way (Hatteras, Wanchese, Salter Path), but we certainly didn't discover it.[8] Residents of the Outer Banks were accustomed to outsiders' recognition long before we arrived, and some people are even prepared to perform the brogue on command. Rex O'Neal, one of eleven boys born to Essie and Harry O'Neal on Ocracoke Island and a featured representative of Outer Banks speech in several of our television documentaries, can "perform" the dialect at his discretion. In fact, Rex's first encounter with Walt Wolfram at a raucous retirement party at the Pony Island Restaurant in the spring of 1993 included a phrase demonstrating salient features of the dialect. Rex recalled that meeting in an interview with one of our fieldworkers a few days after the party.

REX: I got him [Walt Wolfram] going with that "hoi toid on the sound side."
FIELDWORKER: What did he say to that? Did he get all excited?
REX: Oh my god, yeah. Came out there, said, "I'm studying speech." And

I said, "Well it's hoi toid on the sound soid. Last night the water far, to-night the moon shine. No feesh, what you supposed the matter, Uncle Woods?" Well, he got a laugh out of that.[9]

In this quote, Rex performs several dialect traits of Outer Banks speech, including the iconic oi for long i in toid for tide and soid for side, the pronunciation of -ire as ar in far for fire, and the pronunciation of the vowel of fish as feesh. Obviously, he has developed a strong awareness of the sounds to highlight in the dialect for performance purposes. This performance phrase, first recorded in 1993, has continued to serve as a marker of island identity. In our second set of sociolinguistic interviews in the mid-2000s, we were occasionally told by proud parents that a child had the brogue. One even taught his daughter the iconic phrase used by Rex.

To hear Rex O'Neal's performance phrase, visit http://www.talkintarheel.com/chapter/5/audio5-4.php

Rex O'Neal, like many islanders, also has the ability to shift dialect traits. For example, in one conversation, he is conversing with a graduate student who is conducting a sociolinguistic interview with him. As he is chatting with the fieldworker, a couple of his brothers drive up in their pick-up truck and start talking to him. He switches his speech so drastically that it is sometimes difficult for outsiders to understand what they are talking about: a mandarin duck escaped through a hole in the net in which he was confined. The examples of Rex O'Neal's speech show how adroit he is at switching from casual style with an outsider to in-group conversation with his brothers and dialect performance for outsiders who want to hear the brogue. He naturally shifts everything from his vowels to his rate of speech when talking to his brothers.[10]

To hear a younger speaker's (Chante Mason) performance phrase, visit http://www.talkintarheel.com/chapter/5/audio5-5.php

To hear Rex O'Neal interviewed by a fieldworker, visit http://www.talkintarheel.com/chapter/5/audio5-6.php

The Outer Banks Brogue is arguably one of the United States' most distinctive dialects. It is also one of the few dialects spoken in the nation that is commonly misidentified as British . . . or Australian . . . or Irish. Islanders commonly recount stories of tourists asking them what country they are from and acting confused when they respond "right here." The brogue elicits a wide range of comments from people trying to guess where it comes from, but most first-time listeners think that it is from Australia or England, usually in the southwest of England where they pronounce their r's in words like ear or far. At

To hear Rex O'Neal talking to his brothers, visit http://www.talkintarheel.com/chapter/5/audio5-7.php

one point in our study of Outer Banks English, we took the famous British dialectologist Dr. Peter Trudgill to visit the islands, and he took back some speech samples to play for native speakers of British English in Essex. He mixed these passages with samples from five different parts of the English-speaking world. The fifteen listeners unanimously assigned a British English origin to the Outer Banks speakers, with most people opting for a West Country location—that is, southwestern England.[11]

The other part of the story about Outer Banks English is the way in which it is receding, including the commodified status it now has even for natives. To give some historical context, remember that the Outer Banks was the site of the Wright brothers' historic first controlled, powered flight in Kitty Hawk in 1903. The first flight took place on an isolated barrier island in a linguistic context resonating with the sounds of the Outer Banks dialect tradition. In fact, the local residents would have referred to the "Wrights" as *Wroits* and "flight" as *floit*, leaving little doubt about the distinctive dialect surrounding the rudimentary airstrip for a breakthrough aeronautical achievement. The clash of traditional language and technical innovation represented on that occasion has been taking place ever since on these barrier islands as an inundation of tourists and outsiders has flooded the sandbars of the traditional, marine-based culture to change it forever.

Though the brogue was once spoken by the majority of the residents born and raised on the Outer Banks, this is certainly no longer the case. In some areas, particularly the northern islands of the Outer Banks, the vast majority of property is now owned by outsiders and beach development has made ancestral islanders an endangered species. In places like Corolla, Kitty Hawk, and Nags Head, it is hard to find representative traditional brogue speakers. In concentrated communities that retain a community base of ancestral islanders and a few traditional marine-based occupations, brogue speakers can be found if you know where older locals hang out—the fish house, the local convenience store, or a separate building in someone's backyard where local men might congregate to play cards, eat fish caught earlier in the day, and have a few drinks. Because of the rapid change, it is mostly older people who speak the traditional dialect, though there are some middle-aged and even a few younger speakers who have embraced it. Our interviews with ancestral islanders—that is, people whose families go back at least three generations on the island—focused on Ocracoke, where we conducted more than 120 interviews with ancestral islanders ranging from age ten to those well into their nineties, and on Harkers Island, where we have conducted more

FIGURE 5.2. Rex O'Neal of Ocracoke entertains tourists while cleaning fish. (Photograph by Kathleen Angione)

than fifty interviews with speakers again covering a full range of ages. Our archive also includes more than forty interviews of residents of Manteo on Roanoke Island who are mostly part of the African American community dating to the Freedmen's Colony.[12] Based on our interviews with people of different ages, we can hear the obvious decline in many traditional brogue features over time, though there are a couple of exceptions to this trend. Reasons for the retention of the brogue by speakers from diverse communities along the Outer Banks can be quite complex but often relate to a strong sense of island identity.

To hear three generations of speakers from Ocracoke, visit http://www.talkintarheel.com/chapter/5/audio5-8.php

The Roots of Outer Banks Speech

It is not coincidental that the term *foreigner* was once used to describe anyone not from the Outer Banks. In some ways, islanders feel like their separation from the mainland is not just geographical. They like to tell stories about tourists who visit Outer Banks communities thinking that they are on some exotic offshore site. Dale Mutro and Candy Gaskill, both descendants of long-standing Ocracoke families, lightheartedly discuss the more extreme perceptions by outsiders coming to the island for the first time.

CANDY GASKILL: They always ask the ferry guys on the Hatteras ferry whether we take American money over here. I don't know where they think they are going, but they always want to know if they take American money.

DALE MUTRO: I think they think that we're in the outback or something, in the lawless land or something. Most of the time when the fishermen come, they bring a five dollar bill and a pair of drawers, and they don't change either one of 'em.[13]

To view the video of this conversation, visit http://www.talkintarheel.com/chapter/5/video5-1.php

Before paved highways, regular ferry service, and bridges connected the islands to the mainland in the mid-twentieth century, access to the Outer Banks was very limited, though a few resort areas existed long before then; Nags Head, for example, became a resort before the Civil War, which is perhaps one of the reasons it is not a good place for collecting samples of the brogue. The geographic isolation that restricted daily interaction and regular communication between mainlanders and islanders for a couple of centuries is certainly an important part of the story of the Outer Banks Brogue. But given current access to the islands through bridges and ferries, the lore of exotic isolation that frames the dialect is part of a wishful, older perception rather than a contemporary reality. Legendary stories of outsiders' reactions to the islands, exotic portrayals by famous "experts" such as Dr. Beach, and the preservation of selected traditions and historical landmarks by local communities offer a convenient stage for presenting a dialect as different as any in the United States. In this setting, the traditional dialect is an ideal icon, a cultural commodity that is now as significant as the physical and historic artifacts that project the image of traditional quaintness associated with the Outer Banks.

Naturally, the history of language on the Outer Banks does not begin with American English but with the varieties of English that were brought there from the British Isles. Of course, American Indians inhabited the Outer Banks long before Europeans, mostly as temporary rather than permanent residents, but the only linguistic remnants of that period are the place names: *Currituck*, from the Algonquian word *carotank*, meaning "land of the wild geese"; *Hatteras*, an English rendition of the word for "less vegetation"; *Chicamacomico*, from "place of sinking sand"; and others. The name

Ocracoke was most likely derived from the Algonquian term *woccon*, meaning "sacred or powerful," though the legends of the Outer Banks have sometimes led to rather creative folk etymologies.[14] One island resident, born in 1913, offered the following explanation for the naming of Ocracoke: "Well, they always said that Blackbeard laid out here in the inlet. He found out there was a Lieutenant Maynard, I reckon, was after him—I believe that's the way it is. But he wanted to get going, he wanted to get out of the inlet. When the rooster crows in the morning, it's getting closer to daylight. So he said, 'Old cock crow!' And after that the old cock crowed and he went out. But they changed the name around—Ocracoke. That's what I always been taught."[15]

To hear this quote, visit http://www.talkintarheel.com/chapter/5/audio5-9.php

It is likely that early Outer Banks English was influenced by Irish or Scots-Irish English, as well as by dialects from various regions of England that include both East Anglia and southwestern England. However, the most dramatic influence would have come from second-wave migration patterns—settlers who did not come directly from overseas but from an earlier destination location point in North America. Some settlers in Jamestown and eastern Virginia and, to a lesser extent, Philadelphia, migrated southward along the coastal waterways. English-speaking homesteads and communities dotted the Outer Banks relatively soon after the 1607 settlement of Jamestown. Currituck County, the location of Corolla, was established in 1670, and Hatteras and Ocracoke developed in the first decade of the 1700s. Most of the earliest residents on the Outer Banks arrived by water from Tidewater, Virginia. Speakers spreading out from Jamestown settled both the Outer Banks and coastal parts of Virginia, Maryland, and even Delaware, which is why Outer Banks English in North Carolina has such a strong affinity for the speech of residents along the eastern shore of Virginia and Maryland and the Chesapeake Bay communities of Tangier Island (Virginia) and Smith Island (Maryland). We have compared the speech of different Outer Banks island communities with island and coastal communities to the north, to their mainland cohorts, and to the eastern shores of Virginia and Maryland and shown that the dialect area follows the historical migratory path that spread east and south along the estuary waterways leading to the Atlantic Ocean.

Outer Banks communities have naturally changed, sometimes dramatically, since the early days of European settlement. For a time, Corolla was the largest community on the Outer Banks, but after World War II, the population declined steadily, so that today there are about 500 year-round residents.

Duck, like many other Outer Banks towns, was a small fishing village until N.C. Highway 12 reached it, allowing tourists increased access to the town and making it a popular resort. The dynamic geography of the Outer Banks also played a role in its development. During the colonial period, Currituck Banks was cut into several islands by hurricanes. For most of the late seventeenth century and the eighteenth century, Roanoke Inlet by Roanoke Island was the most important inlet on the Outer Banks for ship travel, but natural forces closed it off by 1783. Ocracoke Inlet was once a busy channel for navigating ships through the sound to the mainland by *lightering*—that is, placing the cargo from large, heavy seafaring ships onto smaller, lighter boats at the mouth of the inlet so that the freight could be transported across the shallow waters of the sound to the mainland. When Oregon Inlet to the north was opened by a hurricane in 1846, it became a more convenient channel to the mainland, and Ocracoke Inlet traffic declined.

Some Outer Banks communities were also abandoned for geographical and/or economic reasons. Shackleford Banks on the Core Banks was abandoned in 1902 for Harkers Island and Salter Path because of the constant battering from hurricanes. Portsmouth Island, across the inlet from Ocracoke Island, was abandoned in 1971 because of flooding and a number of its former residents moved to other Outer Banks islands such as Ocracoke.

Economic and cultural continuity and change naturally set the stage for language preservation and transformation. Manteo and Wanchese, two communities on Roanoke Island a few miles apart, illustrate this dynamic. Manteo has become a popular destination for tourists for its historic attractions and boating, and the outsiders seem to overwhelm the few remaining ancestral residents. The smaller fishing community of Wanchese, a few miles south, is the site of one of the largest commercial fishing ports on the North Carolina coast, with only a few modest bed and breakfast accommodations for tourists. Lots of fishermen come in and out on a regular basis, conducting their business with locals in the traditional dialect. Sheltered by an insular industry, Wanchese has become a linguistic cove for the traditional brogue barely heard in Manteo. These two communities, just a few miles apart on the same island, are a microcosm of the language dynamic along the Outer Banks. A confluence of geography, economy, and cultural tradition are at play in both the recession of the dialect in Manteo and its retention in Wanchese.

The concrete transformation of many Outer Banks towns started with the paving of roads, the regular ferry service, and the bridges. Outsiders set

FIGURE 5.3. Early ferry service from the mainland to the Outer Banks.
(Courtesy of the Ocracoke Preservation Society)

up motels, restaurants, and other resort businesses, acquiring prime property that was not protected by the extensive Cape Hatteras National Seashore preservation program that managed to retain large stretches of uninhabited beach. On Ocracoke Island, slightly more than half of the 750 to 800 permanent residents are from off of the island, and in the Ocracoke public school, the majority of students are no longer from ancestral island families. Further eroding the brogue are the marriages between islanders and dingbatters, which create a perfect linguistic storm for diluting the traditional dialect. This is one of the reasons that there are often dramatic differences between generations of speakers and why the traditional dialect can virtually disappear within a couple of generations. The confluence of these social and economic factors leads us to consider the Outer Banks Brogue as an endangered dialect.[16]

To hear the speech of a lifelong (white) Wanchese resident, visit http://www.talkintarheel.com/chapter/5/audio5-10.php

Sounds of the Brogue

Residents of the Outer Banks are relatively easy to identify compared to speakers from other regions of North Carolina. A few iconic vowel sounds are dead giveaways since they are not found elsewhere in the state. The iconic pronunciation trait is, of course, the long *i* vowel sound in words like *time* and *high*, which sound something like *toim* and *hoi*. As noted, one of the traditional labels for people from the Outer Banks, *Hoi Toiders*, involves an imitation of this distinctive vowel sound. Although outsiders often caricature the pronunciation as sounding like the *oy* vowel of *boy* or *toy*, the actual production is more like the combination of the *uh* sound of *but* and the *ee* sound of *beet*, so that the Outer Banks pronunciation of tide really sounds something like *t-uh-ee-d*. Though highly associated with the Outer Banks, it is also characteristic of particular regions in the British Isles and occurs in the English of Australia and New Zealand—and it is one of the reasons outsiders think Outer Banks natives don't sound like they're from the United States. In the South, the pronunciation contrasts sharply with the mainland pronunciation of these vowels without the glide, as in *tahm* for *time* or *tahd* for *tide*, making it highly salient. While Outer Banks residents nowadays may focus on the distinctiveness of the long i to assert their identity as islanders, there are other vowels that may actually be even more distinguishing among American dialects. The production of the vowel in words like *sound* and *brown* is every bit as distinct, but it has not received nearly as much symbolic attention, either by locals or tourists. The vowel sound in the word *brown* actually sounds closer to the vowel in the standard American pronunciation of *brain*, and the word *round* sounds more like *rained*.

Another pronunciation trait is the vowel in words like *caught* and *bought*, which is produced closer to the vowel sound in words like *put* or *book* in the traditional brogue. This pronunciation is unique among American English dialects, sounding similar to the pronunciation of this vowel in many British dialects of English. This may, in fact, be the vowel sound that most strongly leads outsiders to perceive them as British or Australian. But people don't talk about this vowel nearly as much as they do about the vowel of *high tide*. We once conducted an experiment in which we had the vowel in *bought* pronounced in four different ways: (1) the western United States pronunciation in which *caught* and *cot* are pronounced the same as *cot*; (2) the New York City and Philadelphia pronunciation in which it sounds like *c-ooh-ah-t*; (3) the southern rural pronunciation as *c-ah-oo-t*; and (4) the Outer Banks pronunciation where it sounds more like the vowel in *book*. Listeners were puzzled by the Outer Banks pronunciation and thought that it didn't sound like the speaker was from North America.

The pronunciation of *ire* sequences in *fire*, *tire*, and *iron* are usually two syllables in most regions outside of the rural South, something like *fah-eer*, *tah-eer*, and *ah-eer-uhn*. On the Outer Banks, they are more apt to pronounce the

ire sequence as one syllable, something like *far, tar,* and *arn.* This pronunciation is certainly not unique to the Outer Banks and is found in many rural
regions of the South, but it is one of the prominent features associated with
this variety. It is even one of the traits built into the performance style of
the Outer Banks Brogue and the target of some stories of miscommunica-
tion between Bankers and outsiders. For example, a middle-
aged woman from the town of Atlantic reports the following
incident from her days as a university student at East Carolina
University: "When I was in college, we had a tea to go to for
the president and I wanted to *arn* the dress to get the crease
out of it where it had been taked up. And I went to every suite
in that dorm and ask if they had an *arn* I could borree [bor-
row]. Nobody had an *arn.* Come to find out, everybody had
one. They didn't know what I was askin' for. They all had 'I-
rons' but I needed a *arn.*"[17]

To hear speech samples
from this experiment, visit
http://www.talkintarheel.com/
chapter/5/audio5-11.php

Other vowel features found on the Outer Banks affect the
final vowel of words. One pattern leads words like *shallow,*
mosquito, and *window* to be pronounced like *shaller, skeeter,* and
winder. People who have visited the Outer Banks during the
muggy summer season can understand the significance of the
skeeters. As one T-shirt with a picture of a giant mosquito proclaimed, "Send more tourists—the last batch was delicious."
Another pattern turns the final *a* of "soda" and "extra" into
something more like *ee,* as in *sodee* or *extree.* The *ee* can even
occur for some final *ow* sounds, as in *borree* for *borrow* in the
story told above.

To hear examples of Outer Banks
vowels *au, oh,* and *ire,* visit
http://www.talkintarheel.com/
chapter/5/audio5-12.php

To view the video of this quote,
visit http://www.talkintarheel
.com/chapter/5/video5-2.php

There are also a few consonant pronunciations associated with the
brogue that are retentions of older pronunciations once common in English.
For example, the retention of the h in words like *it* as *hit* and *ain't* as *hain't,* or
the t in *oncet* and *twicet* among older speakers, is a relic pronunciation of an
earlier, widespread pronunciation of standard English. These kinds of pronunciations are, however, no longer common in the speech of middle-aged
and younger speakers. These retentions and the final two vowel patterns are
all also shared by the speech of the Appalachian region of North Carolina.

The combination of pronunciation features comprising the Outer Banks
Brogue leads outsiders to perceive it as a peculiar combination of southern and northern features. The vowels of *saind soid* for *sound side* and production of a vowel of *fought* more like *foot* distance it from mainland south-

ern pronunciations, but the pronunciation of *tar* for *tire* unites it with the South, as does the well-known southern pronunciation of *pin* and *pen* with the same vowel—usually the vowel of *pin*. Like most dialects, the unique aspect of Outer Banks English is found in the combination of pronunciation traits rather than individual sounds per se.

As the traditional pronunciations are being lost, the replacement pronunciations sometimes reveal the impact of the new residents. On the island of Ocracoke, outsiders are likely to come from northern states such as New Jersey, Pennsylvania, and Ohio, so when the traditional *hoi toid* vowel is lost, it is usually replaced by the northern pronunciation of *high tide*. But on Harkers Island, where outsiders are more likely to come from mainland North Carolina, islanders are more susceptible to replacing this vowel with the widespread southern *hah tahd*.

Sayin' a Word

People on the Outer Banks who have a propensity for talking or have a reputation as good storytellers are described as *sayin' a word*. But the meaning of all the words they use may not be apparent to outsiders or, in some case, even to people from other regions of the Outer Banks. The general vocabulary of the Outer Banks includes hundreds of distinct words, some used generally up and down the islands and others restricted to local residents of a particular community.

Our lexical confusion on the Outer Banks started early, when someone asked if we had met any of the Midgett family yet. Several days later, we were embarrassed to admit that we had been looking for little people when we should have known that this was one of the prominent historical families who had lived on the Outer Banks for centuries. We have worn the *dingbatter* label ever since.

In chapter 3, we reported our experience with the word *meehonkey* on Ocracoke. Practically everywhere we have been, children play a version of hide-and-seek, but we had never heard it called *meehonkey*. We checked further with the editors of the most comprehensive dialect dictionary ever assembled for American English, the *Dictionary of American Regional English* (DARE), and they had never heard of it either. So naturally, we submitted it as a localized dialect word, and future editions of DARE should include it. We speculated that it may have arisen as an imitation of a goose call, but we can't honestly be sure. As we noted, every word has its own history, and it is sometimes difficult to come up with irrefutable evidence for the origin of a word. Some have histories that go back more than a millennium, and others are recent coinages to fill a descriptive need. Relatively speaking, words like *meehonkey* or *whoop and holler* for "hide and seek" in Ocracoke, as well as terms for local places such as *the ditch* ("mouth of the harbor") or *up the beach* ("off the island") are among the newer items, while *mommuck* and *token* are retentions of older forms in English. However, there are also some unique nuances of meanings assigned to Outer Banks dialect words not shared with other areas. For example, the use of the word *mommuck* (also spelled as *mammock* and *mammick*), an older English word found in the works of William Shakespeare, has developed a meaning on the Outer Banks that sets it apart from both its original meaning and that developed in other regions where it is retained. In the works of Shakespeare it refers to "tearing apart" in a literal sense (for example, "Hee did so set his teeth, and teare it. / Oh, I warrant how he mammockt it" [*Coriolanus*, 1.3.67]), whereas on the Outer Banks its meaning has been extended to refer to mental or physical harassment (for example, "The young 'uns were mommucking me"). This meaning is, in turn, distinguished from that of some mainland dialects of southeastern North Carolina and the western Mountain area of the state, where it means "mess up" (for example, "They mommucked up the house"). On the Outer Banks, the term *fatback* refers to the oily fish "menhaden," often used for crab bait, whereas in the rural areas of southeastern North Carolina, the same term refers to the fatty back of the hog, much like bacon.

Lexical items reinforce the notion that all dialects are a combination of the old and the new. Words like *mommuck*, *quamish* (meaning "uneasy" or "upset," as in "quamished in the gut"), and *token of death* (meaning "an unusual sign of impending death," such as a rooster crowing in the middle of the day) have been in the English language for centuries. On the other hand, words like *dingbatter*, *dit-dot*, or the most recent term adopted for outsiders by some younger speakers, *touron*, are relatively new. Prior to that time, terms like *foreigner*, *stranger*, *woodser* (a person from an area where woods abound—that is, not the Outer Banks), those from *off*, and *away* were used for outsiders.

Though we can focus on some words found exclusively on the Outer Banks, the vast majority of regional lexical items found on the islands are found in other dialect areas or even shared throughout the South. One restricted set of dialect words is associated with the marine ecology—for example, *slick cam* ("smooth water"), *winard* ("into the wind"), *leeward* ("with

To view a vignette about Outer Banks vocabulary, visit http://www.talkintarheel.com/chapter/5/video5-3.php

the wind"), and *lightering* (defined above). Given the interconnected marine-based economy of the area, it is not surprising that most of these terms are shared throughout the estuary system. Some of the lexical items for wind and storms extend beyond the waters of North Carolina—such as *nor'easter* and *sou'easter*, *squall* for "a violent gust of wind with rain," and *boomer* for "thundershower"—were appropriately used to describe the weather conditions.

A few additional samples of some dialect phrases from Ocracoke on the Pamlico Sound and from the southern Core Banks communities of Harkers Island, Atlantic, Cedar Island, Smyrna, and so forth given below illustrate the local, Outer Banks, and more general regional terms. These terms come from dialect dictionaries that we composed with the Ocracoke and Harkers Island communities.[18]

A SAMPLER OF OCRACOKE DIALECT VOCABULARY

across the beach (prepositional phrase). On the beach by the ocean. (*Did you see the shark that washed up across the beach?*) Compare *up the beach*, meaning "travel off the island to the north." (*They went to the doctor up the beach.*)

buck (noun). A good friend, usually a male. (*How you doin', buck?*). Compare with *puck*, sometimes used for a female. (*Hey puck, whatcha doin'?*) Used only on Ocracoke Island.

cattywampus (adjective). Crooked, not square, diagonal. Used mainly in the South. (*That shack is sitting cattywampus.*)

chunk (verb). Throw, particularly natural objects. General southern term. (*Chunk the rock in the water!*)

creek (noun). A small inlet running from the sound through the island. Often appears in proper names for these inlets, such as *Molasses Creek* or *Oyster Creek*.

doast (noun and verb). A cold or influenza, from *dose*. (*I got me a doast today.*) To give or receive a contagious illness. (*Sue Ellen doasted me last night and I feel awful today.*)

goaty (adjective). Foul smelling. From the bad smell of a goat. (*You smell goaty today.*)

mash (verb). To press, smash. General southern usage. (*Chester mashed the wrong button on the computer.*)

off-island (adjective or noun). Not from the island. (*Jeff is an off-island person who studies dialects.*)

pizer (noun). A porch, from Italian *piazza*. (*We sat on the pizer and watched the young 'uns.*)

A SAMPLER OF CORE SOUND DIALECT VOCABULARY

away (adverb). At a different location, someone who lives off-island. (*She lived away for a while.*)

backhouse (noun). Outhouse, privy. (*We used to have a backhouse in the yard.*)

chunk. (See above.)

crowd (noun). Group of two or more people. (*That crowd was not happy with the news.*)

directly (adverb). In a little while. (*I'll be with you directly.*)

drime/droim (interjection). Calling one's bluff, deceiving. (*Drime! You ain't got no winning hand of cards.*)

mash. (See above.)

off (adverb). Not on the island, not from the area. (*That crowd of dit-dots came from off.*)

pizer. (See above.)

whopperjawed/whipperjawed (adjective). Crooked, not square, diagonal. Used mainly in the southern Outer Banks. (*That shack is sitting whopperjawed.*)

The samples from the Ocracoke Island and the Core Banks Island dictionaries demonstrate the layered distribution of items that is fairly typical of community lexicons. Some words are uniquely local (*drime, off, buck, across the beach*), some are immediately regional (*creek* and *slick cam*, for example, are found throughout the Outer Banks), and others are more broadly shared (*chunk, mash,* and *pizer* are all found to some extent throughout the South). Some words seem to be innovations (*drime* or *buck*), while others are repurposed standard English words (*chunk* or *mash*). Some words are old (*pizer*), while others are new (*drime*). As with southern identity discussed previously, Outer Banks identity is layered. One may simultaneously identify as a southerner, a Banker, and an O'Cocker, and the words chosen will likely divulge all levels of this identity. The fact that the isolation of the individual islands has resulted in so many words restricted to a single community makes some of the local words—like *buck* for "friend" in Ocracoke or *drime/droim* "to call someone's bluff" in the Core Sound area—salient enough to allow Outer Banks residents to reasonably identify a speaker's specific island or local community. Outsiders are usually not as perceptive and are content to classify a person from the Outer Banks because of some common pronunciation or grammatical traits. That is not an unusual difference in perceptions and is analogous to what might be found in the western mountains of North Carolina, where locals are more apt to hear differences that differentiate one hollow (or *holler*) from another.

To view a vignette about identifying dialect features, visit http://www.talkintarheel.com/chapter/5/video5-4.php

Surprised by Grammar

The distinctive pronunciations and colorful words and expressions are usually the first things that come to mind when thinking about the Outer Banks Brogue; however, sentence structure or grammar can be quite diagnostic for those who listen intently. Though the grammatical structure of the brogue may not be sanctioned in the schools, these traits often involve intricate systematic patterning in their own right. Like some of the distinctive pronunciations, they may extend from the Core Sound and Outer Banks up to Maryland's Eastern Shore. The use of *weren't* where other dialects use *wasn't*, as in "I weren't there" or "It weren't in the house," is only found among American English dialects in the mid-Atlantic coastal region extending from the coastal areas of Virginia and Maryland in the north to the southern areas of coastal North Carolina. This use reflects a structured reorganization of *was* and *were* where *was* is used in positive or affirmative sentences, that is, I/you/(s)he/we/you/they *was there*, and *were* is restricted to negative sentences as in I/you/(s)he/we/you/they *weren't there*. The alignment of *was* with positive sentences and *were* with negative sentences is quite different from the majority of English dialects, where *was* is used with singular forms (I *was*, he *was*, etc.) and *were* is used with plural forms (we *were*, they *were*, etc.). This feature, restricted geographically, is surprising in part because middle-aged and younger speakers in some Outer Banks communities seem to use it more extensively than older speakers, contrary to the expected pattern of dialect change for different generations of Outer Banks residents. We found this to be the case for both Harkers Island and Ocracoke when we studied different generations of speakers. We also found that islanders, especially women, were more likely to use *weren't* when talking among themselves than with outsiders; men seem less likely to adjust its use according to audience. Curiously, this might actually be one of those Outer Banks structures that endures while the islands' distinctive pronunciations fade.

There are other grammatical patterns that are noteworthy, some recognized and some more subtle. The use of the preposition *to* for *at* to indicate static location—as in "She's to the house tonight" for "She's at the house tonight" or "I think he's to the dock right now" for "I think he's at the dock right now"—is typical of Outer Banks varieties, as is the use of -*s* suffix on verbs with plural subjects in sentences like "The dogs barks every night." The latter pattern is well documented in other remote dialect areas of North Carolina as well. The use of the *uh* sound before verbs ending in -*ing*, called *a*-prefixing, in "The dog was a-huntin' the possum," is also used by older speakers on the Outer Banks but not by younger speakers. Finally, a plural -*s* may be left off of nouns if two conditions are met: the noun must be a measure noun (*inch, mile, quart, pound,* etc.) and must be preceded by a quantifier that notes "how much." Thus, the plural -*s* can be omitted in a sentence like "It's three mile to the light house" but not "It's mile to the light house" (no quantifier) or "Three crab are in the pot" (not a measure noun). The grammar of the brogue may not add many novel dialect features to the dialect mix, but it is certainly part of the overall composition that makes Outer Banks English what it is.

Saying What You (Don't) Mean

Language differences involve more than simple words, sounds, and sentences. There are lots of different ways to say the same thing, and the choice of expression can be dictated by community norms. How we address people, how directly or indirectly we say things, and our selection of particular communication routines for meeting, greeting, and leaving can be an important part of language variation reflected in dialects.

Some Outer Banks families employ a naming practice that involves addressing people, particularly men, by two names, such as *James Barrie* or *David Scott*. In this naming routine, the "middle" name is the surname of their mother's family. This is slightly different from the more general southern practice of using two first names such as *Billy Bob* or *James Earl*. When outsiders unaware of this naming custom address James Barrie as *James* or David Scott as *David*, it stands out. Even James Barrie's wife calls him *James Barrie*, and David Scott's mother always calls him *David Scott*. In some dialects, the use of two names is used mainly when parents are angry, as a parent saying,

"Jake Walter, you stop doing that right now!" In the case of David Scott, a person calling him *David* would be referring to his father, not him. And the use of a nickname like *Jim* or *Dave* for these islanders would probably make them feel like the person wasn't even talking to them. These kinds of naming customs can be tricky, but understanding them is part of knowing how to use a language variety.

One of the ritualized language routines found on the Outer Banks is what is referred to as "talking backwards" or "talking in opposites." In this routine, the speaker uses the opposite adjective, or antonym, to describe an exceptional attribute of, for example, the weather, a situation, or a person. As Houston Lewis, a boat builder from Harkers Island, describes it: "We might talk backwards sometime. We'll say one thing, mean something else. Yeah. You take a purty day, you know, you walk out the house, sun's bright and shiny, you say, 'This is a ugly day, isn't it?' What you mean is a purty day, you know." This use of opposite attributes can be confusing to those unaccustomed to this ritual. In fact, Lewis admits to confusing his wife, who did not grow up on the island: "And she'd say, 'What's wrong with the day?' I say, 'Well, there's nothing with it. It's a purty day.' And she'll, 'Why don't you say that?' Then if you come out the house and it's a-rainin', you say, 'Boy, this is a purty time.' She'll say, 'Well, I don't see nothing purty about it. You know, it's a-raining.' And she, 'Why don't you say what you mean?' It took my wife 'bout twenty years to realize I was talking in opposites. I always, you know, talk in opposite. After a while, she learned it."[19]

To view this quote and the following quote about talking backwards, visit http://www.talkintarheel.com/chapter/5/video5-5.php

The process of reversing the meaning of an attribute or quality in language is not unique to this dialect. Most of us are aware that younger people today may use the term *wicked* or *sick* to mean *good* in a sentence like "That party was sick; we had a great time" or "That concert was wicked." Linguists call this process a "semantic inversion." The difference in this custom on the Outer Banks is that it does not involve a new meaning for a particular word, as in the word *sick* for *good*. Most adjectives and some other words can be used in this routine without extending the conventional meaning of the word as such. Ann Rose, from Harkers Island, describes how this works with the adjective "greatest" in talking backwards: "They could say, 'That crowd had the greatest time.' . . . And the 'greatest time,' it could be not necessarily positive. It coulda been that maybe they were fussing about something and feuding and hollering and screaming and whatever, but 'greatest' means like intensity, you know. And 'time' could be just an occurrence. So 'that crowd had the greatest time,' uh—they coulda been out there just been fussing and fuming or maybe out there fighting over some fish nets or something, you know."[20]

The routine of talking backwards, talking in opposites, or, as they call it farther north on Tangier and Smith Island in the Chesapeake Bay, "over the left talk" is one of those aspects of meaning that comes from understanding a kind of paradox between the obvious situation and the description of it. It should be blatantly obvious to the listener that there is an ironic conflict between the observed situation and the descriptor, so if we are standing in a downpour on the Outer Banks and an islander says, "It sure is a purty day," we should have enough common sense to see the contradiction between the descriptive attribute and the circumstance.

The playful verbal irony sets apart islanders' behavior as "not from the mainland." By conversational design, the paradoxical declarations can confuse outsiders, establishing social distance between community insiders and outsiders and setting up an "us-versus-them" dichotomy. Ancestral islanders often do not feel like they are a part of the mainland society; in a coy, verbal routine, islanders assert—and embrace—their detachment by reversing the role of marginalization linguistically. It may be playful, but it is also a subtly powerful and symbolic behavior that places islanders in opposition to the "standard" uses of English.

Ebb Toid on the Saind Soid

There is often a love-hate relationship between ancestral islanders, tourists, and new residents. Long-term families sometimes feel that their traditional ways of life have been so disrupted that we occasionally hear islanders jokingly wish for a hurricane near the end of the tourist season just so they can reclaim their island. Tourists and those who relocate to the Outer Banks have changed the Outer Banks, and these communities will never be the same.

How dialects weather the social and linguistic reconstruction of Outer Banks communities has been a major theme of our long-term studies. In the social life of language, dialect patterns may represent symbolic shifts that reflect restructured social divisions within communities. For example, we have found that men and women born before World War II use similarly traditional dialect features such as the vowel in toid for tide and the fronting of the vowel glide in brown more like brain).

Those born in the generations during the rapid transformation of the island (1950s through 1970s), however, show a decline in the use of traditional dialect features, with women abandoning traditional features faster than men. During this period, women began to participate extensively in the tourist-based economy, while men began to relinquish their traditional maritime occupations in order to profit from the new economy. However, a linguistic analysis revealed one group of middle-aged men who had linguistically resisted this trend, which we labeled the "Poker Game Network." These men had the highest incidence of the iconic island *toid* vowel; in fact, this group had more extensive use of this vowel than men or women in the previous generation. The members of the so-called Poker Game Network project a highly traditional masculine image and pride themselves on speaking the authentic brogue, and this particular feature allows them to construct this identity linguistically even while they continue to lose other features, such as the pronunciation of *sound* as *saind*.

Among adolescent speakers, women are much less likely to use the traditional vowels since there is little capital for younger women. The traditional dialect may still be tied to notions of "islander identity"; however, that identity has now been reduced to a single type of identity—that which is captured in the image of the rugged fisherman that traditionally has dominated written and visual portrayals of island life. This image is not embraced by all Outer Banks men or by a majority of contemporary women, who find themselves unable to reconcile that identity with some measure of traditional feminine identity. In fact, women may willingly embrace nontraditional language variants, including nontraditional variants of the *hoi toid* vowel, since such variants may represent the demise of traditional, dominant gender roles and definitions on the island. For middle-aged and younger speakers, the brogue has a much more gendered association than it once did—when just about everyone on the Outer Banks used it.[21] We once asked a woman ferry attendant in Cedar Island if she thought men or women used the brogue more. She responded without hesitation: "Men." When we asked her why, she said: "Because it doesn't sound ladylike." That kind of gender association did not always exist, but as the brogue has taken on a more specialized and symbolic role in island life, it obviously has become more associated with male speech. There are, of course, exceptions to this pattern, as we noted for the young girl earlier in the chapter; she performs the brogue in a way that shows an affinity for the traditional dialect.

The description underscores an essential point about dialect recession in island communities—namely, that it takes place in terms of the social dynamics, interpersonal relationships, and symbolic capital of the community undergoing change. Language change in island communities is no different from change elsewhere, and it needs to be interpreted in terms of its social meaning. It is also important to understand that there is more than one path to dialect loss on island communities. Our in-depth comparison of Ocracoke on the Outer Banks with Smith Island, an island in the Chesapeake Bay area of Maryland, reveals radically different responses to dialect endangerment—from the rapid decline of a long-standing dialect within a couple of generations on Ocracoke to the intensification of dialectal distinctiveness in Smith Island. So while some dialect areas of the Outer Banks in North Carolina are rapidly losing most of their traditional dialect features, residents of Smith Island, Maryland, are actually intensifying their use of distinguishing dialect features, including the hoi toid vowel and the vowel of brown and mound as brain and maind.[22] As the traditional crabbing trade has declined on Smith Island, more and more islanders are moving to the mainland, reducing the resident population from approximately 800 to fewer than 300 over the last half century. Those who remain intensify their use of traditional dialect features, perhaps in a linguistic version of the survival of the fittest. Most likely, this intensification reinforces a sense of solidarity, as fewer and fewer islanders remain to follow the traditional Smith Island way of life. Even though the dialect is intensifying rather than weakening, it is in danger of dying out through sheer population loss—along with the fact that land erosion is causing the island to gradually sink into the Chesapeake Bay. The dialect dissipation model of recession found on the Outer Banks generally is more common than the intensification model in language-shift situations, but particular groups of islanders may intensify their dialect as a symbol of islander identity against the rising tide of tourists and new residents who now flood these islands during the extended tourist season, now nine months long.

An Endangered Dialect

The classification of Hoi Toider speech as an "endangered dialect" has sometimes caught the fancy of the media; headline stories such as "Ebb Tide on Hoi Toid" have been circulated by the Associated Press in newspapers (for example, the Raleigh News and Observer, the Norfolk Virginian-Pilot, and the Washington Post), and National Public Radio has done special features on the dying brogue. Is this simply media hype to call attention to the changing status of this traditional dialect, or is an endangered dialect a significant cultural and scientific threat?

Certainly, dialectologists and linguists worry about the disappearance of the brogue and liken language loss to the extinction of biological species.

To view the CBS This Morning segment "Are Americans Losing Their Accents?," visit http://www.talkintarheel.com/chapter/5/video5-6.php

People may argue that they are not the same, claiming that speakers don't give up talking when a language dies, they just use another one. In fact, some people would applaud language death and say that the reduction of the world's languages to just a few would make international communication much more efficient. It is also true that manufacturing would be much more efficient if we all wore the same size and style of clothing, but where would that leave us in terms of the expression of individual and cultural identity?

Dialectologists argue that science, culture, and history are lost when a language or a dialect of a language is lost. In our quest to understand the general nature of language, we learn from diversity, just as we learn about the general nature of life from biological diversity. Studying language diversity can also reveal intimate details of a dying way of life or a rich, untold history. We, as a society, are poorer if these traditions are not preserved. Saying that dialect loss is not as important as language loss is like saying that we should be vitally concerned with the general species *canis familiaris*—or "dogs"—but not worried about particular breeds. After all, dogs come in so many breeds and can be mixed in so many ways that the preservation of a particular breed is not very important. But suppose the choice of dogs was reduced to Great Danes and your favorite dog—and the only kind you've ever had in your home—was a miniature Pekinese. Try telling Walt Wolfram that his home could do without an Australian Labradoodle and that any kind of dog should be adequate. American dialects would not be as diverse, scientifically interesting, and culturally intriguing without the Outer Banks Brogue.

As it turns out, our classification of the Ocracoke brogue as an endangered language variety has challenged the established canon of endangerment in linguistics, bothering those who work on dying languages. After we accepted several invitations to speak at language-endangerment conferences early in our studies and presented the case for labeling the Ocracoke brogue as an endangered language variety, we are now excluded from conferences and workshops on this topic. In fact, after one presentation at a national conference on language endangerment, a colleague congratulated us on the presentation only to follow up with the comment, "Do you think anyone takes you se-

FIGURE 5.4. L. J. Hardy of South River sorts through his shrimp catch. (Photograph by Neal Hutcheson)

riously when you argue that isolated dialects of American English should be considered as endangered?" In fact, we are quite serious and adamant in our position.[23] The first assumption in the language-endangerment canon is that the distinction between a language and a dialect is sufficiently well-defined to make principled decisions about which varieties of language should and should not be included in the endangerment canon. It may be somewhat surprising to the general public that linguists maintain that the difference between a dialect and a language is impossible to determine on structural grounds or even in terms of mutual intelligibility. Instead, linguists maintain that the definition of a language is more typically based on political factors rather than linguistic ones. An oft-repeated adage by linguists is that "a language is a dialect with an army and navy," alluding to the political nature of determining language boundaries.[24] Swedish and Norwegian are mutually intelligible language varieties but considered to be separate languages because of a political boundary between the countries, whereas Mandarin, Cantonese, and Min are not mutually intelligible but are considered dialects because of the national political boundary of China. If, in fact, there is no principled way of determining the distinction between language and dialect, then how can we exclude a variety of a language on the basis that it is a dialect rather than a language?

There is another factor at play in excluding varieties like Outer Banks English from the endangerment canon. As it turns out, dialects of languages have indeed been treated as endangered, but only when the language variety exists in a bilingual context rather than a bidialectal one. For example, a Newfoundland dialect of French is considered endangered because it is surrounded by the English language, or a dialect of Albanian is considered endangered when it is surrounded by Greek.[25] But why can't a dialect of English similarly be threatened by other mainstream dialects of English?

Finally, the endangerment canon seems to assume that the loss of cultural identity and intellectual diversity involved in dialect loss is not nearly as significant as that involved in the loss of a language. One of the important arguments for examining endangered dialects is the fact that when one dies, an essential and unique part of human knowledge and culture dies along with it. In reality, some dialects of a language may have stronger iconic status in terms of their symbolic identity than a separate language. For example, the cultural symbolism of the unique variety of Lumbee English that we describe in chapter 9 is every bit as significant as any other cultural artifact— or as an American Indian language. The Lumbee dialect was, in fact, explicitly recognized as one of the distinctive attributes that marked the community as Lumbee in the 1956 Congressional Act of Congress Recognizing the Lumbee Indians.

Even as we may mourn the seemingly inevitable passing of traditional dialects like the Outer Banks Brogue, however, we can be assured that people— and their ways of speaking—are dynamic and resilient. And communities desiring to assert their uniqueness will also find a way to do it. We know of cases where communities have accommodated their overall ways of speaking but chosen new features of speech to continue to set themselves apart from others. It may be the case that a couple of features of Outer Banks speech might be maintained and redefined in terms of their symbolic significance, or that new features or words will be created to maintain dialect and community distinctiveness.

One thing seems certain about the Outer Banks Brogue: it is an essential part of the culture and people of the Outer Banks and important to the greater North Carolina community, and both Bankers and mainlanders have a right to know about it if they have any desire to stay in touch with the legacy that has made these barrier islands unique. The dialect heritage, including its past and present development, deserves to be documented and preserved—for *Hoi Toiders*, for new residents, and for tourists who wish to understand the past and present status of the island. That is why our activi-

FIGURE 5.5. James Barrie Gaskill of Ocracoke passes on the fishing tradition to his teenage son Morty. (Photograph by Neal Hutcheson)

ties have involved conducting extensive recorded interviews with many different islanders of all ages for documentation and preservation, developing a school-based curriculum for students to learn about their dialect heritage (see chapter 11), writing trade books for popular audiences, producing video documentaries, compiling oral history audio discs, and constructing museum exhibits that highlight the past and present dialect.

6 Mountain Talk

Well, the way people talks around here, I guess it'd be more like what you'd call Hillbilly style or something I guess. I don't know, it's just Mountain Talk.

—MARVIN "POPCORN" SUTTON, quoted in *Mountain Talk*, produced by Neal Hutcheson (Raleigh: North Carolina Language and Life Project, 2004)

To view the quote above, along with other comments about Mountain Talk, visit http://www.talkintarheel.com/chapter/6/video6-1.php

In traveling through the mountains of western North Carolina, we have encountered a number of unforgettable characters, from back-porch musicians to storytellers and moonshiners. One of the noted musical families from the Caney Fork section of Jackson County is featured in the documentary *The Queen Family: Appalachian Tradition and Back Porch Music.*[1] At age ninety-three, shortly before her death, Mary Jane Queen, the family matriarch, received the highest heritage honor from the National Endowment for the Arts for knowledge and preservation of hundreds of ballads that originated in England, Ireland, and Scotland, along with her knowledge of traditional foods, flowers, and medicinal practices. She framed her knowledge in a rich Mountain dialect, including the use of *a*-prefix in sentences such as "We's a-settin' there" and irregular verbs like *clumb* for *climbed* and *tuck* for *took*, wrapped tightly in the Mountain sounds of *braht* for *bright*, *far* for *fire*, and *young 'uns* for *young ones*. She seemed quite aware of the fact that her speech expressed her traditional background, and in one playful exchange with her son while picking on his guitar, he jokingly observes: "Well I know English pretty good, that's about it, and part of it's real old English." She responds, "The part that I know, too, is REAL old English."[2]

Though traditional Mountain speech certainly preserves some older or archaic forms of speech that have fallen out of use in other dialects, it is, like any other dialect, always changing. As we discussed in our explora-

FIGURE 6.1. Mary Jane Queen and her son Henry Queen from Jackson County. (Photograph by Neal Hutcheson)

tion of Outer Banks English, the notion that Elizabethan English, Shakespearean English, or "Old English" can still be heard echoing throughout the Blue Ridge Mountains is not linguistically accurate, and most linguists dismiss it as a romantic myth. But there is a kernel of truth to the idea. Mary Jane Queen and her son are not claiming to speak as the Anglo-Saxons did at the time *Beowulf* was written down; instead, they use it as a convenient metaphor for a language variety that preserves some features lost in other dialects.[3] While it is true that

To view a vignette about Mountain Talk being Old English, visit http://www.talkintarheel.com/chapter/6/video6-2.php

the isolation imposed by the mountains has led to the preservation of some features from earlier forms of English, the notion that the language is unchanged dismisses the vibrancy of a culture that has managed to look both forward and backward.

Probably the most notorious personality we interviewed during our years of recording was the infamous moonshiner Marvin "Popcorn" Sutton, who was apparently nicknamed Popcorn after he damaged a popcorn vending machine with a pool cue in a bar as a young man. Descended from a long line of moonshiners, he was one of the best-known personalities in the mountains of North Carolina and was featured in several documentaries, including *The Last One* by producer Neal Hutcheson.[4] He was a caricature of the moonshiner, a scrawny, chain-smoking, long-bearded character always dressed in

FIGURE 6.2. Famous Maggie Valley moonshiner Popcorn Sutton (right) and his assistant, J. B. Rader, at their still. (Photograph by Neal Hutcheson)

his bib overalls and fedora hat, irreverently commenting on just about any topic, including language. He referred to his speech as "Hillbilly speech" or "Mountain Talk." When Popcorn Sutton referred to Hillbilly speech, he was embracing it as a positive part of his Mountain identity, not a pejorative classification of an undereducated person belonging to an impoverished, marginalized culture.

After a 2009 raid by ATF (Bureau of Alcohol, Tobacco, Firearms, and Explosives) officials on a still across the state line in Tennessee led to his conviction and an eighteen-month sentence for illegally distilling whiskey, Popcorn vowed he would not return to prison. Despite a plea to serve his sentence under house arrest and a petition with thousands of signatures asking that he not be sent to jail, he was ordered to begin his jail sentence. Several days before he was scheduled to be imprisoned, smitten with cancer at age sixty-two, Popcorn Sutton took his own life by carbon monoxide poisoning in a Ford Fairlane painted in John Deere green with bright yellow tires.[5] But his moonshine legacy continues, thanks to Hank Williams Jr., who announced a partnership with Sutton's widow in 2010 to distribute Sutton's whiskey legally.[6] Like Mary Jane Queen, award-winning storyteller Orville Hicks from Watauga County, and a number of other Mountain personalities we have met over the years, Popcorn Sutton's traditional Mountain dialect is a critical part of his persona—as essential as any other cultural trait.

Despite the expansion of roads and the construction of vacation and tourist sites that have led to the appearance of new residents, tourists, and *halfbacks* (northerners who have moved to the South, particularly Florida, during the winter and then move halfway back to the mountains during the summer months), Mountain dialect is not endangered as is the brogue along the Outer Banks of North Carolina. It is changing, and some of the more traditional dialect forms are fading, but there is still plenty of dialect to distinguish those whose families have been connected to the mountains for generations from those from the outside—*foreigners, halfbacks, outsiders, flatlanders, jaspers,* and others.

A Rugged Range

The famed Appalachian Trail runs from northern Georgia to Maine, but the 2,200-mile trail still doesn't traverse nearly the full length of the range, which actually stretches into Alabama at the southern terminus and Newfoundland, Canada, at the northern terminus.[7] This range, once taller than the present-day Himalayan Mountains, now averages around 3,000 feet above sea level, with the tallest stretch running the width of North Carolina and crowned by Mount Mitchell, the highest point in the United States east of the Mississippi at 6,684 feet. This barrier of parallel ridges was one of the most formidable obstacles in the European settlement of the United States, constraining or, at times, entirely blocking westward expansion.

The U.S. Geological Survey (USGS) defines thirteen Appalachian provinces based on geological similarities, including rock type and tectonic forces. Some of these provinces correlate with local definitions of geographical divisions and cultural groups, including, in North Carolina, the Piedmont and Blue Ridge—the latter encompassing what many North Carolinians would differentiate as the Blue Ridge, Roan, Brushy, Great Balsam, and Smoky Mountain Ranges. Culturally, the Appalachian Range is more limited. In the United States, the Appalachian region is generally restricted to parts of Georgia, South Carolina, North Carolina, Tennessee, Kentucky, Virginia, Maryland, Pennsylvania, the whole of West Virginia, and a small slice of southeastern Ohio. Ironically, the name "Appalachia" comes from well south of the range. In 1528 a Spanish expedition encountered an American Indian village near present-day Tallahassee, Florida, that they transcribed "Apalchen" or "Apalachen."[8] This term was briefly used to denote all lands north of Florida, but by Hernando de Soto's 1540 expedition, the name, now

FIGURE 6.3. The rugged terrain of the Smoky Mountains.
(Photograph by Neal Hutcheson)

with the modern spelling, was restricted to the mountains themselves and began appearing on Spanish-made maps. The later British exploration and settlement gave the mountains a competing moniker: the Allegheny Mountains.[9] By the mid-nineteenth century, the older Spanish name had won out, at least in the southern regions of the range.

This chapter focuses on the language spoken in the Mountain region of western North Carolina and surrounding states, where political borders and geologist-defined boundaries do not necessarily align with cultural groups. The Piedmont region of North Carolina, despite being included in the USGS's definition of Appalachia, is quite different linguistically and culturally from the more mountainous areas to the west, and no one living in the Raleigh-Durham area would ever claim to be living in the Appalachian region, even if government-employed geologists insist on it. It is obvious to native and nonnative North Carolinians that Piedmont residents are culturally different from those who live in the highland Appalachian region. Less obvious are the differences within the highland region, though these do exist. Picking up on a core of social and linguistic similarities, many popular portrayals of Appalachia have presented a relatively uniform cultural region with the image of the "hillbilly" at the center. Appalachian storyteller Gary Carden has noted that "Mountain people are either depicted as inbred and stupid variations of the guys in *Deliverance*, or there's the other extreme where they're impossibly noble and remarkable and intelligent." He recounted a friend's frustration with such monolithic portrayals: "Gary, if I lived in St. Petersburg, Florida, and the only thing I knowed about the mountains was what I read in *Foxfire*, I'd think we's all jelly-making dulcimer-pluckers up here."[10]

To view the video of these quotes, visit http://www.talkintarheel.com/chapter/6/video6-3.php

Hillbilly Speech in Appalachia

Stereotypes, caricatures, and myths abound about Mountain life and language. These may include myths about its past and current status, the labels used to refer to people, and even the pronunciations of regional terms. We've already discussed the myth about Mountain speech as *Elizabethan* or even, in some cases, as Old English. In chapter 4, we discussed how the label *country* was used, often in a pejorative way but also in ways that connected it with positive traditions and values. Though Mountain speech is sometimes included in the label *country*, it is more likely to be referred to as *hillbilly*, evoking a set of stereotypes about lifestyle, education, and language. At the same time, the term "hillbilly" is reflective of the complexities and nuances of Mountain life and language. The use of this term predates its association with residents of Appalachia; it first appeared in print around the turn of the twentieth century. In the April 23, 1900, edition of the *New York Medical Journal*, a hillbilly is described as "a free and untrammeled white citizen of Alabama, who lives in the hills, has no means to speak of, dresses as he can, talks as he pleases, drinks whiskey when he gets it, and fires off his revolver as the fancy takes him." In the early to mid-twentieth century, "hillbilly humor" was extremely popular in the United States, and comic strips such as *Barney Google* (later *Snuffy Smith*) and *Li'l Abner* played on more-negative depictions of Mountain folk as lazy, backward, and felonious.[11] But the term has not always been derogatory, and it sometimes carried positive associations tied to resourcefulness, hard work, mischievously good humor, and independence. The 1960s brought a slight shift in the cultural depiction, as television shows like *The Andy Griffith Show* and *The Beverly Hillbillies* relied on archetypal trickster characters who were backward or simple yet wise, and who consistently outwitted or outmaneuvered more urbane, refined fools.[12]

In the quote from Popcorn Sutton to open this chapter, he embraces the *hillbilly style* of speaking as part of his personal presentation. Like some terms we discussed in previous chapters, its meaning can be flipped, or semantically inverted, to indicate a localized, positive identity. For example, hillbilly arts and crafts and music identify particular, positive kinds of customs or genres that reflect Mountain culture. And whole communities may embrace the moniker as a badge of community lifestyle. The Springfield, Missouri, chamber of commerce used to honor dignitaries with an Ozark Hillbilly Medallion, naming them honorary "Hillbilly of the Ozarks." In fact, in 1952 President Harry S. Truman received the Ozark Hillbilly Medallion and certificate from the community.[13]

Even the pronunciation of a single word, *Appalachia* or *Appalachian*, can be implicated in identity. Its pronunciation can vary from ap-uh-LA-chuh(n) to ap-uh- LAY-shuh(n), and even ap-uh- LAY-shee-uh(n) with an extra syllable. As with many phonetic variations, each pronunciation carries symbolic social significance. Most of the residents of the region we have talked to favor the first pronunciation, with the *a* vowel and *ch-* sound, over the other two. They strongly disfavor the final pronunciation with the extra syllable—*lach-ee-uh* versus *lach-uh*—which automatically betrays someone as not being from the area. The preferred local pronunciation, however, differs from those prescribed by dictionaries such as the *Oxford English Dictionary* or *Webster's Third New International Dictionary* (unabridged), which suggest using the most disfavored "lay-shee-uh" pronunciation. How a person pronounces the name of the region is often the first symbolic diagnostic of insider-outsider status, and it is not unusual for those who have contact with native residents to wonder how they should pronounce Appalachia.

To hear insider and outsider pronunciations of "Appalachia(n)," visit http://www.talkintarheel.com/chapter/6/audio6-1.php

Though the pronunciation of Appalachia(n) might be indicative of insider-outsider status, it should be noted that the term itself is mostly used by outsiders who study the region, especially academics, journalists, and newscasters. In the hundreds of hours of audio and video footage we have collected in the mountains of North Carolina, we rarely hear folks from the region itself refer to it by that term. To them, it is simply "the mountains" and "Mountain Talk." In fact, that's why we titled the chapter "Mountain Talk" and not "Appalachian English."

The Linguistic Roots of Mountain Speech

While the mountains of western North Carolina had been home to diverse Iroquoian groups for several millennia, there was relatively little European influence in the area until the mid-eighteenth century, over 150 years later than in the eastern part of North Carolina. It was 1717 before Scots-Irish and German settlers extended the Great Wagon Road, also called the Great Philadelphia Wagon Road, into western North Carolina (see chapter 2 for a discussion of the labels "Scots-Irish" and "Scotch-Irish" and more on the history of these groups' roles in this and other areas of North Carolina) and farmsteads began dotting the western Piedmont; however, it wasn't until the 1761 defeat of the Cherokee by the British that the Scots-Irish and, later, Ulster Scots entered the highland regions in earnest.[14] The stream of settlers intensified so quickly that it wasn't long before some pushed the frontier farther west via the Wilderness Trail, famously established by Scots-Irish legend Daniel Boone. The Scots-Irish, Germans, and Ulster Scots all contributed to modern Mountain Talk, with the speech of the first group being the biggest influence on its patterning and sounds today.

The shift from British colony to American state did not radically change life in the North Carolina mountains. Coves and valleys sprouted small communities whose members intertwined their social and economic well-being, relying only as a last resort on those living on the other side of a single ridge. Many farmstead communities developed as cooperatives instead of individual self-sufficient entities. Communities shared in work, service, religion, and entertainment. Neighbors routinely helped each other with building shelters and planting crops. The latter were sometimes coordinated by a community in order to maximize yield. Small independent religious gatherings also provided a venue for the beginnings of the distinctive music that would eventually become associated with the area. The population growth of the region in the late eighteenth and early nineteenth centuries led to some industrial pursuits, including various mining operations (salt, coal, feldspar, and other resources), hide tanning, and, eventually, ironworks, logging, textiles, and Christmas-tree farming.

Aside from spa resorts found around Hot Springs, a few luxury resorts like the Balsam Mountain Inn and Asheville's Grove Park Inn catering to the nation's elite, and, of course, the Biltmore Estate (built 1889–95), the westernmost part of North Carolina attracted little attention from the average American until a series of ambitious road-building efforts beginning in the 1930s made it possible for the non-elite to travel to the region instead of merely reading about it. Most notably among these projects was the Blue Ridge Parkway, which began construction in 1935 and took more than fifty years to complete.[15] The final piece was the now-famous Linn Cove Via-

FIGURE 6.4. Construction of the Blue Ridge Parkway's Linn Cove Viaduct, 1981. (Courtesy of the National Park Service, Blue Ridge Parkway)

duct, which skirts Grandfather Mountain and is touted on tourism materials as the "most complicated concrete bridge ever built."[16] The parkway and other roads effectively opened a swath of the mountains to tourism, which increased slowly until it blossomed as an industry in the late 1960s—mostly as a result of the Appalachian Regional Commission's work creating an expansive network of roads, touching off a tourism boom that has grown into one of the most important local industries in western North Carolina and even spawned the term *leaf-lookers* for the thousands of tourists who arrive every autumn.

Unlike on the Outer Banks, where tourism has diluted local culture, tourism in the mountains has sometimes had the opposite effect, resulting in an overt intensification of local cultural attributes as a means of meeting outsiders' preconceived notions of the region. Antiques and antiquated lifestyles became profitable commodities, as did local lore and, sometimes, linguistic mythology. Until the mid-1960s, welcome centers in North Carolina distributed a booklet called *A Dictionary of the Queen's English* (1965), which claimed that "you hear the Queen's English in the coves and hollows of the Blue Ridge and the Great Smoky Mountains" (page 3). The idea makes some sense to the casual observer, who might assume isolation has kept the language as "pure" as it has the Mountain way of life (also a romanticized notion). The linguistic and cultural reality is far more complex. As noted above, the pioneers who settled the region were themselves from diverse backgrounds and were not linguistically homogeneous. In fact, the largest group of settlers, the Scots-Irish, would not have spoken "Shakespearean English" even before emigrating from Ulster Plantation. Second, and even more crucial, is that even in isolation, languages and dialects continue to evolve. The Elizabethan language myth, however, has been largely embraced by both those inside and outside the community, though for different reasons. We have even found it among some of our erudite university colleagues who teach literature to college students, somewhat to our chagrin. Outsiders latch onto the myth out of a romanticized desire for the pastoral; insiders may embrace the myth as a means of asserting cultural and linguistic legitimacy amid the "jarringly negative [images]" of the region.[17] Linguist and Appalachian expert Dr. Michael Montgomery understands the usefulness of the myth, as it gives the region and language the respect it deserves: "There's definitely a place for the Shakespearean myth as an education and political tool for the foreseeable future."[18]

It is certainly true that isolation has contributed to the preservation of some older forms of speaking, including the a-prefixing form (the a- is pronounced "uh") in a sentence like "he was a-hunting"; the pronunciation of the word it with an initial h- sound ("hit's gonna rain"); and certain words that have dropped out of mainstream English, such a poke ("bag"), a term borrowed into English from regional French in the thirteenth century and later used by Shakespeare in the play As You Like It ("Then he drew a diall from his poake" [2.7.20]). Though once widespread and standard, poke has been largely regional since the early part of the twentieth century. Though these and other preservations may seem like they build the case for the Queen's English connection, the vast majority of present-day English overlaps with the words and forms of earlier English, and there are plenty of terms that have originated since the Mountain region was inhabited by English speakers. Language change may occur faster or slower in some situations, but language never stands stills.

The past fifty years have marked a substantial shift in Appalachian culture, setting the stage for changes in the dialect as well. Presidents John F. Kennedy and Lyndon B. Johnson were deeply concerned that poverty in Appa-

FIGURE 6.5. Mountain Talk storyteller Orville Hicks of Watauga County. (Courtesy of Orville Hicks)

lachia would forever keep the population from modernizing unless something was done; Johnson began his War on Poverty by announcing, "The Appalachian region of the United States, while abundant in natural resources and rich in potential, lags behind the rest of the Nation. . . . [I]ts people have not shared properly in the Nation's prosperity."[19] A major part of this effort involved the creation of the Appalachian Regional Council (ARC) in 1963 and the passing of the Appalachian Recovery Act of 1965. The ARC is in part responsible for new roads, schools, and improved access to health care, water, sewer, and cheap electricity. Not all of these modern amenities were welcomed at first. Appalachian storyteller Orville Hicks, from Watauga County, recalls: "I think it was 1964. I was fourteen years old before we got electricity at the house. I remember I was fourteen before we got it. I remember the first light bill we got was three dollars. And daddy didn't know how he was gonna pay the light bill. He was going to call and tell them to take the electric back out of the house. But us young 'uns [unintelligible] stuff to help pay the light bill so he wouldn't take it back out. It's better than sitting by the oil lamp trying to read a book or do your homework."[20]

To view the video of this quote, visit http://www.talkintarheel.com/chapter/6/video6-4.php

Similar sentiments can still be heard about other aspects of the government's interventions. Although the ARC was supposed to be culturally sensitive, residents felt as though they were being told they and their ways of life were simply not in line with American ideals. One resident recounts: "Well, I didn't know it was hard, because we had it about the same as everyone else [in the mountains]. We didn't know we lived in poverty until we got grown and Sargent Shriver came in here with Billy Graham and said we were all poverty stricken."[21] Though the ARC's success might be questioned, the 219 Appalachian counties identified in 1965 as economically distressed have been cut to eighty-two currently, including only one North Carolina county.[22]

This transition has not occurred without some changes to the culture, including the effects of tourism, cultural commoditization, and in- and out-migration. The mountains are now a popular retirement locale or vacation-home destination for people with no historical connection to the area. As one lifelong resident notes: "Now we have a lot of influx of people that's come here to get away from wherever they was. And they change it, too. They change it a little bit. And sometimes it's for the better and sometimes it's not. They come here because it's perfect, and some of them try to change it as soon as they get here. You know what I mean? . . . Their attitudes are different, their personalities are different, and their reason's different than ours. They're different then we are. It takes them a while to get used to us or leave 'cause we don't change a lot."[23]

Popcorn Sutton recounted the change to Maggie Valley in Haywood County in dramatic terms: "And now they've got Ghost Town and the Stomping Ground and Fair Child and Carolina Nights and the Thunder Ridge thing. Several attractions now for people to come and see. But I remember when they didn't have nothing. The first attraction in the valley I remember was old man Ted Sutton. He'd get out there on a wooden box he'd made and pick an old banjo and sing. And he was one of the first tourist attractions there was around here. Maggie Valley now is just about Miami."[24] Now Maggie Valley even has an annual "Popcorn Sutton Jam."

Today, many residents of the Mountain region maintain a deep connection to the past, even if it means endorsing potentially negative stereotypes that accompany it. Consider one resident's description: "We are twenty years behind the whole country. But I wouldn't swap places with nobody. I feel much more comfortable here being twenty years behind everybody than I would be a-sitting in a lot of other places and being so miserable. You don't like your neighbor. You don't speak to your neighbor. You're bitter with the world. Atlanta is a good example, or Raleigh. You drive down the street and everybody is wide open blowing their horns and don't

To view the video of these quotes, visit http://www.talkintarheel.com/chapter/6/video6-5.php

know nobody and don't want to know nobody and don't care about nobody. It's quite a bit different up here."[25]

In this discussion, being "behind" is preferable to being modern. As in the literary and pop-cultural images discussed earlier, in "backwardness" there is wisdom, empathy, genuineness, and a keen suspicion that modern is not synonymous with better. It is these cultural values and context that contribute to the currency of Mountain Talk among residents.

Features of Mountain Talk

As mentioned above, the dialect spoken in the Mountain region of North Carolina reflects the settlement of the region, its development, and its innovation from within and without. Its preservation of some aspects of language has led linguists to establish connections to early forms of English, particularly in grammar. Pronunciation is more prone to innovations than is grammar, and vocabulary reflects a mixture; for example, *poke*, which was discussed previously, is an older form, while *boomer* ("red squirrel") or *bald* ("small area without trees") are newer forms. There is a tremendous amount of variation in the

To view the video of this quote, visit http:// www.talkintarheel.com/ chapter/6/video6-6.php

speech of Mountain Talkers, including differences by region, urbanity, gender, ethnicity, class, age, and so forth. As storyteller and artist Gary Carden describes: "[In] every region of Appalachia there is usually—if you come there even from another county, you don't have to come from another state, you can just move from the adjoining county—people use expressions you don't understand. And it means something only to them. And that is one of the delights of Mountain culture."[26]

While we cannot describe precisely the county-by-county differences Gary Carden notes, we will give some information about the ubiquity or restrictedness of various forms. For the sake of illustration, we will also offer some explanation for how forms developed through historical preservation or local innovation.

MOUNTAIN WORDS

If you were to pick up a Middle English copy of Chaucer's *The Canterbury Tales*, written in the late 1300s, you may think you accidently picked up a French translation. Chaucer's writing reflects a time when Norman French had substantial cachet among English nobility. Some of Chaucer's words have remained in the language, oftentimes existing alongside Old English stock. For example, the Old English word *get* works just fine, unless you want to sound a little fancier, in which case you use the French-based *receive*. In a related case, we now use French-based words for many foods, including *pork*, *beef*, *veal*, and *mutton*, but retain Old English words for the animals themselves, including *pig*, *ox*, *calf*, and *sheep*. Previously, each word could refer to either the animal or the meat of that animal (much like the word *chicken* today). The different domains reflect the roles of the Old English farmers who raised the animals to be eaten by the French nobles. While some of the French words that Chaucer used have remained in English, a good many of the rest dropped out. Picking up an Early Modern English copy of a Shakespearean play, it is readily apparent that the French influence was far less dramatic. Also, it is apparent that notwithstanding changes in spellings and meanings, the words Shakespeare used are still, for the most part, used today.

It is easy to focus on the few words and phrases we do not recognize and, in the process, underestimate or miss just how much has stayed the same. To say that separation from other communities in the mountains has allowed Shakespearean English to be preserved misses the fact that Standard English has preserved the majority of the language in which Shakespeare wrote. When we focus on differences, we often think about a word or phrase being preserved in one dialect, but it is equally appropriate to think about that same word being lost in other dialects. The latter raises questions about what other word may now be used as a synonym—and if there is none, why not? Occasionally in regional dialects, certain word differences are maintained out of local usefulness where these are merged in the general lexicon in other communities.

Dialects often differ dramatically in the words they use to categorize people. We looked at examples from the Outer Banks that differentiate insiders from outsiders (*off*, *dit-dotters*, *dingbatters*, etc.) in chapter 5 and will look at examples of Lumbee terms (*Lum*, *cuz*, *buddyrow*, etc.) in chapter 9, including words to refer to different internal groups (for example, *on the swamp* and *Brickhouse Indian*). The Mountain terrain helped to impede communication networks and would keep some areas just as isolated as the Outer Banks islands from the mainland. In fact, the ferry system that connected the Outer Banks with the mainland predates the ARC's road-building initiative in the mountains by about fifteen years. This may explain why there seem to be fewer Appalachian words for community insiders and outsiders, though it may also relate to the kinds of relations that developed between the groups. Some communities still use the word *residenter* to describe a person who comes from long-established families. The term dates to the fifteenth century, originally used in a religious context as a member of a church. In the mid-seventeenth century, it started to be attached to the Scots-Irish groups, meaning something akin to "pioneer."[27] Meanwhile, some common terms to differentiate outsiders, like *jasper*, *peckerwood*, and *halfback*, developed. The first two are terms for people who are transient to the area—perhaps a tourist, salesman, or other unfamiliar person—but the latter, as introduced earlier in the chapter, is used to describe someone who takes up seasonal residency in the mountains, usually starting in the North or Midwest and relocating to a place like Florida, only to finally settle "halfway back home," which happens to be in the mountains. For obvious reasons, *halfback* is a more-recent innovation. The other two terms, *jasper* and *peckerwood*, are sometimes used to differentiate the type of visitor. According to storyteller Gary Carden, "If it's somebody [my mother] didn't like she'd call him a peckerwood. Or if there's somebody she didn't know, but he's probably alright, she didn't have any animosity for him, she'd say, 'he's a jasper.'

'There's this jasper come by here this morning and knocked on the door.' You know, but if it was a salesman, 'there's this peckerwood out there on the porch.'"[28] These terms have been around longer than *halfback*. *Jasper* is documented in the late nineteenth century with a definition of "rustic" or a "hick." *Peckerwood* seems to predate them all, being used with derogatory connotations since the 1850s.[29]

To view the video of this quote, visit http://www.talkintarheel.com/chapter/6/video6-7.php

As on the Outer Banks, there are many local terms in the mountains to describe the topography of the region. *Bald*, introduced above, is used metaphorically to describe a treeless area on a mountain. Its usage can be found in texts from the 1600s, including the Shakespearean play *As You Like It*. In Mountain Talk, the term can be used as a noun, referring to a specific place. Previous to about 1850, however, the term was used as an adjective to describe a place. Local innovation allowed Charles Egbert Craddock (a pen name of Mary Murfree) to write in *Prophet of the Great Smoky Mountains* (1885): "She paused often, and looked idly . . . at the great 'bald' of the mountain" (page 2). The term *scald* is sometimes used in the same way, and a *fire scald* is a bare area that is created by a fire. Other terms for Mountain topography include *cove* or *hollow*, usually pronounced *holler*, to describe a gap between ridges (used with this definition as early as 950 and 1550, respectively), and *drain*, meaning a small stream (used in this sense since the early 1700s).

Local plants and animals often have names not used outside the area as well. The term *boomer* for a small red squirrel native to the region seems to be an innovation within Appalachia, whereas the use of *polecat* for skunk is due to the similarity between the North American skunk and the European polecat (*Mustela putorius*), an equally putrid-smelling animal. A cicada may be called a *jarfly*, a groundhog may be called a *whistle pig*, and certain turtles may be called *tarpins* (from "terrapin"). Rhododendrons are occasionally called *lettuce* or, more commonly, *laurels*, a term also used for the similarly shaped but unrelated plant the mountain laurel. A thicket of rhododendrons or mountain laurels may be referred to by various names, including *lettuce bed, laurel bed, laurel hell, laurel slick, laurel rough, rough,* or *rough slick*.

Other Mountain terms are recognizable but seem quaint or antiquated outside the region, including *varmint/varment* ("an objectionable creature, mischief maker"), *vittles* ("food"), *spell* ("a period of time or weather"), *hussy* ("spiteful woman"), or *nary* ("none at all"). Others, especially the preservations of older terms, may seem totally unfamiliar to outsiders. A few of these terms are *airish* ("cool, breezy"), derived from a form used by Chaucer; *beal* ("a festering sore"), probably related to "boil" and used as early as the 1400s; *brogan* ("a leather shoe"), from Irish and Gaelic *brògan* ("little shoe"); *gaum* ("sticky or dirty mess"), used in this sense in the late 1700s; *mommuck/mommick* ("mess up, confuse, tear up"), found in Shakespeare and other writers as early as the 1500s; and *poke* ("a small paper container"), used as early as the 1300s, including in Chaucer's *The Reeve's Tales*.

Some terms are rooted in cultural traditions, such as the term *Jack tale*, which is a traditional story involving one or both of the trickster characters Jack and Molly. Many of these tales seem to derive from Celtic oral tradition, and it is possible that the Scots-Irish became familiar with these terms while still working in Ulster.[30] Other innovations are less clear, such as the term *sigogglin*, introduced in chapter 1, with alternate spellings/pronunciations *sygoggly* and *sigodling*, which means "crooked, not plumb, or askew." In Pittsburgh and some areas of the South, the related word *antigoglin* is used to mean the same thing. The terms seem to derive from the word "google," which meant "to roll one's eyes" in the 1300s and which took on connotations of dizziness or swaying in the 1500s.[31] In the early 1900s, it was used to describe a swerve or a break in bowling.

Dialect words for crooked things are common, as are words for making a mess. So it is not surprising that *gaum* is used for messy, dirty, or sticky things. By the same token, things can be *redd up*, or tidied up and cleaned, if they get too *gaumed up*. Though *redd up* tends to be associated today with

North Midland dialects in Pennsylvania and Ohio, its Irish-English roots are in the hills of southern Appalachia. And it is a well-established term documented as early as the 1400s.

The term *yonder*, while not restricted to the Mountain region, is used commonly enough there that it is associated with the area. Typically meaning "over there" or "more distant" in Standard English, it can take on additional meanings. Furthermore, it can be pronounced both as *yonder* and

To view the video of this quote, visit http://www.talkintarheel.com/chapter/6/video6-8.php

yander, though, as Vester McGaha noted in *Mountain Talk*, the latter is the preferred pronunciation: "Instead of saying yonder, you know, over yonder, it's over yander." Orville Hicks captured this pronunciation in a recollection from his childhood: "Yeah, I say way over yander. My mama used to come up to us when we was little. And she'd say 'goose or gander?' And she'd pull each ear. If you'd say 'goose,' she'd say, 'pull it a-loose,' and for gander she'd say, 'pull it over yander.'"[32]

To view a vignette about Mountain Talk vocabulary, visit http://www.talkintarheel.com/chapter/6/video6-9.php

Other residents also have commented explicitly on the pronunciation and local usages of some terms, as the late Jim Tom Hedrick did for the use of *sigogglin* and *yonder*: "They'll stand back and look if something isn't right—and say, 'That thing is sigogglin.' They'll say, 'I want you to look.' Say, 'What is it?' if you're building some[thing] . . . and say, 'That thing is sigogglin right yonder.'" He further described how the term *yonder* can be used to mean "arrive" or "here," as in: "They all know me, they say yander comes him a-riding that Harley-Davidson." Finally, it may locally be used to reference a specific location, as in: "That's the way you can tell the Mountain people from your outsiders, by their language they use. Say 'I'll see you over yonder,' it means, 'I'll see you like in Waynesville,' it's the Mountain Talk calling."[33] Word histories sometimes follow the most sigogglin paths, once again echoing the each-word-has-its-own-history refrain.

THE SOUNDS OF MOUNTAIN TALK

In discussing Mountain Talk vocabulary, we could not avoid referring to the ways in which some of these words were pronounced, such as the pronunciation of the term *hollow* as *holler*. This pronunciation, however, is not an idiosyncratic departure from standardized English pronunciations; instead, it reflects a process in which unstressed word final *o* sounds can be pronounced as "er," giving rise to *yeller*, *feller*, *winder*, *(to)mater*, *(po)tater*, and *skeeter* (from *mosquito*). The same pattern can even be applied to borrowings from other languages, so it is now possible to order a *burriter* (*burrito*) for lunch in Appalachia. *O* sounds that are stressed cannot undergo this change in pronunciation, so words like *throw*, *go*, and *bestow*, for example, are never pronounced with an "er" sound.

In the mountains of western North Carolina, like in other parts of southern Appalachia, words that end in a sound like "uh" are sometimes pronounced with an "ee" sound instead. Thus, *soda* becomes *sodee* and *Florida* becomes *Floridee*. As one older resident commented, "Oh a dope, you're talking about like a sodee pop, sodee water."[34] The term *dope* in this sentence is a distinctive older Mountain word referring to soda or *pop*.

As in Outer Banks English and other rural dialects, the two-syllable sequences in words like *fire*, *tire*, *briar*, *liar*, and *higher* are commonly pronounced with one syllable, as *far*, *tar*, *brar*, and so on. The related vowel sequence in the word *hour* is subject to a similar change, so that the words *flour* and *flower* are pronounced as *flar* and *shower* as *shar*.

Two consonant features heard in Appalachia are preservations of older pronunciations once common in English. The words *it* and *ain't* are often pronounced with an *h* sound at the start of the word, as *hit* and *hain't*.[35] The loss of the initial *h* sound of these words in Standard English is not surprising, as many other words have also lost this sound, including *hraven*, *hleap*, *hneck*, and *hlady*.[36] A second consonant feature preserved from older productions includes the *t* sound in words that now end in an *s* sound, as in *oncet* and *twicet*. These are forms that could be heard in various English dialects beginning by about 1300. Other English dialects never included these pronunciations, but they are common in English dialects that had contact with the Irish. In places where this pronunciation has remained common, it occasionally spreads to other words that end in *s* or *f*, provided that the *-s* is not related to a plural, possessive, or verb marker. Examples include *cliff* as *clift* and *across* as *acrosst*. All of the pronunciation features described thus far can also be heard in the speech of older Outer Banks residents; however, they all remain much more robust in Mountain Talk.

One of the most commonly cited aspects of southern speech involves the pronunciation of the long *i* vowel in words like *ride*, *tight*, or *time*, as introduced in chapter 3 and discussed in other chapters. In the mountains of North Carolina, the unglided *i* occurs in all contexts, which contrasts with the more restricted pattern found in the Piedmont area of North Carolina. Only Mountain Talk speakers would use the unglided *i* in *tight*, *nice*, and *price* (they would pronounce these as *taht*, *nahs*, and *prahs*). This pronunciation of the unglided i may have been a relatively recent change in Mountain Talk as well as other southern dialects, apparently spreading during the mid-nineteenth century.[37]

The final pronunciation feature discussed here is important because it helps explain the Mountain term *you'uns*, which has various pronunciations, including something more like *yunz* or even *yinz* in Pittsburgh, a city that has had its speech intimately affected by Mountain Talk. This use, for second-person plurals, serves as a Mountain Talk version of the iconic southern plural *y'all*. Like *y'all* elsewhere in the South, *you'uns* or *yunz* has developed local social meaning among native speakers of the Mountain dialect since it can be more closely connected to Mountain identity. This phrase started out as *you ones* and over time underwent a contraction similar to that which gives us a word like *gonna* (from "going to"). However, this particular contraction is noteworthy because it is associated with words that begin with a *w* sound, as *one* (*wuhn*) does. When unstressed, a *w*- sound at the beginning of a word is prone to reduction, which helps explain contractions such as *he'll* or *she'd* for "he will" and "she would." This can also extend to the reduction of the *w*-sound of *was*, as in "he's there yesterday" for "he was there yesterday."

GRAMMAR IN THEM THAR HILLS

While the distinctive vocabulary and pronunciations of Mountain Talk reflect a mix of preservation and innovation, the characteristic grammatical patterns that distinguish this variety tend to be preservations. This does not mean, however, that speakers in the mountains do not acquire newer grammatical innovations. For example, the use of quotative *be like* in "She's like, 'where are you going?'" introduced in chapter 4 is generally found among speakers under forty to fifty years of age, just as it is in other dialects of American English.

Some of the grammatical features preserved in Mountain Talk were common across many English dialects, while others were restricted to a few often stigmatized dialects. However, it is important to note that at no time in its history has the grammar of English been uniform across its dialects.

There is no grammatical form more synonymous with Mountain Talk than the use of an *a*-prefix with words ending in *-ing*, as in "he was a-hunting this morning," where the *a*- is pronounced as "uh." So common was this usage that in 1925, early Americanist scholar Dr. George Philip Krapp reported of Appalachian English—somewhat overzealously—that "in popular speech, almost every word ending in -ing (usually pronounced as in') has a sort of prefix a-."[38] While the form is found in other dialects, including North Carolina's coastal varieties, it is far more ubiquitous in Mountain Talk, though it doesn't occur nearly as much as Krapp suggested. The form derives historically from a pattern of Standard English whereby the -ing form of verbs was used with the preposition on or at. Thus, it previously would have been standard to say something like, "He was on/at hunting this morning." Over time, on or at was reduced to "uh" and then, in Standard English, was removed altogether. Reductions of this type are common, and a similar process of reduction has given us the present-day indefinite articles a and an, which are merely reduced forms of one. Typically, the a-prefix can only be used with -ing verbs and not -ing words that are other parts of speech such as adjectives ("the child's behavior was a-shocking to her parents") or nouns ("I like a-hunting"). Second, there cannot be an additional preposition preceding the -ing verb. It would be acceptable to say "People destroy the mountains a-littering" but not "people destroy the mountains by a-littering." The third rule governing this pattern is that the primary stress for the -ing verb must be on the first syllable. Thus it would be acceptable to say "they were a-HOLlering the chant" but not "they were a-reMEMbering the chant." Amazingly, though speakers of the dialect follow these rules, they have little to no conscious knowledge of the rules themselves. The feature is still strongly associated with Mountain culture and language, but it seems to be used less and less in the younger generations (though it may be used robustly by people of all ages in storytelling settings).

The online *Dictionary: Southern Appalachian English* lists entries such as *blowed, borned, catched, heared, knowed, seed,* and *throwed* as the past tense form of the verbs *blow, born, catch, hear, know, see,* and *throw.*[39] Categorizing these as idiosyncratic lexical differences neglects the systematic and powerful linguistic process whereby irregular verbs often become regular; in this case, verbs with irregular past-tense forms are made past tense with the same *-ed* ending that the majority of English verbs take. By making these verbs regular, Mountain Talk is extending a process that has been at work in the language for hundreds of years. A similar process of regularization also affects nouns with irregular plurals. In Mountain Talk, it is common to hear an *-s* ending on nouns that typically do not have one, such as *deers, oxes, foots,* etc. At the same time, a plural *-s* may be omitted altogether from measure nouns that occur with a quantifier. In Mountain Talk, as in Outer

TABLE 6.1. The Merging of Past-Tense and Past-Participle Forms in Mountain Talk

Past Tense	Traditional Past Participle	New Past Participle	Sample Sentence
mowed	mown	mowed	I have mowed the lawn.
sawed	sawn	sawed	She had sawed the board.
strive	striven	strived	He has strived to do well.
heave	hove	heaved	We had heaved the log in the lake.

Banks English, it is possible to have constructions such as "We bought twenty pound of flour" but not "We bought pound of flour" (meaning multiple pounds) or "We bought twenty apple," since *apple* is not a noun of measure.

Another common pattern in Mountain Talk is to merge the use of past-tense and past-participle forms of verbs that have different forms in Standard English. It is worth noting that Standard English is currently replacing many past-participle forms with past-tense forms. The examples in Table 6.1 illustrate this shift clearly.

Over the past couple of centuries, hundreds of English verbs have lost the distinction between past-tense and past-participle forms. Mountain Talk often extends this pattern to verbs that still have distinct forms in Standard English. For example, *drank* can be used instead of *drunk* ("I had drank my milk"), *fell* can be used instead of *fallen* ("she has fell down"), and *took* can be used in place of *taken* ("they had took the book to school"). Occasionally, other innovated forms are used in place of a past-tense or past-participle form. For example, some speakers may use *drug* instead of *dragged*, *eat* instead of *ate* or *eaten*, *holp* instead of *helped*, and *retch* instead of *reached*. Such verbal forms typically arise due to some related pattern in the standard or via a systematic sound change in a dialect and are not merely idiosyncrasies; further, they are most certainly not corruptions of the language.

The verb *to be* is the most irregular verb in the English language, so it often shows variation in dialects. Standard English maintains six forms of the verb: *am, is, are, was, were,* and *been.* Some dialects use fewer forms, making the irregular pattern more regular. In Mountain Talk, it is common to weaken the distinction between *was* and *were* by using *was.* This is demonstrated in this passage from a local resident: "Well, that's the Mountain customs are definitely a thing that is being lost. And it's a tragedy as far as the people that was born raised in the mountains like myself." The preference for the single form *was* is also found in Outer Banks and Lumbee English; however, in these dialects, as described in chapters 5 and 9, *weren't* is regularized for all negative uses of past tense *be* (for example, "I weren't there"; "she weren't there"). This feature offers a nice illustration of the grammatical differences among different dialects.

Another common grammatical feature of Mountain Talk involves adding an *-s* to the end of verbs when no *-s* is required in Standard English. Standard English uses this suffix only in the present tense with a third-person singular subject, as in *he/she/it/the car runs*. In Mountain Talk, the *-s* is used in this standard context but also commonly with conjoined subjects ("me and my sister gets in a fight sometimes"), collective subjects ("the way people talks around here" [Popcorn Sutton] or "Old people says you put it in a poke" [Carl Presnell]), and other plural subjects ("all those kind of things has poisoned the outside world's view of the mountains").

Many other grammatical features are found in Mountain Talk, some of which are shared with other southern dialects due to the shared Scots-Irish settlement. *Done* may be used to mark an occurrence that has been completed or for emphasis, such as "I done sent the letter weeks ago" or "We done forgot where it was." Certain helping verbs may be used in tandem where they are not in Standard English, often to convey a different meaning, as in "You might should clean your room" or "I might could do that." These "double modals" offer a polite way of issuing a command and declining a request. To a native speaker, the first sentence leaves no doubt as to the importance of the request, while the second sentence offers a diplomatic way of declining a request or offer without using the word "no." *Liketa* and *supposeta* are used in a wide variety of contexts but most commonly to indicate something was close to happening but didn't, as in one sample we recorded: "Oh, he liketa had a fit. He said, 'My God, you done killed that man's horse.'" As we noted in chapter 4, these forms also commonly serve as a metaphorical or hyperbolic means of describing an occurrence, as in "It was raining so hard I liketa drowned" or "It was so cold I liketa froze to death." All of these grammatical features are more common in older speakers than in younger speakers.

In the 2001 movie *Zoolander*, the title character (played by Ben Stiller), discouraged with the world of high fashion modeling, returns to his childhood home in an Appalachian coal-mining town. After spending one day in the mines with his father and brother, he reports: "I think I'm getting the Black

Lung, Pop. It's not very well ventilated down there." This scene captures an interesting pattern of Mountain Talk, whereby the definite article "the" can be used with all names of illness or disease. Standard English does this in talking about "the flu," "the mumps," and "the measles," but throughout the Appalachian region, it is also possible to hear "the cancer," "the toothache," "the cold," "the stomachache," and so forth.

There are many other grammatical structures that unite Mountain speech with southern grammatical structures that we have discussed in previous chapters, including the personal use of an object pronoun in "She likes her some dogs"; or the use of *but* as an adverb meaning something like "only" in "She ain't but three years old"; or the use of the intensifying adverbs *right* and *plumb* in "She's right bright" and "She's plumb stupid." Though there are a limited number of structures found prominently in Mountain Talk, the vast majority of its grammar is shared with other southern varieties.

The Future of Mountain Talk

The physical erosion of the Appalachian Mountain range is an apt metaphor for its English-language history. Over time, the mountains may have changed, but many regions remain rugged and physically imposing. As the mountains have succumbed to the elements and the incursion of roads, the heart of the mountains has remained. The language of Mountain residents, too, has been affected, not so much by the flow of wind and water but by the flow of tourists and transplants. Nonetheless, the distinct voices of the language still echo throughout the hollows and coves of the mountains. Younger speakers tend to use fewer of the traditional features than their forebearers, but they often retain an intimate connection to the place and language of their home. Speakers who rarely use many older Appalachian forms are able to incorporate them into retellings of traditional stories. And while the Elizabethan English myth is losing its traction, the variety is now validated through a celebration of the pioneering spirit that led to the settlement of the region and the rich culture that developed there. In fact, Dr. Kirk Hazen, a professor of linguistics at West Virginia University, has established the West Virginia Dialect Project in part to preserve and celebrate Mountain Talk.[40] His work includes academic research as well as public engagement and curriculum materials for schools to learn about the past and present states of Mountain culture and talk. In North Carolina, Mountain Talk is one of the featured regional dialects in our *Voices of North Carolina* curriculum. Responses to our documentary *Mountain Talk* (2004) provide evidence that there is tremendous local and general pride in the enduring Mountain culture and speech. As the late Jim Tom Hedrick, from Graham County, put it: "Everybody hears about Graham County, don't they? How good the people is. How they'll help you. I'll run into people I don't know, I've never seen in 'em in my life and I help them any way I can. Somebody once said, 'You'll get knocked in the head.' I said, 'Well, if I do, I'm just knocked.' They're just good-hearted. Everybody you meet, just 99 percent of 'em. If I didn't live here, I'd move, wouldn't you?"[41]

To view the video of this quote, visit http://www.talkintarheel .com/chapter/6/video6-10.php

7 African American Speech in North Carolina

Particularly in the African American community, there is this idea that, yes, you can speak in a much more relaxed, intimate black speech in certain spaces. And then in other spaces you have to speak a much more common English. For some people, there's an internal struggle about, should you really do that? Should you really be trying to talk like white folk? Or should you always, all the time, no matter what setting you are in, speak the same way, speak the same way your momma taught you to speak?
—**RICHARD BROWN OF DURHAM**, quoted in *Voices of North Carolina*, produced by Neal Hutcheson (Raleigh: North Carolina Language and Life Project, 2005)

To view the video of the quote above, visit http://www.talkintarheel.com/chapter/7/video7-1.php

In the documentary *Voices of North Carolina*, North Carolina statesman Bill Friday introduces a vignette on African American English by observing: "Language is an important part of all social and cultural groups, but it seems to have a special place in the African American community." That may be an understatement. For more than a half century now, the topic of African American speech has been a hot-button topic. Everyone has an opinion—just ask people what they think about "Ebonics" and you'll get an earful.[1] The controversy about African American speech is not surprising since language serves as a proxy for deeper political and social concerns. At its core, debate about the legitimacy of the speech of African Americans is really about the adequacy of African American history, culture, and people. This is not unlike the connection between language and Mountain culture discussed in the last chapter, but issues touching on race in American society always heighten the stakes.

African American English remains by far the most controversial dialect of American English. Flare-ups related to the variety have mostly happened outside the state—like in the late 1970s in Ann Arbor, Michigan, and in 1996–97 in Oakland, California—though North Carolinians have certainly been aware of these controversies and the ongoing debates even in the absence of overt local uproar.[2] Few North Carolinians realize, however, how important African American communities in North Carolina have been in contributing to our understanding of the history and current development of African American speech in the United States. In fact, we have demonstrated that information from small communities in North Carolina has provided new and critical information about the past and present development of African American English.[3]

In the urban areas of Charlotte, Greensboro, Durham, and Raleigh, the speech of African Americans tends to be similar to other southern metropolitan regions and, in fact, more general urban areas across the United States. There are similarities that unite the urban speech of African Americans from Los Angeles to New York City, and even more similarities among African Americans in the urban South. These similarities are striking enough that many linguists once thought that African American English was quite homogeneous across the United States.[4] However, as we looked closely at the speech of African Americans in rural areas of North Carolina, particularly in the rural coastal regions and in the western mountains, we found a different story. These unique situations led the way to a new understanding of the effect of region, isolation, and communication networks on the evolution of the speech of African Americans.

We have conducted interviews in communities from the far eastern and western edges of the state and many places in between. These include the first town incorporated by blacks in the United States, Princeville, in Edgecombe County to small enclave Mountain communities and coastal communities of African Americans.[5]

These studies led us to one of the most unusual situations of isolation that we have uncovered in almost a half century of sociolinguistic fieldwork: the case of the Bryant family, a lone African American family living on the island of Ocracoke for almost 150 years.[6] Map 7.1 gives the locations of different rural sites where we have now conducted more than 300 interviews with African American residents of the state. As the map shows, our interviews have been conducted in all the major regional dialect areas of North Carolina, giving us good regional distribution. In addition, in most communities we have interviewed people representing different generations, cover-

FIGURE 7.1. Princeville, the first town in the United States incorporated by blacks, celebrates an anniversary. (Photograph by Neal Hutcheson)

ing more than a century in time. Thanks to these interviews, we now have a much better understanding of how language variation, regional distinctiveness, and ethnicity are negotiated.

Popular Myths and African American Speech

African American English—or, more popularly, "Ebonics"—is the most talked about and politicized American English dialect. Even its name has become contentious. Among the labels attached to this variety over the past five decades are Negro Dialect, Nonstandard Negro English, Black English, Vernacular Black English, Afro-American English, African American (Vernacular) English, and African American Language. Though it is now popularly referred to as Ebonics, most linguists prefer not to use this label because of the strong emotional reactions it evokes, which have, unfortunately, given license to racist parodies of various types. For example, there are a number of so-called "Ebonics Translators" found on the Internet that usually offer inaccurate, mocking renditions that rely on slang terms rather than faithful translations into the grammar of this variety.[7] Most linguists prefer to use more-neutral references like African American English or African American Language, though there are problems with any label assigned to a language variety with ethnic associations. At the very least, social class, age, and region intersect with ethnicity and identity in the definition. When using a term like African American English, most people are referring to working-

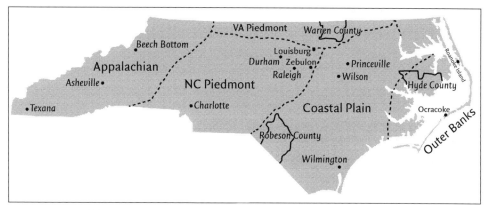

MAP 7.1. African American Communities Studied
by the NCLLP within North Carolina Dialect Regions

class, urban youth speech, although this is just one, often somewhat limited perspective on the language used by African Americans. As is true for any group, the use of language is highly varied among African Americans.

Everyone seems to have an opinion about African American English, but a lot of the popular ideas are based on assumptions that have little to no basis in linguistic reality. Linguists argue contentiously about the details of language structure, including dialect differences, but there is a remarkable consensus about the fundamental nature of African American speech—or any dialect for that matter. All linguists agree that differences in language use by African Americans are not due to genetic or physical differences. Dialectologists point to cases in which African Americans reared in European American communities talk no differently from their European American peers; conversely, European Americans who learn their language from African American English speakers adopt the features of this language vernacular variety. Yet myths persist, mostly in hushed whispers rather than in public acclamation, so there is a continuing need to debunk claims about the physical aspects of language and race.

It also needs to be understood that there is great variation in the speech of African Americans, just as there is among European Americans. Though people tend to homogenize the speech of African Americans, no one should really talk about African American speech as if it is a uniform language variety. There is great variation in African American speech in North Carolina based on a range of social factors, and even more variation exists as we consider the speech of African Americans beyond the state's borders. As mentioned, the variety of African American speech at the center of most of the dialect storm is that of working-class rather than middle-class speakers and tends to be associated with urban youth culture. No one would argue against the low social evaluation of this speech on an institutional level; language attitudes are enmeshed with established social hierarchies, and strong opinions about African Americans—especially urban African American youths— are held by a large segment of Americans. As one linguist puts it: "It is not language per se, but its power to function as a 'proxy' for wider social issues which fans the flames of public disputes over language."[8] Linguists do not deny the social reality of the status of race and ethnicity in the United States; they merely point out that social acceptability is a totally different issue from linguistic validity.

One of the persistent myths about African American English is that it has no patterning or rules governing the use of structures, but it is obvious to anyone who has ever had an introductory course in linguistics—or read other chapters in this book—that all languages and dialects have systematic and complex patterning. African American English is no different. In fact, saying that some dialects have no rules or patterns would be like a physicist maintaining that there are some people who are not bound by physical laws such as gravity, or a mathematician claiming that two plus two does not equal four. Such assertions contradict our basic scientific and mathematical knowledge and as such would be dismissed by specialists and nonspecialists alike. Unfortunately, linguistics is not taught in our core curriculum, so we tend to have less knowledge about language than we do about basic science and math. The universal patterning of all language varieties is one of the rudiments of linguistics, which is why we said that all linguists, regardless of political persuasion, are absolutely united in maintaining that there are patterns that guide the use of vernacular African American English.

The patterning of vernacular African American English can be illustrated by the use of a sentence like "Sometimes my ears be itching," which is an idiom that captures a feeling of suspicion that someone is talking about the speaker behind his or her back. Most middle-class speakers who hear this sentence react by thinking that this use of *be* results from the speaker's ignorance of the rules for conjugating *be*. But a systematic linguistic examination of this form in everyday interaction demonstrates that the use of *be* actually refers to an action that takes place more than once—a "habitual" activity. The speaker would not, for example, use this *be* form to refer to a one-time event, such as "My ears be itching right now." The user acquires this pattern intuitively without explicit instruction—spoken language is always naturally learned—and will use the form in accordance with this pattern without ever explicitly recognizing the intricacies of it. We can demonstrate the patterning of the feature by asking speakers of this variety to choose which sentence sounds "better" with *be* in a sentence pair: one with the adverb *usually* or the one with *right now*. The speakers will use their inner knowledge of language—or "language intuitions"—to choose the sentence that refers to the habitual activity.[9] We once asked a group of thirty-five fourth-grade African American speakers in a working-class urban area to choose which sentence "sounded better" in the sentence pairs listed below. The number of students who chose each sentence is given for each pair of sentences.

They usually *be* tired when they come home. (32)
They *be* tired right now. (3)

When we play basketball she *be* on my team. (31)
The girl in the picture *be* my sister. (4)

My ankle *be* broken from the fall. (3)
Sometimes my ears *be* itching. (32)

The choices reveal that the students were not simply guessing at the correct sentence, even though they may not have had any notion of what "habitual aspect" is.[10] The fact that the sentence associated with habitual action was identified as the "correct" sentence about 90 percent of the time indicates that there was a systematic basis for the students' choices. They recognize what the pattern is from inner knowledge about language structure, an intuitive skill quite different from the ability to talk about the structure using technical linguistic labeling. When we gave the same sentence pair test to seventy-six middle-class European American speakers, only twenty-nine (38 percent) chose sentences like "Sometimes my ears be itching" over "My ears be itching right now," suggesting that they had no intuitions about the structure and were simply choosing randomly.[11] Only those who use this English variety regularly would internalize the rule for habitual *be* use, and speakers of other dialects simply don't have the inner knowledge to guide their selection. It is important to understand the fundamental validity of African American English as a linguistic system apart from its social valuation and educational utility.

Rural and Urban African American Varieties

While modern African American English is strongly associated with urban culture, studying the speech of rural African Americans can help shed light on its origins and development since African American culture in the South was largely found in rural areas. The results of this research point to some interesting, and perhaps counterintuitive, conclusions.

Most people think that they can accurately identify the ethnicity of working-class African Americans from a sample of speech, and a number of experiments support this claim. Using speech samples from urban areas, studies show an accuracy rate of between 85 and 95 percent on ethnic identification—for both European American and African American listeners.[12] These results suggest that there is a significant ethnic dimension that distinguishes African American speech from the white regional dialects of English that surround it. But a different picture emerges when speech samples from rural settings in North Carolina are included in such experiments.

At one point, we conducted some interviews with people from rural mainland Hyde County, where whites and blacks have been living in the same coastal region since the early 1700s.[13] Population density in Hyde County is sparse, with fewer than ten people per square mile. Today, there are slightly over 5,000 residents of Hyde County—less than 1,000 more than the 4,120 people in the 1790 census. Throughout the centuries, the percentage of African Americans in this county has ranged from 30 to 45 percent of the population, suggesting a fairly stable ethnic proportion from the antebellum period to the present. In fact, many of the surnames in Hyde County are still shared by white and black families—Spencer, Mann, Gibbs, and Bryant—because of the legacy of naming slaves with the surname of the owner. The majority of black and white families in Hyde County have lived there now for almost three centuries.

During our interviews in Hyde County, we talked to speakers from different generations, ranging from age five through 102. In one instance, we interviewed four different generations of speakers from the same African American family and spliced short passages from our interview onto a CD.[14] We also included samples of white speakers of comparable ages and mixed up the order of presentation for the voices.

To hear the speech of four generations of an African American family in Hyde County, visit http://www.talkintarheel.com/chapter/7/audio7-1.php

We then asked listeners simply to identify whether they thought the speakers sounded black or white. The results were

FIGURE 7.2. The marshy coastal mainland of Hyde County, North Carolina.
(Photograph by Bryan Conrad)

stunning. The speech of the great-grandfather of the African American family, who was born in 1910 and lived all of his life in Hyde County, was identified by more than 90 percent of the listeners from the Piedmont area of North Carolina as sounding "white." Over 95 percent of the listeners identified the older and younger white speakers as white as well. In contrast, the great-granddaughter of the Hyde County African American, who was born in the 1970s and also lived all of her life in Hyde County, was identified as African American over 90 percent of the time by the same group of listeners.[15] How can it be that the speech of different generations of the same family can evoke such dramatically different ethnic associations when the four generations of speakers grew up in the same household in the same community all of their lives? We have had similar ethnic misidentifications of African American speakers

To hear the speech of a European American in Hyde County, visit http:// www.talkintarheel.com/ chapter/7/audio7-2.php

from some of the communities we have studied in the mountains of North Carolina, where black speakers in Appalachia tend to be identified as white in ethnic identification tasks.[16] These kinds of results suggest that African American English is not nearly as homogenous as it is sometimes perceived by the American public. It further indicates that the urban-rural division is important and that age and generational factors must enter into an authentic description of African American speech.

North Carolina's propensity for small towns and communities turns out to be a sociolinguistic treasure for examining the rural heritage of African American speech. Among the numerous small towns of North Carolina, there have been a surprising number of long-standing African American communities that were established in some of the remote lowland estuaries and in the highland mountainous terrain. These out-of-the-way communities can tell us a lot about the earlier history of African American speech in the rural South. The two most revealing kinds of situations for historical reconstruction are those involving the once-remote coastal communities by the sounds and the sea on the east and those in the mountains in the far west region of the state. From the examples above, we hear that older versions of the variety may have been more similar to European American Englishes than modern African American English. With urbanization, the speech of these groups has diverged, and this divergence has continued—and accelerated—even after the desegregation of public schools. A more-detailed look at groups of African Americans across the state reveals insights about the history, development, and role of African American English.

African Americans on the Coast

It may not be apparent to most beachgoers, but African Americans have played a vital role in the development of the waterways of coastal North Carolina. African Americans by the sea have often been invisible despite the fact that they comprised almost 50 percent of the total population of the sixteen tidewater counties between 1800 and 1860. There are some long-standing African American communities and families that have been, and continue to be, a significant part of the coastal tradition, culture, and language. African Americans have fished the waters of the sea and sound, piloted ships around the dangerous shoals and through the narrow channels of the waterways, harvested crops from the fertile coastal mainland soils, and safeguarded the coast.[17]

As we reported in chapter 2, most of the first African Americans in the coastal region were brought there as slaves from Virginia and Maryland starting in the early 1700s. By the mid-1700s, records indicate that African Americans made up one-quarter to one-third of the overall population of coastal North Carolina. Through the Civil War, even the Outer Banks islands had significant slave populations. Ocracoke had a population that included over 100 slaves at the time of the Civil War, and mainland Hyde County near the Pamlico Sound had a single plantation with over 200 slaves.

Many African American slaves became skilled watermen and were heavily involved in fishing, ferrying, and piloting, and their expertise was essen-

FIGURE 7.3. The Pea Island Life-Saving Station, the first all-black station, was formed in 1871. (Courtesy of the National Park Service, Cape Hatteras National Seashore)

tial to the maritime culture and economy of coastal North Carolina. As we noted earlier, recent studies led by historian Dr. David Cecelski have indicated a strong undercurrent to their life on the water: a maritime version of the Underground Railroad that flourished along coastal waterways of North Carolina between 1800 and the Civil War. The combination of skillful African American watermen and a conspiring network of freedmen, fugitive slaves, and sympathetic ship pilots within the complex geography of rivers, estuaries, pocosins, and tidal marshes along the coast offered an opportunistic topography for a maritime route to freedom. By the mid-1800s, this coastal escape route had become such a common passageway to freedom that one Wilmington correspondent noted that it was a regular occurrence for African Americans to take passage on a boat and go North.[18]

Although the Civil War changed the lives of many African Americans on the Outer Banks and altered the demographics of particular coastal communities, the proportion of African Americans to whites in the overall coastal population did not change appreciably. For example, the black populations of island communities such as Hatteras, Portsmouth, Ocracoke, and Hark-

FIGURE 7.4. The coastal estuary provided the environment for a marine-based Underground Railroad. (Courtesy of the State Archives of North Carolina)

ers Island were decreased dramatically during this time, but Roanoke Island became a large enclave for ex-slaves and the site of a freedmen's colony. Today, a number of small maritime African American communities still dot the coastal mainland, but on the Outer Banks, a number of islands are represented by a single, long-term family. In the twentieth century, Ocracoke, Hatteras, Hog Island, Cedar Island, and Portsmouth Island have all had only one permanent black family on their respective islands. In most cases, the family simply stayed on the island when freed slaves left the islands en masse after the Civil War.

The little-known history of African Americans on the coast of North Carolina turns out to be a unique linguistic resource as we examine the speech of different generations of speakers. We already examined the dialect of the Outer Banks in chapter 5, giving examples of distinctive vowel pronunciations, grammar, and vocabulary. But what about the speech of coastal African Americans, some of whom have lived along the coast for centuries? Is their speech the same as their white neighbors?

To answer this question, we return to the great-grandfather (born in 1910) of the long-term African American family in Hyde County and note why he was identified as white by the vast majority of listeners. At one point in the conversation, he was talking about an incident that took place and said: "I was *behind* him. I was stunting that *time*, and I run up *behind* 'im." His pronunciation of the long i in *behind* and *time* is quite like a hoi toider would produce this vowel (*behoind* and *toim*). That is just one aspect of this man's overall vowel system that sounds like an Outer Banker. At another point, he said: "He was taking up for the boy, but he weren't takin' up for me." As we noted in chapter 5, the use of *weren't* for "wasn't" strongly indexes Outer Banks speech. His speech is heavily embedded in the distinctive dialect of the region where he and his family have spent generations. For older African American residents from that region, regional identity clearly trumped ethnic identity. While there are moments where his speech diverges from European Americans of the community, salient vowels and grammatical structures are similar enough to lead most listeners to conclude that he is white. In mainland Hyde County, whites and African Americans have lived near each other for well over 200 years, but in the tighter confines of the Outer Banks islands, African Americans and whites have lived in more intimate contact, offering a complementary perspective on the development of African American English.

The Bryant Family of Ocracoke

Lone African American families on the Outer Banks islands had a different level of social acceptance when compared to groups of African Americans on the mainland. Outer Banks African Americans were included in many community activities, with virtually no reported acts of overt hostility toward them. At the same time, there was a complicit understanding of differential social roles for African Americans based on the existence of statewide Jim Crow laws barring blacks from attending the white schools during segregation and prohibiting interracial marriage.

Each isolated Outer Banks African American family is a unique story. One of these exceptional stories involves the Bryant family of Ocracoke. As the slave population of Ocracoke dispersed after the Civil War, a former slave family from Blounts Creek, located near Washington, North Carolina, came to Ocracoke on a steamboat and settled there in the mid-1860s. Harkus (Hercules) Blount was a boat builder and carpenter, and his wife, Winnie Blount, was a domestic and picked clams from their shells at the Doxee Clam Factory in Ocracoke. They had two children, one of whom, Acey Jane, stayed on the island, where she met her husband, Leonard Bryant. Originally from Engelhard in mainland Hyde County, Leonard Bryant had come to the island to work for the Doxees, loading and unloading the clam boats. He and Acey Jane Blount fell in love, married, and had nine living children, five boys and four girls.[19]

Most of the children left the island when they became adults, returning only for brief visits. One of the most newsworthy events involved the oldest son, Artis Bryant, who was born on Ocracoke in 1902. He left the island for Philadelphia in 1916 to work on the dredges and rarely if ever visited the island. During World War II, he served on an all-black crew of a merchant marine ship that was torpedoed by German U-boats in the Atlantic Ocean near the coast. The lifeboat carrying the survivors beached at the closest land, which turned out to be his homeland island of Ocracoke. According to the reports of his sisters who were living on the island at the time, he left the next day and never again returned. Newspaper accounts at the time verify the fortuitous, albeit brief, return of Artis Bryant to Ocracoke.[20]

Though most of the Bryant children left, several stayed and became part of the island community. For example, one son, Jules, born in 1921, participated in many traditional Ocracoke male activities—fishing, playing poker, drinking homemade meal wine, strumming his guitar, and singing traditional island songs. He is remembered fondly by islanders as "one of their family"—perhaps a slightly generous assessment given that he could not attend the legally segregated school or marry an island woman. His relationship to the island community did, however, have family-like aspects that were generally not afforded to African Americas on the mainland. For example, he learned to read, as did his brothers and sisters, from volunteer teachers after school hours, and he was regularly included in poker games, fishing, and other community activities. His sister, Muzel Bryant, born in 1904, lived on the island all of her life, with the exception of a couple of years when she moved to Philadelphia as a teenager. She died just short of her 104th birthday, the oldest resident of the Outer Banks at the time of her passing. She was a gracious, generous woman, with a remarkable aptitude for recounting historical events and dates. At age 103, she could recall all of the birth dates of her siblings and remember many details of past events that had faded in the memories of other islanders. Though mostly invisible to outsiders, she was well-known and greatly appreciated by islanders who had known her all their lives. On the occasion of her 100th birthday, she was driven from her home to the school in a limousine for what was described as the largest party ever hosted in the gym. Ironically, it was the same school that she could not attend because of segregation.

FIGURE 7.5. Muzel Bryant, Ocracoke resident born in 1904. (Courtesy of the Ocracoke Preservation Society)

For the last ten years of Muzel's life, we regularly visited her on the island and conducted a number of recorded interviews. Her story is fascinating, but as linguists, we were particularly interested in her dialect as an African American who lived for a century on a historically isolated island surrounded by a unique dialect. Was her speech completely like the community members who surrounded her, or was her family an isolated ethnic enclave that retained some semblance of historical African American speech from the mainland? We also discussed with her how she perceived her own speech compared to other islanders. In the following passage, MB stands for Muzel Bryant and KH and WW for the two interviewers talking to her.

To view a tribute to Muzel Bryant (from the documentary *Carolina Brogue*), visit http://www.talkintarheel.com/chapter/7/video7-2.php

KH: Did your daddy sound like the other islanders? Or did he sound different?

MB: He sounded a little bit different than what the uh, uh—

WW: Do you think your family talked a little different from the other islanders?

MB: Yes, I do, yes, uh huh.

WW: What was it about it that was different?

MB: I don't know, they just speak a little bit different than us in a way I guess.

KH: Uh huh. And your mom—your mother also spoke a little different?

MB: Yes, she did.[21]

To hear this conversation with Muzel Bryant, visit http://www.talkintarheel.com/chapter/7/audio7-3.php

Muzel Bryant's perception tends to match those given by outside listeners. About 70 percent of the listeners in an ethnic identification experiment identified her as African American even though she has identifiable features of Outer Banks speech, including some of the traits of the brogue. Jules passed away before we began doing interviews on Ocracoke; however, through good fortune, an islander was able to provide us with a recording of Jules singing traditional songs that he had made as a gift for a few islander friends. When we played these songs to people from the Piedmont, they generally identified him as a European American islander based on his use of hoi toider vowels in his songs, such as the way he pronounces the long i in the word "pine tree."[22]

To hear Jules Bryant singing "When They Cut Down the Old Pine Tree," visit http://www.talkintarheel.com/chapter/7/audio7-4.php

Though Muzel and Jules Bryant used some island vowels and other features of Outer Banks speech, both had a few traits exclusive to African American English, such as the absence of the linking verb *be* (for example, "she nice") and the absence of *-s* on verbs ("she'll be comin' 'round the mountain when she come"). The story of the Bryant family is an inspiring personal story, but it also turns out to be highly instructive for sociolinguistic history. Obvious assimilation from the regional dialect of the community occurred, but the social divide of blacks and whites—even on a small, isolated island—managed to sustain the effect of ethnically distinctive speech for 150 years.

African Americans in the Mountains

The stories of small, enclave African American communities nestled in the mountains of North Carolina mirror the stories of African Americans on the other side of the state, providing insight into the regional and historical context of African American speech in North Carolina. Beech Bottom is a small, receding Mountain community in a hollow of the southern Appalachian Mountain range. Located about thirty-five miles southwest of Boone along the Tennessee border, Beech Bottom was home to more than 100 African American residents in the early 1900s, but the population dwindled to about ten in the early twenty-first century. The diverse heritage of Beech Bottom defies the homogeneity stereotype of the region, so it is an ideal community for the study of the relationship between European American Appalachian speech and the speech of nonwhites through history. Beech Bottom was established in the 1870s during a time when Appalachia was developing its own diverse roots, with establishments by English, Scots-Irish, German, and Dutch pioneers. African American slaves were brought to the area earlier from other parts of North Carolina and from Virginia. The Beech Bottom black population from 1900 to 1940 ranged from eighty to 110 people, and the primary industry was mining feldspar, a mineral used in ceramics and glassmaking. As the mines began to close in the early 1940s, residents migrated to the North to seek work. Beech Bottom's primary industry now is Christmastree farming, with a couple of large farms of about 100,000 trees each employing several community residents full-time; other residents tend trees on a part-time basis. The regional dialect context of Beech Bottom, however, is a variety of Mountain Talk.[23] The Beech Bottom African American community is much smaller than many other communities, but it still offers insight about language and ethnicity. When we interviewed different speakers, we found that they used many of the iconic Mountain dialect features, pronouncing *white rice* as *whaht rahs* along with other vowel traits characteristic of Mountain speech. They also used some of the grammatical traits of southern Appalachia, such as the absence of *-s* with nouns of weights and measures ("four acre of corn" or "two mile down the road a piece") and *-s* with plural subjects (as in "people goes there a lot"). There are also tokens of Mountain Talk vocabulary, as in the use of *a piece* ("a distance"), *bald* ("a bare of treeless area on a mountain summit"), *holler* ("a gap between mountain ridges"), and other vocabulary associated with Mountain speech.

To hear an older and younger speaker from Beech Bottom, visit http://www.talkintarheel.com/chapter/7/audio7-5.php

About 150 miles to the southwest of Beech Bottom is Texana, the largest African American community in the Smoky Mountains, though it only numbers about 150 people. As we noted in chapter 3, Texana dates to the 1850s, when the McClelland family moved there from neighboring Avery County, a stretch to the north. After the family's initial settlement, Texana quickly developed into an African American enclave, and the population has remained relatively stable for over a century. The community is situated on a hillside overlooking the Cherokee County seat of Murphy, North Carolina, placing it squarely within the Smoky Mountain region of Appalachia where a variety of southern highland English—or Mountain Talk—is the prevailing dialect norm. Community life in Texana is largely focused on interaction with friends and family. Texana residents pride themselves on their friendliness and welcoming spirit, and according to them, even if you are not related to them, you are still treated like family. As one young female resident put it: "In Texana, if you're not kin, you're kin."[24] The high level of community solidarity shared by Texana residents is also reflected by the pride they take in their community. Older residents in particular are dedicated to building among the young residents a sense of ownership and respect for Texana as a strong black community; similarly, they are determined to keep the young residents from losing a sense of their black heritage. A few years ago, community members began an oral history and quilt project that brought older residents and young people together to preserve stories of kinship and history in the community.[25]

In Texana, the language situation is a little more complicated than it is in Beech Bottom because there are different groups in the community, including one group oriented toward urban African American culture and another toward the local rural church. We still find regional Mountain Talk well represented in the speech of the more-conservative group associated with the church. So the pronunciation of vowels in *white rice* and grammatical features like "people goes to church" or "two mile down the road a piece" mirror those described for speech in Beech Bottom. However, the groups that are oriented more outwardly show some departure from these localized pronunciations and grammatical uses, suggesting that there can be tremendous variation even in relatively small communities as regional, ethnic, and community identities are negotiated.

Small enclave communities of African Americans, like those in the mountains and along the coast, underscore the importance of region as well as the urban-rural distinction for African American speech. Older, rural African Americans tend to sound a lot more regionalized than some of their urban counterparts.

White and African American regional dialects sound more alike in long-standing rural communities of North Carolina. But there are also aspects of vernacular African American English that may differ, and the African American community is generally well aware of the significance of these differences. One of the leaders in the African American community in Durham made the following observation about dialect differences in different regions of speakers in the state: "Even inside the African American community, when you go from region to region there're really different voices and sounds. You can tell the difference between an African American who lives in Northeast [North Carolina] 'cause they say 'skraight,' which is not something you'd hear in Durham, or you'd hear in Winston-Salem, or you'd hear in Fayetteville, but if you hear 'skraight' or 'skreet,' you know exactly where they came from."[26]

To view the video of this quote, visit http://www.talkintarheel.com/chapter/7/video7-3.php

Here again, a distinction is made between urban and rural speakers: rural speakers are more likely to say *skraight* for *straight* and *skream* for *stream*, differentiating some rural communities from their urban counterparts. Even as the distinction between urban and rural speech is lessened for some young rural African Americans, there remains a noticeable difference in the speech of these groups.

Another insight from the study of these rural communities relates to the history of African American English. The origin and early development of African American English had been hotly contested by linguists for a half century now, but speech data from North Carolina's diverse rural communities help resolve some of this mystery. After briefly reviewing some of the distinctive features that are associated with contemporary vernacular African American English, we consider the rural and urban status of African American speech.

Vernacular African American Speech in the City

The speech of African Americans in urban areas often has less regional flavor than that in rural areas. In urban areas, particularly among the younger speakers, there seems to be a unifying set of linguistic traits. Some of the dialect traits that characterize these populations include the following.

Habitual *be*, especially with verb -*ing*:
Sometimes my ears be itching. They be acting all cool.

Absence of *are* and *is* forms of *be* verb:
She acting silly. You good.

Absence of -*s* on verb forms following third-person singular subjects:
She go to school every day. Malcolm like school.

Absence of possessive -s forms:
Nona hat is strange. The dog tail was wagging.

Remote time *been*:
I been known him forever. He been took the medicine.

Multiple negation:
I ain't do nothing. She don't never do nothing.

Reduction of word final consonant blends:
wes' en' ("west end"); *col' ac'* ("cold act")

f for *th* in syllable final position:
birfday ("birthday"); *toof* ("tooth")

r-loss after vowels:
feauh ("fear"); *sistuh* ("sister")

To view a group of Princeville residents talking about growing up in Princeville (from *This Side of the River*), visit http://www.talkintarheel .com/chapter/7/video7-4.php

The list of structures cited here is restricted, and there are lots of qualifications that need to be made. The full inventory of structures make up a coherent dialect system rather than a list of unrelated traits; a comprehensive inventory based on studies across the United States would be at least five times longer than this list, with each feature being the subject of multiple research articles. There are several dozen articles written about the use of the habitual *be* and the absence of linking verb *be* alone—and even more written about the reduction of consonant blends (for example, *wes'* for *west* or *wil'* for *wild*). A remarkable finding from this research is that the same set of core structures has been documented in urban areas around the country, including larger and smaller metro areas of North Carolina from Raleigh and Durham to Princeville, Louisburg, Texana, and mainland Hyde County. But variation does exist; as we will discuss later, age, social class, social interaction, and many other demographic, social, and psychological factors go into understanding how these features are actually used.

The History of African American English

The present state of African American English is a lot easier to document than its past, but that does not diminish the significance of the past for understanding the present. There are several major questions: (1) What was it like at its origin? (2) How did it develop during its earlier history? (3) What kinds of changes are currently taking place? The broad trajectory of historical language shift seems obvious: Africans speaking a rich assortment of West African languages—such as Mandinka, Mende, and Gola, among many others—learned English. Many learned some English prior to their shackled voyage from Africa to America through the Middle Passage while still speaking a language from their homeland on the West Coast of Africa. But the specifics of this language shift during the period are full of speculation and mystery, and the description of the early development of African American speech has proven to be an elusive historical, linguistic, and political challenge. Slave traders were hardly thinking about documenting their exploitation of human cargo for the historical and linguistic record, and most references to speech in the early slave trade were connected to its role in moving and marketing human merchandise. Furthermore, literacy for African Americans was illegal for generations, so firsthand accounts are rare and of questionable reliability. The written records run the gamut—from racist caricatures that exaggerate stereotypical differences to those that faithfully attempt to represent spoken language and authentic written accounts by slaves and ex-slaves during and shortly after the antebellum period.

Two major explanations have dominated the debate about the origin and early development of African American English. The "Anglicist Hypothesis," originally set forth by prominent American dialectologists during the mid-twentieth century, argues that African American speech can be traced to the same sources as earlier European American dialects of English—varieties of English brought to North America from the British Isles.[27] The position assumes that slaves speaking different African languages simply learned the regional and social varieties of English spoken by the adjacent contact groups of white speakers. In most cases, this would have been a socially stigmatized variety of English spoken by poor rural whites who were working as indentured servants on the same plantations and farms as the slaves. It further assumes that over the course of a couple of generations, only a few traces of the ancestral African languages remained, following the typical American model of language shift explained in chapter 10. In this model, the first generation remains relatively monolingual in the heritage language, the second generation is bilingual in English and the heritage language, and the third and subsequent generations are monolingual in English.

In the mid-1960s and 1970s, a prominent group of language researchers who studied creole languages in the Caribbean (for example, Jamaican, Barbadian, and Trinidadian Creole) and creoles spoken in West African countries such as Liberia and Sierra Leone claimed that African American English derived from a creole language, leading to the "Creolist Hypothesis."[28]

A creole language is a kind of hybrid language that develops from a contact situation where speakers do not share a common language of communication. Typically, the lexical stock comes from the language of the socially dominant group in the contact situation, so we have English-based (for example, Jamaican Creole, Krio), French-based (Haitian Creole, Antillean Creole, Louisiana Creole), Dutch-based (Negerhollands, Berbice), and Portuguese-based (Papamiento, Saramaccan) creoles, among others. In the initial stage, when there are no native speakers of the language, the grammar is drastically reduced, but when this variety—called a "pidgin" by linguists—becomes the first language of some speakers, the grammar becomes more expansive to the point that it rivals that of any language.[29]

Amid the slave trade, a number of the English-based creoles were developed from trade routes that grew along the coast of West Africa and throughout the African diaspora. The slave trade brought together many different ethnic groups that were, in Africa, not at all homogeneous; in fact, in many cases, former adversaries found themselves united in bondage. These groups began to use shared resources, including English, to communicate out of necessity, leading to a pidgin, or what may also be called a "medium of interethnic communication." Over time, this language variety would develop and become more useful as a tool to be used among the oppressed to resist the power of the oppressors (at least in some ways). Thus what was developed out of necessity emerged as a "medium of ethnic solidarity," erasing what were once radically different ethnicities and giving birth to a new one: African American.

From the beginning, then, it seems that African American English may have had power in its distinctiveness; by being shared by the slaves and not entirely accessible to the white overseers, the language could be used by slaves to communicate in ways that subverted the overt power structures. There is a parallel situation in the way modern slang works as a means of marking a group via shared linguistic vocabulary while actively excluding from that group those who do not know the terms. It might be unsurprising, then, that African American speech is the source of lots of modern slang, including many

To view an excerpt with John Baugh from *Do You Speak American?*, visit http://www.talkintarheel.com/chapter/7/video7-5.php

words that have become so widespread that they can hardly be considered slang anymore, such as "cool" and "hip," or even more youth-restricted terms like "crib" to mean one's home.

Linguists studying creole languages have noted that conditions of slavery were hardly like those of Europeans who came to the continent by choice and blended with other European groups. Instead, the extreme circumstances of caste subordination led to the development of pidgin and creole languages that developed in the African diaspora, extending from West Africa to the Middle Passage in the Caribbean and then to North America. Today, creoles are still spoken in regions that extend from West African countries such as Sierra Leone and Liberia through the Caribbean to the Sea Islands of South Carolina and Georgia, where the creole language Gullah (apparently named for the town Gola in Sierra Leone) or Geechee (from the town Gizi) is still spoken. Under the Creolist Hypothesis, this creole was once more widespread, sprawling throughout the plantations of the American South. This widespread creole was the basis for the development of African American English in the regions away from the isolated Sea Islands where Gullah still exists. Creole researchers have argued that the creole inscription is still detectable in a number of language traits characteristic of vernacular African American English: the absence of the linking verb *be* in sentences like "She nice"; the absence of *-s* suffixes on verbs as in "She go to the store" and possessives such as "the dog mouth"; and distinctive verb particles such as *done* to indicate completed action in "He done went," or the use of *been* to designate distant time as in "She been known him forever." All of these traits are typical of well-known English-based creoles—from Gullah on the Atlantic coast and Jamaican Creole in the Caribbean to Krio (the dominant creole language of Sierra Leone) and Liberian Kreyol. The Creolist Hypothesis naturally stands in stark opposition to the Anglicist Hypothesis; however, there is no reason to suspect that African American English was ever homogenous, and it is possible that in different ecological and social conditions (for example, high concentrations of African slaves in the South Carolina lowlands vs. the relatively lower concentrations of African Americans in the Piedmont plantations), the English of the earliest slaves was markedly different.[30]

Reassessing History

New linguistic and historical information has challenged traditional viewpoints on the origin and early development of African American English. One expanding source of information comes from written texts of ex-slaves, including an extensive set of ex-slave narratives collected by interviewers under the Works Project Administration (WPA) in the 1930s, more recently discovered letters written by semiliterate ex-slaves in the mid-1880s, and other specialized texts—such as court testimony and amanuensis accounts where a scribe attempted to capture the voice of the speaker. In addition to these texts, some archival audio recordings have been uncovered, including a set of tapes recorded by WPA workers in the 1930s and other collections of recordings with ex-slaves.[31]

To hear a passage from an ex-slave narrative (from the Library of Congress), visit http://www.talkintarheel.com/chapter/7/audio7-6.php

A very different source of information comes from the examination of the speech of groups of black expatriates who lived in relative isolation after their exodus from the United States in the 1820s. For example, in the 1820s, a group of blacks migrated from Philadelphia to the peninsula of Samaná in the Dominican Republic, where they were relatively isolated and continued to speak English until recent decades. More than 20,000 African Americans also migrated from the United States to Canada in the early 1800s, and some of their descendants continue

To hear a speaker from Samaná, visit http://www.talkintarheel.com/chapter/7/audio7-7.php

to live in out-of-the-way areas of Nova Scotia. It is assumed that secluded groups will be relatively conservative in their language and thus provide a window into the earlier state of the language.[32] There were also expatriate groups who migrated to Liberia and Sierra Leone in West Africa in the 1820s that may provide information about earlier African American speech.

The initial study of expatriate speech in the Americas revealed similarities to the speech of some earlier European American varieties of English, leading to a new version of the Anglicist Hypothesis. The reincarnated Anglicist position maintained that while earlier African American English was virtually identical to the speech of earlier European American English speakers, African American speech diverged from its earlier alignment with European American speech during the twentieth century, so that contemporary African American speech is now more ethnically marked. Divergence, however, was a product of language evolution rather than the maintenance of earlier differences between African American and European American speech.[33]

The remote situations in North Carolina are comparable in some ways to other expatriate situations, but they also offer an advantage in their long-term continuity. For example, in mainland Hyde County, African Americans and European Americans have coexisted since the early 1700s—a full century before any of the expatriate communities emigrated to Nova Scotia and Samaná.

As we have pointed out, our interviews in Hyde County and enclave Mountain communities cover over a century of time in terms of the age of the participants. In interviewing the oldest white and black speakers, we hoped to get an idea of the earlier dialect used by African Americans and European Americans, since dialects learned during childhood tend to persist throughout life. Comparing younger speakers with older speakers gives us an idea of how the dialects have changed over time because most speakers establish their dialect for life during their adolescence and early adulthood. The selection of speakers of different generations to represent different time periods is called "Apparent Time." While it does not replace following the same speakers chronologically, it is the next best way of getting time depth in a study of a community. Our findings suggest that the speech of older African Americans was substantially influenced by the regional dialect of the area. Recall the great-grandfather from Hyde County whose Outer Banks pronunciations (for example, *high tide* as *hoi toid*) and grammatical structures ("I weren't there" or "She weren't there") led listeners to identify him as white over 90 percent of the time. Likewise, in the mountains, African Americans and European Americans share characteristic regional traits such as the pronunciation of *fire* as *far*, the pronunciation of *white rice* as *whaht rahs*, and the use of the prefix *uh-* in "He was a-huntin' and a-fishin'." This kind of evidence might seem to offer strong support for the Anglicist Hypothesis, but there are some other details that reveal a more subtle relationship. At the same time that details of regional dialect assimilation are revealed, especially for the production of vowels, there are some characteristics that have apparently distinguished whites and African Americans for centuries. For example, the absence of the suffix *-s* in verbs ("She go to the store") and possessive nouns ("man hat"), the absence of the linking verb *be* in "She nice," the loss of the final consonant in *wes' en'* for *west end*, and the pronunciation of the sequence *skr* for *str* in *skreet* for *street* are traceable to remnants of the original contact situation between English and West African languages. These features coexist with the regional vowel traits and some grammatical and lexical components of Outer Banks speech, and listeners will often overlook these features in ethnic identification tasks. As African languages and English collided, there was an obvious assimilation of regional manifestations of English. Regional accommodation was quite transparent, but the imprint of the original impact of language contact was also indelible, though more subtle. This phenomenon is hardly remarkable in a language-contact situation. The English vowels of the earlier Scandinavian settlers in Minnesota and Wisconsin have been embraced and perpetuated, bearing the imprint of their ancestral languages as part of the regional dialect in current-day speech; and in southeastern Pennsylvania, the regional dialect still reflects German-language influence in constructions such as *Are you going with?* for "Are you going with me?" and *It's all* for "It's all gone" long after German ceased to be used regularly in the area. In more segregated circumstances, like those between African American and European American communities, the likelihood of a lingering effect would even be higher.

The revised understanding of the earlier history of African American English, inspired by our conclusions from the remote enclaves of African American communities in North Carolina, suggests that the truth about African American English rests somewhere between the extremes of the Anglicist and Creolist Hypotheses. Earlier African American speech was influenced by the regional speech where speakers were implanted at the same time that it continued to bear the imprints of an unusual contact situation and ethnic division. For the record, this interpretation of history has been labeled the "Substrate Hypothesis" since it maintains that there was a persistent, enduring effect from the original language contact situation, called "substrate," along with regional dialect assimilation in earlier African American speech.[34]

Contemporary African American Speech

We noted that the ethnic perception of the African American speaker born in Hyde County in the 1970s was the opposite of her great-grandfather who was born in 1910—despite the fact that she was born and raised in the same home as her great-grandfather. How can that be? Can language change that drastically over a couple of generations? The story of change in African American speech is a dramatic one, and its modern trajectory of change is every bit as intriguing as its origin and earlier history.

Most linguists agree that the distinctive traits of African American speech are stronger at the beginning of the twenty-first century than they were a hundred years ago. Over the last century, regional traits prominently marking older speakers were exchanged for a more trans- or supraregional English variety that is now culturally centered in the larger metropolitan areas of the United States rather than its rural southern roots. The fact that ethnicity now seems to trump region in African American speech is one of the great stories of modern dialectology. It is not just true in North Carolina; it is happening across the nation. Younger speakers in the outlying region of Hyde County, for example, now tend to reject the regional pronunciation of *hoi toid* and the use of *weren't* for *wasn't*, trading them in for the habitual use of *be* in sentences such as "They be trippin'," the use of *-s* absence in verbs as in "She go there," and the absence of the linking verb in "She nice."[35] This does not mean that African American English does *not* have a regional dimension, because speakers from different areas may certainly be identified by some regional traits, but these have taken a backseat to the ethnic dimension of speech identity. Our studies of communities on the coast of North Carolina show how the distinctive traits of African American English have intensified and the regional traits of the Outer Banks Brogue have diminished in rural Hyde County over the past century. During that period, regional attributes have been subsiding as the ethnically distinctive qualities have intensified, resulting in the divergence of white and black speech. Ironically, the period following the institutional integration of Hyde County schools in the early 1970s paralleled the most dramatic divergence of black and white speech. We typically assume that languages in contact converge, but in this case, they actually diverged. Students may have gone to the same schools, participated in the same activities, and ridden on the same buses, but they clearly maintained different social groups apart from this institutional integration. They continued to hang out in separate groups, go to different churches, and socialize in segregated family groups. The trajectory of divergence suggests that speech became much more marked for ethnicity during this period and that black youth did not want to "sound white."

In the process of becoming associated with ethnic identity during the twentieth century, the cultural center of African American speech was transformed into an urban variety strongly associated with youth culture. Thus, the speech of urban black youth in cities like New York, Philadelphia, Detroit, and Los Angeles shows a core set of structures that make them more alike than they are to the neighboring white varieties of English spoken in these cities. In North Carolina, the speech of urban youth in Raleigh, Durham, Greensboro, and Charlotte share patterns that transcend some of the regional distinctions found throughout the state. The core of grammatical and pronunciation traits noted above are shared in these urban areas. The shared vocabulary of urban slang—from terms for friends (*dude, bro, girl-*

FIGURE 7.6. Patrick Douthit from Winston-Salem, better known as hip-hop producer and artist 9th Wonder, shares a moment with his daughter. (Photograph by Neal Hutcheson)

friend, *homie*) to adjectives and nouns (*stylin'*, *bomb*, *ugly*, *dope*) to describe objects, events, and attributes—is worthy of a book in its own right, though most linguists are more interested in entrenched, systematic grammatical and pronunciation patterns.[36] The traits strongly associated with urban youth are now diffusing to the black youth in rural areas who model urban norms of behavior, including speech.

In the late 1990s, when we were interviewing young African Americans in rural Hyde County, our most animated conversations were about the purported deaths of Tupac Shakur and Biggie Smalls, two iconic rappers who were engaged in an East Coast–West Coast feud during that period. When we talked about the data at conferences, many of our colleagues—who are unconnected to urban culture—didn't even know what we were talking about when we mentioned the controversy about the reported deaths of these hip-hop icons. Speech followed the path of urban culture, as the youth of this community adopted a much more ethnically identifiable dialect association over recent decades. So the youngest Hyde County speaker embraced these features and is identified as African American by outside listeners, though some African American listeners in Boston and New York noted that she sounded "kinda country."[37] That is because there were still a few remnants of the traditional regional speech of Hyde County in her vowels and some other subtly lingering traits in her speech.

There are several reasons for the emergence of African American English as a transregional, ethnically based dialect of English. There was also expanded intersectional mobility of African Americans in the last century that connected speakers from different regions, making it easier for language spread to take place. The connection between rural southern and urban northern African Americans is fluid. People return for homecoming, family reunions, and other events that keep them connected with their heritage in the South, and some move back South. At the same time, the pattern of persistent, de facto segregation has actually intensified the density of African American populations in many urban centers of the North and South, and the informal social networks of most African Americans remain highly segregated, making these urban communities a fertile social environment for developing a distinct ethnic variety.[38] African Americans and European Americans may go to school and work together but, for the most part, they still party, worship, and mourn separately.

Population demographics, however, are not the only story. Over the past half century, there has been a growing sense of ethnic identity connected with African American English, supported by a variety of social mechanisms that range from community-based social networks to stereotypical media projections of African American speech. In the process, regional dialects and standardized English have become associated with white speech. The development of an "oppositional identity," in which behavior associated with white norms is avoided, has become an important part of the ethnic divide.

Dialect and Identity

The differentiation of white and black cultural behavior has taken on increased significance in recent decades, and "acting white" and "acting black" now seem to be solidified cultural constructs in our society. Comedic parodies of the "other" ethnic group are common—for example, by black comedians going back to Flip Wilson in the 1970s and Richard Pryor in the 1980s—so black and Latino comedians have parodied "white behavior" as an oppositional culture, and white comedians such as Robin Williams have parodied black culture. Part of the caricature always involves the use of dialect, underscoring the significance of notions such as "talking white" and "talking black." As one Internet post on the Sistahs University website noted about black college students: "Trust me, at some point of your collegiate career someone is going to tell you that you 'sound white.' When—not if—but when someone tells you that you sound white, it may very well be a compliment that means, 'You're a very bright, intelligent person'; OR, it may be a shot at you that means 'You're a sell-out, and you've forgotten where you came from.'"[39]

A study conducted in an inner-city high school in Washington, D.C., in which the students were asked to list some of the attributes of "acting white" found, not surprisingly, the top characteristic associated with acting white was "talking white."[40] There is no stronger association with black and white cultural behavior than speech. As one of our interviewees from Durham noted: "I think it's one of the many markers that people use to decide whether you are part of the in-group or out-group."[41] We have now heard countless stories of people who did not sound like others thought they should in terms of their ethnicity and were ridiculed because of it. One African American high school girl in an urban school reported that she stopped speaking in class because every time she spoke she was mocked for "talking white." In a National Public Radio interview with a prominent black comedian who was raised by a white family, the comedian was asked if he had been made fun of for sounding white while growing up. His response: "Every day!" These common occurrences highlight the significance of language in terms of ethnic identity, particularly for young people who are subject to peer pressure. It also has implications for teaching standardized English as a skill and helps us understand why some students can be resistant to learning standardized English at certain stages in their lives. Learning standardized English is more than an academic skill; for better or worse, it is also adopting an identity.

In one study conducted with the Frank Porter Graham Child Development Institute in Chapel Hill, we tracked the first twenty years in the lives of seventy African American youths who grew up in the Piedmont.[42] They entered the study when they were between six months and one year old, and speech samples were collected at yearly or biannual intervals throughout their schooling. Interviews were even conducted after they finished high school to see how their language continued to change throughout their lifespan. We had access to extensive information about family background and school performance, and we interviewed them with their mothers as well as their peers in middle school and secondary school to get a full range of information about the social and educational contexts that might affect speech. This unique longitudinal study has given us exceptional insight into how language has played a role in their family, education, social life, and personal development. Some of the findings confirmed common-sense hunches, such as the important role of caretaker speech in early language and the role of peers in later speech. We used a specially developed scale called a "Dialect Density Measure" to measure speakers' use of vernacular African American English traits, coding the number of core features of African American speech and then counting how many features occurred per each sentence or utterance.[43] Part of our goal was to determine how their vernacular dialect changed over the course of their school life. Though there has been a lot of speculation about when the use of vernacular dialect is most and least extensive, there was previously no study that actually followed the same individuals for the first twenty years of their lives.

We found a couple of prominent trajectories of vernacular dialect use from the age of four through their post-secondary school life. Twenty of the thirty-two speakers in this sample followed the pattern that we refer to as the "roller-coaster pattern." That is, they came to school using a moderate level of core vernacular features. During the first few years in school, when teachers are a primary language model, the level of dialect features receded, and then there was a dramatic upturn during the middle-school years, when children generally orient toward their peers' speech for models. Another decrease in vernacular use occurred in high school.

The results of this study demonstrate that schools, with their emphasis on standardized English, have an apparent effect on speech during the early grades, then peer influence seems to take over during middle school. In secondary school, students may adjust their dialect based on the adult life choices that young people make, including post-secondary education and career paths. These paths of African American English use reveal that it is not just a matter of education into standardized English that determines the use of vernacular dialect but how people situate themselves ethnically and the social group with which they identify.

It might seem ironic that standardized English would be associated with "white speech," but it signifies the symbolic role that dialect has assumed as part of the African American experience. It is also an indication of an enduring cultural clash between dominant mainstream institutions and people of color in American society. Language is one of the strongest indicators of the past and present voice of African American culture, but it is rarely celebrated because of the strength of overt, mainstream institutional values.

Admittedly, it is a complicated struggle of identity, as Richard Brown describes in the quote at the opening of this chapter: "[T]here's an internal struggle about, should you really do that? Should you really be trying to talk like white folk? Or should you always, all the time, no matter what setting you are in, speak the same way, speak the same way your momma taught you to speak?"[44]

The Legacy of 8
American Indian Languages

They did speak in Cherokee mostly all of 'em way back when I was growing up. They wasn't too many people that speak in English, just a few of 'em, and you go to the home, they'd all speak in Cherokee. Everywhere you went. And now, you can't go nowheres and they'd say, "I don't know how to speak it." —MANDY SWIMMER, Eastern Band of the Cherokee, quoted in *Voices of North Carolina*, produced by Neal Hutcheson (Raleigh: North Carolina Language and Life Project, 2005)

From Hatteras and across the Pamlico Sound, up the Neuse River, past the Sauratown Mountains, and all the way to Cherokee County, American Indians have left imprints of their ancestry on the place names of North Carolina. The remnant reminders capture a fleeting glimpse of the linguistic and cultural diversity that existed in North Carolina before the arrival of Europeans who brought their own notions about and names for

To view the video of the quote above, visit http://www.talkintarheel.com/chapter/8/video8-1.php

the land. The intertwining of American Indian and European names seems appropriate, however, when one considers just how connected the groups have been since the arrival of European explorers and settlers. American Indians at times have welcomed the European explorers, guided them, taught them, and even saved them from starvation. They fought alongside the British against the French and alongside the French against the British. They fought on both sides of the American Revolutionary War and the Civil War. At the same time, American Indians suffered greatly at the hands of their sometime allies, with many tribes even suffering extinction. The tribes who survived often did so barely, with many groups losing more than 80 percent of their population to diseases such as smallpox, measles, typhoid, and tuberculosis.[1] In some cases, the remnants of once-independent groups merged in order to survive, and American Indian populations moved voluntarily and involuntarily throughout the known historical periods, making it difficult to recount their histories.

The language history of the American Indian in North Carolina is even more elusive than in other parts of the country thanks to their relatively early encounters with Europeans in this region. In 1929 linguist and anthropologist Dr. Edward Sapir described the incredible diversity of American Indian languages: "Few people realize that within the confines of the United States there is spoken today [in 1929] a far greater variety of languages . . . than in the whole of Europe. We may go further. We may say, quite literally and safely, that in the state of California alone there are greater and more numerous linguistic extremes than can be illustrated in all the length and breadth of Europe."[2] It is estimated that there were around 400 distinct native North American languages at the time of the European arrival.[3] Nearly half of these languages are now extinct, and about 70 percent of the remaining languages have few if any younger speakers.[4] Less than 0.1 percent of North Carolina's population speak a language native to North Carolina, and the majority of that small group are Cherokee.[5] Even among those enrolled in the Eastern Band of Cherokee, fewer than 10 percent speak the language with moderate proficiency, and a much smaller percentage speak it fluently. Current estimates of fluent Cherokee speakers from tribal members range from 200 to 300.

Countering the dire predictions is an unprecedented interest in preserving American Indian languages. Around the country—including in the mountains of North Carolina—there are concentrated efforts to bridge the generation gap so that American Indian languages do not die with the passing of the current elders. In addition to preserving currently spoken but endangered languages, another remarkable trend is occurring: some tribal groups are attempting to revive previously dead languages (languages with no speakers). Such rejuvenation projects are truly remarkable to linguists. Linguist Dr. Osborn Bergin observed in 1969 that "no language has ever been revived, and no language will ever be revived."[6] He may not be wrong, but there is knowledge, pedagogy, and deep investment by some tribes in reviving certain languages. Given the connection between language and culture, it may be possible that a dead language could in fact be revived and become an important part of the daily lives of people, especially in an enclave setting.

To view the trailer for the documentary We Still Live Here, visit http://www.talkintarheel .com/chapter/8/video8-2.php

What's in a Name?

Every label for race or ethnicity is fraught with complicated connotations. Those outside the group being named often feel uneasy as they search for the best—or at least the safest or most "politically correct"—term to use to describe members of a group. The fact is, based on the roles of race and ethnicity in societies, there simply are no "neutral" labels. Labels tend to be reductively simple, whereas ethnicities are varied and complex. Beyond this is a host of other problems related to etymology, connotation, and traditions of past usage. For the groups discussed in this chapter, many options for names are problematic—or overtly offensive. At various times, the following labels have all been used to refer to the same groups: "Indians," "Injuns," "Redskins," "Redmen," "American Indians," "Native Americans," "Native American Indians," "First Nations," "Indigenous Peoples," "Aboriginals," "Aborigines," and "Amerindians."

The etymologies of the most common terms hint at the various problems associated with each label. The term "Indian" draws on a geographical mistake in which these groups were once thought to inhabit part of Asia. This term was used in Europe to describe those from India for more than 200 years before Columbus's voyages, but the geographical mix-up remains encoded in the name of the Caribbean area explored by Columbus, now referred to as the West Indies.[7] A second explanation for the origin of the name "Indian" claims that it derives from the pronunciation of a Spanish phrase erroneously attributed to Columbus. The legend goes that when Columbus encountered the native populations, he wrote of them in his journal: "una gente in Dios" ("these are people of God").[8] The final part of the phrase, "in Dios," then merged to form "Indian." David Wilton, in his book *Word Myths: Debunking Linguistic Urban Legends*, reports the phrase does not exist in any of Columbus's writings.[9]

"Native" brings a different set of connotations—and problems. In the literature of colonization, the term "native" is commonly synonymous with such terms as "primitive," "savage," and "non-Christian," all of which assume a Eurocentric notion of normalcy. It also has implications about the power inequality between colonizer and colonized and is fraught with problematic assumptions interpreting cultural difference as cultural deficiency. While history sometimes recounts westernization as improving the lives of native groups, it must also be contextualized and evaluated in light of the decimation of the native populations—between 88 and 97 percent for the groups between Louisiana and North Carolina from 1685 to 1790.[10]

"America" is the Anglicized form of the name of Italian explorer and cartographer Amerigo Vespucci, who explored the coast of what is now South America in 1501. Thus, names that include "America" are honoring a European and European power instead of recognizing and celebrating the indigenous cultures. There is also a question of geography, as many American Indian groups do not feel connected to other indigenous groups of the Americas, including those in South America and Alaska. To differentiate indigenous populations in the two Americas, some academics have employed the somewhat cumbersome terms "North American Indian" and "South American Indian."[11]

So what about "Native American" or "American Indian" as labels? The *Oxford English Dictionary* (OED) offers this note on the choice between these most common options: "The term *American Indian* has been steadily replaced, esp. in official contexts, by the more recent term *Native American*. The latter is preferred by some as being a more accurate description (the word *Indian* recalling Columbus's assumption that, on reaching America, he had reached the east coast of India). *American Indian* is still widespread in general use, however, partly because it is not normally regarded as offensive by American Indians themselves." Despite the OED's preference for the term "Native American," it combines two problematic words. Furthermore, the noncapitalized "native American" dates to the seventeenth century, during which the term is used both for reference to indigenous populations and reference to those of European heritage who were born in the area that would become the United States. Perhaps more troublesome than the etymology of each word is the fact that the label itself was a creation of the federal government for grouping together populations that would not reflect the divisions made by the indigenous populations. The capitalized, fused version "Native American" became prominent during the Civil Rights Movement and eventually replaced "Indian" in many governmental usages. It has been used by the federal government to describe the indigenous populations of the forty-eight contiguous states, Alaska, and, sometimes even Hawai'i and Samoa.[12]

Though the term "Native American" has been seen as the preferred (or at least "safest") term, it has not been the preferred term of the groups it describes. "Indian," even with its obvious geographical misnomer, seems to be the more familiar term, and "American Indian" or "North American Indian" offers some sense of understanding of the variation that exists within the population. Sir Walter Raleigh was one of the first English authors to adopt the term "Indian," which he used for indigenous populations from what is now the United States and from the Caribbean.[13] It is a term that American Indian groups have been familiar with and have used for centuries and tends to be restricted to groups from the contiguous states.

The controversy over these labels gathered steam with the founding of the American Indian Movement in 1968. A delegation from this group met in Geneva, Switzerland, in 1977 and unanimously voted the term "American Indian" as the preferred term for self-identification. Among this group was the well-known Oglala Sioux activist Russell Means, who in 1998 wrote a treatise on the terms titled "I am an American Indian, not a Native American." In it, he writes: "I abhor the term Native American. It is a generic government term used to describe all the indigenous prisoners of the United States. These are the American Samoans, the Micronesians, the Aleuts, the original Hawaiians, and the erroneously termed Eskimos, who are actually Upiks and Inupiats. And, of course, the American Indian." In no uncertain terms, Means states his preference for a label, embracing its political implications: "I prefer the term American Indian because I know its origins. . . . As an added distinction the American Indian is the only ethnic group in the United States with the American before our ethnicity. . . . We were enslaved as American Indians, we were colonized as American Indians, and we will gain our freedom as American Indians, and then we will call ourselves any damn thing we choose."

Means's opinion on the name mirrors that of the plurality of American Indians, though of course there is no consensus. The U.S. Census Bureau conducted a survey of indigenous groups in 1995, to which just under 50 percent of respondents claimed they preferred the term "Indian," compared to 37 percent who preferred "Native American" (the remaining chose "some other name" or "no preference").[14] Many U.S. academics seem to prefer the term "Native American," and Canadian scholars favor "First Nations." We sometimes get disapproving looks when we use the term "American Indian" at academic presentations, but our considered opinion is that folks ought to choose what they want to be called and that scholars should respectfully follow their lead.

Modern Cherokee artist and activist Christina Berry offers this advice on her website, "All Things Cherokee."[15] We take this to heart with respect to the selection of labels in this book:

FIGURE 8.1. Russell Means, activist and leader of the American Indian Movement. (Courtesy of the *Rapid City Journal*)

In the end, the term you choose to use (as an Indian or non-Indian) is your own personal choice. Very few Indians that I know care either way. . . . [W]henever possible an Indian would prefer to be called a Cherokee or a Lakota or whichever tribe they belong to. This shows respect because not only are you sensitive to the fact that the terms Indian, American Indian, and Native American are an oversimplification of a diverse ethnicity, but you also show that you listened when they told what tribe they belonged to.

When you don't know the specific tribe simply use the term which you are most comfortable using. The worst that can happen is that someone might correct you and open the door for a thoughtful debate on the subject of political correctness and its impact on ethnic identity. What matters in the long run is not which term is used but the intention with which it is used.

In this book, we have conformed to the wishes of the American Indian Movement over recommendations from the federal government and the OED and employ the term "American Indian" with the understanding that it is imperfect and imprecise. Whenever possible, following the suggestion of Berry and others, we use the tribal names for the groups we reference.

Other Labels and Characterizations

Given the prominence—and controversy—of a few other labels (for example, "Redskin") and related usages (such as "Injun"), we consider briefly these uses. The pronunciation of "Indian" as "Injun" is a result of two common phonetic processes in English; it is also more pronounced in the English dialects that have settled the Appalachian Mountains. In standard pronunciation, the d in *Indian* is followed be a high front vowel *ee* sound. When d and other consonant sounds produced at the ridge after the teeth (t, s, z) are followed by the vowel *ee* or *y*, there is a tendency to change the place of articulation closer to the position of the vowel. This process—called *palatalization* because the consonant moves closer to the palatal position of the vowel—is common in English and many other languages of the world. For example, "recite" becomes *recitat(sh)ion* and "divide" becomes *divis(zh)ion*, triggered by the following *ee* of *-ion*. Informal speech productions of "got you" as *gotcha* or "what you" as *whatcha* are also examples of this natural process at work. In some areas of Ireland today, the country "India" is referred to as "Injia." The second process at work in changing *Indian* to *Injun* reduces the pronunciation from three syllables to two. In English dialects, it is common to drop syllables that receive little stress, so most Americans pronounce *family* not as "fam-uh-ly" but as "fam-ly." So, the pronunciation "Injun" probably arose organically and without any phonetic malice.

"Injun" is first recorded in writing with that spelling in 1812 by a colonel recounting his encounters with people from Tennessee.[16] The pronunciation is perhaps most strongly tied to the writings of Mark Twain, who used it first in his 1872 work *Roughing It*, in which he writes: "'Heap' is 'Injun-English' for 'very much.'" More famously, Injun Joe appears as the main antagonist of *The Adventure of Tom Sawyer* (1876). Because Injun Joe is the villain of the novel, it is possible that Twain was instrumental in the term eventually becoming not just a regional pronunciation but a pronunciation that is stigmatized and derogatory. There is now a strong stigma attached to the use of the term, and usage guides caution against using the pronunciation. Its use remains questionable in the compound form "Honest Injun," which is used to mean something like "I swear" or "I promise." Ironically, the first written attestation of this usage comes from *The Adventures of Tom Sawyer*, the same work that may have started the stigmatization of the term in the first place. When Ben asks Tom to let him whitewash a little of the fence, Tom replies: "Ben, I'd like to, honest injun; but Aunt Polly." The phrase jumped the pond and eventually showed up in the writings of Irish writers George Bernard Shaw and James Joyce (in *Ulysses*).[17] It seems that the negative connotations arose in the mid-twentieth century and likely stem from its use in Western movies that depicted the American Indians in a negative light.

Like "Injun," the term "Redskin" has relatively innocent origins. The etymology of compounding two English words is transparent. However, it is not clear that it was entirely an English invention. In the writings of various explorers, there are transcriptions in American Indian languages of individuals using the term to describe themselves: "I am a person with red skin" or "I have red skin."[18] Similar descriptions appear in the writings of French trappers, suggesting it was a relatively widespread descriptive label used in the eighteenth century along with such related terms as "Redman" and "red people." In dictionaries today, all of these terms carry labels such as "offensive," "slang," and "disparaging." When did these terms become so socially stigmatized? A court case filed in 1992 seeking to compel the National Football League's Washington Redskins to change their name claimed that at the time the team name was trademarked in 1967, the term was "a pejorative, derogatory, denigrating, offensive, scandalous, contemptuous, disreputable, disparaging and racist designation for a Native American person."[19] Though the initial ruling was in favor of the plaintiffs, the case was resolved in 2005, allowing the team to continue using the name not because the term was not offensive in 1967 but because the claim was not filed until so much later.[20] In a sense, the court suggested that if the term were as negative as the case claimed, it would have been challenged much earlier. While this decision certainly does not pinpoint when "Redskin" became offensive, the historical and literary records seem to suggest that, like "Injun," the negative connotations are largely a product of the twentieth century. Yet, despite the near universal recognition of the taboo nature of the term to refer to American Indians, a 2004 poll conducted by *Sports Illustrated* found that 90 percent of American Indians deemed the usage to be acceptable when restricted to the team name.[21]

Other sports teams have also had their mascots or nicknames challenged. At the professional level, relatively few changes have occurred, as is apparent by the continued use of the names/mascots of the Washington Redskins, the Kansas City Chiefs, the Cleveland Indians, the Atlanta Braves, and others. Teams such as the Golden State Warriors and the Chicago Blackhawks have dropped or modified their Indian iconography; for example, the Blackhawks still use an American Indian profile on their jerseys but now use a hawk as the actual mascot.[22]

In 2005 the National Collegiate Athletic Association (NCAA) banned the use of American Indian mascots in sanctioned events (the only place they could enforce the ban).[23] Since then, a number of universities have changed their mascots, though there are a few notable holdouts. In North Carolina, the University of North Carolina at Pembroke successfully petitioned the NCAA to allow it to continue to use its mascot and the nickname "Braves," citing support from the Lumbee tribe and its historical roots as an Indian Normal School.[24] The University of Illinois ("Fighting Illini") and Florida State University ("Seminoles") have made similar claims with backing of local American Indian groups and have been allowed to continue to use their names. Ironically, Florida State University once considered adopting the nickname "Crackers"; one can only wonder how southern white folks would have responded to that.[25] The Oklahoma branch of the Seminole tribe remains opposed to Florida State's continued usage of "Chief Max Osceola" as well as the practice of naming a homecoming chief and princess.

The American Indian community is split on the issue of team names and mascots. Some suggest that the mascots draw attention to positive attributes of the culture in the same way that Fighting Irish, Vikings, Spartans, or Musketeers do for other groups. Others equate the war paint to blackface. The issue has deep cultural, historical, and linguistic implications. The controversy is not limited to sporting events. In 2012 Victoria's Secret received a brief flurry of negative press when one of their models was dressed in a war bonnet, a garment traditionally worn only by males.[26] Ironically, this story broke only weeks before elementary schoolchildren were dressed up as pilgrims and American Indians for school Thanksgiving feasts, a holiday remembered quite differently by representative groups. Perhaps more than anything, these examples highlight the ongoing struggle over cultural self-definition versus imposing European notions of civilization that align metaphorically with historical struggles over land, freedom, and basic human rights. In this regard, the commonly remembered history is as sanitized as the grinning image of the Cleveland Indians' Chief Wahoo. Yet an insensitive or inaccurate portrayal may "open the door for a thoughtful debate."

American Indian Demographics Past and Present

Estimates of the number of American Indians in North America at the time of the European arrival range from 2.1 million to 18 million.[27] Using even the most conservative estimates, the population of American Indians in 1890, the first year for which there is somewhat reliable census data for such an analysis, was 12 percent the size that it was before the arrival of Europeans. Disease was probably the greatest reason for the depopulation, but federalized efforts that included wars and removals also played roles. From 1900—the nadir of the population according to U.S. Census data—until about 1960, the identified American Indian population grew steadily but slowly to about 524,000. Starting in the 1960s, the population of identified American Indians grew quickly, so that in 2010, there were 5.2 million self-identified "Native Americans" according to the U.S. Census.

The Status of American Indians Today

Perhaps no group has been more consistently stereotyped than American Indians, thanks in part to the media. American Indians tend to be portrayed through a small set of iconic artifacts and behavioral traits, including teepees, headdresses, dancing, chanting, and papooses. Many of these images stem from Plains Indians tribes and are not accurate for other American Indian cultures, but that does not seem to stop the media. In every medium, American Indians have been cast to look the same, dress the same, act the same, and even to speak the same.

To view Tony "Iron Eyes" Cody in the *Keep America Beautiful* public service announcement, visit http://www.talkintarheel .com/chapter/8/video8-3.php

One of the more famous American Indian icons of the silver screen was Tony "Iron Eyes" Cody, who claimed Cherokee-Cree ancestry and played an American Indian in over 200 films.[28] He may be best known as the "crying Indian" in the 1970s "Keep America Beautiful" television public-service announcement in which litter is thrown from a car and lands at Cody's feet, which causes a tear to fall from his stoic face. Shockingly, in 1996 Cody, at the age of ninety-two, was revealed to have been born Espera Oscar de Corti, the son of Italian immigrants. Despite having no American Indian ancestry, Cody lived as an American Indian and was even honored by Hollywood's American Indian community in 1995. While Cody's story is remarkable in its own right, it sadly illustrates the monolithic view many Americans have of American Indian culture.

FIGURE 8.2. Powwows emphasize traditional icons of dress, dance, and chanting. (Photograph by David Oxendine)

In many ways, Americans tend to romanticize American Indians, evoking such adjectives as noble, wise, spiritual, peaceful, and so forth. So alluring is this connection to pre-European authenticity that many Americans have eagerly claimed American Indian heritage even in the face of dubious evidence. The recent controversy surrounding the revelation that Elizabeth Warren—today a U.S. senator from Massachusetts—had claimed to be one-thirty-second American Indian on everything from her law school application to her professional applications highlights just how eager Americans are to claim a connection to the pre-European inhabitants of the land.[29] Singer and actress Dolly Parton offers another example, claiming to be one-eighth Cherokee in her authorized biography.[30] It was embarrassing when her sister-in-law, Dorris Parton, later traced the family genealogical history and could not find any connection to the Cherokee.[31] Many celebrities have claimed Cherokee ancestry, including Kevin Costner, Johnny Depp, James Earl Jones, Chuck Norris, Cameron Diaz, Jimi Hendrix, and Della Reese. None of these celebrities, however, is enrolled in any Cherokee tribe.

Between the 1990 and 2000 censuses, the number of people self-identifying "Native American" more than doubled, according to the U.S. Census. This growth occurred almost exclusively because respondents were allowed for the first time to check multiple "race" boxes on the census forms. On the 2010 census, 1.7 percent of the population self-identified as completely (0.9 percent) or partially "Native American," the label used in the census question. Yet reporting on a census form typically requires a level of proof beyond that required for retelling family lore. Less than half of those who self-identify as American Indian are registered on a tribal role in the United States (about 2 million people, or 0.7 percent of the population, are enrolled).[32] Various large-scale DNA studies have suggested that somewhere around 4 to 5 percent of the population has some identifiable American Indian ancestry. Scientists from Cornell University, the location of one of the leading projects, report that the vast majority of Americans who expect to confirm their believed American Indian DNA are disappointed.[33] This phenomenon is so common that it has been nicknamed the "Cherokee Grandmother Syndrome." Sociologists use a more academic term—"ethnic shopping"—which is probably equally amusing to nonsociologists.

What is the source of this deep desire among Americans to find a connection to American Indian culture? And what is actually required for a genetic connection to be recognized by a tribal council? While the United States maintains a version of the "one drop rule" for African American identification, Indian tribes set different heritage levels for admittance onto tribal roles, from five-eighths (more than one full-blooded parent) to one-thirty-second (one great-great-great-grandparent), while other groups allow registration for any direct descendent of an enrolled member. The Eastern Band of the Cherokee requires one-sixteenth (one great-great-grandparent), while the Cherokee Nation in Oklahoma follows the any-direct-descendant criterion. While blood quantum measures are now the purview of American Indians, the history of this practice began with Ulysses S. Grant, who shifted the federal government's policy from elimination via genocide to elimination via breeding.[34] Early in the reservation era, the federal government offered benefit incentives for groups that became "less Indian" by marrying whites. Even before this policy, the acceptance of the white populations by some American Indian groups had already resulted in a dilution of cultural purity. John Ross, the leader of the Cherokee Nation in the 1838–39 Trail of Tears removal, was often said to be seven-eighths Scottish.[35]

Amid ethnic shopping and the American romanticization of American Indian culture, many American Indian groups are struggling with their own identities in the modern world. The iconic imagery of the Plains Indian has so defined Americans' views of American Indians that many coastal Indian groups have started to adopt Plains traditions to meet the expectations of those seeking iconic images of Indians—most notably, tourists. In no way is this identity struggle more keenly apparent than in language. American Indian groups across the nation are rushing desperately to attempt to revitalize languages that are on the verge of becoming extinct. Bo Parris, an "honorary" Eastern Band of the Cherokee member who moved to the tribe when he was a teenager, describes his fear of extinction of the Cherokee language: "Every time someone that spoke Cherokee dies— there's been quite a few, more and more, as they get older— makes me feel kindly bad. So now, we use it some here, not like we did. We only have one preacher that could preach Cherokee without any English, only one left. We had two and one died a few months ago."[36]

To view the video of this quote, visit http://www.talkintarheel .com/chapter/8/video8-4.php

The transition to English was due in part to the educational mandates that the federal government imposed on American Indians, which included such measures as cutting hair, renaming children with English names, and punishing students for speaking Cherokee in school. Sarah Margaret Sneed, a member of the Eastern Band of the Cherokee Indians in North Carolina, writing about her interviews with elders from the communities, discovered that the "English-only" policy was sometimes enforced as strictly in the home as it was in the schools.[37] The elders she interviewed who attended the Cherokee Boarding School in the early twentieth century recalled some incidents of children being punished at school for speaking Cherokee, but the real threat to the language came from the school-instilled sense of shame the Cherokee felt for speaking their language. Sneed's parents, who had attended the school in the 1920s, refused to teach her or her siblings any of the Cherokee language. They further refused to justify their decision aside from claiming that knowing the language would lead to trouble. Thus the threat to the language moved from forces external to the community to those within the community: most of the intervening two generations of Cherokee would not be exposed to the language in the home. Elderly Eastern Band of Cherokee Indian member Mandy Swimmer, in the opening epigraph to this chapter, described the onslaught of English as relatively recent and extremely quick.

To view an excerpt about the Cherokee boarding-school rules, visit http:// www.talkintarheel.com/ chapter/8/video8-5.php

Alfred Welch, a North Carolina Cherokee, recalled how he struggled to maintain Cherokee with his own children: "My youngest one, all he knew when he first talked was Cherokee, and he picked up English from these other kids, before he even started school."[38] More will be said about the

FIGURE 8.3. Cherokee speaker Mandy Swimmer of Qualla Boundary
with her grandson. (Photograph by Neal Hutcheson)

Cherokee revitalization program later in this chapter, but this discussion
highlights the stark difference between the reality of the American Indian
situation and the perception of it by outsiders.

Gary Carden, a white artist and storyteller from the Appalachian Mountains of North Carolina who has lived near the Eastern Cherokee, recounts
some of his experience with cultural impostors and how readily the public
accepts them:

> There's an awful lot of fake Cherokees, now, guys making a good living
> pretending to be Cherokees and that are really extroverted or sorta show
> people. You can usually identify a fake Cherokee by his name. You know,
> if it's a beautiful name, "Floating Eagle Feather," you know, "Snow Bear,"
> you know, beware, beware, beware. Because the Cherokee names, there
> are some colorful ones, but what you hear more often is "Tooni," "Crow,"
> "Big Meat," "Smoker," "Stomper," "Swimmer"—it doesn't, don't have
> the drama that people like in a colorful name, "Princess Pale Moon,"
> oh look out! [laughs]. Course there's a genuine effort in Cherokee to
> give you the true Cherokees, but lots of times tourists aren't interested
> in that, they want bloody tomahawks and scalping and they want what
> they're accustomed to off the TV, they wanna see Deer Slayer, right there

on main street, you know, and if you tell 'em the Cherokees were sophisticated and agrarian, they raised cotton, uh they had their own alphabet,
syllabary, and their own newspaper back in the 1820s, uh they get bored,
that's not really what they want. That's not the image they want.[39]

It is this oversimplified vision of American Indians that has
allowed non–American Indians such as those described by
Carden, as well as someone like Iron Eyes Cody, to appropriate
the culture relatively easily. Despite the monolithic views and
To view the video of this quote,
portrayals of American Indian culture and language, it is worth
visit http://www.talkintarheel
noting that American Indian languages are more diverse—in
.com/chapter/8/video8-6.php
terms of language families and dialects—than the sum of all nonindigenous
languages currently spoken in the United States. The real allure of culture is
in its diversity, and the linguistic diversity of American Indian groups offers
one way of learning about the American Indian heritage of North Carolina.

As we have noted, the most enduring linguistic imprint of American Indians in the United States is in place names. Over half of the states in the nation have names that derive from American Indian words, as do at least ten
North Carolina counties, including a few named after major American Indian
groups of the area, such as the Cherokee, the Catawba, the Chowan, and the
Pamlico. Other contributions from American Indian languages now used in
English describe some of the many things that were foreign to the European
explorers, including, but not limited to *tobacco, tomato, maize, hominy, chili, succotash, raccoon, chipmunk, coyote,* and *canoe*.[40] While these borrowings into English are noteworthy, focusing solely on these contributions minimizes the
importance of the American Indian cultures and the languages that existed
and still exist in the United States and, in particular, North Carolina.

Earlier American Indian Languages

Three major groups of Woodland Indians—Siouan, Iroquoian, and Algonquian—inhabited most of what would become North Carolina. A fourth
group, the Muskogean, were a Mississippian group who occupied a small
slice of the southwestern part of the state concurrently with the Woodland
groups. These groups can be seen on Maps 8.1 and 8.2. Major language
families are given in Map 8.1 and specific languages in Map 8.2.

Language families are made up of distinct languages that are, in turn,
made up of various dialects. Each of the four language families of Ameri-

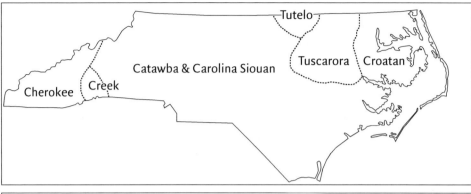

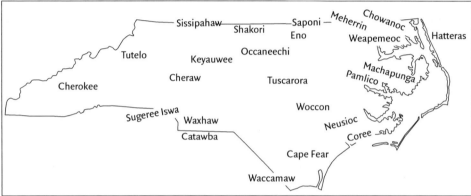

(top) MAP 8.1. Historical Distribution of American Indian Language Families
in North Carolina; (bottom) MAP 8.2. Historical Distribution of American Indian
Languages in North Carolina

can Indians in North Carolina consisted of multiple tribes operating independently of each other despite linguistic and historical connections. Thus,
when Thomas Harriot wrote in 1595 that "the language of every government
is different from any other, and the further they are distant the greater is
the difference," he was probably describing the different language varieties
used by groups of the Pamlico or Croatan Indians, who were members of
the Algonquian language family.[41] A modern analogy helps illustrate the notion of "language family," "language," and "dialect:" the languages French,
Spanish, Italian, and Portuguese, as well as others, belong to the Romance
language family, meaning they all derived from a common source—in this
case, Latin. Each language within the language family might then have different dialects spoken by particular groups. What Harriot was describing
would be both different languages and different dialects within languages.

In the eastern part of the state, the Algonquian language family was prominent. It stretched northward from North Carolina to northern Canada and dipped into what is now the Midwest. The local language group, commonly known as Carolina Algonquian, included speakers of the Croatan or Pamlico languages as well as the Powhatan language that may at one point have spilled over into North Carolina from Tidewater Virginia. These would have been the first American Indians encountered by Sir Walter Raleigh's expeditions and the language of Manteo and Wanchese—the two American Indians who were brought to England after the 1584 expedition. Other groups of Algonquian Indians have been identified by various names, many of which should sound familiar to North Carolinians: Hatteras, Roanoke, Cape Fear, Coree (the basis for "Core Sound"), Chowanoke, and Mattamuskeet/Machapunga. Perhaps because of the early encounters and the study of the language of Manteo and Wanchese, the Algonquian languages have had a number of words preserved in modern English, including *moccasin, moose, opossum, papoose, pecan, raccoon, skunk, squash, squaw,* and *wigwam.*

The grammar of Algonquian languages was very unlike English and not at all like the stereotypical portrayal of American Indian language in twentieth-century media. Instead of using multiple words to mark grammatical distinctions, Algonquian languages tended to rely on a system rich with prefixes and suffixes. Complex thoughts and English sentences could be expressed by what English might describe as a single word. A single example illustrates the vast difference between English and Algonquian languages. The sentence nikîkakwêwâpamikawin êmêkwânîmihitoyân translates into English as "I tried to be seen while dancing." The pieces of words and grammar fit together as follows (dashes are used to separate individual units of meaning):

ni—kî—   kakwê—wâpam—ikawi—   n—   ê—   mêkwâ—
nîmihito—yân

I—past tense—try   —see   —I action—   speech act—
complementizer (*that, which*)—   while—   dance—   I

Today, only three of the eighteen known eastern Algonquian languages still exist, and two are in severe danger of extinction; one has fewer than 500 speakers and the other has seven.[42] Given their location on the East Coast, these Algonquian groups suffered heavily from diseases brought by Euro-

To view an excerpt of spoken Algonquian (from *We Still Live Here*), visit http://www.talkintarheel.com/chapter/8/video8-7.php

pean explorers and settlers. They also would have had earlier and more opportunity to assimilate into the newly arriving European communities before hostility between the groups escalated.

The Coharie are a state-recognized tribe with a little more than 2,500 registered members located mostly along the Little Coharie River in Harnett and Sampson Counties in southeastern North Carolina.[43] The Coharie speak English, having lost their native language early on. Given their historical proximity to other American Indian groups, it is thought that the modern Coharie are composed of American Indians from a number of tribes, including the Algonquian Coree, the Iroquoian Tuscarora, and the Siouan Waccamaw. In this region of the state where the Europeans arrived first, many groups suffered severely from European diseases, leading previously diverse groups to band together for survival. In fact, this is one of the speculations about the Lumbee that we discuss in chapter 9.

THE TUSCARORA

To the west of the Carolina Algonquian groups were the Tuscarora, who spoke an Iroquoian language. The Iroquoian languages historically were concentrated around the St. Lawrence Seaway, Lake Ontario, and Lake Erie and stretched southward along an inland trail to North Carolina and the areas surrounding the present-day towns of Goldsboro, Kinston, and Smithfield. Tuscarora is still spoken by about a dozen speakers on each side of Niagara Falls. At the Tuscarora Elementary School in Lewiston, New York, students are taught the language from preschool through sixth grade; however, despite formalized revitalization efforts, the language remains critically endangered.[44]

Unlike many of the other American Indian groups, the Tuscarora left North Carolina on their own terms. The Five Nations of Iroquois had established a well-protected homeland in New York by the beginning of the eighteenth century. Incursions by the Five Nations as far south as South Carolina helped reunite them with their long-lost cousins the Tuscarora, who, because of their common language, were welcomed northward as the Sixth Nation. Beginning in 1713, the Tuscarora began leaving North Carolina, settling a village at what is now Martinsburg, West Virginia, on what is still known as Tuscarora Creek. It is thought that the last Tuscarora left North Carolina in 1803 to live on the reservation that was established in New York.[45] In the past thirty years, a number of groups have arisen in North Carolina claiming Tuscarora heritage, including the Southern Band Tuscarora Indian Tribe (in the town of Windsor), the Hatteras Tuscarora, the Tuscarora Tribe of Indians Maxton, the Tuscarora Nation of Indians of North Carolina, and Tuscarora Nation One Fire Council in Robeson County; however, neither the state nor the official Tuscarora tribal offices in New York have granted recognition to any of these groups. The Meherrin Nation, located in northeastern North Carolina, is a state-recognized tribe of about 900 who are thought to be related to the Tuscarora.[46] While their language, Meherrin, has been lost, it is believed that it was similar to Tuscaroran. The Cherokee are also an Iroquoian group but will be discussed after the tribes of the Piedmont.

SIOUAN

In the Carolina Piedmont, the dominant American Indian tribes were Siouan, including groups of Tutelo, Catawba, Cheraw, Waxhaw, Waccamaw, Saponi, Saura, Occaneechi, Monacan, and Manahoac speakers, though the latter two groups were likely restricted to what is now Virginia. These groups spread as far west as the Yadkin River and beyond the northern and southern boundaries of modern North Carolina. The histories of some of these groups, such as the Saura and the Waxhaws, are not well known, but their linguistic imprint on the state is clear; for example, we have the Sauratown Mountains, and Waxhaw is a town in Union County and also the name of the geographical area south of the Uwharrie Mountains. The Siouan-language-family speakers found themselves sandwiched by the British arriving in the east and the Scots-Irish arriving in the west. With their numbers declining, various groups merged and became collectively known as Tutelo-Saponi. By about 1730, these merged groups left North Carolina for a more peaceful existence in Pennsylvania and New York, where many eventually were accepted by the Cayuga people, an Iroquoian group. The last fluent Tutelo speaker died in Ontario, Canada, in 1871 at the age of 106. However, before the speaker's death, ethnologist Horatio Hale documented as much of the language as he could. Hale later used other related languages to publish a grammar of Tutelo in 1883, which has served as the basis for attempts among twenty-first-century descendants to revive the dead language.[47]

It was widely reported that the last native Catawba speaker, Red Thunder Cloud, died in 1996. Shortly after his death, however, it was revealed that Red Thunder Cloud was an African American from Rhode Island who became fascinated with American Indian culture as a teenager and lived the rest of his life claiming an American Indian identity. While not a native speaker—and apparently not a fluent speaker—Red Thunder Cloud, born Cromwell Ashbie Hawkins West, extensively studied the language in written form and was able to speak it with some authenticity.[48]

It is now widely held that Robert Lee Harris, a Catawba chief who died in 1954, was the last native speaker of the language. However, like Tutelo, members of the Catawba Nation (centered in South Carolina just across the border from Charlotte) are trying to resurrect the native language.

Many of these Siouan groups are still present in North Carolina today, though in many cases they do not have a continuous historical tradition and in all cases do not share a native language. Four tribes are recognized by the state: the Haliwa-Saponi, the Occaneechi Band of the Saponi, the Sappony, and the Waccamaw Siouan.[49] The farthest east of these groups is the Waccamaw Siouan, who number about 2,300 individuals living mostly in Columbus and Bladen Counties, especially in the area between the Green Swamp and Lake Waccamaw. The Haliwa-Saponi draw the first part of their name from a blend of the counties in which they reside: Halifax and Warren. They have about 3,800 members, most living within a few miles of the town of Hollister. A few counties west of the Haliwa-Saponi are the 250 or so members of the Sappony, previously known as the Indians of Person County. The Sappony were the first of these Siouan groups to receive state recognition in 1911. The most recent of these groups to be recognized by the state are the Occaneechi Band of the Saponi. The group of about 700 members, centered in Mebane, received state recognition in 2002.

MUSKOGEAN-SPEAKING GROUPS

It is thought by many that the Algonquian, Iroquoian, and Siouan language families may all derive from a common ancestral language. At the very least, the three language groups existed in close proximity for long enough to develop similarities in their structure. The fourth language family present in North Carolina, Muskogean, is historically unrelated to the other three. The tribes of the Muskogean family were most prominent in what are now areas of Mississippi, Alabama, Georgia, Tennessee, South Carolina, and northern Florida. Collectively, this group is known as the Southern Appalachian Mississippian. Other Mississippian groups extended into Louisiana, Missouri, Michigan, and Ohio. These groups are distinct from other American Indian groups in a few ways. First, they were mound builders who used the earthworks for burial and ceremonial purposes. They were also among the most advanced agrarian cultivators of all the American Indian groups, and their large-scale maize agriculture afforded them stability and power.[50] It was primarily this Mississippian culture that Hernando de Soto encountered in his 1539–41 explorations in what is now the United States, making him one of the first and last European observers of pre-European Mississippian culture. The culture changed radically throughout the sixteenth century, perhaps largely because of the mass deaths caused by the introduction of European diseases by de Soto and other explorers. This change led to the drastic reduction of the population of American Indians in the east, even resulting in the death of entire tribes.[51]

At the time of European exploration in North Carolina, the Muscogee, sometimes called Creek, were centered in what are now Polk and Rutherford Counties, though the Town Creek Indian Mound near present-day Mount Gilead (Montgomery County) suggests that they extended into the eastern part of the state before the arrival of the Woodland groups described above; in fact, some believe that the Pee Dee of South Carolina are the descendants of these early Mississippian mound builders.[52] The Muscogee were seen as having an especially developed civilization, which led to their selection as the first tribe for "civilization" under President George Washington and his secretary of war, Henry Knox. In Washington's view, the American Indians were equal people but practiced an inferior culture. He believed that if the American Indians would practice private ownership of land, build permanent houses, farm, formally educate their children, and convert to Christianity, they would be embraced by Americans.[53] Absent from Washington's plan was a requirement that all American Indians learn English, and it certainly did not demand abandonment of indigenous languages. This plan was eventually extended to four other American Indian groups: the Cherokee, the Seminole, the Choctaw, and the Chickasaw. Under the plan, the federal government was to protect the rights of these groups against imposing American expansion.

It did not take long for tensions to mount between the "Five Civilized Tribes" and the encroaching American settlers. In 1811 Tecumseh, a Shawnee leader, attempted to organize American Indians to fight for an independent Indian state. He convinced a faction of the Muscogee to join him, causing a rift in the tribe that would lead to a civil war that would become entangled in the conflicts of the War of 1812. In 1814 the Muscogee tribe was crushed under overwhelming force from Andrew Jackson's forces, aided by the Choctaw and Cherokee tribes. Andrew Jackson would again figure prominently in Muscogee history, as it was during his presidency that the series of forced removals to Oklahoma from 1830 to 1838, commonly known as the Trail of Tears, were carried out.[54] A few groups of Muscogee remained in the east, settling in Florida, where they were absorbed into the Seminole tribe, and Alabama, at what is now the Poarch Creek Reservation.

The Muskogean language family is quite different from the Algonquian languages. Whereas the Algonquian languages used a large number of prefixes and suffixes for grammatical relationships, Muskogean languages relied more heavily on syntax. English syntax typically follows a Subject-Verb-Object pattern (for example, "I—held—a cat"), whereas the general pattern in Muskogean languages is Subject-Object-Verb ("I—a cat—held"), with the verb coming after the subject and object. Muskogean languages also have more tenses than English does, which include a separate tense for immediate past (within the past day or so), middle past (within the past few weeks), distant past (within the past year), and remote past (more than a year ago). Muskogean is still spoken by at least 4,000 speakers in Oklahoma.

The Cherokee

The Cherokee (also spelled Tsalagi), speaking an Iroquoian language, inhabited the western portions of North Carolina at the time of European arrival. There are a few theories of the origin of the term "Cherokee"; one suggests it comes from "Chalakee" in the Choctaw language, meaning "the people who live in the mountains." Choctaw, a Muskogean language currently found in Oklahoma, was originally located in the southeastern United States before the Indian Removal Act of 1830. Another theory posits that it comes from the Muscogee word for the tribe, "Cilokki," which translates roughly as "people with another language." The Cherokees' name for themselves was *Aniyunwiya*, which translates literally as "the people" or "the real people," though there is some evidence that the use of Tsalagi for self-identification occurred quite early.[55]

Scholars disagree about whether the Cherokee migrated southward from the Great Lakes region, where other Iroquoian groups lived at the time of European settlement, or whether the Cherokee and perhaps the Tuscarora remained in North Carolina while the other Iroquoian groups moved to the Great Lakes region.[56] The linguistic differences between Cherokee—the only Southern Iroquoian language—and Tuscaroran and other Northern Iroquoian languages are substantial, suggesting that the split between Cherokee and other Iroquoian groups took place a long time in the past, perhaps 3,000 to 4,000 years ago. However, it also seems to be the case that at least part of the Cherokee land in North Carolina was previously inhabited by the Muscogee, raising questions about the location and range of the Cherokee from about 1800 B.C.E. to at least 1000 C.E.

The English language met the Cherokee language in the early eighteenth century. The Cherokee tribe sided with the British against their Iroquoian cousins in the second Tuscarora War (1711–15). The war was fought over land and pushed the Tuscarora away from lands in the Coastal Plain and Piedmont, opening the area for German, Dutch, and British settlers. This cooperation led to an amicable relationship between the Cherokee and the British that would eventually lead to Moytoy of Tellico (born Amo-adawehi) being named "emperor of the Cherokee" in 1730, after which he and a small group of other Cherokees were taken to England to meet King George II.[57] The relationship with the British garnered protection from French encroachment and other American Indian groups, especially the Muscogee, but it brought disastrous consequences as well. A smallpox outbreak in 1738–39 left nearly half of the Cherokees dead. Misunderstandings following the French and Indian War led to a breakdown in the British relationship and eventually to the Anglo-Cherokee War of 1758–61, in which a number of Cherokee towns and fields were burned to the ground. Additional skirmishes throughout the remainder of the eighteenth century would see many more Cherokee towns destroyed and the European settlement—largely by the Scots and Scots-Irish—encroach farther onto the Cherokee's traditional lands. In 1805, in an effort to reach some resolution, the Cherokee ceded their lands between the Duck and Cumberland Rivers in Tennessee.

Despite the acrimonious end to this period, some English had begun to see the Cherokee as different in some fundamental ways from other American Indian groups of North Carolina. Early American historian Dr. Alexander Hewatt noted this difference in 1779:

It may be remarked, that the Cherokees differ in some respects from other Indian nations that have wandered often from place to place, and fixed their habitations on separate districts. From time immemorial they have had possession of the same territory which at present they occupy. They affirm that their forefathers sprung from that ground, or descended from the clouds upon those hills. These lands of their ancestors they value above all things in the world. They venerate the places where their bones lie interred, and esteem it disgraceful in the highest degree to relinquish these sacred depositories. The man that would refuse to take the field in defence of these hereditary possessions, is regarded by them as a coward, and treated as an outcast from their nation.[58]

Their deep connection to the land is one of the factors that have led to the Cherokee to become the only American Indian group with a land trust, the Qualla Boundary—commonly called the Cherokee Reservation—in North Carolina.

Like the Muscogee, the Cherokee were selected as one of the five tribes for "civilization." Also like the Muscogee, they were one of the tribes forcefully removed from their lands in the Trail of Tears. There is an irony to the attempted "civilization" of the Cherokee in that they were in some ways more like the Europeans than some of the other tribes.

CHEROKEE LANGUAGE AND LITERACY

Since Cherokee is the only American Indian language spoken regularly in North Carolina, we describe it in some detail. Cherokee is quite different from English. Depending on the dialect, speakers of English typically have

between eleven and eighteen vowel sounds, more than most languages. Cherokee has six vowel sounds, which are roughly similar to the ones found in the following English words: *beet*, *bait*, *bat*, *boat*, *boot*, and *but*. Thus Cherokee does not have the vowel sounds in words like *bet*, *bought*, *book*, *boy*, *bout*, and a few others.

To view footage of Cherokee being spoken, visit http://www.talkintarheel.com/chapter/8/video8-8.php

Consonant sounds further differentiate the two languages. English has consonant sounds that Cherokee lacks, and Cherokee has consonant sounds not found in English. Though there is some variation among current dialects of Cherokee, traditionally, the language has not had the following consonant sounds that English has: *b*, *p*, *r*, *f*, *v*, *z*, *th*, *ch*, *sh*, *j* (as in *Jeff*), and the middle sound in "measure" or "vision." It is possible to hear the lack of an *r*- sound in the Cherokee children's rendition of "America the Beautiful," in which the word "America" sounds something like "Uh-my-yi-ya."

To view children singing "America the Beautiful" in Cherokee, visit http://www.talkintarheel.com/chapter/8/video8-9.php

Many English consonants do exist in Cherokee: *g*, *k*, *h*, *l*, *m*, *n*, *qu*, *s*, *d*, *t*, *w*, and *y*. In addition to these sounds, Cherokee has a few sounds that either do not exist in English or are used only sporadically in words that have been borrowed from other languages. One such sound is ts-, which appears in the loan words "tsar" (Russian) and "tsetse" fly (Setswana). Cherokee also has consonants that sound like dl, tl, hw, hy, hl, and hn.

Cherokee is further distinguished by being a tonal language, meaning that the same vowel and consonant sounds pronounced with different contours of pitch can mean very different things. Mandarin Chinese is another tonal language. Whereas Mandarin has four tones, Cherokee has six: low and level, high and level, rising from low, falling from high to low, falling from high to mid, and falling from low to lower. In some cases, the tone can signal the difference between two words, while in other cases, the tone can signal a difference in grammar. For example, the falling from high to mid tone can denote uncertainty in the same way that the word "might" does in English. These tones can be exceptionally hard for nonnative speakers to master.

The syllable structures of Cherokee are also quite different from English. English is a little unusual in that it allows for lots of combinations of consonants both before and after the vowel of a syllable. For example, the word "street" has three consonants before the vowel and one after. The most common syllable pattern in the languages of the world allows one or two consonants before a vowel but few consonants after a vowel. Hawaiian is one such language, which gives English such words as "a-lo-ha" and "wi-ki" (as in "Wikipedia"), "hu-la," and "u-ku-le-le." Cherokee is closer to the pattern of Hawaiian than English, so that all consonant sounds appear before the vowel of the syllable, and only a few (d, g, l, n) can occur at the end of a syllable.

Given the syllable constraints, there are eighty-five different combinations of consonants and vowels in modern Cherokee. Its writing system takes advantage of the relatively limited number of syllables in the language. English is written with an alphabet, where one symbol (letter) corresponds to roughly one sound. Ancient Egyptian hieroglyphics, by comparison, used one symbol (a picture) for every word. Cherokee uses a syllabary, which is a writing system in which each symbol corresponds to one syllable. Thus modern Cherokee is written using a script that has eighty-five symbols. In the early part of the nineteenth century, Sequoyah developed this writing system over twelve years, completing a workable syllabary by 1821.[59]

To view a video about Cherokee syllabary sounds, visit http://www.talkintarheel.com/chapter/8/video8-10.php

The syllabary was remarkably successful. Within a few years, many Cherokees had learned to read text written in the syllabary, and by 1830, a mere nine years after it was introduced, three-fifths of the Cherokee were literate, growing to about 90 percent by 1850—which made the Cherokee the most highly literate group in America at the time.[60] American-born European Americans as a group did not reach this level for another fifty years, and America as a whole took until 1910.[61] This statistic may seem somewhat shocking given common portrayals of American Indians as uncivilized populations who refused to accommodate to European norms. With the syllabary, the Cherokee began printing a newspaper in 1828 called the *Cherokee Phoenix*, an image of which is reproduced in Figure 8.4.

The paper was published in both Cherokee and English and distributed in North Carolina and neighboring states. This newspaper predates the *New York Times* (1851); the *Sentinel*, which became Raleigh's *News and Observer* (1865); the *Washington Post* (1877); and the *Charlotte Observer* (1886). It was also the first newspaper published by any American Indian group and the first written in an American Indian language. The paper's publication was interrupted by state agents in 1834, and shortly thereafter the Georgia Guard confiscated the printing press to ensure that it could not be used to stir up pro-Cherokee sentiment during their forced removal, but the paper was resurrected in Oklahoma by the Cherokee Nation. Other works also appeared using the syllabary. A Cherokee almanac was published yearly from 1836 to

To view the official music video for "Know Me" by Cherokee rapper Litefoot, visit http://www.talkintarheel.com/chapter/8/video8-11.php

1861, and school texts, such as *Cherokee Elementary Arithmetic*, appeared shortly thereafter. In modern times, Cherokee has an increasingly rich, living literary tradition, with novels, plays, histories, songs, and poems all appearing in Cherokee. The Cherokee rapper Litefoot even incorporates Cherokee into his raps, and Cherokee (along with a syllabary keyboard) is now included as a language in word-processing programs and on smart phones, allowing speakers to text in Cherokee.[62]

The sounds and writing system of Cherokee are quite different from English, and the grammar is even more different. As with the Algonquian languages described above, Cherokee relies on a Subject-Object-Verb word ordering ("I—a cat—held"). Also, Cherokee can express full, complex sentences with a single word. Transliterated into English spelling, *ga-wo-ni-ha* is a single word meaning "she is speaking" or "he is speaking" (Cherokee, unlike English, does not make gender distinctions).

There are two major dialects of Cherokee currently spoken in the United States. The Cherokee in North Carolina (Eastern Band of the Cherokee) speak what is known as Kituhwa, while the Cherokee of Oklahoma (Cherokee Nation) speak Otali. Kituhwa is, in general, the more conservative branch of

FIGURE 8.4. The *Cherokee Phoenix*, May 21, 1828.

the language and has fewer innovations (changes) than the western variety. The group that stayed in North Carolina at the time of the forced removal had already separated from the rest of the Cherokee over what they saw as a departure from traditional cultural norms. There are also far more Cherokees in Oklahoma than in North Carolina (288,000 compared to 13,000).[63] And the Cherokee in North Carolina have traditionally been more insulated from other American Indian groups that might influence their spoken and written Cherokee. The two groups have now lived more than 750 miles apart for nearly 175 years, resulting in some significant dialect differences between the groups, but the language varieties are still mutually intelligible.

Diseases transmitted by Europeans were certainly the decimating events for American Indian populations, but most of this was unintentional. Disease spread among the American Indians because they lacked immunity from the diseases, but there is some evidence to suggest that toward the end of the eighteenth century, Europeans began using this knowledge to intentionally infect populations in what amounted to biological warfare. Perhaps even more reprehensible were the forced removal polices enacted by Andrew Jackson's Indian Removal Act. Under this act, President Jackson was granted authority to negotiate the terms by which American Indians would cede their lands in the east to the federal government in exchange for a number of benefits—including land—west of the Mississippi, mostly in what is now Oklahoma (itself deriving from the Choctaw roots okla ["people"] and homma ["red"]). Under the act, the removal was to be voluntary. The Choctaws were the first group to accept the proposal in 1830, but the other four members of the Five Civilized Tribes held fast in the face of increasing anti-Indian sentiment. Jackson's landslide reelection in 1832 emboldened him to increase the pressure on the American Indian groups, resulting in the "treaties" signed in 1832 detailing the terms of the removals of the Chickasaw, Muscogee, and Seminoles. These groups were removed primarily by force over the next few years, suffering great hardships and high death tolls along the way and leaving only small populations behind.[64]

The Cherokee who remained in the east were able to do so by different means. A small group of perhaps 100 simply evaded the government officials in charge of the removal, using the rough terrain to their advantage. Another group of perhaps 400 Cherokee were able to legally stay on land held for them by William Holland Thomas, a white man who had been adopted into the tribe as a child. The split between the Eastern Band of the Cherokee and the Cherokee Nation originally arose as a cultural dispute, and the two groups governed themselves independently beginning in 1819.[65] Anticipating the impending removal treaties, the Eastern Band asked Thomas to be their legal representative to ensure they could remain on the 640 acres they negotiated in a previous treaty with the government. Being white, Thomas had the right to own land, an entitlement not extended to American Indians. The tribe transferred land to him and used his money and money from other Cherokees to purchase a second tract on which the Cherokee could live. This would eventually become the Qualla Boundary, which is still home to about two-thirds of the members of the Eastern Band of the Cherokee. The Qualla Boundary is commonly referred to today as the Cherokee Reservation, but it is not a true reservation since the Cherokee legally purchased and maintained ownership of the land. Instead, the land is now held in a trust and overseen by the Bureau of Indian Affairs.

The Cherokees who remained in North Carolina were not immune from continued pressures to accommodate to European norms, including language. The path to gaining civil rights was long. American Indians were nominally granted citizenship in 1924, but it was not until 1948 that they were granted full citizenship along with the right to vote. In the decades between the removal and citizenship, the Eastern Band of the Cherokee, like other American Indian tribes, were subject to continued attempts by the government to make them think and act like the dominant white populations. This effort eventually included mandatory education at state-run boarding schools. The Cherokee Boarding School was opened in 1882 on the Qualla Boundary. Despite the close proximity to their family homes, children were boarded at the school to separate them from their native language and culture. Children had their hair cut in the style of whites and were required to wear European-styled uniforms, often renamed with English names, given unfamiliar food, and forbidden from speaking Cherokee.

Cherokee historian Sarah Margaret Sneed recounts her mother's and other community members' memories of the school in an article titled "Uniform Indians." Her mother tells of how at age five, she was picking blackberries when a school officer forcibly took her and her sister to school without their mother's knowledge or permission.[66] She was served macaroni, which she thought was a plate of worms. Her refusal to eat the food earned her a knuckle-rapping reprimand. She would not see her mother again until Christmas of that year despite her mother's attempts to visit her at the boarding school. Such was the harsh reality at American Indian boarding schools across the United States. Sneed's interviews with the tribe's elders reveal just how deeply the Eastern Band of the Cherokee cared about education. The elders interviewed by Sneed consistently recounted the harsh, militaristic treatment they received at the school while still adamantly insisting they appreciated the skills they learned there. Though the school was designed to strip them of their culture, for many, the inhumane attempts at Americanizing them actually led them to a deeper devotion to and appreciation of their traditional tribal ways and lands. The elders had less-consistent accounts of how and when the use of Cherokee was punished. Some could not recount a single instance where a child was punished for speaking Cherokee, while others described various punishments, from being struck with a belt to having their mouths washed with lye soap. Beginning in the 1930s, the Cherokee Boarding School began allowing nonboarding students, a policy that it continued until it closed in 1954.

CHEROKEE LANGUAGE REVITALIZATION

The English-only policies of the boarding schools were largely effective in achieving their purpose with respect to language. Across the United States, the vast majority of American Indian languages that survived the initial contact period have been lost or are currently endangered. Even among reservation groups, few people under fifty speak the heritage language. For example, a 2002 survey of the Cherokee Nation in Oklahoma found only about 10,000 fluent Cherokee speakers—almost all of whom were older than fifty—out of a population of 288,000.[67] The situation is not much better in North Carolina. The 2000 U.S. Census reported 1,147 of the approximately 12,500 Cherokee in North Carolina as having some fluency in the language; however, a 2005 survey conducted by the tribe identified only 460 fluent speakers—of whom 72 percent were over fifty—a number that tribal elders claim has since dwindled to somewhere between 200 and 300.[68] The tribe estimates that even with its preservation efforts, they are still losing an average of three Cherokee speakers a month.

To view this quote by Myrtle Driver, as well as the quote below by Jean Bushyhead, visit http://www.talkintarheel .com/chapter/8/video8-12.php

This stark finding launched an intensive, community-based language revitalization project. For the community, more than the language is at stake. Native Cherokee speaker Myrtle Driver notes: "Our language is who we are. Once you start learning the language, it branches out to all other areas—history, culture, traditions. So, when they're learning the language they're learning, you know, everything about the Cherokee people as well."[69]

The revitalization project has a number of initiatives, the first of which is the Kituwah Academy, an early childhood immersion program that teaches parents and children from seven months to age five to speak and read together in Cherokee.[70] This early childhood component prepares the children for a total immersion curriculum that extends from preschool to fifth grade. To support the teaching of this program, the community has partnered with Western Carolina University, which boasts strong programs in elementary education and the Cherokee language so that students can now learn to deliver elementary school content in Cherokee. Jean Bushyhead, a local teacher, is optimistic about the chances for success in preserving the language: "The Cherokee culture and language will survive because of the great emphasis that has been going on for the last five or six years. And I think that we are getting to the children at the right time. And that is [from] birth . . . on."[71] Although the program directs most of its efforts toward young children, since 2007 all Cherokee students have been required to speak Cherokee in order to graduate from high school. While students sometimes resist such imposed mandates, and success in language learning is closely tied to a person's desire to learn the language, in the case of Cherokee, many students are eager to learn. One student, Harley Young, notes: "All our elders know it. . . . [I]f we don't learn it, nobody'll know it, and it's like our heritage is gone." He goes on to describe the pride he feels in learning the language: "Not many people can say they have— they can speak two different languages, and I mean, especially a Native American language, and I think it's pretty cool that . . . we're learning our heritage."[72] His classmate Pat Smith offers this slightly more pragmatic take on the usefulness of learning Cherokee: "And like, well no offense, but if we see white people and start talking to each other about 'em, they don't know. I don't know, it just kinda feels good to have our own language that nobody else can understand."

To view the video of this quote and others about knowing Cherokee, visit http://www.talkintarheel.com/chapter/8/video8-13.php

The community has also begun adult education programs on the Qualla Boundary as well as intergenerational events that bring together the older and younger speakers of the language. And there is a Cherokee summer camp in the Snowbird community an hour south of Qualla Boundary where the children produce a play in Cherokee by the end of the summer. The Cherokee in North Carolina have also reached out to Cherokee groups in Oklahoma to create workshops to discuss their common language and help adapt it to the modern world. The program's tasks include adding new words to Cherokee so that it can be used to teach state-mandated curricular content. The Cherokee Language Consortium, for example, has designated new Cherokee words for English words like cell phone, plastic, CD, computer, amoeba, galaxy, axis, biology, and astronaut.[73]

Despite the current incentive, it is impossible to know what the future holds for the Cherokee language. The Kituwah dialect of Cherokee remains below the critical mass of speakers that would allow us to comfortably predict it will continue to be a viable and flourishing language. However, a 2010 report on the results of the first five years of intensive work to revitalize the language made a number of positive observations, including the dedication of key partners within and outside the community; the effectiveness of the educational materials and programs; and, most promising from our point of view, the observation that Cherokee has emerged as important in the everyday lives of community members.[74] Other evidence also inspires optimism. In seven years, the Kituwah Academy has grown from a single classroom to an independent academy and from seven students to fifty-eight, with waiting lists for students at every age group. Renissa Walker, Kituwah Preservation and Education Program director, notes: "There's not enough words to describe how we feel on our seventh anniversary. But, then again, there aren't words to describe how we feel when we walk into a room and you see children counting in Cherokee."[75]

Linking the Past to the Present

To many, American Indian history seems located in the distant past. Americans now seem to view these diverse peoples with a sense of reverence, perhaps because we now recognize their right to the land that was earlier denied. With that right, a sense of authenticity is more concrete and accessible. We have mentioned how remarkable it is that many people have laid claim to an American Indian heritage and history that does not belong to them. Further, they do so without truly realizing the hardships such groups endured at the hands of governmental and citizen groups alike. Lost in this admiration is the understanding that this painful history is not altogether distant, and American Indian groups are still fighting to overcome many of the burdens that have been placed on them by those who arrived after they did.

It is hard to imagine a governmental policy today that would result in massive deaths among any population, as the Indian Removal Act did for the American Indians. Likewise, it is hard to imagine a policy that would intentionally strip so many people of their cultures and languages. Yet some of the rhetoric of the English-only movement we discuss in chapter 10 advocates this kind of governmental policy, now directed at Latino populations. It is common to hear such statements as "They're here, they should learn English" without any regard for the fact that we previously thrust our English on a group that is the actual native population. With an entwined history with American Indians of more than 450 years, English speakers

FIGURE 8.5. Young Cherokee speakers sing at a Veterans Day celebration.
(Photograph by Danica Cullinan)

are at a point where they see in their rearview mirrors a little of the cultural
and linguistic loss caused by such policies. Outside of relatively isolated
enclaves, English has been thrust on the vast majority of immigrant and indigenous people alike with irreparable consequences to language and culture.

The persistence of the Eastern Band of the Cherokee
against the backdrop of history and adversity is a story that
all North Carolinians should celebrate, whether or not they
have a "Cherokee grandmother." North Carolina's modern
and past linguistic diversity—with its variety of different languages and many dialects—is a cultural resource that deserves to be honored.

To view the full Cherokee
vignette from *Voices of
North Carolina*, visit http://
www.talkintarheel.com/
chapter/8/video8-14.php

9 Lumbee English

Tar Heel American Indian Dialect

It's like an immediate identification mechanism. Can I talk to this person? Can I trust this person? Do we share a common experience? Do we have a common bond? —KARL HUNT, Lumbee artist, Pembroke, North Carolina, quoted in *Indian by Birth: The Lumbee Dialect*, produced by Neal Hutcheson (Raleigh: North Carolina Language and Life Project, 2001)

To hear the above quote and others, visit http://www.talkintarheel.com/chapter/9/video9-1.php

Robeson County is the most ethnically diverse county in North Carolina, with minority groups constituting the majority of the population. Contributing to the county's diversity is the largest American Indian population east of the Mississippi River—the Lumbee, whose tribal members, now approaching 50,000, make up 39 percent of the Robeson County population, with the rest composed of non-Hispanic European Americans (25 percent), African Americans (25 percent), and Hispanics (8 percent).[1] The first three ethnic groups have lived side by side for several centuries now, enduring long periods of legal and de facto segregation—three seating areas in the movie theater; three school systems; and, most recently, three homecoming kings and queens. As the ninth-largest tribe in the United States—and the largest nonreservation tribe of American Indians—the Lumbee Indians of Robeson County are the reason that North Carolina ranks seventh among all states in terms of its American Indian population. But the Lumbee have been largely ignored by the federal government, the Bureau of Indian Affairs, and people outside of North Carolina, who rarely know who they are.

Traveling south on Interstate 95 in North Carolina through Robeson County seems routine and monotonous. Nine hundred and forty-six square

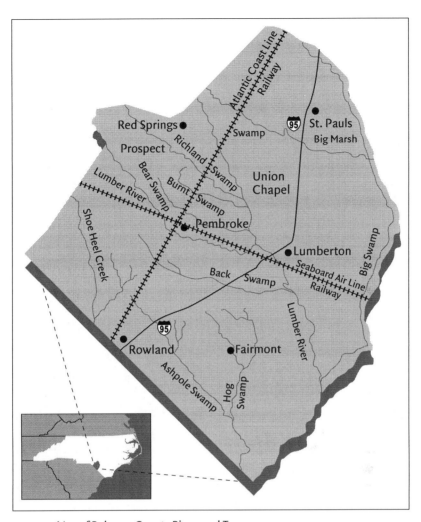

MAP 9.1. Map of Robeson County Rivers and Towns

miles of flatlands and sandhills in the state's most expansive county stop abruptly at the South Carolina border. As drivers speed south on the most traveled north-south corridor on the East Coast, attention is drawn to gaudy billboard advertisements featuring infamous, stereotypical caricatures of Pedro beckoning drivers in accented English to take a break "South of the Border," a garish amusement park and rest stop across the state line in South Carolina. The chain of billboards and the repetitive landscape obscure a small green sign sitting modestly by a well-disguised bridge marking the Lumber River. The meandering river flowing sluggishly under the concrete

FIGURE 9.1. The meandering Lumber River. (Photograph by Neal Hutcheson)

slabs of I-95 is easy to miss, like the American Indian group whose cultural homeland is intimately connected to the river. As investigative journalist Fergus M. Bordewich put it: "It is hard to believe now that the plain and forthright flatlands of Robeson County could have hidden an entire people for generations."[2]

Exit 17 off of I-95 steers drivers west onto Route 117, leading through a procession of tobacco fields, cotton fields, and cornfields toward Pembroke, occasionally interrupted by a new, somewhat ostentatious house that sits gauchely in the middle of a field where a dilapidated barn might seem more appropriate. Approaching Pembroke, ten miles west of the interstate, a couple of newly constructed strip malls and billboards advertise the Lumbee presence. Murals on a couple of buildings depict American Indian figures, and the prominent new edifices of the Lumbee Guarantee Bank and Lumbee Regional Development Association starkly rise above the single-level structures on the outskirts of Pembroke, a town not quite like other small towns in North Carolina.

At the railroad intersection of the east-west and north-south crossing of the Union Pacific, Southern, and CSX railways lies the heart of what seems at first to be just another small southern town center. But it is hardly that. About 90 percent of the 2,500 people living within the town of Pembroke are Lumbee Indians. Crossing the railroad tracks, a flashing sign at the edge of the campus of the University of North Carolina at Pembroke advertises up-

(top) FIGURE 9.2. Indian murals on oil tanks in Robeson County. (Photograph by Neal Hutcheson); (bottom) FIGURE 9.3. Indian State Normal College, now the University of North Carolina at Pembroke. (Courtesy of the State Archives of North Carolina)

FIGURE 9.4. Downtown Pembroke during the Lumbee Homecoming
Parade. (Photograph by Neal Hutcheson)

coming events at one of the fastest-growing universities in the state. The
school was established in 1887 as the Croatan Normal School to train American Indian public school teachers, opening with one teacher and fifteen students.[3] Today, it educates almost 7,000 students in the liberal arts and sci-
ences. It has always been known as an Indian school, although it was not
until 2005 that the governor of North Carolina signed a declaration officially
making it "North Carolina's Historically American Indian University."[4]

The flickering sign projects the digital profile of an Indian in headdress
and welcomes newcomers to the "Home of the Braves." The juxtaposition of
the towering modern university across the tracks from the traditional town
center featuring small, family-run businesses and services is symbolically
transparent.

To view the introduction to the
documentary *Indian by Birth*,
visit http://www.talkintarheel
.com/chapter/9/video9-2.php

The signage on billboards and buildings in Pembroke recy-
cles names—Oxendine, Locklear, Lowry, Hunt, Chavis, Bray-
boy, and Bullard are all common Lumbee names. And yes, the
name Locklear also is shared by the famous blue-eyed, blonde
actress Heather Locklear through a paternal grandparent from
Robeson County. Heather Locklear's appearance represents
the ambiguity of the tribe's legacy to outsiders who expect to
encounter more phenotypical Indian features, dress, behavior,
and language. Instead, Lumbee features range from blue-eyed, light-skinned
blondes to brown-eyed, dark-complexioned people with tightly curled hair.
From their appearance and cultural heritage to their official status as Indi-

ans, the Lumbee Indians seem ambiguous and ironic. At least that is what many outsiders would have us believe.

Who Are the Lumbee?

When we started conducting linguistic interviews with residents of Robeson County in the early 1990s, our goal was to compare the English of the Lumbees with that of European American and African American residents to see if the groups used distinct ethnic varieties of English. In addition to more than 100 interviews with Lumbees of all ages, we conducted about fifty interviews with European Americans and twenty-five with African Americans, generally directed by fieldworkers of the same ethnicity.[5] On more than one occasion, after the tape recorder was turned off, white or black interviewees would take us aside, lower their voices, and offer us some confidential information about the Lumbee: "I'm going to tell you something that you need to know about the Lumbees for your study. They like to think that they're Indian but they're just a mixed breed that doesn't want to be black." Ambiguity and suspicion—even from other residents of Robeson County—seem to be synonymous with the Lumbee label. Perhaps journalist Fergus M. Bordewich summed it up best in his chapter "We Ain't Got Feathers and Beads" about marginalized American Indian groups: "The Lumbees' century-long quest for identity is a story as serpentine as the jungled Lumber River, whose swampy course shielded, and perhaps even created, them and their ambiguous world. . . . There is, in fact, nothing at all about the Lumbees that fits conventional notions of what it means to be Native American. Yet for as long as any Lumbee can remember, they have possessed an unflagging conviction that they are simply and utterly Indian, a tenacious faith that is troubled only by the failure of most other Americans to recognize it."[6]

Suspicions people have about Lumbee identity are not lost on the Lumbees themselves, and the response to this skepticism is consistent and predictable. By legacy, tradition, and self-definition, they have no doubt about who they are. While other people—ranging from physical anthropologists in the 1920s who measured their skulls to see if they were real Indians to current DNA geneticists who strive to objectify their genetic uniqueness as a people—may question their authenticity, the Lumbee are steadfast in their belief that they are "simply and utterly Indian."[7] They are used to, if not comfortable with, the persistent doubts about their Indianness. As one Lumbee told an inquiring reporter seeking to determine the exact American Indian roots of the Lumbee: "We know who we are, we know, we have always known; y'all are the ones who are trying to identify something."[8]

To view Lumbee commentary on Lumbee identity, visit http://www.talkintarheel.com/chapter/9/video9-3.php

Outsiders, including the federal government, have been debating the Lumbees' precise ethnic status and historical origin for well over a century now, but the issue is largely a matter of external speculation rather than internal confusion, and identity to the Lumbee means more than simply having family ties. As Lumbee artist Karl Hunt noted in his comments about the status of actress Heather Locklear: "I mean, you know, this Heather Locklear thing, Heather Locklear ain't no Lum, I don't care what nobody says, I don't care if her granddaddy or great-granddaddy or what-what came from here. She's never lived as a Lum, she's never been involved in this community, she's never certainly had to experience the things that are just gonna be a part of your life experience if you are a Lum and live in Robeson County. . . . You just gotta be a part of this community, even if it is from a distance. I guess what I'm trying to say is that you gotta have the genetics and the culture."[9]

After two decades of interaction with people in Robeson County, we have yet to encounter a Lumbee who has any doubt about his or her identity as American Indian. Lumbee curator and storyteller Barbara Braveboy-Locklear, summarizes it appropriately: "Who are the Lumbee? Our identity is rooted in our Native American culture. Our struggle to prove our identity is caught between continuous theoretical debates on our origin. Yet we know who we are and recognize our own."[10] They may defy some conventional stereotypes as an Indian group, but the Lumbee maintain a resolute sense of who they are as an Indian people.

The quest for cultural respect and federal recognition continues amid lingering questioning. Perhaps Lumbees should have been less peaceful in their dealings with the federal government historically and required a treaty, one of the conditions for federal recognition. If they had, they probably would have gained recognition more than 125 years ago. In 1885 the North Carolina General Assembly recognized the Indians of Robeson County as Croatan, an American Indian tribe, preceding even the recognition of the Cherokee in North Carolina. Just a few years later, in 1888, the Lumbee petitioned the U.S. government for recognition and assistance. They were denied by the Bureau of Indian Affairs due to a lack of funding. That was just the start of repeated, failed petitions for federal recognition that have routinely taken place since then. Finally, in 1956, they were officially recognized by a congressional act that ironically managed yet again to underscore their marginal status.[11] The Lumbee Recognition Act (H.R. 4656) recognized the Lumbee as having American Indian origins and designated them as the Lumbee Indians of North Carolina, but it stipulated that "nothing in this Act shall make such Indians eligible for any services performed by the United States for Indians because of their status as Indians."[12] Since that time, several new petitions for full recognition have been submitted, and in 2009 the U.S. representative from Robeson County, Mike McIntyre, introduced legislation (H.R. 31) intended to grant the Lumbee Indians full federal recognition.[13] The bill garnered the support of more than 180 cosponsors, and in June 2009, the U.S. House of Representatives voted 240 to 179 for federal recognition for the Lumbee tribe, acknowledging that they are the descendants of the Cheraw tribe. This time the bill included a no-gaming clause and no provision for reservation land. Needing only the approval of the Senate—both North Carolina senators supported the bill—and the president before becoming law, the Senate adjourned for 2010 without taking action. Just when the Lumbee thought it was a done deal, the deal was broken. The seemingly endless quest continues as this book goes to print.

If the Lumbee had a heritage language that they still used or that they were familiar with, their argument for full federal recognition would have been settled in their favor long ago. In fact, the Congressional Lumbee Act of 1956 does mention language as one of the defining traits of the Lumbee, but the reference is to a distinct dialect of English rather than an ancestral American Indian language: "Whereas by reason of tribal legend, coupled with distinctive appearance *and manner of speech* . . . shall after the ratification of this Act, be known and designated as the Lumbee Indians of North Carolina" (emphasis ours).[14] We will see how the dialect of English spoken by many Lumbees has become a natural part of who they are and how they define themselves. However, unlike those situations described in the previous chapter, it is not an American Indian language. Instead, a distinctive dialect of English marks their cultural and regional identity.

The Term "Lumbee"

The word "Lumbee" itself is perhaps the best index of the Lumbee circumstance. Outsiders assume that this is simply the latest label for a group of Indians who can't figure out what they want to be called; the group has previously been known as "Croatan" (1885) or "Croatoan Indians," the "Indians of Robeson County" (1911), the "Cherokee Indians of Robeson County" (1913), and the "Cheraw Indians." The 1956 Congressional Lumbee Act is the first official use of the term "Lumbee Indians." But was it really a new term at the time? In fact, the term "Lumbee" was attested well over a century ago, when the Lumber River was formerly referred to as the *Lumbee River*. State legislator and historian Hamilton McMillan wrote in 1888 that "at the coming of the white settlers there was found located on the waters of the Lumbee, as the Lumber River was then called, a tribe of Indians speaking English."[15] American Indian groups often share names with bodies of water—for example, Santee, Wateree, Congaree, and Pee Dee—so it may well be the case that Lumbee is an enduring reference to those who lived by the Lumbee River. Further, many names for American Indian groups in the region end in a final -*ee*, though this spelling may be pronounced in several different ways. After examining the possibility that the term Lumbee may have come from an American Indian language, Catawban-Siouan language specialist Dr. Blair Rudes speculated that Lumbee derives from a coastal dialect form of Catawban meaning "bank of a river" (phonetically yãʔbe in Piedmont Catawban, pronounced something like *yahmp-bee*, though it is impossible to give exact equivalent sounds in English). According to Rudes, this name was assigned during the time of the expansive, multilingual Cofitachequi chiefdom that stretched from the Atlantic Seaboard to the Appalachian Mountains at the time Hernando de Soto first reached the Piedmont area of the Carolinas in 1541.[16] Whatever the origin of the term Lumbee, it is not a recent innovation. We can speculate that European Americans took the American Indian name for a river and a people, "Lumbee," and assumed that it was related to the term "lumber" in a process we described in chapter 5 as "folk etymology." In Charlotte, North Carolina, the name of a well-known creek, "Sugar Creek," from the Sugaree Indian word "sugaw" (meaning "group of huts") is a potentially parallel folk etymology.[17] English speakers heard the American Indian word "sugaw" and simply assumed it was related to the similar-sounding English word "sugar." It is not far-fetched to think that European Americans may have heard the indigenous term Lumbee and modified it into a word that made sense to them: "lumber." The modification of the term "Lumbee" into "Lumber" certainly would make sense in terms of the county's largest city, Lumberton, so named because of its role in the early lumber industry. Whatever its historical roots might be, the term Lumbee is not a recent innovation. Further, it surely has come to be uniquely associated with an American Indian community strongly linked historically and culturally to the river once called Lumbee.

Ancestral Language

The historical circumstances surrounding the Lumbee make it difficult to trace the roots of their indigenous, ancestral language. Little documentation of the languages of the Lumbee River region exists, and linguists can't even be certain about what language or languages the Lumbee spoke in the past. Some American Indian languages were documented in North Carolina as early as the sixteenth century, but the region by the Lumbee River was not included in this effort. Another problem is the early acquisition of English by the Lumbee. By the mid-1700s, the Lumbee apparently were no longer reliant exclusively on their ancestral language for communication, at least in their interactions with outsiders, and that would have masked their ancestral language roots. As one observer put it, as early as the 1730s, white settlers encountered a group of Indians in present-day Robeson County "speaking English, tilling the soil, owning slaves, and practicing the arts of civilized life."[18]

An additional problem comes from the cultural dynamics of the area. According to archaeological and linguistic evidence, the Lumbee River region was a zone of cultural interaction for different American Indian groups, so that it is quite possible that the Lumbee community developed not from a single, unitary cultural group but from a conglomerate of American Indians.[19] This possibility does not quite match the American stereotype of tribal purity, but it does reflect the reality reported in chapter 8: there were many cases of cultural convergence as well as independence among American Indians for reasons that range from trade and economic interdependence to wars and disease. As we discussed, languages from Algonquian, Siouan, and Iroquoian language families were represented in this region of North Carolina where the Lumbee community eventually developed, making it difficult to pinpoint a particular ancestral language without earlier documentation.

To view a clip about ancestral Indian language families in North Carolina, visit http://www.talkintarheel.com/chapter/9/video9-4.php

Though there is no documentation of when the present-day Lumbee community was formed, one popular theory is that today's Lumbee Indians were originally situated on the coast and then migrated to the area that became Robeson County. According to this interpretation, the group of Roanoke colonists who disappeared during the two years when John White traveled back to England from Roanoke Island in 1587 blended their culture with that of the coastal Indians, who then migrated south and inland toward the

FIGURE 9.5. Mixing the past with the present. (Photograph by Neal Hutcheson)

Lumbee River. According to Lumbee historians Adolph Dial and Dr. David Eliades, "the survival of colonists' names, the uniqueness of the Lumbee dialect in the past, the oral traditions, the demography of sixteenth-century North Carolina, the mobility of the Indian people, human adaptability and the isolation of Robeson County, all prove the 'Lost Colony' theory."[20]

Another theory argues that the Lumbee and their ancestors inhabited the Robeson County area continuously for a much longer period. Archaeological, cultural, and linguistic evidence suggest continuous American Indian residency in the Robeson County area since prehistory. This does not, however, mean that there was a single group of American Indians there; in fact, the archaeological evidence suggests otherwise, so it is quite possible that the Lumbee developed from a blending of American Indian cultures existing in the region, and that more than one language was spoken in the area at an earlier period. The two explanations are not necessarily incompatible, since it is possible that a migrating group from the Outer Banks speaking an Algonquian language encountered an Eastern Siouan tribe residing in Robeson County at the time. The Lumbee River was not too far removed from the Iroquoian language, Tuscarora, to the north and Siouan languages to the west, along with the Algonquian languages by the coast. The location of the Lumbee and the navigational routes available through the Lumbee River and the Cape Fear River to the north permitted direct travel to the coast.

Cultural groups existing in multilingual language situations are no less real than those that come from monolingual ancestral communities. In fact, the majority of language situations in European history reflect mixing of quite different languages, including the development of English in the British Isles. If the condition of mixing language invalidated a language, then it would annul English, which arose in part from a mixture of Germanic languages and has subsequently mixed extensively with other languages, including French during the Norman invasion in 1066. In fact, fewer than half of the current words of English come from Old English. The same standard should be applied to the Lumbee. The long-standing existence of American Indians along the Lumbee River and the persistence of the current-day Lumbee community are sufficient testament to their cultural and linguistic validity.

Roots of Lumbee English

How did Lumbee English develop its distinctive dialect traits? Are there any vestiges of a heritage Native American language in the English dialect? How does it compare with other dialects of American English—including the dialects of European Americans and African Americans in the immediate area and other historically and cultural distinct regions of North Carolina? There are lots of questions that we have asked and been asked by those curious about the Lumbee dialect of English.

Our team of researchers has attempted to answer some of these questions based on several kinds of language information. As noted earlier, since 1993 we have been conducting interviews with Robeson County residents of all ages and ethnicities. Each of these interviews of forty-five to ninety minutes in length has been analyzed in minute detail to document examples of particular dialect structures, and detailed instrumental analysis of vowels and other features has been carried out.[21] Additional data sources have complemented our own fieldwork, including interviews conducted in conjunction with several oral history projects—including one set by Adolph Dial, the Lumbee historian and community leader, from 1969 to 1971, and another set from a separate oral history project conducted in the late 1960s and early 1970s.[22] Earlier recordings are of special interest since they provide a historical perspective on the development of Lumbee speech. A ninety-year-old speaker interviewed in 1970 would reflect what Lumbee English might have been like when the speaker learned language in the late nineteenth century, since speakers tend to retain many features of the dialect they learned as a child. The earliest records of speech we have, in fact, include speakers who were born in the 1860s, giving a time depth of a century and a half.

One of the most frequently asked questions is whether there are any traces of a heritage American Indian language in present-day Lumbee English. The reasoning behind this question is fairly obvious. If there are vestiges of an ancestral language in their English, it would help authenticate an American Indian lineage. This hopeful expectation is balanced by a couple of practical observations. Although American English has certainly adopted some terms from American Indian languages in the course of its development, as discussed in chapter 8, these terms are derived from different American Indian languages and—with the exception of place names and native flora, fauna, and game—they are relatively restricted. For obvious political reasons, borrowing from other European languages was much more rampant in the development of the dialects of American English, but the original imprint of American Indian names still stands as a kind of linguistic archaeology in North Carolina and elsewhere.

Linguistic influence from an ancestral language can vanish completely in a couple of generations, so it stands to reason that no American Indian language influence would remain many generations after the heritage language was no longer used. It would be quite surprising to find lingering influence from an ancestral language given the relatively early shift to English by the Lumbee. Our studies did find one possible exception to this general trend in a highly detailed analysis of the pronunciation of final consonant blends in words like *find*, *rest*, and *act*. In a careful, quantitative examination of the absence of the final consonant, for example, pronouncing *find* as *fin'*, *rest* as *res'*, or *act* as *ac'*, Dr. Benjamin Torbert found that Lumbee speakers born before World War I are more prone to leave off the final consonant than those born in the mid- and later twentieth century.[23] This reduction of final consonant combinations at the ends of words is a fairly typical holdover effect in English when the heritage language does not have these types of consonant combinations, and it has been documented in the English of American Indian communities elsewhere.[24] This is a very subtle dimension of language that would not be very noticeable to the ordinary listener but only to a linguist doing very detailed statistical analysis. But it is also reasonable to attribute this pronunciation tendency among the oldest speakers of Lumbee English to the holdover effects of ancestral language influence. We would not expect to find the effects of a language lost generations ago to be prominently displayed, but the possibility of subtle lingering effects cannot be dismissed.

With respect to English dialect influence, there are a number of sources for the creation of Lumbee English. To begin with, a couple of dialect traits show a connection with Outer Banks English. Perhaps the most obvious case is the pronunciation of the vowel in *time* and *side* like *toim* and *soid* by older speakers in communities such as Prospect and Union Chapel in Robeson County, but there are other similarities as well.[25] The use of *weren't* in sentences such as "I weren't there" or "She weren't nice" is also a prominent Outer Banks feature. These traits are probably due to the fact that the dialect areas of North Carolina now associated with the Outer Banks once extended well into the mainland area of southeastern North Carolina. While the current dialect profile has changed somewhat, the dialect boundaries that emerge from earlier records are still evident today, particularly in a culturally isolated group like the Lumbee.

It might be tempting to conclude that the dialect connection with the Outer Banks supports a Lost Colony origin for the English of the Lumbee, but the facts are much more complex. The dialect associated with Outer Banks speech was not formed until the early 1700s at the earliest, when English settlers from Maryland and eastern Virginia traveled down the coast by water and established permanent residence along the Outer Banks and coast of North Carolina. That was well over a century after the disappearance of the Lost Colony. Many of the dialect features of the Outer Banks are shared not only with Lumbee English but with other dialects that preserve earlier features of English because of geographic and cultural separation. Ironically, the island dialects on the coast often have more in common with the Mountain dialects in the western part of the state than the intervening Piedmont area, but not because of their historical connection. Instead, they shared a type of isolation and similar kinds of English settlement groups that fosters the retention of some of these earlier forms. The use of the prefix *a-*, pronounced as an *uh* sound as in "She was a-fishin,'" is a well-documented structure of Lumbee English, Appalachian English, and Outer Banks English. In this instance, the different dialects simply share the preservation of an older structure.

Another preserved form is the use of *be* as a helping verb where other dialects use *have*, particularly in sentences such as *I'm been there* for "I've been there." But it is also wrong to conclude that these forms in Lumbee English are simply static vestiges of earlier English since language is always undergoing change. While retaining some earlier uses of *be* for "have," Lumbee English now uses it in ways that it was not used originally.

Some of the surrounding regional English dialects of the area certainly influenced the development of Lumbee English. The use of *bes* in sentences such as "Sometimes it bes that way" or "Dogs bes doing that" was once prominent in a region that included Robeson County and some of the surrounding counties in the vicinity, such as Horry County to the south in South Carolina.[26] It was particularly prominent among descendants of the Highland Scots and can still be found in use by elderly Scottish-heritage residents of Robeson County. However, it has receded among Scottish descendants in Robeson County while remaining quite robust, and even intensifying in use, in Lumbee English over the past couple of generations.

No doubt, some early contact with African Americans has also influenced the development of Lumbee English to some extent, since both the Lumbee and African Americans have been residents of Robeson County for several centuries and, at various points in their history, have been subjugated to similar social oppression. The absence of the verb *be* in sentences such as "You nice" or "She gonna go there," a well-known feature of African American English, is also present to some extent in Lumbee English. This feature has usually been attributed to a vestige of African language influence, although it might have derived from American Indian language influence as well.

Obviously, several different varieties of English have provided input into the development of Lumbee English, not only in its past but also in its present form. At the same time, Lumbee English also developed on its own, apart from the input from surrounding dialects. This is true for some dialect words that refer to social distinctions within the community—for example, the use of the terms *Lum*, *brickhouse Indian*, *on the swamp*, and so forth—as well as some grammatical and pronunciation features. The grammatical construction *weren't* in "I weren't there" seems to be developing of its own accord within the community and is becoming more robust among some younger speakers.[27] The precise contributions of various sources to the development of Lumbee English cannot be calculated, but it is apparent that a particular set of donor language varieties available in the area at the time the Lumbee were learning English combined with the Lumbee language adaptation and innovation to forge a distinct variety of English.

Identifying Lumbee Speakers

When twenty-year-old singer Charly Lowry from Pembroke was a semifinalist on the popular television show *American Idol* in 2004, she seemed quite conscious of her Lumbee dialect. Before she performed, she noted: "I think my accent has made me quite distinctive from the other contestants, but I want them to recognize me for my talent, not the way I talk." When she completed her rendition of "Chain of Fools," one of the judges, Randy Jackson, commented on her dialect: "You know, Charly, I love your speaking voice. It reminds me of my southern heritage. Say something to these fine people." Though they probably didn't realize it, Randy Jackson and Charly Lowry's encounter on national television encapsulated how listeners react to the Lumbee dialect. Those who hear it for the first time think of it as a deep southern dialect that sounds a little quaint. But Lumbees recognize it as more than that: as a socioethnic dialect uniquely associated with the Lumbee Indians.

To view a clip about Lumbee dialect recognition, visit http://www.talkintarheel.com/chapter/9/video9-5.php

After conducting many interviews with speakers in Robeson County, we decided to construct an experiment to test how listeners classified the ethnicity of speakers from the three dominant ethnic groups in the county. First, we excerpted speech samples from longer interviews with twelve different speakers: four Lumbees, four African Americans, and four whites. Each ethnic group was represented by one older and one younger male speaker and one older and one younger female speaker, making a nice symmetrical sample of ethnic representation, gender, and age. The anonymous passages were twenty to thirty seconds long and avoided any topic of discussion that might reveal ethnic identity based on the content of the passage. We then asked groups from two different locations in North Carolina simply to identify each speaker as Lumbee, African American, or white. One group of forty-five listeners was from Robeson County, mostly Lumbees; the other group of thirty-eight listeners was from Raleigh, about 100 miles away. The group from Raleigh had heard about the Lumbee but had never spent time in Robeson County. The group from Robeson County had lived there all of their lives.[28]

To take the perception test, visit http://www.talkintarheel.com/chapter/9/audio9-1.php

The experiment revealed some interesting results. Both groups identified white and African American speakers with approximately the same level of accuracy. African Americans on the tape were correctly identified more than 90 percent of the time and European Americans between 70 and 80 percent of the time. Though there were no differences in identifying the whites and blacks by the two listener groups, they differed significantly in identifying Lumbees. The group from Robeson County correctly identified Lumbee speakers more than 80 percent of the time, but the Raleigh listeners correctly identified them only 38 percent of the time, which indicated that it was a random guess. When the Raleigh group misidentified Lumbees, however, they typically identified them as white, not African American, indicating that they were associating them with southern European American speech. The results of this experiment support a claim commonly heard from Lumbees—namely, that they can indeed identify other Lumbees by the sound of their voice. We also see that Robeson County insiders and outsiders differ in their ability to correctly identify Lumbee speakers but not whites or African Americans.

Part of the strong sense of dialect identity among the Lumbee may be related to the role that self-definition has played in their cultural identity. We noted earlier that outsiders often express skepticism about the status of the Lumbee as "real Indians" due to their early loss of many conventional American Indian customs and their ancestral language. The Lumbee response to this suspicion has led to an especially strong role for self-definition in asserting their identity. The Lumbee further embrace dialect distinctiveness as one of the behavioral indicators of their cultural uniqueness. But this dialect role is mostly lost on outsiders—including Randy Jackson, who thought of the dialect as simply "down-home southern." In the South, the primary ethnic division is biracial and focused on white and black, not on American Indian. Listeners may be attuned to regional dialect dimensions that differentiate the South from the North, the Outer Banks from the mainland, or the mountains from the plains and coast, but ethnic distinctions have tended to center on the black-white racial dichotomy. In Robeson County, people are attuned to the basic triethnic character of the county, where people were socialized early and continuously into three sociocultural entities.

Features of Lumbee English

In defining the Lumbee dialect, it is important to understand that it is differentiated primarily by the combinations of structures rather than by the existence of uniquely Lumbee expressions. Over the past couple of decades, our research team has studied the distinctive dialect structures in great technical detail, offering us important insights about the way that these structures are used by vernacular Lumbee speakers, European Americans, and African Americans in Robeson County.[29]

At its core, Lumbee English is a southern regional dialect, sharing many features of general southern speech. But it compares more with geographically and socially isolated groups—such as those in the mountains and on the coast—than it does with the southern speech found in the Piedmont and Coastal Plain. In fact, visitors hearing the dialect for the first time often think that it sounds like Mountain Talk in certain ways and Outer Banks English in others. Though outsiders may think of it as quaintly southern, they do not usually associate it with a distinctive American Indian language variety.

VOCABULARY

Most popular descriptions center on the words of Lumbee English, and one of our first publications on Lumbee English, produced with Hayes Alan Locklear, was a dictionary of Lumbee English.[30] As we have noted throughout this book, words can be stubbornly independent in their evolution. There is a limited set of words that we have found only among the Lumbee, though we are sometimes surprised to find that words we thought were unique at first sometimes turn out to be shared by other dialects. Some unique Lumbee words are local innovations for places and social relations within the community, such as *on the swamp*, a metaphorical extension of the swampy terrain that now means "neighborhood." Many proper name locations include swamp in their name: *Burnt Swamp, Hog Swamp, Ashpole Swamp, Gum Swamp, Saddletree Swamp*, and so forth. The term *Lum*, a shortened form of "Lumbee," is reserved for those who have identified with their Lumbee cultural heritage; it also indicates a sense of community and peoplehood that distinguishes the Lumbee from other groups and therefore is significant in designating insider-outsider status. That is one of the reasons the Lumbee artist quoted in our earlier discussion about Lumbee status felt confident in exclaiming that "Heather Locklear ain't no Lum."

As is often the case in culturally distinct communities, social differences within the community are also embodied in some of the vocabulary items. The term *daddy*, for example, is used for close peer friends as well as a parent, and teenagers may greet one another with "What's up, daddy." The term *cuz*, shortened from "cousin," is similar in its extension of a kinship term to refer to good friends. Social distinctions within the community are captured by terms like *brickhouse Indian* and *swamp Indian*, which refer to higher and lower status in the community; these are combined with the common southern phrase *above your raisin's* (or *above your raisin'*) to refer to someone who "puts on airs." In the Lumbee community, we've heard the expression *your head's in the pines* to mean the same thing as *above your raisin's*. The fact that a number of the unique Lumbee expressions refer to social relations, including extended kinship, says a great deal about the internal social order and the strength of kinship ties. On first meeting other Lumbees, it is not uncommon for someone to ask "Who's your people?" so that they can be situated in terms of their extended family ties.

Other terms, such as *fine in the world* ("doing well"), *sorry in the world* ("doing badly" or "not feeling well"), *ellick* ("coffee," usually with sugar), or *yerker* ("mischievous child") also separate Lumbee English from the dialect of other communities. We have searched far and wide to find where *ellick* might have come from, including a Gaelic origin, but have not yet come up with a reasonable etymology. For dialectology detectives, it is an unsolved mystery, and we're still searching for good leads.

Some words have a shared but restricted regional interpretation. For example, the term *kelvinator* is a brand name for a "refrigerator" that has been extended to refer to refrigerators in general, largely because a Kelvinator factory once existed in the area. The residents of Robeson County simply extended the proper name to all refrigerators, just as people in other areas use the term *frigidaire* for refrigerators in general or people across the country use *kleenex* for "facial tissue." As we noted in chapter 3, the term *juvember* ("slingshot") is probably used more by the Lumbee than by other residents of Robeson County, but it is also known some by other groups in southeastern North Carolina. Terms like *fatback* ("fat meat of a hog" or "bacon") and *head'nes'* ("overwhelming, very bad") are shared with other dialects in the southern Coastal Plain and beyond. For older people, if you really want to refer to bad times, one can talk about the *Hoover Days* ("the period of the Great Depression").

Another set of words demonstrates the potential contact of the Lumbee with some of the earliest English inhabitants of North Carolina. Terms like *mommuck*, *toten*, and *gaum*, which can be traced back centuries in the English language, have been retained in Lumbee English, just as they have in other geographically and culturally isolated groups to the east and west of the Lumbee. However, some subtle shifts in meaning have taken place in the different regions. *Mommuck*, as described in chapter 5, had an original literal meaning of "tear to shreds" during the 1600s. On the Outer Banks, this meaning has been extended figuratively to mean "harass physically or mentally," as in "Stop mommucking me," while in Lumbee English and Mountain Talk, it has been extended to mean "make a mess," as in "You sure mommucked the house." The common etymological origin of this word has been subjected to slight shifts in meaning that now subtly define its use in the different dialect communities while reflecting its archaic status. The term *token*, which can be traced back a millennium in the English language to the word *tacen* ("show, explain, teach"), is another relic form that has undergone a shift in meaning. In Lumbee English, where it is more likely to be pronounced as *toten* than *token*, it refers to a spirit or ghost; it can also refer to a sign or foreshadowing of death, as it does on the Outer Banks of North Carolina.

Finally, there is a large set of more-general vocabulary items that Lumbee English shares with a wide range of southern English dialects. Uses of *mash* ("push") and *cut off/on* ("turn on/off"), as in "We mashed the button to cut on the lights," are fairly widespread southern rural uses that set them apart from nonsouthern dialects. Similarly, terms like *swanny* ("swear"), *carry* ("accompany"), *young 'uns* ("children"), and so forth are simply words that define a broad-based area of the South, including the major ethnic groups in Robeson County. Lumbee English vocabulary exists within the general context of southern speech while setting itself apart in a few significant ways.

To view a vignette about Lumbee vocabulary, visit http://www.talkintarheel.com/chapter/9/video9-6.php

PRONUNCIATION

For the most part, the pronunciation of Lumbee English follows southern dialects of English found in the Coastal Plain of the South, although the mix of these features with other traits associated with historically isolated dialects makes its pronunciation somewhat different from other dialects in the immediate region. The pronunciation of the long i of words like *time* or *side*, one of the most distinctive sounds associated with the development of the South, is a case in point. Older speakers in more traditional Lumbee communities such as Prospect and Union Chapel may still pronounce these vowels like *toim* or *soid*, the pronunciation strongly associated with the Outer Banks.[31] The passage from an older Lumbee speaker from Prospect given in the grammar section of the chapter illustrates this pronunciation for the *soid* pronunciation for *side*. The more common southern pronunciation of this vowel among the Lumbee, however, is without the vowel glide, so that *time* is pronounced as *tahm* and *side* as *sahd*. This is the tendency among younger Lumbees, aligning them with European Americans and African Americans in Robeson County.

To view a vignette about Lumbee pronunciation, visit http://www.talkintarheel.com/chapter/9/video9-7.php

A detailed analysis of the pronunciation of the long i over four different generations of Lumbee speakers (born before World War I, born between

World War I and World War II, born after World War II but before school integration in 1972, and born after school integration) reveals that there are subtle ways in which the pronunciation of this vowel differs based on ethnicity. All Robeson County ethnic groups unglide the vowel of *time* and *side* to *tahm* and *sahd*, but younger Lumbee speakers are more likely to unglide the vowel in words like *white* and *bright* so that they are pronounced as *whaht* and *braht*, thus distinguishing them from the other ethnic groups.[32] This kind of realignment shows how Lumbee English may shift over time while still maintaining ethnic distinctions. It also points to the subtle distinctions that fine-grained linguistic analysis can sometimes reveal when subjected to instrumental acoustic analysis—differences that are not always immediately apparent to the ear of the casual listener.

The analysis of r-loss in words like *fouh* for "four" or *feauh* for "fear" is also one of those cases where detailed comparisons reveal the subtle ethnic distinctions. Older, more traditional dialects in the Plantation South typically dropped their r's, but the current generation of Southerners has abandoned this pronunciation pattern. Although speakers from the three major ethnic groups of Robeson County exhibit r-loss, the careful measurement of thousands of cases reveals that the relative level of r-loss is different for each of the groups. The relative frequency of r-loss in words like *cah* for "car" and *feuh* for "fear" is the highest for Robeson County African American speakers and lowest for Robeson County European Americans. Lumbee speakers fall in between, distinguishing themselves quantitatively from the other groups, who show more extreme differences. Differences in r-loss can be quite subtle, and we have found that speakers sometimes adjust their levels of r-loss based on the person they are talking to, what they are talking about, and the kinds of relationships that speakers have to each other.[33]

The instrumental acoustic analysis of the vowel system of Robeson County Lumbee, European Americans, and African Americans has shown that the Robeson County Lumbee vowel system is more like Robeson County European American speakers than it is like Robeson County African Americans, helping explain one of the results of the listener-identification test that showed that the Lumbee who are misidentified in terms of ethnicity are categorized as white rather than as African American. The pronunciation of the vowels in *boot* and *boat* sound more like *biwt* and *bewt*, produced at a more front position in the mouth than the typical pronunciation of these vowels found in the northern pronunciation, and vowels like those in *bed* and *bid* may sound more like *beyd* and *biyd*, following the southern vowel shift we described in chapter 3.[34]

The vernacular version of Lumbee English often shows an affinity with the traditional dialects of geographically and socially isolated dialects such as Appalachian English and Outer Banks English. For example, the retention of an h in words like *hit* for *it* or *hain't* for *ain't*; the intrusion of a t in *oncet*, *twicet*, or *clifft*; and the use of the plural *-es* with words like *postes* for *posts*, *roastes* for *roasts*, or even *woodses* for *woods* (illustrated in the passage below in the grammar section) are characteristic of isolated varieties in regions quite removed from the area now occupied by the Lumbee. The connection between these dialects is further strengthened by the pronunciation of the final r in *yeller* for *yellow* or *feller* for *fellow*, *right here* as *right chere*, and *big 'uns* for *big ones* or *second 'un* for *second one*.

A comparison of Lumbee English with other dialects of the South, and to the east and west in North Carolina, shows that there is very little about the pronunciation of words in Lumbee English that is unique. At its core, it is embedded in the traditional dialects of the South, but it sometimes has more in common with the dialects of the Outer Banks and Appalachia than it does with some of the dialects of non-Lumbee residents within Robeson County. When all of the elements are combined, it is, however, identifiable as Lumbee—especially to those who live in the general vicinity of Robeson County.

GRAMMAR

Although the overwhelming majority of the grammatical traits of Lumbee English are, once again, shared with other English dialects, there are several features that seem to be distinctly Lumbee, at least in the context of southeastern North Carolina. As with pronunciation, Lumbee grammar is much like that of the dialects of the state's historically remote regions. For example, *a*-prefixing in constructions such as "She was a-huntin' and a-fishin'" is a fairly common archaic form of English found in historically isolated rural dialects. Sometimes, you can hear some fairly creative expressions using the *a*-prefix, as illustrated in the following passage taken from an interview with a Lumbee woman from Prospect born in 1925.[35] In the excerpt given below, notice how she also converts the noun *ditch* to a verb and then adds the *a*-prefix in the structure "two men in a ditch a-ditchin'." A couple of other verb uses are also highlighted in the excerpt, including the use of *come* for *came* and the use of an -s on *says* with the first person pronoun I, which is often used with personal narratives.

> And, children, there *come* a man in the big broad daylight. I could see him as pretty as I'm *a-lookin'* at you. *Come* all the way down that ditch bank. I *says* to myself, I *says*, I kept *a-lookin'* at the man; he was *a-lookin'* in the ditch just like there was somebody in there ditchin'. You know how a man would walk. Could you imagine a man—two men in the ditch *a-ditchin'* and a man *a-walkin'* down side of that ditch *a-lookin'* at them in there throwing that dirt? That's just the way he was *a-lookin'* into this ditch, this man was, in the broad open daytime. And, honey, he *come* right on down that ditch. And I spoke and I *says*, "How in the world did Uncle Pat get through in here by mule?" I knew he couldn't 'cause there *wasn't but one* road *a-comin'* into my place, back in them *woodses*. I says "He couldn't, I *don't see no car nor nothin'*." And when he got to the—uh, crossed this ditch. He crossed the ditch and went halfway to the field and come on down this other ditch. There was a little path through, went through my yard and went all across the *woodses* there. Well, when he got halfway to that little ditch on this side, before it *come* out here to the road, I was *a-lookin'* at him *plumb* good. Honey, by the time you—if you'd have said to me, "Lucille, that's Harley Locklear." Honey, I *ain't* never got so—he had on a brown coat, he had on a pair of brown britches, he had on a brown hat, just like if you'd have spoke to me and said, "Lucille, that's Harley Locklear." Honey, I *ain't never* got so scared in all the days of my life.

When a passage like this is compared with African American and white speakers just a few miles away, we see striking differences in the use of grammar and other dialect features.[36]

To hear this passage, visit http://www.talkintarheel.com/ chapter/9/audio9-2.php

Although some of the structures of Lumbee English were once widespread in English, in the regional context of southeastern North Carolina, they have now become associated with Lumbee English. One of these is the use of *be* as a helping verb for *have* in sentences like *I'm been there before* for "I've been there before" or *We're got it already* for "We've got it already." Although this may sound strange to contemporary speakers of English, this kind of alternation was once common in the English language. It's also common in isolated varieties of English around the world, from isolated island communities on Abaco Island of the Bahamas to the small volcanic island of Tristan da Cunha, the world's most remote inhabited island, lying more than 2,000 miles from South Africa and Argentina in the South Atlantic.[37] So the form itself is not unique to Lumbee English but has come to index this dialect in the regional context of southeastern North Carolina. It is barely, if ever, used by African American and European American speakers in this region. Lumbee English simply took advantage of available grammatical resources of English and crafted them into a distinctive sociocultural dialect.

To hear an African American speaker from Robeson County, visit http://www.talkintarheel .com/chapter/9/audio9-3.php

Lumbee English is also distinguished from other dialects in the area by how the verb *be* is used in the past tense. *Be* is the most irregular verb in the English language, with different forms for the present tense (*am, is, are*) and past tense (*was, were*). This irregularity makes it a good candidate for changes that tend to make it more regular, and just about all vernacular varieties of English throughout the world regularize this

To hear a white speaker from Robeson County, visit http://www.talkintarheel.com/ chapter/9/audio9-4.php

verb, as in "I/you/(s)he/we/you/they was there." But Lumbee English, like Outer Banks English, is one of the few dialects in the United States that uses a different pattern for regularizing this verb. With negatives, the form *weren't* is used to form sentences like "I weren't there," "she weren't there," "it weren't there," and so forth. Once again, we see an indicative similarity with a grammatical pattern found on the Outer Banks of North Carolina. No other dialect this far inland has this pattern or *weren't* use, though it is robust in coastal island communities that extend from the Chesapeake Island communities of Smith Island (Maryland) and Tangier Island (Virginia) to the Core Sound Harkers Island dialect.

One other grammatical structure shows how Lumbee English has molded the forms made available to them during an earlier formative period. This is the form *be(s)* in sentences like "She bes here" or "Sometimes babies bes born like that." This use of *be* where other dialects use *is* or *are* apparently dates back to early Highland Scots and the Scots-Irish English influence on the dialects of the region, and it has been found in neighboring European American varieties across the border in Horry County, South Carolina.[38] Although it is now rare in European American varieties in Robeson County, it is still prominent in Lumbee English. *Bes* shows a relationship to Scots and Scots-Irish dialects prominent in the area historically, but it also converges with a similar form in African American English—the use of *be*, as described in chapter 7, to refer to habitual activities in sentences such as "Sometimes she be going to the store" or "They be taking the dog with them all the time."

In African American English, the form *be* occurs with verb constructions such as *be talking*, *be tripping*, and so forth, to designate repeated actions. Among Lumbee speakers, particularly younger speakers, it is being modified in the direction of the African American English use, but it remains subtly distinct in a couple of ways. In Lumbee English, *be* can take the *-s* suffix, as in "It bes like that," whereas in African American English, it usually occurs without an *-s*, as in "She be talking." Also, some speakers of Lumbee English still preserve the use of *be* for *have*, as in *She be got it* for "She has got it" or *I might be lost some inches* for "I have lost some inches." So vernacular Lumbee English is distinct in its use of *be*—both from the habitual *be* in the African American community and from its near-extinct status among European Americans.[39] The shaping of *be(s)* in Lumbee English once again reveals how dynamic a dialect community can be in utilizing past and present linguistic resources to mold and maintain cultural uniqueness through changing social and linguistic circumstances.

To view a vignette about Lumbee grammar, visit http://www.talkintarheel.com/chapter/9/video9-8.php

The Future of Lumbee English

What will happen to Lumbee English in the future? Although the speech in many historically isolated dialect communities like Ocracoke and Harkers Island are now eroding because of outside influences and social pressures of the school, this process is not as pronounced in Lumbee English. The set of dialect structures associated with Lumbee English has naturally shifted over time, but the dialect is still robust. And there are even some structures that seem to be increasing rather than receding. The use of *be* for *have* in "I'm been there before" and the use of regularized *weren't* as in "I weren't there" are still quite productive among some young people, even in the face of school's attempts to eradicate vernacular Lumbee English. As Dr. Linda Oxendine, longtime Lumbee educator and former director of the American Indian Studies Program at the University of North Carolina at Pembroke, put it: "Since 1887, there's been an attempt to standardize Lumbee English, and they haven't been successful. So there has to be something in terms of it being embedded in the culture, engrained in the culture, because you would think after 100 years of public education that something would have changed, when in fact, it hasn't."[40]

To view a video of this quote by Linda Oxendine and a quote by Stan Knick, visit http://www.talkintarheel.com/chapter/9/video9-9.php

One of the reasons that Lumbee English remains so vibrant is the crit-

FIGURE 9.6. Lumbee English remains a cultural marker, even as it changes over the generations. (Photograph by Neal Hutcheson)

ical mass of speakers in Robeson County and the neighboring counties of Hoke, Cumberland, and Scotland. With over 50,000 Lumbees in the region and some dense Lumbee school populations, the dialect is not nearly as threatened as other dialect areas now overwhelmed by outsiders. Several elementary schools in Robeson County have more than 90 percent Lumbee students and mostly Lumbee teachers, and Purnell Swett High School near Pembroke has a student population that is more than 80 percent Lumbee.[41] Furthermore, Robeson County does not get a lot of tourists or visitors from outside areas, so many small towns and villages within the county remain largely segregated and culturally in-

To hear a passage by a young Lumbee speaker, visit http://www.talkintarheel .com/chapter/9/audio9-5.php

sular. These concentrated populations and social conditions are conducive to maintaining a unique dialect. Though Lumbee English today may be different from that of previous generations, it is alive and well.

Language is symbolic of Lumbee status itself, caught in a kind of double jeopardy. The community lost its ancestral language heritage originally to accommodate the sociopolitical and economic exigencies of European encroachment. Regrettably, their early adoption of English was subsequently used against them, as they were denied full federal recognition as an American Indian tribe in part because they didn't have a native language to establish their continuous legacy as a cultural group. But they did not lose their linguistic identity. Instead, they creatively crafted the English language from available resources to mark and maintain their ethnic distinctiveness. However, this variety of English has been rejected institutionally by an educational and social system that dismisses it as an unworthy approximation of standard American English rather than a natural linguistic outcome of their maintenance of cultural uniqueness. While Lumbee English is undeniably different from Standard English, it is much more than just another nonstandard dialect of English. Lumbee English did not come about from a conscious ceremonial decision made by the tribal elders in a long house. Instead, it was the ordinary and natural development of a distinct cultural group that manifested its socioethnic distinctiveness by molding the linguistic resources of English to serve as a sociocultural marker. In this respect,

To view a video of the quote by Hayes Allan Locklear, visit http://www.talkintarheel.com/chapter/9/video9-10.php

Lumbee English is no different from the English of other ethnic groups. And the dialect remains one of the most transparent and authentic markers of cultural and ethnic identity, even as the Lumbee embrace other physical and cultural artifacts of the American Indian cultural renaissance. Despite persistent institutional efforts to repress and obliterate any linguistic traces of cultural distinctiveness in their language and dialect, the Lumbee have maintained a distinct manner of speech as a symbolic indicator of their identity. As Lumbee artist Hayes Allan Locklear put it: "[The dialect is] how we recognize who we are, not only by looking at someone. We know just who we are by our language. You recognize someone is from Spain because they speak Spanish, or from France because they speak French, and that's how we recognize Lumbees. If we're anywhere in the country and hear ourselves speak, we know exactly who we are."[42]

To view a homecoming speech by a Lumbee (from *Indian by Birth*), visit http://www.talkintarheel.com/chapter/9/video9-11.php

Carolina del Norte 10
Latino Tar Heels

By mixing two languages, you get a mixed way of speaking that mirrors the identity of a person who feels that they're a part of two different cultures. We call that code-switching. —DR. CARMEN FOUGHT, quoted in *Spanish Voices: Spanish and English in the Southeastern United States*, produced by Danica Cullinan (Raleigh: North Carolina Language and Life Project, 2010)

[Interviewer:] Tell me a little about how you ended up in Ocracoke, where you came from, how you got here and so forth.

[Franco Garcia (pseudonym)]: Well, I come from Mexico and I'm coming here find, looking for job, you know what I'm saying? Well, I'm working first in Germantown, yeah, in one plant open oyster. I don' like this work, you know and I coming to Little Washington. Somebody going to Little Washington and I tell him, "Man, where you from?"

He say, "From Ocracoke."

"Oh, you see job over there? Man, give me one favor. Give me ride to Ocracoke."

He said, "Okay I give you ride, but I don't give you my house."

"Hey man, you just put me in Ocracoke and I'm survival, ok?"

"All right," he say, the guy.

He give me the ride to here, to Ocracoke. My first night I'm sleeping in bushes, yeah, in the bushes. Yeah, it's fine. In 2000 I coming here, I think so, in March, something like that. I'm working, well, I'm listen, know somebody, the guy needed people, you know, for work, you know, for packing fish, and I'm see him and he told me yeah, "I give you job," *pero* he told me, "I no give you place for sleep, you know?" I don't care.

243

I'm thinking I don' care, I gonna sleep in the bushes, maybe two weeks. I like it, for me it's no problem. When you, when you coming from Mexico, you know, when you say bye to your family, you ready for everything, you know. Maybe die, survive, or whatever. *No sé.* Now I no good but I'm stay okay, and I got a job, I got a friend in Ocracoke, yeah, it's good, I think so for me.[1]

To hear this interview excerpt, visit http://www.talkintarheel .com/chapter/10/audio10-1.php

Franco Garcia heard from a friend in Washington, North Carolina, that there might be work on Ocracoke Island, so he put his belongings in a backpack and hitched a ride to the island. Once there, he slept in the bushes, out of sight of residents, for several weeks. At daybreak, he walked the island in search of work. Arriving at the onset of the tourist season, he had little trouble finding work as a busboy, in the fish house, and at a variety of other jobs. More than a decade later, he still lives on Ocracoke, now residing in a permanently docked sailboat on the Silver Lake pier, the small inlet where ferries from Swan Quarter and Cedar Island dock. He supports himself with jobs that range from painting houses to construction, repair work, and net mending. And he readily talks to islanders and visitors in his heavily accented English, openly discussing the path that brought him to the island.

Ironically, Franco's living quarters his first weeks on the island were probably not unlike those of the first Spanish travelers who set foot in North Carolina. Almost 500 years earlier, a lawyer and nobleman from Spain, Lucas Vasques de Ayllon, sponsored several explorations to the "New World" that included an expedition that landed on the coast of North Carolina near the Cape Fear River. Their stay in the Carolinas, however, was much briefer than Franco's due to their general disenchantment with the region and the diseases that plagued their attempts at settlement.[2] Today, the most enduring Spanish legacy of the early expeditions along the coast of North Carolina is probably the wild horses roaming on Shackelford Banks and other Outer Banks communities.[3] Ocracoke still has some ponies that may have descended from the early Spanish settlement attempts; they are now confined to a pen about five miles north of the village.

Franco Garcia's initial destination point was Germantown, a cluster of houses at an intersection of roads in mainland Hyde County where he shucked oysters in one of the few remaining plants. Following a short stay in Washington in Beaufort County, often referred to as "Little Washington" to avoid confusion with the nation's capital, he made the trip to Ocracoke, where he has lived since then. His journey is just one of the personal stories that might be told by the 800,000 Hispanics who now call North Carolina home. The first modern migrants came based on word-of-mouth promises of work—from Mexico, El Salvador, Honduras, Guatemala, and other countries in Central and South America. Some immigrants started their journey to North Carolina based on a report of work from a friend or a "recruiter." Most often, the intention was to return to their home or to be joined by their families in the United States once their financial situation allowed. In an interview, Garcia described his own experience:

GARCIA: No problem. Yeah, I'm, I'm good here in Ocracoke. I think so working couple more years, go home Mexico.
INTERVIEWER: Do you have family back in Mexico?
GARCIA: Yeah, I got a wife. I got a two kids. Yeah, two kids.
INTERVIEWER: How old are they?
GARCIA: Yeah, I got my first—my older son, he have twenty-six. My daughter have twenty-two. Eh, my younger son have sixteen year old.
INTERVIEWER: Do they ever come up? Do they ever come up to visit you?
GARCIA: He is in Mexico. Yeah, my wife and him, she no like here. Well I'm, I'm talking with her every two week, every week, and I tell 'em, "Hey, come here." And she told me, "No, you come back here." Yeah, she loves too much the babies.
INTERVIEWER: Do you have a place of work back there? Work back in Mexico? What part of Mexico are you from?
GARCIA: Tabasco. Yeah, in Tabasco. Yeah, I'm thinking work a couple more year and go home. Maybe no come back anymore.[4]

The story is not unlike those told by immigrants who came from Europe during the early twentieth century in waves that far exceeded the recent Hispanic immigrants in terms of population percentage.[5] In 1992, when we first started our dialect research on Ocracoke, there was not a single Latino on the island; in 2000, when Franco Garcia arrived, Hispanics were less

To hear this passage, visit http://www.talkintarheel.com/chapter/10/audio10-2.php

than 2 percent of the island's 800 residents. Today, approximately 20 percent of the Ocracoke population is from Latin America, and more than 30 percent of the student population in the Ocracoke School is Latino. Spanish is heard daily among Latino workers in motels and restaurants, and it is routinely taught in the schools. There are also classes in English as a second language (ESL) and programs for Spanish speakers and English speakers to learn language from each other. Many native islanders who employ or work with Spanish speakers know at least a few useful phrases that they use in instructions related to work or in limited social interaction. Ocracoke offers jobs in the service industry, mostly manual labor in the motels, restaurants, and local shops. And there are now probably as many Latinos in the school as there are students who come from long-standing Ocracoke families, a transformation that was totally unanticipated a couple of decades ago.

There are similar—and even more-dramatic—community transformations that have taken place in other small towns in North Carolina. Siler City, where the mix of black and white populations has not changed since the Reconstruction era, is one such community. In the 1990s, Latinos were drawn to the town by jobs in the chicken slaughterhouses and the textile mills.[6] The initial trickle of immigrants turned into a flood of approximately 4,000 new residents since the 1990s, making Latinos the largest ethnic group and approximately half of the 8,000 residents now living in Siler City. The makeover is apparent in the Spanish-speaking churches, restaurants, and stores—and in the echoes of the Spanish heard just about everywhere in town now, as well as on a couple of Spanish-language radio stations.

Schools, churches, and other agencies have implemented ESL programs for students and adult learners. Some of the immigrants came directly from Mexico and Central America, but others came from other areas of the United States, including Texas and California, to settle in towns in the mid-Atlantic and southeastern United States, where permanent immigration by Spanish-speaking people was formerly rare. Wilfredo Hernandez moved to Siler City from California with his wife and two children at the urging of a cousin. In a newspaper article in the *Miami Herald* titled "Hispanic Wave Forever Alters Small Town in North Carolina," Hernandez offered one of his main reasons for relocating: "'I could never dream of buying my own place in Los Angeles,' said Hernandez, 35, a native of El Salvador who builds trailer homes by day and on weekends helps his growing Hispanic Baptist congregation erect a sleek new church building. 'After three years here, I saved enough to buy a mobile home. . . . I'm really happy.'"[7]

These stories of Latinos celebrating festivities and holidays, such as the Easter Day celebration in Siler City depicted in Figure 10.2, illustrate several important points. Garcia's story from Ocracoke puts a face on the hundreds of thousands of Latino residents in North Carolina today. Some stories are less dramatic, but some include harrowing tales of traumatic experiences

FIGURE 10.1. Spanish-language radio stations now air throughout North Carolina. (Photograph by Neal Hutcheson)

crossing the border, narratives of hazardous and lonely journeys to eventual destinations, and descriptions of struggles to find work and a place to live—to say nothing of the cultural and linguistic shock of living in an alien country.

The descriptions of immigration to small, rural areas further emphasize that the dispersion of Latinos is not simply an urban phenomenon. Reflecting a broader national trend, Latinos are now settling in the rural regions in North Carolina while also continuing to settle in urban areas such as Charlotte, High Point, Greensboro, Durham, and Raleigh.[8] The influx of Latinos has been felt from the fishing and tourist industry on the coast to the Christmas-tree farms in the hills and mountains of North Carolina. As farmer Blan Bottomly from Sparta reported in a news story about the flow of Latinos into rural North Carolina: "If it weren't for the Hispanic people, I couldn't farm, couldn't do nothing."[9] The Latino population in Alleghany County in the foothills of the Blue Ridge Mountains grew by 90 percent from 2000 to 2010, a testament to both the sizable numbers of immigrants and the paucity of Latinos in the area previously. North Carolina is now third among states—behind Texas and New Mexico—in terms of its rural, or more specifically, "nonmetro," population of Latinos.[10] It is not simply a matter of the number of new arrivals that makes the statistics seem dramatic; it is equally important to recognize how few Latinos there were in the Southeast previously. North Carolina and Georgia are the states most dramatically trans-

FIGURE 10.2. An Easter celebration in Siler City, 1999. (Photograph by Paul Cuadros, University of North Carolina–Chapel Hill Archives)

formed by the influx of Latinos over the past two decades. Between 2000 and 2010, the Latino population of North Carolina more than doubled, after more than quadrupling in the decade before. North Carolina is currently the tenth-largest state in terms of total population, and it now has the eleventh-largest population (by number) of Latinos. In terms of the percentage of U.S. states' Latino populations, however, North Carolina only ranks twenty-fourth.[11]

Nonmetro Latinos typically recount their stories in heavily accented English, portraying the language challenge for Latinos who must accommodate to a culture in which English is usually the exclusive language used for communication. There are structural barriers to learning English, especially in rural areas, from the lack of available classes to the overcommitted work schedule that offers little time for scheduled classes. Unless they come from another region of the United States, most Latinos come to North Carolina speaking minimal English. In fact, because the dramatic increase in Latino population is such a recent phenomenon, North Carolina currently has the highest percentage of monolingual Spanish speakers of any state. That will naturally change as more Latino children are born in North Carolina and the use of Spanish follows the natural path of decline for languages other than English in the United States. This pattern of language recession has been repeated hundreds of times in the history of the United States and will no doubt apply to the use of Spanish in North Carolina.

Over the decade that we have known Franco Garcia, his English has improved, but no one would consider him highly fluent in English. Speaking English remains a struggle, but he gamely uses his current knowledge and learns new English words and phrases that even include a few dialect words peculiar to the Outer Banks. The use of Spanish and the emerging English of Spanish speakers in the regional dialect contexts of North Carolina is, of course, one of the unfolding language stories of the state.

The Name Game

One of the recurrent themes in this book is the labels used for dialects, particularly sociocultural varieties. There are issues related to historical and current sociopolitical relationships, socialized attitudes, and in-group and out-group status that often make the choice of labels to describe people and their ways of speaking problematic. Contrary to the trivialization of labels in the "sticks and stones" childhood nursery rhyme, names can hurt—socially, emotionally, and even physically at times. And some names are "fightin' words." Labels are, however, quite fluid, and their denotative and connotative meaning can vary greatly over time and space. On one level, ethnic labeling practices are as integral to the dialectology enterprise as the difference between the use of *butter bean* or *lima bean*; they just happen to carry a lot more social and political baggage than terms for material objects.

The labels used for people of Spanish descent in North Carolina carry the same social and political significance as labels for other groups. The most common terms used for the Spanish-heritage population in North Carolina are probably "Hispanic," "Latino," and "Mexican." In our own studies, we have fluctuated between the use of the terms "Hispanic" and "Latino," sometimes also using the variants "Latino" and "Latina" to avoid the use of a masculine suffix to refer to males and females. The term "Hispanic" is conventionally used to refer to persons of Spanish ancestry in general, while "Latino," derived from "Latin American," is used to refer to persons from South and Central America, including Brazilians who speak Portuguese. The use of these terms, however, tends to be limited to the United States; they have no currency outside of the United States, where people are referred to simply by country of origin—"Mexican," "Salvadoran," "Guatemalan," and so forth. In their countries of origin, there are other ethnic designations that are primary, particularly those between indigenous and Spanish-heritage populations; people only become "Hispanic" or "Latino" once they migrate to the

United States. These labels do not recognize the complex language profiles of individuals who come from Latin American countries and who may speak a language other than Spanish as their first language—such as, for example, Otomí, an indigenous language spoken in Oaxaca, Mexico; or Tzeltal, spoken in Chiapas. At least 10 percent of Mexicans speak an indigenous language, and there are immigrants in the United States who come from Mexico who do not speak Spanish as their first language. The Mixtec, Nahuas, Otomí, Purhépechas, and Triques are among the largest indigenous groups migrating to the United States, and in a study conducted in 2004, it was estimated that about half a million indigenous immigrants in the United States came from the Mexican state of Oaxaca alone and were native Otomí speakers.[12] Such ethnolinguistic diversity is obscured in homogenizing labels for people from different Latin American countries and distinct language backgrounds within these countries.

The term "Hispanic" was first used in 1970 by the U.S. Census to unite the diverse groups of people who came to the United States speaking the Spanish language. Under this term, an African-heritage "black" Spanish-speaking Dominican and a European-heritage "white" Spanish-speaking Chilean would be "Hispanic," while an equally black creole-speaking Haitian would be something else. In other words, the category labels have in effect created the group that they name, demonstrating the politics of labeling categories.

The preference for "Hispanic" or "Latino" seems to be quite regional; "Hispanic" is used primarily on the East Coast and is fairly common in mid-Atlantic states like North Carolina. Dr. Carmen Fought, a California-based linguist who has done extensive research on Chicano English in California, uses the terms "Mexican American," "Chicano," and "Latino" in her study of Spanish-heritage speakers in California in an attempt to follow the community use of "ethnic terms that are viewed positively by the members of the ethnic group in question."[13] She also admits that she found a "surprisingly wide range of opinions" when she asked community members about the meanings and connotations of various labels. The same might be said for speakers in North Carolina, though the options for labels are different. The term "Chicano," widely used in the U.S. Southwest, does not appear among the label options in North Carolina. The terms "Chicano" or "Chicana" are used to refer to U.S. residents of Mexican descent, particularly those with parents born in Mexico. It gained popularity during the so-called Chicano Movement in the late 1960s and early 1970s when César Chávez led farmworkers in a series of strikes against unfair labor practices in California. There are probably a number of reasons the label hasn't caught on in the Southeast. Immigration is a much more recent phenomenon in the Southeast, so the population of Latinos born in the United States whose parents were born in Latin America is still emerging and not already established. According to Fought, "Chicano" also carries some strong political associations associated with the civil revolt of the Chicano Movement that are now uncomfortable for some people

The term "Hispanic," commonly used in North Carolina and elsewhere in the Southeast, is often avoided in the Southwest. In fact, Fought notes that "the main term which some speakers dislike was 'Hispanic.'"[14] They describe it as "a white person's word"—or a word used by researchers writing about the group—and not a term chosen by community members themselves.[15] We saw a similar reaction to the term "Appalachian" among residents of the mountains in chapter 6 and to the term "Native American" in chapter 8. The terms "Hispanic" and "Latino," however, appear to be more neutral labels in the Southeast, showing how regionalized terms can be in both their denotative and connotative meanings.

In North Carolina, Spanish-heritage people are sometimes referred to generically as "Mexicans." In fact, we have even heard immigrants from other Latin American countries refer to themselves by this term, as one car mechanic from Panama did when he told a customer simply to "ask for the Mexican." To some people, however, this reference is offensive because it indiscriminately lumps together people of Spanish descent into a single nationality, whether they are from Mexico, El Salvador, Honduras, Guatemala, or one of the other Central or South American countries. Immigrants from Mexico are certainly the largest group of Latinos, but they still only make up about half of the Spanish-heritage population in North Carolina. So the use of "Mexican" to refer to any person of Spanish ancestry is a kind of ethnic stereotyping that fails to recognize the diversity of nationalities and heritages represented by the Latino population. Dr. Thomas Bonfiglio, in his 2002 book *Race and the Rise of Standard American*, discusses (in a style befitting of a literary critic) the tendency to homogenize social groups: "The illusion of homogeneity is largely a function of secondary revision that glosses over differences and constructs a linear metanarrative, an overgeneralization that suppresses differences and unites the percepts in a structure of wish-fulfillment; i.e., there is something in the popular consciousness that desires to see a unity of geography, ethnicity, and language."[16]

Though the use of the term "Mexican" may be viewed as a kind of stereotyping with negative connotations, there may be other social meanings based on setting. Dr. Phillip Carter, who conducted a comprehensive ethnographic study of the use of Spanish and English among students in a Durham County middle school, observed that the popular term among all students was "Mexican" despite the fact the Latino population in the school included a substantial number of Salvadorans, Guatemalans, and Hondurans. Carter notes that "in the discursive context of the school, differences in nationality tend to be erased and, correspondingly, the popular term among students for all people of Latino origin is 'Mexican.'"[17]

To view the vignette about diversity in the Latino community (from the documentary *Spanish Voices*), visit http://www.talkintarheel.com/chapter/10/video10-1.php

The labels used for social groups are naturally carried over to linguistic labels. In North Carolina, the distinctive variety of English used by Latinos is often referred to as "Hispanic English" or "Latino English," derived directly from the labeling of the ethnic group. Someone has suggested that we might avoid making a decision by calling it "Hispanic Latino English," following the lead of a couple of cultural organizations, but this "safe" choice seems a bit overdone to others. We also see references to "Latino" as "Latina" or "Latino/a" to avoid using the generic masculine reference, but these nuances seem to be lost in everyday conversational reference. Carmen Fought reports that the spelling "Latin@" is popular in Southern California, although she confesses that she has no idea how to pronounce it.[18] To be honest, we've mostly heard professors and researchers use these variants at academic conferences, not folks from the community itself.

In our discussion, we have chosen to use the term "Latino English" to discuss the variety of English used by Spanish-heritage speakers. We choose "Latino English" over "Hispanic English" simply because it seems to be more generally preferable throughout the United States and especially locally.

Spanglish

Most sociolinguists would probably like to eliminate the term "Spanglish" from the vocabulary, but we don't have any power over people's word choices. Generally, "Spanglish" refers to the mixing of Spanish and English in the speech of people who know both languages quite proficiently. But some people also use it to refer to Spanish speakers who have limited proficiency in English, and it is also used to refer to an ethnically marked dialect of English that we prefer to call "Latino English." The reason that sociolinguists cringe is largely due to the fact that it often carries some pejorative associations, referring to an unworthy, corrupted version of English and Spanish. "Spanglish" is often considered "bad English and bad Spanish" in the ways that some native English vernacular dialects of English are referred to as "bad English." Comments such as "They don't speak either English or Spanish, they just speak Spanglish" or "Spanglish isn't a real language" reveal more about attitude than they do about language. In fact, these kinds of comments embrace some misconceptions about bilingual behavior, including the notion that there are no rules about switching between languages.

Linguists find that switching follows systematic patterns and that there are rules for where speakers can switch. Switches take place at certain positions in the sentence, for example, at edges of phrases rather than within them.[19] So a person might say that "We came to *Carolina del Norte* from Mexico," but they would not say "We came to *Carolina del North* from Mexico." In other words, a person doesn't switch to the English word "North" in the middle of the phrase "Carolina del Norte." Switches between languages follow patterns based on linguistic structure; they are not without "hard or fast rules," as is sometimes assumed in references to Spanglish. Switches can also serve a strong social and psychological function in establishing and maintaining cultural solidarity and identity between speakers. Carmen Fought observes:

> We know language represents identity, and it's one of these cases that are so neat, where a language perfectly represents identity. By mixing two languages, you get a mixed way of speaking that mirrors the identity of a person who feels that they're part of two different cultures. We call that code-switching. Spanglish is just the term that the community gives to that, to a mixing of Spanish and English. People tend to think that when they hear someone speaking Spanglish that they don't speak English or Spanish well, or something like that. But in fact, that's not true. In order to do a code-switch variety, in order to speak Spanglish, you have to know both Spanish and English.[20]

To view a video of this quote and more, visit http://www.talkintarheel.com/chapter/10/video10-2.php

To view a vignette about "Spanglish," visit http://www.talkintarheel.com/chapter/10/video10-3.php

Speakers may not be thinking consciously about where and why they switch from one language to another, but there are specific structural patterns and complex social and psychological forces at work. In fact, the research literature on bilingualism includes hundreds of articles on this topic, making it a flourishing research field. Many of these articles are dedicated to describing the structural linguistic and social factors that govern the shift from one language to another.

The Spanish Incursion

Until a couple of decades ago, the language experience of most native North Carolinians was securely monolingual, especially in the nonmetro regions of the state. Apart from a few tourists and some foreign-born students (who also spoke English), language diversity was vested primarily in the dialects of English. Former settlements of German speakers in the Winston-Salem area and other enclaves in the western part of the state had transitioned to monolingual English communities, and only a few hundred Cherokees in the western mountains still spoke Cherokee. Foreign languages were simply a requirement in high school, and the vast majority of North Carolinians lived their lives far removed from a multilingual world.

But the demographic changes that have resulted in the Latino population now accounting for more than 8 percent of the state population has changed that, and Spanish can now be heard from Manteo to Murphy. This language transformation has raised questions that the state has rarely, if ever, confronted. It also, inevitably, has raised some tensions, as traditional monolingual communities encountered a language they could not understand even if they took a couple of years of high school Spanish. The rapidity of the Spanish language influx and its diffusion into the rural regions of the state led to cultural and linguistic shock for residents mostly accustomed to interacting with long-term community residents who shared their regional dialect of English. Reactions have been swift and varied, from those who welcome the cultural diversity and who benefit economically from the presence of Latinos to those who feel threatened and resent the unforeseen change to their traditional community. Some welcome the opportunity to be engaged with people from a different culture who speak a different language, but others view it as a threat to their traditional way of living and speaking: "The Spanish language has somehow become THE popular symbol of threat in recent years—a threat to English and, ipso facto, a threat to US, TO OUR WAY OF LIFE, and to the version of America constituted by and through the English language."[21]

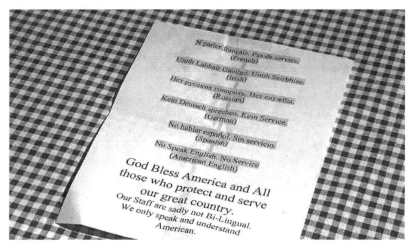

FIGURE 10.3. "No Speak English, No Service" sign at Reedy Family Diner, Lexington, North Carolina. (Courtesy of FOX8 News)

Reactions to the wave of Spanish speakers are not limited to individual opinion. Several local governments have adopted ordinances making English the official language of the government, and local businesses have sometimes become part of the reaction. One restaurant in Lexington, North Carolina, posted a sign in the door that said "No Speak English, No Service" in a way that parodies the use of the Spanish *no* in negative sentences.[22] The sign also explained in multiple languages that the servers only speak "American English," showing an ironic dexterity with languages other than English. After receiving some threatening calls, the owner removed the sign, but the emotional response to the posting is indicative of the tension that has persisted.

The English-Only Movement

Most people are surprised to learn that the United States does not have an official or national language. Many nations have one or more official languages, meaning that the affairs of the government are conducted in these languages. In India, where Hindi is the official language of the republic and English is an "additional" language used for government affairs, each state within the nation can authorize its languages, and there are more than twenty different languages that have official status in India. In the United States, Hawaii has passed a state law making Hawaiian and English official languages, New Mexico has laws providing for the use of both English and Spanish, and Louisiana has laws providing for the use of English and French. But the United States has never passed any legislation as a nation on an official language or languages, though there is little doubt that English is the de facto national language.

Attempts to legislate English as the official language of the United States are hardly new, and numerous attempts have been undertaken to pass a constitutional amendment that would make English the official language. In all cases, movements to make English the official language have arisen from the reaction to a wave of non-English-speaking immigrants. In the early 1900s, for example, in reaction to the large number of immigrants to the United States from southern and eastern Europe, there were movements to make English an official language. In 1920 the state of Nebraska, motivated by the anti-German sentiment at that time, adopted a constitutional amendment declaring English as the official state language. By 1923, thirty-four states had laws that declared English as the language of school instruction, but the movement eventually lost steam as the flow of immigrants diminished and the children of immigrants became monolingual speakers of English.[23]

During the 1980s, there was renewed interest in the Official English Movement, or the so-called English-only amendment that would make English the official language of the United States. This movement was a reaction to the large number of Spanish and Asian immigrants who were moving to the United States for economic or political reasons. In 1981 Senator S. I. Hayakawa, a Canadian-born academic-turned-politician, introduced a constitutional amendment to make English the official language.[24] Ironically, Hayakawa's academic life was spent as a linguistic semanticist, and he wrote a popular book, Language in Action, that was well known by linguists of his generation.[25] The amendment was ratified by twenty-eight states, mostly during the 1980s, but it fell well short of the thirty-eight states needed for its adoption as a constitutional amendment. As the movement gained momentum, North Carolina, without much fanfare, voted to ratify this amendment in 1987.[26] At the time that North Carolina voted for the amendment, the state was still largely monolingual and the vote seemed relatively benign, but the status of English has now become much more controversial since the recent wave of Spanish immigrants. In the last decade, several towns in North Carolina, including Mint Hill and Landis, proposed English-only ordinances that would explicitly recognize English as the language for use in local government affairs. It passed in Landis in 2007.[27] These kinds of acts seem to be symbolic of a language stance with respect to immigrant groups, though it is difficult to determine precisely what legal significance they might have in terms of local government since other laws protect the right to translation services in legal and other proceedings.

The rationale for the English-only amendment seems fairly straightforward: it is intended to unify the nation under a common language. The seeds for such a perspective have been sown and nurtured for well over a century. In fact, in 1907 U.S. president Theodore Roosevelt wrote in his memorial, published in 1926: "We have room for but one language in this country, and that is the English language, for we intend to see that the crucible turns our people out as Americans, of American nationality, and not as dwellers in a polyglot boarding house."[28] English is presented as the common, unifying language of the United States and an empowering economic and social tool for immigrants.

On first glance, an amendment to make English the official language of the United States seems like a simple ratification of the de facto status of English in the United States, but the proposal has turned out to be highly controversial, particularly in regions where other languages are used in everyday conversation. Linguists, along with many other citizens concerned with human rights, view the amendment as inconsistent with values of cultural and linguistic inclusion. Historically, the unity of the United States has rested on overarching political and social ideals, not language unity, though this unity might sometimes be questioned during political campaigns. Furthermore, the amendment assumes that the status of English in the United States is threatened by other languages. In fact, historically, the opposite pattern is the case. In chapter 8, we discussed the brutal cultural and psychological effects of the government's forced assimilation programs of American Indians, which contributed to the eradication of many American Indian languages and the erasure of many cultural legacies. Other European languages that have come to the United States, including German, Polish, Irish, Italian, and French, often before or concurrent with the arrival of English, have all quietly given way to English's dominance. English has maintained its rule without ever being pronounced sovereign; historically and currently, languages other than English are the ones threatened by extinction in the United States, and there is no reason to think that this situation will change with respect to Spanish.

The Linguistic Society of America is just one of the professional organizations that voiced strong opposition to the English-only amendment, passing a resolution in 1987 that included the following:

> **Be it therefore resolved** that the Society make known its opposition to such "English only" measures, on the grounds that they are based on misconceptions about the role of a common language in establishing political unity, and that they are inconsistent with basic American traditions of linguistic tolerance. As scholars with a professional interest in language, we affirm that:
>
> The English language in America is not threatened. All evidence suggests that recent immigrants are overwhelmingly aware of the social and economic advantages of becoming proficient in English, and require no additional compulsion to learn the language.

The resolution goes on to state that "it is to the economic and cultural advantage of the nation as a whole that its citizens should be proficient in more than one language, and to this end we should encourage both foreign language study for native English speakers, and programs that enable speakers with other linguistic backgrounds to maintain proficiency in those languages along with English."[29]

It might also be pointed out that the government needs proficient speakers in a host of languages for missions abroad, both in times of peace and in times of conflict; in fact, the U.S. Central Intelligence Agency and the National Security Agency have both claimed that their missions have been hampered by a lack of bi- and multilingual agents. Linguists have been quite resistant to, and adamant in their opposition to, the English-only movement, viewing it as a symbol of suspicion and resentment toward immigrants. They view the amendment as unnecessary and redundant. As linguist Dr. Geoffrey Pullum writes: "Making English the official language of the United States of America is about as urgently called for as making hotdogs the official food at baseball."[30]

An amendment making English the official language of the United States is not, however, as innocuous as designating a state's official bird, song, or vegetable. It potentially limits access to governmental services for newly arrived residents who may need language assistance in crucial services—for emergency medical assistance, public health, legal services, and other official and unofficial interactions that involve the use of language. Though it is difficult to imagine that this could ever take place in the United States, there are countries—for example, Slovakia and Latvia—where speaking a language other than the official language (Slovakian and Latvian, respectively) can lead to fines or even imprisonment. In the case of Slovakia, there is a sizeable population of Hungarian speakers in the southern region who are penalized by this rule, while in Latvia there are many Russian speakers who are punished by the law.[31] With such potential stakes, it is understandable why those who value linguistic diversity would stand so strongly in their opposition to a constitutional amendment making English the official language of the United States.

Shifting Language

Though it is sometimes imagined that there is adamant resistance to learning English, we are still looking for our first Spanish-heritage speaker who actually expresses this sentiment. In fact, there is a well-documented pattern of language shift found in study after study in which experts in demography and population studies "have consistently found a shift to English by the second or third generations among Spanish-speaking and other immigrant groups in the United States."[32] The first generation comes to the United States speaking a language other than English, the second generation is bilingual, and the third generation is dominant in English and, in most cases, monolingual unless there are direct strategies to maintain bilingualism.

Walt Wolfram's parents came to the United States in the 1920s from Germany as adults speaking only German. They settled comfortably in a German-speaking neighborhood in Philadelphia, Pennsylvania, worked in German-speaking factories, attended churches where the services were in German, and socialized in their home only with people who also spoke German as their first language. The first language of their six children was German, but the children rapidly abandoned German when they starting attending school. The children all became English dominant, despite the fact that the parents exposed them to the German language at home, at church, and in the community. Walt and his wife, Marge, who comes from the same German community where she spoke German as her first language, spoke almost no German to their children, and today these children only recognize a few German swear words and the German commands barked to their dog. This is the typical pattern regularly repeated with immigrants who come to the United States speaking a language other than English, be it Polish, Mandarin, or Spanish.

Children of Spanish-speaking parents born in the United States use more and more English as they mature, and our interactions and interviews with the Spanish-speaking community in North Carolina lead us to predict that the next generation of Spanish-heritage residents in North Carolina will probably be monolingual English speakers. The prospect of linguistic assimilation to English is much more inevitable than any threat of Spanish to the sovereignty of the English language in the United States.[33]

Rapid language shift can sometimes have practical consequences for families. When monolingual Spanish grandparents and their children and grandchildren from Latin American countries interact with monolingual English second- and third-generational children, they are left without a common language for communication. In the process, a language integral to immigrants' cultural heritage is lost. In this respect, the United States is the exception, where only 6 percent of its population is raised bilingually.[34] Over two-thirds of the rest of the world is raised bilingually, a rate that is ten times higher than that of the United States. It is curious that some Americans are proud of their monolingualism since there are intellectual and practical benefits to knowing a language other than English in an increasingly global economy. There are even advantages at the later stages in one's life span. A study in 2010 showed that being bilingual had the effect of delaying the onset of Alzheimer's disease by four-to-five years, just as doing crossword puzzles or learning a musical instrument tends to boost the brain's cognitive reserves.[35] There are cognitive, social, and economic reasons for encouraging the maintenance of bilingualism apart from the obvious cultural heritage it embodies.

Tar Heel Latino English

Ana (pseudonym) is a nine-year-old girl who lives in a rural area outside of Hickory in Catawba County. Her parents are from Mexico, but she has lived mostly in the United States. She is fully bilingual, but naturally uses much more Spanish at home than in school, where she strongly favors English. In some respects, she is typical of an increasing number of children of Latino parents who are being raised in the United States—bilinguals who use English and Spanish in different settings. In an interview conducted by one of the staff members of the North Carolina Language and Life Project, Ana talks about her involvement in Girls on the Run, a recreational program devoted to promoting physical and mental health among girls by raising self-esteem. In the passage, we indicate some of the sounds she produces with modified spelling. The italicized words are intended to mark some of the distinctive pronunciations and grammatical features in the passage: "I'm just *doin'* it here. It's Girls on the Run. Last *tahm* we had a race, but I didn't want to *gew*. It was *tiw* chilly. And—but this *tahm*—it's gonna be this Saturday—I'm gonna *gew*. It's, like, you *dew* runs for *fahv* mile, or, one day I did a run for *fahv* miles and it's real hard."[36]

To hear this passage, visit http://www.talkintarheel.com/ chapter/10/audio10-3.php

The first impression of Ana's English is that it is very southern and somewhat rural. She produces the *ing* of "doing" as *in'*, unglides her long *i* in *time* and *five* to *tahm* and *fahv*, and pronounces the vowels of *go* and *do* as *gew* and *diw* in a way that reflects the southern rural pronunciation described in chapter 3. In her grammar, she leaves the plural *-s* off of the noun *mile*, following a southern rural pattern in which the plural *-s* is not required for nouns of weights and measures when the word is preceded by a number or quantifier, as in *five mile* or *six bushel*. Her speech sounds so characteristically southern that it might be tempting to say that she doesn't sound Latina at all. But when we listen closer, there is something about the rhythm of her speech that doesn't quite sound like a native English speaker, leaving a detectable trace of Spanish influence. We'll say more later about the rhythm in Latino English, because it turns out to be one of the more persistent traces of Spanish heritage that might be sustained in the long term.

To hear an exercise on detecting bilingual versus monolingual status, visit http://www.talkintarheel.com/ chapter/10/audio10-4.php

The passage from Ana raises questions about the kind of English that Spanish-heritage speakers adopt in North Carolina. Do speakers just adopt the dialect of the community where they learn English? Do they lose all traces of Spanish as time goes on? In other regions of the country, such as the Southwest or New York City among Puerto Ricans, a distinct ethnic dialect of Latino English has arisen, even among monolingual English speakers.[37] If such a variety has developed in North Carolina, what southern traits may be incorporated into the language, and how consistent will these appear? Perhaps surprisingly, it is often impossible to tell the difference between bilingual and monolingual native English speakers by listening to them speak English. In our studies of North Carolina Latino English, we have found a number of cases where listeners cannot tell whether a young speaker was born in North Carolina or Latin America.

Listeners have a tendency to attribute any feature linked to Spanish to the acquisition of English as a second language. Research on Chicano English in

FIGURE 10.4. Honduran immigrant Maria Punch sounds southern to listeners on the phone. (Photograph by Danica Cullinan)

the Southwest, however, shows that traits derived from Spanish historically are not a matter of inadequate English learning but an integration of heritage linguistic features into American English in order to construct a distinct ethnic identity tied, in part, to a unique variety of English.[38] Will this be the case in North Carolina as well? Only time will tell what will happen in North Carolina, but we have now been studying the emergence of Latino English since the early 2000s in order to follow the possible development of a Tar Heel version of Latino English. We have conducted interviews with Latinos from the coast to the mountains, including urban areas such as Durham and Raleigh and nonmetro areas from Hyde County on the coast to Catawba County in the west. The results of our studies show some noteworthy trends of both dialect assimilation and distinction.[39]

Dialect Mix and Match

Acquiring English as a second or other language in the context of a local dialect community is a complicated process. For speakers who learn English as adults, it is practically impossible to acquire an unaccented variety of English, despite the fact that a speaker may be completely proficient in understanding and producing English. As Walt Wolfram's mother would say, fifty years after settling in the United States: "They know I'm from Germany the minute I open my mouth." Most adult learners of English never rid themselves of the influence of their first language, reaching a plateau of accented English that seems to be frozen or "fossilized" for life. For children, however, it is a different language game, and they can become proficient in English that sounds quite native in a relatively short time.

The extent to which this happens is determined in part by a person's social situation, including family life, social life, school life, and individual identity. Because there are so many factors involved in this process, it is difficult to project a common path for Spanish-heritage speakers learning English. We do know, however, that certain traits from Spanish are likely to "transfer" to their English. Below are passages from two nine-year-old children from Siler City, one born in the Siler City community and one more recent immigrant who came to the United States from Mexico a couple of years prior to the interview. For the sake of illustration, we'll focus on the marking of past tense in verbs, one of the major features of language acquisition for all learners of English as a second language. In the passage, verbs that follow the standard English norm are bolded and those that are not marked for past tense are italicized.[40]

NINE-YEAR-OLD SPEAKER BORN IN SILER CITY

To hear this passage, visit
http://www.talkintarheel.com/
chapter/10/audio10-5.php

The little mermaid when, she *rescue* a boy. And then they, they—she *help* him, then she *start* singing to him. Then, 'cause the boat they **were** on, they—it **started** on fire and it *go* under water and he **couldn't** breathe under water so she **took** him over there, and her daddy **said** to them, "Rescue humans or nothing." And she don't—and then a bird **came** and he **said**, "He's dead." Then, um, his grandpa **came** and he *wake* up the boy and he **was**, uh, he **said** a girl **was** singing. Then she *turn* into a human.

Some of the verbs are marked for past tense and some are unmarked, showing variation in the attachment of past tense in her English. Though highly variable, there are patterns to this fluctuation so that, for example, irregular verbs such as *be*, *take*, and *say* are more likely to be marked for past tense than regular verbs such as *turn* or *help*. We have studied this kind of variation in marking past tense in a number of different language-learning situations, and it follows a highly predictable pattern related to general strategies of language learning that happened to apply both to first- and second-language learning.[41] In this case, the pattern is closely related to pronunciation patterns, though it is often interpreted instead as a speaker struggling with grammar.

To hear this passage, visit
http://www.talkintarheel.com/
chapter/10/audio10-6.php

NINE-YEAR-OLD SPEAKER,
TWO YEARS IN THE UNITED STATES

Like the other day I **went** to Waltmar and she **was** there, and we *say* hey to each other, and we **wanted** to spend the night one time at my house but she **couldn't** cause she *haded to go with her family. They **were** gonna go somewhere. But I **don't** when **she's** gonna spend the night with me. One time I *spend* the night at her house. Oh, it **was**, um, a sleepover. We **had** all kinds of friends we *invite* all of her friends, I *invite* mines so she *invite* hers and we **had** a sleepover. Whoever—whoever, um, *sleeps*, whoever *wake up* late, they **were** the ones who **gotta** cook for them and clean up the room, and paint their face. So, I know I *wake up* early. I always wake up at five o'clock. So I *didn't had to clean the room. I *didn't even had to go in back.

The two speakers show quite similar patterns of fluctuation in their use of past tense, despite the fact that one was born in the United States and the other had come from Mexico just a couple of years before the interview. Both speakers lived in homes with Spanish-dominant speakers, so Spanish was the norm for speaking at home. The second speaker, in addition to unmarked past tense, has some double marking of past tense (marked by *) in forms like "I didn't had to and she haded to go," a kind of overgeneralization fairly characteristic of second-language learning. At the same time, she also demonstrates her acquisition of the southern greeting form *Hey* when she notes that she said "Hey" to her friend in Walmart—or, in her rendering, *Waltmar*. We can't be sure, but the use of *mar*, which means "sea" in Spanish, may be a carryover from Spanish or the product of eliminating a final consonant, a preferred pattern in Spanish pronunciation.

Local regional greetings in English may be among the early dialectal forms that are acquired, as well as the iconic *y'all*. It is not unusual for speakers to incorporate *y'all* into their speech within the first year or two, so we were not surprised when a Latino server at a local pizza shop in Siler City came to our table and asked in heavily accented English, "Can I help y'all?" Local dialect words and phrases can be conveniently incorporated into the most accented English. In fact, one of our former students, Becky Moriello, titled her master's thesis "'I'm Feeksin' to Move': Hispanic English in Siler City," quoting from a conversation she had with a Latino resident.[42]

In one study of language acquisition among Latinos, linguists Dr. Mary Kohn and Hannah Franz looked at the acquisition of the relatively new use of *be like* in English to introduce directly reported speech, thought, emotions, mimetic expression, and so forth.[43] For many American English speakers under the age of forty to fifty, the use of *be like* has largely replaced *say*, as in "My brother was like, 'You're a scaredy cat,'" instead of "My brother said, 'You're a scaredy cat.'" The use of *like* to carry along a narrative (for example, "We were at the mall, like, just hanging out, and like, we saw these people . . .") or to introduce a quotation is one of the things that older speakers love to rail about in the speech of younger Americans. For sure, some speakers can use it quite frequently. Kohn and Franz report that a young Latina woman in Hickory used so-called quotative *be like* eighty-nine times in a relatively short interview with her, as illustrated in the following excerpt: "Yeah, and I *was like*, 'What are you talking about?,' and *she's like*, 'I know the Apple laptop cost like nine hundred dollars so don't tell me this is—,' and I *was like*, 'You know how much that purse cost?,' and *she's like*, 'What? Like thirty?' And I *was like*, 'Read the label!' And *she's like* . . ."[44]

The same speaker introduced only three cases of directly reported speech with the more traditional verb *say*, showing how prominent the use of quotative *be like* can be among some speakers. At the same time, it can be one of the earlier features of American English acquired by Latinos. The study of Latino middle school students in Durham shows that their use of African American English features can be quite robust, though it varies with the social group.

To hear this passage, visit http://www.talkintarheel.com/chapter/10/audio10-7.php

We have also compared the process of ungliding for the long i in *tahm* for *time* and *sahd* for *side* in different Latino community settings and found that rural speakers are more likely than their urban cohorts to unglide their long i following the traditional Tar Heel model. But there is also a lot of variation among speakers that relates to their social affiliation and person identity—or "agency."

Finally, we've looked at the timing system for the production of speech in different communities. Timing, or rhythm, relates to the beat of syllables in a way that is parallel to how long we "hold a note" in musical patterning. Languages can have quite different timing patterns, ranging from those that assign approximately the same beat to each syllable to those that hold stressed syllables longer than others. Languages that produce all syllables approximately the same are referred to as *syllable-timed languages*, and those that hold stressed syllables longer than the unstressed ones are referred to as *stressed-timed languages*. Spanish is typically described as a syllable-timed language and English as a stressed-time language, though this distinction is not an absolute one. If we take a sentence like "Juan and Billy like to eat ice cream," the difference in syllable timing and stress timing might be represented by the length of the line under the syllables. The most-stressed syllables are capitalized and bolded, the next-most-stressed syllables are capitalized, and other syllables are relatively unstressed. The second production follows the pattern of Spanish syllable timing and sounds somewhat "syncopated" to a native speaker of English.

Stress-timed pronunciation:
JUAN and **BILL**y LIKE to EAT **ICE** CREAM

—   -   —   -   —   -   —   —   —

Syllable-timed pronunciation:
JUAN and **BILL**y LIKE to EAT **ICE** CREAM

—   —   —   —   —   —   —   —   —

To hear the stress-timed pronunciation versus the syllable-timed pronunciation of this sentence, visit http://www.talkintarheel.com/chapter/10/audio10-8.php

With more-recent advances in the instrumental measurement of sounds, we can measure the length of each syllable quite precisely in milliseconds. After measuring hundreds of syllable pairs like this, we can arrive at an average score for syllable timing for a speaker. Using this method, we have calculated the timing for a number of varieties of English and other languages. We have found that ethnic varieties of English like Latino English occupy an intermediate position between timing in the heritage-language Spanish and the English target norms of North Carolina European American and African American English. We also have found that syllable timing in a developing Latino community in North Carolina matches that for a long-standing Latino community in southern Texas, suggesting uniformity for this trait for Spanish-heritage speakers across different regional settings. In fact, we have found that syllable timing seems to be one of the most persistent and sustainable features of Latino English in different regions in the United States, and that, in some cases, it may carry over to monolingual English speakers. It is certainly too early to predict how an eventual dialect of Latino English in North Carolina might stabilize, but it seems to be gaining currency as a sociocultural variety of English with a formative contribution from the southern dialects and Spanish heritage in North Carolina.

Symbolic Dialect

Speakers of Spanish learning English make dialect choices. There are different norms and models for speaking English in their emerging linguistic environment, from the dialect-minimized Standard English of ESL instructors to the regional and ethnic varieties spoken by neighboring socioethnic groups. We have noticed that many ESL teachers in North Carolina speak nonsouthern varieties of English, while other teachers in schools show considerable variation, ranging from regionalized varieties of southern speech to midland and even New England dialects of English. Students learning English in the schools are further exposed to the dialects of their student peers that include vernacular regional and ethnic dialects. The variety of dialects offered in a single school or community setting provide a number of options for modeling English. From the onset, emerging English speakers make choices based on a full range of social and psychological factors. Children from the same family who attend the same school may make quite different dialect choices based on their engagement with social structures, sometimes referred to as "speaker agency." Individuals have the capacity to act independently and to make their own choices, but these are naturally influenced by social structures related to class, ethnicity, gender, and so forth.

Consider the simple dialect choices made by an eleven-year-old girl and her thirteen-year-old brother in the use of the long i in *time* and *ride*. The siblings lived in Siler City at the time of our interview with them. Their parents came from Mexico, but the children lived all of their lives in the North Carolina Piedmont, moving a couple of times in Durham County before settling in Siler City. At the beginning of our interview, we asked them to count to ten in order to make sure the tape recorder was working properly. This is how they counted:[45]

Eleven-year-old girl: One, two, three, four, five, six, seven, eight, nine, ten.
Thirteen-year-old boy: One, two, three, four, *fahv*, six, seven, eight, *nahn*, *tin*.

In addition to the ungliding of i, the brother also merged the pronunciation of the *pin* and *pen* vowel in the pronunciation of *ten* as *tin*, and he used a kind of raspy voice that is often associated with a style of speech used by

To hear these passages, visit http://www.talkintarheel.com/ chapter/10/audio10-9.php

young African American males. The boy, who also indicates many other southern vernacular features in his speech, identifies strongly with a local version of "jock" culture of adolescent boys, projecting a strong "macho" image, while his sister is much more oriented toward to mainstream American institutional values sometimes referred to as "nerd." Such cases demonstrate the symbolic choices that speakers may make as they mold their identities in relation to those around them and make choices about self-presentation, even within the same family. This case might also suggest a role for gender in this equation, since the brother's choice aligns him with a typically more masculine identity in addition to his decidedly southern orientation.

Speakers, however, are not static, and they may change over time and situation. In one remarkable case study, linguist Phillip Carter interviewed a young Latina over the course of several years, starting at age ten. She migrated from Mexico to Raleigh when she was eight, staying with relatives until she was reunited with her parents at age ten.[46] At the time that Carter started recording her speech, she lived in an insular, Spanish-speaking community and attended a predominantly white school in a suburb of Raleigh. She was one of only two Latinos in her class and one of a handful of Latino students in her school. She then moved to a new, ethnically diverse community and changed schools, attending a middle school that is approximately 50 percent African American, 30 percent Latino, and 20 percent white or other ethnicity. When Carter first started studying her speech, Maria (a pseudonym) had, for the most part, acquired the English of her classroom cohorts—mainly white children whose parents had moved to the region from the North. The suburban school was viewed as a school of northern transplants, and Maria's speech sounded nonsouthern—like most of her peers. A couple of years later, Carter noticed that Maria had acquired not only a new urban, hip-hop style of dress and hairstyle but also a new dialect to go with it. Carter notes that "for the first time since meeting Maria, she sounded, impressionistically more, rather than less, Latina and for the first time in my presence she referred to herself as Mexican."[47] She now embodied difference, including an "attendant metamorphosis in language." Her vowels and other features of her dialect had become much more symbolically Latina. Carter notes that Maria's current presentation of self is not simply about her adoption of dialect or style but the agency she assumed within the social milieu of a North Carolina middle school divided into racialized social groups. At one pole of the so-

FIGURE 10.5. The Quinceañera has become a part of Latino festivities in North Carolina. (Photograph from Danica Cullinan)

cial spectrum are the "nerds" who are categorically "white" regardless of academic achievement, and on the other end of the spectrum are various gangs that are categorically African American and Latino. In between are the "Latino nerds," the "average" Latinos, the "average" and "nerd" African Americans, and so on. Maria underwent a transformation as she abandoned the peer norms of her first school for a new middle school with a different social order, showing how an adolescent can change her voice according to new situations and choices about her presentation of self.

Stability and Change

Predictions about trends in language are about as reliable as the weather report. At the same time, there are historical tendencies and sociolinguistic movements that suggest a long-term trajectory for the speakers of Spanish who currently live in North Carolina. With the largest group of non-English-language speakers ever to live in the state, there should be a lasting effect. However, the number of speakers of Spanish will no doubt decline sharply, following the typical pattern of immigrants who come speaking another language and end up monolingual English speakers after a few generations. Instead of Spanish persisting as a commonly spoken language in North Carolina, there is a good chance that a socioethnic variety of Latino English will flourish, as it has in the Southwest United States. It has certainly happened for other socioethnic varieties of English in North Carolina, like Lumbee English and African American English, so there is no reason to think it could not happen for Latino English. Some subtle traits from the Spanish heritage language will probably persist—perhaps the timing of syllables and other

To view a discussion of Latino English from *Spanish Voices*, visit http://www.talkintarheel .com/chapter/10/video10-4.php

nuanced phonetic traits—but other significant traits in the mix will no doubt bear the imprint of southern English. The blend of southern-based English and Spanish-language heritage should continue, not only by bilingual speakers, but by future monolingual speakers of English who perpetuate their Latin American heritage. Latino English should be one of North Carolina's most significant sociocultural varieties for some time to come.

Celebrating Language Diversity 11

And if you listen to me for another minute, you can hear me smile at you.

—**DR. BOYD DAVIS**, quoted from *Voices of North Carolina*, produced by Neal Hutcheson
(Raleigh: North Carolina Language and Life Project, 2005)

From a safe distance, the middle-aged man stopped and stared
at our exhibit at the State Fair. His greased, dark hair and rebel
flag insignia on his black leather jacket and upturned collar
made us wonder if we were about to confront the occasional
visitor who reacts negatively to our celebration of language diversity. Though he was our only visitor at the time, he stood in
the middle of the lobby, glaring intently at our panels about

To view the full quote by
Boyd Davis, visit http://
www.talkintarheel.com/
chapter/11/video11-1.php

Spanish, Cherokee, Lumbee English, and African American English, among
others. Eventually, he inched toward our staff, and we braced ourselves for
his reaction. Instead, he sweetly asked: "Do y'all accept donations for your
work? I really appreciate what y'all are doing to preserve our language tradition." He proceeded to tell us how his family has lived for hundreds of
years in the Piedmont region of Chatham County and how proud he was
of his heritage. We happily accepted his donation and gave him a DVD of
Voices of North Carolina in return. After he left, we confessed to each other that
we had shamefully prejudged him because of his appearance. At the same
time, it made us realize the broad base of interest in language and dialect
differences.

Why Language?

In a world confronting challenges like global warming, terrorism, and hun-
ger, language may seem like a relatively trivial matter. But it is not. The

FIGURE 11.1. Discussing language at the North Carolina State Fair in Raleigh. (Photograph by Liang Zhang)

choices we make in language have a tremendous impact on how we go about solving problems. Heated political, social, or scientific debates often revolve around which word we use or whose definition is privileged. In politics, an indiscreet word or phrase can cost an election, and word choice can lead to a libel suit costing millions of dollars. Polls reveal that a little difference in language can make a huge difference in perception; Americans are very much against a government-imposed "Death Tax" but are more accepting of the same tax under the name "Estate Tax."[1] It is no exaggeration to say that there are wars—literal and metaphorical—fought because of language.

The use of language to set apart and bring together is not a recent phenomenon. Chapter 12 of the book of Judges in the Christian Old Testament includes an account from somewhere between 1070 and 1370 B.C.E. in which language was used as a means of differentiating groups that led to the deaths of 42,000 Ephraimites. In the account, the Ephraimites, having just suffered a military defeat at the hands of the Gileadites, attempted to return to their homeland on the other side of the Jordan River. The Gileadites controlled the river crossing and used language as a means of identifying Ephraimites from other travelers. Before being allowed to cross the river, each traveler was asked to say the word "shibboleth," a Hebrew word meaning "grain." The Ephraimites' dialect did not have the "sh" sound, so

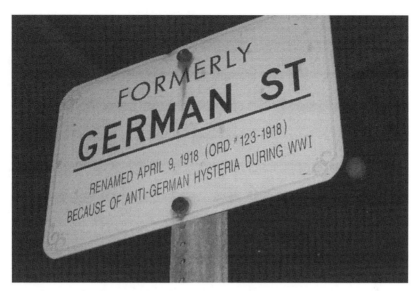

FIGURE 11.2. Sign from Cincinnati, Ohio, describing the linguistic heritage of the area. (Photograph by Jerome Strauss)

they would pronounce the word as "sibboleth"—after which they were immediately killed.

Language has continued to serve a strategic role in identifying group membership. American soldiers at the Battle of the Bulge used the ability to talk about baseball as a means of separating other American soldiers from Germans in American uniforms.[2] In World War II, Americans used the term *lollapalooza* to try to root out Japanese who had infiltrated their ranks, exploiting the tendency for speakers of Japanese to pronounce their l's as r's.[3] Linguistic identifications like these have been used by national groups around the world where identification was critical to national security. Of all the markers of identity, language may be the most revealing—and the hardest to fake—of our cultural distinctiveness.

Other war-related linguistic responses reveal as much about our nation's fears and hopes as they do about the power of language to unite and divide. The renaming of German foods like "sauerkraut" and "hamburgers" as *liberty cabbage* and *liberty sausage* during World War I seems a bit humorous in retrospect, but such renaming was a means of effectively fostering American solidarity.[4] This anti-German zeal spilled over into the streets, literally. Hundreds of streets that were renamed during this time have never been returned to their German-sounding origins. In 1995 Cincinnati, Ohio, considered un-

FIGURE 11.3. Freedom Fries spread to Wilmington, North Carolina.
(Photo by David Bailey)

cloaking its German heritage by reverting streets to the original names. The reversal lacked popular support, but now some secondary signs around the city offer a short history of the street name, such as: "English Street. Formerly German Street, renamed April 9, 1918, because of Anti-German hysteria during WWI."

We are not immune from such displays of linguistic renaming today. In 2003 U.S. representative Robert Ney, who oversaw the congressional cafeterias, ordered that all menus change "French fries" to "Freedom Fries" in "a small but symbolic effort to show the strong displeasure many on Capitol Hill have with our so-called ally, France."[5]

The grave consequences of linguistic differences depicted here are, thankfully, not the norm. But that does not diminish the serious consequences of linguistic differences. While sentencing people to death over dialect differences is not something we do today in America, we still use language variation as a means of grouping and judging others, resulting in significant effects on housing, education, and access to services. We note one example here to build the case for the importance of studying language scientifically.

Given current sensibilities, it is shocking to read today how bilingualism—and by extension, those who spoke with an identifiable "foreign accent"—was formerly viewed in the United States. In 1926, in one of the top journals of psychology, Dr. Florence Goodenough, a pioneer in the field of developmental psychology and a major contributor to early intelligence and standardized testing, published findings in which bilinguals scored lower on IQ tests than those who spoke only English. She concluded that there are essentially two explanations for this: "The use of a foreign language in the home is one of the chief factors in producing mental retardation. . . . A more probable explanation is that these nationality groups whose intellectual ability is inferior do not readily learn the new language."[6] We know now that it was the tests—not the nationalities—that were "inferior." In the introduction to one of the first major linguistic studies of bilingualism, linguist Dr. Uriel Weinreich in 1953 cataloged widespread "scholarly" assertions about the effects of bilingualism, which included inevitable poor fluency in two languages, excessive idleness, moral depravity, left-handedness, low intelligence, emotional troubles, and excessive materialism.[7] Subsequent empirical research overturned every one of these conclusions and subsequently demonstrated that there are cognitive benefits associated with bilingualism. The gulf between linguistic lore and linguistic reality is the same gulf between the lore that the Earth is flat and the scientific reality that it is spherical. Flat-earth thinking has few dire consequences, however, whereas linguistic lore has many. So pervasive is language lore in our culture that one of the founders of modern linguistics, Swiss linguist Dr. Ferdinand de Saussure, noted: "In the lives of individuals and of society, language is a factor of greater importance than any other. For the study of language to remain solely the business of a handful of specialists would be a quite unacceptable state of affairs. In practice, the study of language is in some degree or other the concern of everyone."[8] This same sentiment was echoed by Dr. Dwight Bolinger, a Harvard linguist and former president of the Linguistic Society of America, who concluded: "Language should be as much an object of public scrutiny as any of the other things that keenly affect our lives—as much as pollution, energy, crime, busing, and next week's grocery bill."[9]

Language is obviously a topic worthy of scientific and social scientific investigations, and the implications of language-related research are significant in a wide range of venues: child language acquisition; educational achievement; reading and writing instruction; urban development; civil rights; bilingual educational policy; poverty; criminal justice; access to housing, goods, and services; and so forth. Language pervades all areas of life, from the courts' opinions on "ear-witness" testimony to those who experience linguistic profiling over the telephone or in the classroom. The pervasiveness and clandestine nature of language-based discrimination are so acute that Dr. Rosini Lippi-Green writes that language discrimination "can be found everywhere in our daily lives. In fact, such behavior is so commonly accepted, so widely perceived as appropriate, that it must be seen as the last back door to discrimination. And the door stands wide open."[10]

Linguistic Plurality

North Carolina's rich tapestry of language diversity is truly one of its great resources, and as such, it should be a source of pride for its residents. It is not, however, always viewed in such a positive light. When we tell people we meet that we are linguists, we often hear a response like this: "Oh, well, I better watch my grammar around you." In our research and travels, we often encounter people who apologize for their "country accent" or recount to us a story about a time they felt uncomfortable speaking, not because they

To hear the pronunciations of cot and caught merged and unmerged vowels, visit http://www.talkintarheel.com/chapter/11/audio11-1.php

didn't know what to say but because they were afraid the way they said it would be ridiculed. Many residents of North Carolina have gone out of their way to practice pronouncing pen and pin differently, even though it causes only an occasional, momentary confusion in conversation. A similar type of linguistic feature—a merger of two vowels—managed to go unnoticed for twenty years to Jeff Reaser, who learned in his first linguistics class that many people do not pronounce cot and caught the same way.

To view the video of the quote from American Tongues, visit http://www.talkintarheel.com/chapter/11/video11-2.php

Neither the pin/pen merger nor the cot/caught merger cause much conversational confusion, so what is the source of the negative stereotypes of speakers who use the pin/pen merger that we hear from southerners, including most native North Carolinians? Language use is different than the use of other types of knowledge. It is commonplace to hear people admit humorously, "I can't balance my checking account," but have you ever heard someone playfully admit, "I can't conjugate my verbs"? Even people who are quite secure in their personal identity in other ways can exhibit linguistic insecurities such as these. In the documentary American Tongues, a man from New Orleans captures this sentiment perfectly: "You know, I mean, it's not a matter of pride or anything, but I mean I don't want to go through the process of making my tongue do this stuff you have to do to talk right, I mean, you know why put forth the effort? Everybody knows me."[11]

In our documentaries on North Carolina speech, we hear many similar sentiments. In our documentary *Mountain Talk*, Appalachian resident Kyle Edwards (quoted in chapter 6) notes that he "wouldn't swap places with nobody" and feels "much more comfortable here being twenty years behind everybody than I would be a-sitting in a lot of other places and being so miserable."[12]

To view the video of this quote, visit http://www.talkintarheel .com/chapter/11/video11-3.php

It is clear that these gentlemen are exactly where they most want to be. They are who they want to be. But they position themselves as somehow deficient or behind where others would think they should be. There is nothing deficient in the language of these folks, nor in the language of those who merge *pin* and *pen*. It is for social reasons—not linguistic reasons—that these prejudices about dialect differences exist.

One of the goals of our research, and of this book, is to raise awareness about the historical, cultural, and humanistic explanations for language diversity in North Carolina so that we, collectively, become proud rather than ashamed of our linguistic differences. We truly love the differences we hear in and among languages, as those differences tell about who we are and where we came from, who our ancestors were, where they came from, and who we hope to be. The now-deceased editor of the *Dictionary of American Regional English*, Dr. Frederic Cassidy, notes in *American Tongues* how dull a world we would live in without linguistic diversity: "The little differences that are with us everywhere we go are not likely to be changed, as long as they don't prevent comprehension. As long as they don't keep you from knowing what somebody else is saying or what you are saying to somebody else. As long as they don't spoil communication, then we're not going to change them. Why should we? I don't want to sound like somebody from some other part of the country. I don't know what's wrong with my own speech. We don't have to all talk alike."[13]

To view the video of this quote, visit http://www.talkintarheel .com/chapter/11/video11-4.php

We are not inspired simply by the old cliché that "variety is the spice of life." Language variety allows us to do the things that make us distinctly human. We can create and interpret, discover and teach. Without mentioning it, our voice conveys clearly how the world is to understand us. As we saw in the quote by Dr. Boyd Davis that opened this chapter, our voice can convey a smile, a frown, or a scolding. It can connect us to others or distance us from them. There are times when we rely on our voices to give hugs or dry tears over the telephone. There are few tools more useful, weapons more powerful, or balms more soothing than speech. The pen is said to be mightier than the sword, but spoken words "have more power than atom bombs."[14] Malleable and diverse speech can reflect the deep cultural and personal beliefs and rituals that are fundamental to our being and doing.

One of the aspects of language that makes it so appealing is that it is at once personal and communal. From birth, we are exposed to language and eventually start to take what we hear and make it our own. Very quickly, we arrange words in ways that we've never heard spoken before—we are creators, not merely imitators. Beginning at birth, we create our own language, called an *idiolect*. Yet, despite the individuality of dialect, it is also understood by the community that also speaks that language. Because language acquisition happens naturally and without much direct instruction, we typically assume that others have had linguistic experiences similar to us. If we fail to make a distinction in the pronunciations of *cot* and *caught*, we assume others do not either, at least until it is pointed out to us that most people do make such a distinction. Because of humans' remarkable language faculty, we are able to be highly effective language users even while we might consciously know very little about the structure of our language or how we are using it.

The lack of conscious thought about language leads us to develop what psychologists term *implicit attitudes* about it.[15] Implicit attitudes derive from our experiences, though we do not have conscious memories of how they were formed. They're the sort of thing that "you just always knew." Furthermore, they affect all of our social views and interactions without any conscious thought. The downside of these implicit attitudes is that, once formed, they can have serious and long-lasting societal repercussions.

In 1514 Copernicus published observations that postured, contrary to conventional wisdom and theological doctrine, that the Earth revolved around the Sun and not vice versa. Galileo confirmed this in 1610, which led to his eventual imprisonment in 1633. It was not until 1835, more than 300 years after Copernicus, that the prohibition against teaching the heliocentric model in European schools was lifted.[16] Ideologies change slowly and only through expansive educational efforts. In fact, even today, about one in five American high school graduates adheres to the "common sense" understanding of the sun revolving around the earth rather than the scientific explanation.[17] The knowledge—accurate or inaccurate—that we draw from our observations is remarkably powerful in shaping how we construct our lives and our and others' roles in it. Marcus Aurelius, the Roman emperor and philosopher, nearly two millennia ago was said to have cautioned us against trusting our own observations too much: "Everything we hear is an opinion, not a fact. Everything we see is a perspective, not the truth."[18] A second analogy can be drawn from more recent history. One only has to consider how "common sense" notions of men's and women's "natural roles" have evolved over the past 100 years to recognize the role of scientific research in overturning common-sense ideologies—albeit through a slow process. Dr. Albert Einstein warned us about common sense, defining it as "nothing more than a deposit of prejudices laid down by the mind before you reach eighteen."[19]

A final example offers insight into another goal of our public education programs. At one time, public information about American Indian culture and history was selective and limited. Today, while we still have plenty we could learn about these cultures, we do not consider education, documentaries, or museum exhibits dedicated to American Indians to be unusual. Misinformation may still persist, but the value of studying and learning about these diverse cultures is widely accepted. Our goal is parallel: we hope that through our efforts, readers will come to understand language diversity as something worthy of study and respect. We also hope that people will come to see research on language to be commonplace and essential as opposed to trivial and esoteric. We do not expect everyone to celebrate linguistic diversity the way we do, but our efforts are well spent if we convince people that language diversity is worth knowing about.

We are not interested in criticizing or confronting people's beliefs but in shining a positive light on language variation. We realize that research suggests that such beliefs change very slowly—and mostly through experience or discovery, not traditional education. We admit that even linguists can struggle with implicit attitudes about language. Once Walt Wolfram, while watching an interview with the great college and professional basketball player Larry Bird during his playing days, remarked that Larry Bird must be dumb. One of Walt's sons, who was in high school at the time, reacted impressively, first asking why Walt had said that. After Walt admitted that it was due to how Bird sounded, his son pointed out that Walt had always told his children not to judge others' intelligence based on how they spoke. The point is not really about Walt's obvious (and acknowledged) hypocrisy but about the fact that language attitudes change slowly, and prejudice is hard to eradicate even for those of us who study language variation. In spite of this reality, we endeavor to continue preaching the linguistic gospel to every willing audience and in every available venue. The North Carolina State Fair, for example, has recently become an additional stage for us to celebrate the linguistic di-

FIGURE 11.4. Young State Fair visitor Owen Reaser proudly displays his dialect buttons. (Photograph by Jeffrey Reaser)

versity of the state. Our exhibit has drawn equal interest from those who are from North Carolina, who often have a personal story connected to something they see in the exhibit, and those who are not, who often leave saying, "I didn't know that." The reactions of people are truly gratifying to us and viewed as a seed sown for linguistic tolerance that may eventually bear fruit.

To view a vignette from the NCLLP State Fair exhibit, visit http://www.talkintarheel.com/chapter/11/video11-5.php

Given the serious social and educational consequences language variation can have, it is sometimes tempting to preach fire and brimstone. We prefer to remain focused on the positive associations and use entertainment, humor, and anecdote as a means of beginning critical conversations about the seriousness of language diversity, which we see as just another way of exploring our humanity. Everyone has an anecdote about an awkward or funny conversation stemming from some linguistic misunderstanding. Maybe that story involves having to spell a number, street name, or word. Maybe it became an unintended punch line to a joke. Northerners who move to the South may be unfamiliar with grits, and when faced with the question "Potatoes or grits?," they may respond, "What's a grit?" No matter what dialect we speak, there has been a time where someone misunderstood us, at least momentarily. And no one is immune from linguistic blunders. These moments of misunderstanding or humor often open candid discussions that quickly move from language to culture or history and reveal much about ourselves in the process.

Such misunderstandings are universal, but southerners often have experiences that speakers of other dialects rarely have. They've probably been asked questions at some point just so the listener could hear a little more of their speech. Or maybe they've attracted the ears of overhearing outsiders who are intrigued by the accent. It is a bit of a paradox that southern English is at once stigmatized by outsiders and associated with positive characteristics such as hospitality and politeness. These various southern dialects are intriguing to outside ears because they intimately remind us of a past that is sometimes viewed as pastorally idyllic. Listeners may describe southern speech with a word like "quaint," evoking simultaneously two radically different visions of the South: the Andy Griffith South and the slave plantation South. Reactions to the dialect—to all dialects—are much more complex and deep-seated than they may seem on the surface. That's because we're not really reacting to the dialect in and of itself; we're reacting to the type of person whom we expect to speak that dialect in a social and historical context. Once we distill it in this way, it is more straightforward to accept that our reactions to people are not always consistent, fair, or simple. At that moment, we may then accept that our reactions and judgments about dialects are equally problematic.

Though dialects can lead to occasional miscommunications, we are usually good at adjusting our listening and quickly understanding what's being said, both in general and in detail. Furthermore, we recognize that some ways of speaking bear a social tax in some situations while carrying tremendous social currency in others. Since dialects are a part of our culture, time, and place, they are one way that we define ourselves both as individuals and as members of a community.

Linguistic Equality

Our public education efforts aim beyond documenting and celebrating linguistic diversity. Language remains one of the few areas where we commonly discriminate against others, as was noted in the opening section of this chapter. Language discrimination has been found to be pervasive and extremely damaging in complex and sometimes seemingly invisible ways. One such example, termed *linguistic profiling*, involves making assumptions about a person's race or ethnicity over the phone and then illegally discrim-

To view a public-service announcement about linguistic profiling from the U.S. Department of Housing and Urban Development, visit http://www.talkintarheel.com/chapter/11/video11-6.php

inating against that person in the housing, employment, or service marketplace.[20] It is estimated that such discrimination takes place thousands of times a day in the United States—between 2 and 4 million times a year in housing alone. So widespread is this problem that the U.S. Department of Housing and Urban Development partnered with the Ad Council to create print and television public-service announcements that show listeners reacting in a discriminatory manner to housing applicants representing different social and ethnic varieties of English.

Following Hurricane Katrina, which hit the Gulf Coast in 2005, the displaced populations of Louisiana, Mississippi, and Alabama faced remarkably different experiences depending on their race. A study conducted over five states found that two-thirds of housing-related test calls treated the test caller differently based on perceived ethnicity. White callers were offered lower rental rates, waived application fees, and even free flat-screen televisions, while African American callers instead received stricter minimum-income requirements and additional background checks or simply were told that there was no apartment available.[21]

We argue that language variation is crucially entwined with our failures and successes, often in invisible ways. In many ways, the public education system has the largest effect on perpetuating linguistic inequality. In schools, students are expected to accommodate to the social and linguistic norms of the institution, which mirror those of middle-class whites. Anyone outside this group is expected to figure out and accommodate to these behavioral expectations with virtually no instruction other than overt correction. Those students who arrive from the least privileged backgrounds are expected to learn more than their privileged counterparts, often without any formal instruction on how to learn this information.[22] Even in our modern world, in which we overtly value diversity education, no state currently has a mandated program that includes information about linguistic diversity. Teachers remain underprepared for the linguistic diversity of students in their classes and continue to interpret difference as deficit. The psychological research on *confirmation bias* and *self-fulfilling prophecy* is compelling and sobering. More than thirty-five years ago, Dr. Robert Rosenthal and Lenore Jacobson linked teacher expectations to individual student achievement, yet teachers are never asked to consider how their attitudes about dialects affect their expectations of and interactions with individual students.[23] If the most consistent predictor of student success is teacher expectations, there is nothing more damaging to minority children than a teacher who believes that dialect is "broken English," "sloppy," "slang," "ghetto," or "ignorant."

A lack of cultural understanding, including linguistics, can have tremendous effects on the learning of students in a class and in determining their attitudes toward formal education in general. A famous example involves well-meaning teachers on American Indian reservations who were "put off" by their students who had different cultural traditions of appropriate language use. Different cultural expectations about behavior (such as making eye contact), classroom rituals (for example, raising hands or call-and-response questions), and topics of discussion (such as predicting future historical events) can undermine the student-teacher dynamic in ways that are disastrous to the student's sense of self and his or her perspective on education.[24] The common-sense prejudices of well-meaning but linguistically unaware educators have even graver effects.

Language has been at the heart of many public debates on education. The 1996–97 Oakland Ebonics controversy, described in chapter 7, was one such moment. The national debate on the role of language variation in the classroom ignited a media maelstrom fueled primarily by "common sense" and raw emotion rather than empirical evidence. The program was created in an attempt to close the achievement gap while adhering to a 1979 federal court mandate from *Martin Luther King Junior Elementary School Children v. Ann Arbor School District Board*. The arguments of the plaintiffs in that case were based in part on the 1974 Equal Educational Opportunity Act, which includes the following statement: "No state shall deny equal educational opportunity to an individual on account of his or her race, color, sex, or national origin . . . by failing to overcome language barriers that impede equal participation by its students in its instructional programs" (1703[f]). The judge found that the Ann Arbor School District failed "to recognize the existence of the language system used by the children in their home community and to use that knowledge as a way of helping the children learn to read Standard English. . . . No matter how well intentioned the teachers are, they are not likely to be successful in overcoming the language barrier caused by their failure to take into account the home language system, unless they are helped."[25]

Oakland was attempting to create a program that would help the teachers learn about the language variety of the students and develop appropriate pedagogy to effectively teach them how to use Standard English in academic contexts. Popular linguistic ideology and media-perpetuated misunderstandings about the program converged to block low-income minority children from accessing a program that was based on educational models found to be successful around the globe. While these children may not have been killed on the spot, they certainly were not allowed to cross the Jordan River.

Other language-centric debates further demonstrate the critical role that language plays in creating and justifying inequality in our society. The modern English-only movement described in the previous chapter has parallels with other Official English movements that date back to the 1700s. However, it was xenophobia—not Americans' love of English—that fueled violence against those who spoke German, Irish, Italian, Polish, and Chinese and who now speak Spanish and Arabic. In each case, language becomes the vehicle by which we enact agendas of ethnic discrimination. If we accept this to be true, we must also accept the fact that our society will never achieve social equality if we accept linguistic inequality.

We are all aware of the benefit of being able to alter the way we speak for various situations. Dr. Robert C. Pooley defines good language use as "success in making language choices so that the fewest number of persons will be distracted by the choices."[26] With respect to language, it quickly becomes apparent that the more different spheres one wishes to navigate, the broader his or her linguistic repertoire must be. For those people who have a privileged language variety as their native dialect, less switching is required of them. In fact, typically, speakers of other dialects will accommodate more to these privileged speakers than vice versa. We are often critical of others if they make language choices that mark them as too urban, too rural, too low class, or too haughty. Yet inside each of those groups, the local or ethnic dialect is the language choice that is least distracting to the largest number of people. The truth is that there is a social tax associated with using vernacular forms in a standard context as well as a social toll on using standard forms in a context that demands more informal language usage. Therefore, we have to allow that all language varieties have social currency, even those we eschew.

Dialects all along the periphery—urban and rural, and lower- and upper-class—carry a steep social levy when used with people from outside that group. But they are the appropriate dialects to use when members of those communities speak to one another? There is linguistic danger in speaking "above your raisin'"—or, as they say in Robeson County, "with your head in the pines"—as well as linguistic danger in an outsider attempting to take on a dialect of a relatively closed group. We may understand this for ourselves but struggle to understand it for those of different communities.

The linguistic reality is simple: every dialect is as patterned and systematic—or "rule-governed"—as every other dialect (including Standard English). To the extent that we can apply logic to a language to evaluate its goodness, many dialects are more consistent or logical than Standard English. Isn't it more "logical" or consistent to use only one past tense form of *be* (like virtually every other verb in English) instead of alternating between *was* and *were*? Why then are "we was there" and "she weren't there" stigmatized forms in mainstream America? Every dialect, and every language, has roughly the same ability to express knowledge about the world or our innermost thoughts. Why then do we make children communicate in something other than the language of their hearts? It is the social application of the linguistic reality that is difficult. To be blunt, the privileging of one language variety over another is never based on the goodness or logicalness of a language per se but instead on the perceived goodness of the group of people associated with that dialect. Since the determination of language goodness is sociopolitical, it is not surprising that language becomes a venue for discrimination. We cannot correct all of the ills introduced into society through public, nonscientific perceptions of language diversity, but our outreach programs aim to plant seeds of awareness that may, over time, lead individuals to more-nuanced perspectives on how language diversity is a resource rather than a handicap.

Sharing Voices

The most immediate goal of our research and outreach is to share a linguistic-cultural resource that is inherently intriguing but seldom discussed formally or scientifically. Documenting the linguistic landscape of North Carolina—or of any place—is an arduous and time-consuming task. The formal research we have conducted, hidden in scholarly journals in library archives, is often inaccessible to people who do not have graduate degrees in linguists, but socially responsible professionals have now been challenged by a couple of principles that include the *principle of debt incurred* and the *principle of linguistic gratuity*.[27] Social scientists have a debt to give back to the communities that have inspired and fueled their research studies, and linguistic researchers should "pursue positive ways in which they can return linguistic favors to the community."[28] The descriptions in this book represent a culmination of two decades of scholarly work that we hope will educate and instill pride in the fascinating and rich linguistic landscape of North Carolina. We are only able to do this work because of the generosity of North Carolinians who have given us their time and shared their stories.

In pursuing language diversity, we've had to consider history, sociology, geography, anthropology, and psychology, among other disciplines. At the convergence of these scholarly pursuits are people: the present and past citizens of what is now North Carolina. Studying how they talked and continue to talk tells us a lot about what it means to be human, what it means to be a southerner (or a Yankee, for those of us who are nonnatives), and, most important, a little bit about what it means to be a North Carolinian. In this sense, we hope that at the very least, we have been able to preserve something of the rich—and sometimes wild—history enjoyed by those who have inhabited North Carolina and continue to make the state their home.

We are sometimes asked if our work aims to preserve languages or dialects before they die out. The answer is emphatically yes. We have created museum exhibits detailing the present and past of language varieties and the people who have spoken them. Sometimes language seems peripheral to the other information we include in the exhibit. One such case was our *Freedom's Voice: Celebrating the Black Experience on the Outer Banks*, which was hosted at the Outer Banks History Center in Manteo in 2006–2007. The exhibit documented the Freedmen's Colony and the development of the black community on the Outer Banks along the coastal region of North Carolina described in chapter 7.

At other times, language is the center of the exhibit. Our permanent exhibit on Lumbee English at the Museum of the Native American Resource Center at the University of North Carolina at Pembroke is one such exhibit. Visitors can learn about Lumbee history and American Indian heritage, but the centerpieces of the language exhibit focus on the distinctive words, pronunciations, and grammatical patterns of the Lumbee dialect presented in chapter 9.

Our documentary work also exhibits both language and life. A few of our documentaries are most immediately about language, including *The Ocracoke Brogue, Mountain Talk, Hyde Talk*, and *Spanish Voices*.[29] Some documentaries, such as *Indian by Birth: The Lumbee Dialect* or *Cedars in the Pines: The Lebanese of North Carolina*, blend language and life.[30] Other documentaries have grown out of our cooperation with communities and have little to no overt focus on language, instead highlighting cultural and historical institutions. These include such documentaries as *Princeville Remembers the Flood, This Side of the River, The Queen Family*, and our latest feature, *Core Sounders*.[31]

FIGURE 11.5. Freedom's Voice exhibit at the Outer Banks History Center. (Photograph by Charlotte Vaughn)

We have even, at a community's request, created a video tribute to celebrate the life or mourn the death of an important, perhaps even historic, person. In one case, described in chapter 7, we compiled a video documenting the 100th birthday of Muzel Bryant, the last remaining African American resident on Ocracoke Island.[32] In another case, we compiled a posthumous tribute to local performer Roy Parsons (also of Ocracoke), while our talented producer, Neal Hutcheson, won an Emmy for his documentary *The Last One*, featuring the infamous moonshiner Popcorn Sutton, who lived for many years in Maggie Valley.[33]

To view an excerpt from Neal Hutcheson's documentary *The Last One*, visit http://www.talkintarheel.com/chapter/11/video11-7.php

Oral histories are yet another way in which we can share the diverse voices of North Carolina. With the help of community members, we have complied CD collections of stories that reminisce, celebrate, and entertain. The staff of the North Carolina Language and Life Project created two such compilations a decade apart for Ocracoke, *Ocracoke Speaks* and *Ocracoke Still Speaks*; a similar project, *Voices of Texana*, in Texana, North Carolina; and two CD complications combining the stories and music of Appalachia, *An Unclouded Day* and *The Queen Family: Back Porch Music*.[34]

To view a tribute to Roy Parsons, visit http://www.talkintarheel.com/chapter/11/video11-8.php

We have created a sociolinguistic archive of more than 2,000 interviews with North Carolinians. We have even distilled much of this knowledge about North Carolina's language heritage into a state-approved curriculum for eighth-grade students in North Carolina.[35] The multimedia curriculum has been proven to be able to be taught effectively by classroom teachers without any specialized linguistic knowledge or training. This curriculum is a first step toward achieving our goal of every eighth-grade student in North Carolina learning about language heritage alongside learning state history. We wonder how a student can learn about the history of North Carolina without including a good dose of the language that has been used by the different social and ethnic groups. The curriculum is the first of its kind in the nation, and it, along with the informal educational efforts detailed previously, make North Carolina the nation's leader in dialect-education programs and a model for language preservation and celebration in places around the country, including West Virginia, Pennsylvania, Alabama, Mississippi, Washington, California, and South Carolina.

We are, on occasion, fortunate to do more than preserve a voice; we also preserve memories. As mentioned, many times we have been called on to help honor the life of a community member after his or her passing, as we did with our video tribute to Roy Parsons. On other occasions following a death, we've had family members contact us for a copy of an interview we had conducted with their beloved family member. The power of language is, perhaps, best illustrated in the tears that accompany listening to the voice of a lost loved one.

As we document and preserve the past and present, we are aware that our efforts may have little effect on the steady march of language change. No community, no matter how isolated, is ever frozen in time, and no language variety is ever static. In 1747 Samuel Johnson undertook a project that would culminate in the most advanced and remarkable dictionary of English of its time. In his published plan, he described his goals, which included tracing etymologies, standardizing spellings, and offering standard pronunciations. His vision was that his dictionary would "preserve the purity" of English so as to "fix the English language" forever, by which he meant to make it permanent or without change. By the time his dictionary was published in 1755, Samuel Johnson had come to realize the folly in his plan.[36]

> Those who have been persuaded to think well of my design, require that it should fix our language, and put a stop to those alterations which time and chance have hitherto been suffered to make in it without opposition.

FIGURE 11.6. Teaching the *Voices of North Carolina* dialect-awareness curriculum to Ocracoke eighth graders. (Photograph by Sarah Hilliard)

With this consequence I will confess that I flattered myself for a while; but now begin to fear that I have indulged expectation which neither reason nor experience can justify. . . . With this hope, however, academies have been instituted, to guard the avenues of their languages, to retain fugitives, and repulse intruders; but their vigilance and activity have hitherto been vain; sounds are too volatile and subtle for legal restraints; to enchain syllables, and to lash the wind, are equally the undertakings of pride, unwilling to measure its desires by its strength. The *French* language has visibly changed under the inspection of the academy. . . . Total and sudden transformations of a language seldom happen; conquests and migrations are now very rare: but there are other causes of change, which, though slow in their operation, and invisible in their progress, are perhaps as much superior to human resistance, as the revolutions of the sky, or intumescence of the tide. . . . [C]onsider that no dictionary of a living tongue ever can be perfect, since while it is hastening to publication, some words are budding, and some falling away.

By the end of his short lexicographical career, Johnson had come to understand a tremendous amount about the reality of language variation and change. No authoritative book, guide, or academy, let alone a couple of linguists, have the power to "fix" a language. We seek to preserve history, culture, and language, but we have no delusions about being guardians of things that simply do not belong to us. We—along with community residents—may feel sadness as we hear the Outer Banks Brogue or Mountain Talk slowly fade away, but the members of a community are the ones who have the capability to maintain a historically based language variety into the future. And it is clear that many such communities may adapt to mainstream linguistic norms for good reasons, while, perhaps, signaling their authentic connections to the past in other ways.

There will not come a time when all Americans speak alike, contrary to the often-repeated questions by reporters about the homogenization of English in the United States. Nor will there come a time when all North Carolinians speak alike. However, just as traditional ways of life have vanished, some dialects will as well. We cannot guard these dialects from change any more than we can stop day from giving way to night. Though change is inevitable, we hope to continue to document the languages and lives of North Carolinians—both old and newly arrived—so that the state has a record of its cultural and linguistic heritage, a heritage marked by as much or more dialect diversity as any other state in the country. Being powerless to stop linguistic change in no way impedes our ability to celebrate linguistic diversity. We do not need to be linguists to join in this celebration. In fact, we do it every time we hear a smile in a dialect. Our hope is that the joy and respect we have for the linguistic life of the Tar Heel State will bring a few smiles to some faces.

Notes

All URLs are accurate as of July 14, 2013.

Chapter 1

1. See chapter 2 for a discussion of the terms "Scots-Irish" and "Scotch-Irish."

2. *Creecy Family Papers*, 1861–1865, http://www.lib.unc.edu/mss/inv/c/Creecy_Family .html.

3. John Stephen Farmer, *Americanisms, Old and New: A Dictionary of Words, Phrases and Colloquialisms Peculiar to the United States, British America, the West Indies, Etc.; Their Derivation, Meaning and Application, Together with Numerous Anecdotal, Historical, Explanatory and Folklore Notes* (London: Thomas Poulter & Sons, 1889). Text available at http://archive.org/stream/americanismsoldnoofarmuoft/ americanismsoldnoofarmuoft_djvu.txt.

4. Reported in William S. Powell, "What's in a Name? Why We're All Called Tar Heels," *Tar Heel Magazine*, March 1982. Available online at http://alumni.unc.edu/ article.aspx?sid=3516.

5. Cackalacky Spice Sauce, "Our Story," http://www.cackalacky.com/#!our-story/ cr22.

6. N.C. Department of the Secretary of State, "Sweet Potato—North Carolina State Vegetable," http://www.secretary.state.nc.us/pubsweb/symbols/sy-sweet.htm.

7. Jonathan Byrd, "Cackalack," http://www.cdbaby.com/cd/jonathanbyrd.

8. The six-volume *Dictionary of American Regional English*, ed. Frederic G. Cassidy and Joan Houston Hall (Boston: Harvard University Press), is published in alphabetical increments (vol. 1: A–C [1985]; vol. 2: D–H [1991]; vol. 3: I–O [1996]; vol. 4: P–SI [2002]; vol. 5: SK–Z [2012]). Volume 6 (2013) is dedicated to supplemental materials that include contrastive maps, an index to entries, a questionnaire, and fieldwork data. An online index is available at http://dare.wisc.edu/?q=content/ index-labels-region-usage-and-ethymology-dare.

9. See chapter 8 for a discussion of the terms "American Indian" and "Native American."

10. Nicholas Sparks, *Nights in Rodanthe* (New York: Random House, 2002).

11. John L. Sanders, "Talk Like a Tar Heel: North Carolina Place Names," http:// www.lib.unc.edu/ncc/ref/resources/tlth.html.

12. Guy Bailey, "The Relationship between AAVE and White Vernaculars in

the American South: Some Phonological Evidence," in *Sociocultural and Historical Contexts of African American Vernacular English*, ed. Sonja Lanehart (Philadelphia and Amsterdam: John Benjamins, 2001), 53–92.

13. Rosina Lippi-Green, *English with an Accent: Language, Ideology, and Discrimination in the United States*, 2nd ed. (New York: Taylor and Francis, 2012), 66–74.

14. Dennis Preston, "The South: The Touchstone," in *Language Variety in the South Revisited*, ed. Cynthia Bernstein, Thomas Nunnally, and Robin Sabino (Tuscaloosa: University of Alabama Press, 1997), 311–51.

15. George W. Harris, *Sut Lovingood: Yarns Spun by a "Nat'ral Born Durn'd Fool,"* available at http://docsouth.unc.edu/southlit/harrisg/gharris.html.

16. Walt Wolfram, "Language Ideology and Dialect: Understanding the Ebonics Controversy," *Journal of English Linguistics* 26, no. 2 (1998): 108–21.

17. *Raleigh News and Observer*, September 8, 2009, C-1.

18. Quoted from Neal Hutcheson, producer, *Voices of North Carolina* (Raleigh: North Carolina Language and Life Project, 2005).

19. Ibid.

20. Migration Policy Institute, "Migration Facts, States, and Maps," http://www .migrationinformation.org/datahub/state2.cfm?ID=nc.

Chapter 2

1. See, for example, William S. Powell, *North Carolina: A History* (Chapel Hill: University of North Carolina Press, 1988); William S. Powell, *North Carolina through Four Centuries* (Chapel Hill: University of North Carolina Press, 1989); and Milton Ready, *The Tar Heel State: A History of North Carolina* (Columbia: University of South Carolina Press, 2011).

2. Judith A. Bense, *Archaeology of the Southeastern United States: Paleoindian to World War I* (New York: Academic Press, 1994).

3. The Ice Age climate was much cooler than today's, allowing large game to live in what is now North Carolina.

4. Isaac Randolph Daniel Jr., "The Archeology of Early North Carolina," *Tar Heel Junior Historian* 45 (Fall 2005): 3–5.

5. Cèllere Codex, as part of "The Written Record of the Voyage of 1524 of Giovanni da Verrazano as Recorded in a Letter to Francis I, King of France, July 8th, 1524," in Lawrence C. Wroth, *The Voyages of Giovanni da Verrazzano, 1524–1528* (New Haven, Conn.: Yale University Press, 1970), 134. Translation by Susan Tarrow.

6. Ibid., 134.

7. Giles Milton, *Big Chief Elizabeth: How England's Adventurers Gambled and Won the New World* (London: Hodder and Stoughton, 2000).

8. Thomas Harriot, *A Brief and True Report of the New Found Land of Virginia* (1588), 35.

9. Ibid., 36.

10. For three competing theories, see David B. Quinn, *Set Fair for Roanoke: Voyages and Colonies, 1584–1606* (Chapel Hill: University of North Carolina Press, 1985); Karen Ordahl Kupperman, *Roanoke: The Abandoned Colony* (New York: Rowman & Littlefield, 1984); and Lee Miller, *Roanoke: Solving the Mystery of the Lost Colony* (New York: Arcade

Publishing, 2000). The most recent take on the disappearance of the Lost Colony came in 2012 after the discovery of a new clue on an old map. See, for example, http://www.newsobserver.com/2012/05/01/2041723/north-carolina-and-british-researchers.html.

11. For a more complete history of the settlement of Jamestown, see, for example, James P. P. Horn, *A Land as God Made It: Jamestown and the Birth of America* (New York: Basic Books, 2005).

12. Kathleen M. Brown, "Women in Early Jamestown," http://www.virtualjamestown.org/essays/brown_essay.html.

13. Thirteen/WNET New York, Educational Broadcasting Corporation, "Slavery and the Making of America, Time and Place: The Beginning," http://www.pbs.org/wnet/slavery/timeline/1619.html.

14. Powell, *North Carolina through Four Centuries*, 49–50.

15. Quoted in ibid., 18–19.

16. There are many excellent accounts of piracy in North Carolina, including popular texts such as Terrance Zepke, *Pirates of the Carolinas*, 2nd ed. (Sarasota, Fla.: Pineapple Press, 2005), and more scholarly treatments, such as Lindley S. Butler's *Pirates, Privateers, and Rebel Raiders of the Carolina Coast* (Chapel Hill: University of North Carolina Press, 2000).

17. Quoted in Powell, *North Carolina through Four Centuries*, 59.

18. Ibid., 105.

19. James G. Leyburn, *The Scotch-Irish: A Social History* (Chapel Hill: University of North Carolina Press, 1962), 172–73.

20. For a more complete account of the formation and history of the Ulster Plantation, see Leyburn, "The Plantation of Ulster, 1610 and After," chapter 6 of *The Scotch-Irish*.

21. Quoted in Leyburn, *The Scotch-Irish*, 329.

22. Michael Montgomery, "Scotch-Irish or Scots-Irish: What's in a Name?," *Tennessee Ancestors* 20 (2004): 143–50.

23. Ibid.

24. For a more complete account of the emigration from the Ulster Plantation, see Leyburn, "The Migration," chapter 6 of *The Scotch-Irish*.

25. Estimates of the proportion of indentured servants come from Abbot Emerson Smith, *Colonists in Bondage: White Servitude and Convict Labor in America* (Chapel Hill: University of North Carolina Press, 1947), 336.

26. *Laws of the Commonwealth of Pennsylvania, from the Fourteenth Day of October, One Thousand Seven Hundred* (London; reprinted by John Bioren, 1812), 312.

27. Powell, *North Carolina through Four Centuries*, 104–5.

28. Ibid., 110–11.

29. Marvin L. Michael Kay and Lorin Lee Cary, *Slavery in North Carolina, 1748–1775* (Chapel Hill: University of North Carolina Press, 1995), 203–4.

30. Powell, *North Carolina through Four Centuries*, 112.

31. Ibid., 112.

32. Ibid., 113.

33. "Stories of the American South: Slavery in North Carolina," http://www.lib.unc.edu/stories/slavery/story/index.html.

34. Powell, *North Carolina through Four Centuries*, 333–34.

Chapter 3

1. *Raleigh News and Observer*, July 29, 2012.

2. David S. Cecelski, *The Waterman's Song: Slavery and Freedom in Maritime North Carolina* (Chapel Hill: University of North Carolina Press, 2001).

3. William S. Powell, *North Carolina through Four Centuries* (Chapel Hill: University of North Carolina Press, 1989), 169–70.

4. NBC News, May 2, 2012.

5. See North Carolina Language and Life Project, "Princeville, N.C.," http://www.ncsu.edu/linguistics/ncllp/sites/princeville.php.

6. See, for example, the map of the Appalachian Mountain region provided by the U.S. Geological Survey, http://3dparks.wr.usgs.gov/nyc/images/fig51.jpg.

7. See Town of Rhodhiss, http://www.main.nc.us/townofrhodhiss/.

8. Nan K. Chase, *Asheville: A History* (Jefferson, N.C.: McFarland, 2007).

9. See North Carolina Language and Life Project, "Texana, N.C.," http://www.ncsu.edu/linguistics/ncllp/sites/texana.php.

10. William Labov, Sharon Ash, and Charles Boberg, *The Atlas of North American English* (Berlin: Mouton de Gruyter, 2006).

11. Walt Wolfram and Natalie Schilling-Estes, "Parallel Development and Alternative Restructuring: The Case of *Weren't* Intensification," in *Social Dialectology*, ed. David Britain and Jenny Cheshire (Philadelphia and Amsterdam: John Benjamins, 2003), 131–54.

12. H. Kent Craig, "What Is North Carolina–Style BBQ?," http://www.ncbbq.com/Modules/Articles/article.aspx?id=20.

13. For more detail about vocabulary on the Outer Banks, see Walt Wolfram and Natalie Schilling-Estes, *Hoi Toide on the Outer Banks: The Story of the Ocracoke Brogue* (Chapel Hill: University of North Carolina Press, 1997), 29–49.

14. The most exhaustive lexicon on Mountain speech is Michael B. Montgomery and Joseph S. Hall, *Dictionary of Smoky Mountain English* (Knoxville: University of Tennessee Press, 2004).

15. Angus Bowers, "Feature Erosion and Ethnolinguistic Alignment: The Case of Bertie County" (M.A. thesis, North Carolina State University, 2006).

16. See North Carolina Language and Life Project, "Crusoe Island, N.C.," http://www.ncsu.edu/linguistics/ncllp/sites/crusoeisland.php.

17. Quoted in sociolinguistic interviews of the North Carolina Language and Life Project, http://ncslaap.lib.ncsu.edu.

18. Ibid.

19. For details on these atlases, see Hans Kurath, *Handbook of the Linguistic Geography of New England* (Providence, R.I.: Brown University, 1939); Hans Kurath and Raven I. McDavid Jr., *The Pronunciation of English in the Atlantic States* (Ann Arbor:

University of Michigan Press, 1961); and Labov, Ash, and Boberg, *The Atlas of North American English*.

20. See Michael Montgomery and Margaret Mishoe, "He Bes Took up with a Yankee Girl and Moved up There to New York: The Verb *Bes* in the Carolinas and Its History," *American Speech* 74 (Fall 1999): 240–81.

21. See National Park Service, "Gullah/Geechee Cultural Heritage Corridor," http://www.nps.gov/guge/index.htm.

22. See Labov, Ash, and Boberg, *The Atlas of North American English*, for details.

23. As noted in chapter 1, the landmark work on lexicon is, of course, the six-volume *Dictionary of American Regional English*, vols. 1–6, ed. Frederic G. Cassidy and Joan Houston Hall (Boston: Harvard University Press, 1985, 1991, 1996, 2002, 2012, 2013). This reference work also includes many observations about pronunciation and grammar.

24. Wolfram and Schilling-Estes, *Hoi Toide on the Outer Banks*.

25. See Montgomery and Hall, *Dictionary of Smoky Mountain English*.

Chapter 4

1. Quote from Neal Hutcheson, producer, *Voices of North Carolina* (Raleigh: North Carolina Language and Life Project, 2005).

2. See Stephany B. Dunstan, "The Influence of Speaking a Dialect of Appalachian English on the College Experience" (Ph.D. diss., North Carolina State University, 2013). Also see Lauren Hall-Lew and Nola Stephens, "County Talk," *Journal of English Linguistics* 40, no. 1 (2012): 1–25.

3. The earliest usages (1570) cataloged in the *Oxford English Dictionary* (online edition) suggest the term (alternatively spelled "bunkin") was a humorous designation for a Dutchman. How the term came into English is not certain, but it may have been a borrowing of the Dutch term *bommekijn*, which meant "little barrel." It is easy to see how it evolved into the description of a "short, stumpy" person. In the eighteenth century, it shifted again, this time into its modern American usage to mean "rustic" or "clownish."

4. Quoted from Hutcheson, *Voices of North Carolina*.

5. Song written by Kyle Fleming and Dennis Morgan. Lyrics from http://www .metrolyrics.com/i-was-country-when-country-wasnt-cool-lyrics-george-jones.html.

6. For technical details, see Robin Dodsworth and Mary Kohn, "Urban Rejection of the Vernacular: The SVS Undone," *Language Variation and Change* 24, no. 2 (2012): 221–45.

7. Quoted from Hutcheson, *Voices of North Carolina*.

8. Ibid.

9. See Raymond Arsenault, "The End of the Long Hot Summer: The Air Conditioner and Southern Culture," *Journal of Southern History* 50, no. 4 (1984): 597–628.

10. U.S. Census Bureau, "State and County QuickFacts: North Carolina," http:// quickfacts.census.gov/qfd/states/37000.html.

11. Quoted from Hutcheson, *Voices of North Carolina*.

12. Ibid.

13. Ibid.

14. See William Labov, *The Social Stratification of English in New York City* (Washington, D.C.: Center for Applied Linguistics, 1966).

15. See Frank S. Anshen, "Speech Variation among Negroes in a Small Southern Community" (Ph.D. diss., New York University, 1969).

16. Barry Saunders, "What's up with Pols Talkin' Down," *Raleigh News and Observer*, August 13, 2012, http://www.newsobserver.com/2012/08/12/2265927/whats-up-with-pols-talkin-down.html.

17. Meghan Deanna Cooper, "Pre-Lateral Merging and the Southern Shift in Forsyth County" (unpublished manuscript, Raleigh, N.C., 2013).

18. Andy Griffith, "What It Was, Was Football," originally performed in 1953, available online at http://www.youtube.com/watch?v=0NxLxTZHKM8.

19. See Malcah Yaeger-Dror, Lauren Hall-Lew, and Sharon Deckert, "It's Not or Isn't It? Using Large Corpora to Determine the Influences on Contraction Strategies," *Language Variation and Change* 14, no. 1 (2002): 79–118.

20. Lyrics from http://www.metrolyrics.com/dont-get-above-your-raisin-lyrics-flatt-and-scruggs.html.

21. See one example at http://www.reflector.com/content/bless-your-heart-121754.

22. Quoted from Hutcheson, *Voices of North Carolina*.

Chapter 5

1. The CBS sitcom starring Carroll O'Connor as Archie Bunker and Jean Stapleton as his wife, Edith, ran from 1971 through 1979, coinciding with the time that the Outer Banks started receiving regular television. Archie Bunker often referred to his wife as "dingbat," giving rise to the application of the term "dingbatter" for outsiders who have little "common sense" for living in Outer Banks communities.

2. David Stick is the most well-known historian of the Outer Banks, and his books, such as *Graveyard of the Atlantic: Shipwrecks of the North Carolina Coast* (Chapel Hill: University of North Carolina Press, 1952) and *The Outer Banks of North Carolina, 1584–1958* (Chapel Hill: University of North Carolina Press, 1990), are still quite popular. The David Stick Collection and Papers at the Outer Banks History Center has more than 25,000 books and pamphlets and 150 cubic feet of correspondences, business records, and research notes. See http://www.obhistorycenter.ncdcr.gov.

3. See David S. Cecelski, *The Waterman's Song: Slavery and Freedom in Maritime North Carolina* (Chapel Hill: University of North Carolina Press, 2001); and David Wright and David Zoby, *Fire on the Beach: Recovering the Lost Story of Richard Etheridge and the Pea Island Lifesavers* (Oxford and New York: Oxford University Press, 2000).

4. See report at http://www.prweb.com/releases/Ocracoke-Beach/Best-Beach-List/prweb531647.htm.

5. Associated Press, June 8, 2007, 1.

6. From the oral history CD *Ocracoke Still Speaks: Reflections Past and Present*, compiled by Jeffrey Reaser, Paula Dickerson Boddie, and Walt Wolfram from the North

Carolina Language and Life Project and DeAnna Locke, Chester Lynn, and Phillip Howard from the Ocracoke Preservation Society (Raleigh: North Carolina Language and Life Project, 2011).

7. From the oral history CD *Ocracoke Speaks: The Distinct Sounds of the Hoi Toide*, compiled by Helen Marie Cloud, Becky Childs, and Walt Wolfram (Raleigh: North Carolina Language and Life Project, 2001).

8. See Walt Wolfram and Natalie Schilling-Estes, *Hoi Toide on the Outer Banks: The Story of the Ocracoke Brogue* (Chapel Hill: University of North Carolina Press, 1997), and Walt Wolfram, Kirk Hazen, and Natalie Schilling-Estes, *Dialect Maintenance and Change on the Outer Banks*, Publications of the American Dialect Society, no. 81 (Tuscaloosa: University of Alabama Press, 1999).

9. From Cloud, Childs, and Wolfram, *Ocracoke Speaks*.

10. Rex O'Neal's performance style has also been studied as a case of highly conscious style shifting by linguist Dr. Natalie Schilling-Estes in "Investigating 'Self-Conscious' Speech: The Performance Register in Ocracoke English," *Language in Society* 27, no. 1 (1998): 53–83.

11. Conversation with Peter Trudgill reported in Wolfram and Schilling-Estes, *Hoi Toide on the Outer Banks*, 53.

12. All of these interviews are archived at the Sociolinguistic Archive and Analysis Project website, http://ncslaap.lib.ncsu.edu/.

13. Quoted from Neal Hutcheson, producer, *The Carolina Brogue* (Raleigh: North Carolina Language and Life Project, 2008).

14. A folk etymology is a process in which a word or phrase is modified so that it makes sense in terms of already-existing words. For example, "Alzheimers Disease" is reinterpreted as *Old Timer's Disease*, "garter snake" as *garden snake*, or "hook and lateral" as *hook and ladder* in football.

15. From Cloud, Childs, and Wolfram, *Ocracoke Speaks*.

16. Walt Wolfram and Natalie Schilling-Estes, in "Moribund Dialects and the Endangerment Canon: The Case of the Ocracoke Brogue," *Language* 71, no. 4 (1995): 696–721, have argued strongly for the inclusion of vanishing dialects in the language endangerment canon, but, for the most part, their arguments have not been recognized.

17. From Hutcheson, *The Carolina Brogue*.

18. See Wolfram and Schilling-Estes, *Hoi Toide on the Outer Banks*, 29–49, for more examples of vocabulary differences. The North Carolina Language and Life Project has also produced dialect lexicons for Ocracoke and Harkers Island; see Walt Wolfram, Natalie Schilling-Estes, and Kirk Hazen, *Dialect Vocabulary in Ocracoke* (Raleigh: North Carolina Language and Life Project, 1994), and Kevyn Creech, Walt Wolfram, and Natalie Schilling Estes, *Harkers Island Dialect Vocabulary* (Raleigh: North Carolina Language and Life Project, 1994).

19. From Hutcheson, *The Carolina Brogue*.

20. Ibid.

21. See Natalie Schilling-Estes, "Reshaping Economies, Reshaping Identities: Gender-Based Patterns of Language Variation in Ocracoke English," in *Engendering*

Communication: Proceedings of the Fifth Berkeley Women and Language Conference, ed. Suzanne Wertheim, Ashlee C. Bailey, and Monica Corston-Oliver (Berkeley, Calif.: Berkeley Women and Language Group, 1999), 509–20.

22. Technical details supporting this interpretation are found in Natalie Schilling-Estes and Walt Wolfram, "Alternative Models of Dialect Death: Dissipation vs. Concentration," *Language* 75, no. 3 (1999): 486–521.

23. See Wolfram and Schilling-Estes, "Moribund Dialects and the Endangerment Canon."

24. This usage is attributed to a public lecture given by the Yiddish linguist Max Weinriech in "A Shprakh iz a Dialect mit an Armey and Navy," *YIVO Bleter* 25, no. 1 (1945): 13, but the origin is uncertain.

25. See Ruth King, "On the Social Meaning of Linguistic Variability in Language Death Situations: Variation in Newfoundland French," in *Investigating Obsolescence: Studies in Language Contraction and Obsolescence*, ed. Nancy C. Dorian (Cambridge, UK: Cambridge University Press, 1989), 139–48.

Chapter 6

1. Neal Hutcheson, producer, *The Queen Family: Appalachian Tradition and Back Porch Music* (Raleigh: North Carolina Language and Life Project, 2006).

2. Quoted from Neal Hutcheson, producer, *Mountain Talk* (Raleigh: North Carolina Language and Life Project, 2004).

3. *Beowulf*, perhaps the most well-known literary work of Anglo-Saxon culture, is a heroic epic poem traditionally told orally. The poem was transcribed by two anonymous scribes between the eighth and eleventh centuries C.E., which corresponds with the period of the language that linguists recognize as Old English (roughly 450 C.E. to 1100 C.E.).

4. Neal Hutcheson, producer, *The Last One* (Raleigh: Sucker Punch Productions, 2008).

5. See one media account at http://www.citizen-times.com/article/20090319/NEWS01/903180322.

6. See http://www.nytimes.com/2012/02/21/us/popcorn-suttons-whiskey-once-moonshine-is-now-legal.html.

7. See, for example, the map of the Appalachian Mountain region provided by the U.S. Geological Survey, http://3dparks.wr.usgs.gov/nyc/images/fig51.jpg.

8. George R. Stewart, *Names on the Land: A Historical Account of Place-Naming in the United States* (New York: New York Review of Books, 2008), 17–18.

9. Ibid., 334.

10. Both quotations from Hutcheson, *Mountain Talk*.

11. *Barney Google* (later *Snuffy Smith*) was created in 1919 by Billy DeBeck and was continued by Fred Lasswell after DeBeck's death in 1942. John R. Rose has been drawing the strip since 2001. *Li'l Abner* was created in 1934 by Alfred Gerald Caplin, who was better known as Al Capp. The strip ran through 1977.

12. See chapter 1 for more on the trickster archetype.

13. Harry S. Truman Library and Museum, "Public Papers of the President,

Number 157: Remarks at a Breakfast of the 35th Division Association, Springfield, Missouri," available online at http://www.trumanlibrary.org/publicpapers/index.php?pid=2414.

14. James G. Leyburn, *The Scotch-Irish: A Social History* (Chapel Hill: University of North Carolina Press, 1962), 219.

15. A digital archive of images and documents detailing the construction of the Blue Ridge Parkway can be found at http://docsouth.unc.edu/blueridgeparkway/.

16. See, for example, "Linn Cove Viaduct," http://www.highcountryhost.com/linn-cove-viaduct/

17. Michael Montgomery, "In the Appalachians They Speak Like Shakespeare," in *Language Myths*, ed. Laurie Bauer and Peter Trudgill (London: Penguin, 1999), 75.

18. Ibid., 76.

19. Full text of Appalachian Regional Council, "United States Code Title 40 Subtitle IV–Appalachian Regional Development," is available online at http://www.arc.gov/about/USCodeTitle40SubtitleIV.asp.

20. Quoted from Hutcheson, *Mountain Talk*.

21. Ibid.

22. Appalachian Regional Council, "County Economic Status and Distressed Areas in Appalachia," available online at http://www.arc.gov/appalachian_region/CountyEconomicStatusandDistressedAreasinAppalachia.asp.

23. Quoted from Hutcheson, *Mountain Talk*.

24. Ibid.

25. Ibid.

26. Ibid.

27. *Oxford English Dictionary* (online edition), http://www.oed.com.

28. Quoted from Hutcheson, *Mountain Talk*.

29. *Oxford English Dictionary* (online edition), http://www.oed.com.

30. See, for example, Richard Chase, ed., *The Jack Tales* (New York: Houghton Mifflin, 1943).

31. *Oxford English Dictionary* (online edition), http://www.oed.com. This term has a different etymology from the Internet search engine named "Google," which derives from the math term "Googol" (the number 1 followed by 100 zeroes), although the thought of such a large number is, indeed, dizzying.

32. Both quotations from Hutcheson, *Mountain Talk*.

33. All quotations from ibid.

34. Quoted from ibid.

35. *Hain't* and subsequently *ain't* are derived from the standard contraction of *have* and *not*, which explains why the h sound was pronounced originally.

36. These spellings, with the exception of the h, are modernized.

37. Erik R. Thomas, *An Acoustic Analysis of Vowel Variation in New World English*, Publication of the American Dialect Society, no. 85 (Durham, N.C.: Duke University Press, 2001), 117.

38. *The English Language in America* (New York: Frederick Ungar Publishing Company), 226.

39. *Dictionary: Southern Appalachian English*, available online at http://artsandsciences.sc.edu/engl/dictionary/dictionary.html.

40. West Virginia Dialect Project, http://dialects.english.wvu.edu/.

41. Quoted from Hutcheson, *Mountain Talk*.

Chapter 7

1. See the articles discussing the 1996–97 controversy in Oakland at Dr. John Rickford's website, http://www.stanford.edu/~rickford/ebonics/. Also see Walt Wolfram, "Language Ideology and Dialect: Understanding the Ebonics Controversy," *Journal of English Linguistics* 26, no. 2 (1998): 108–21.

2. See Charles Wycliffe Joiner, Ann Arbor Board of Education, and the Center for Applied Linguistics, *Ann Arbor Decision: The Memorandum, Opinion, and Order and the Educational Plan* (Washington, D.C.: Center for Applied Linguistics, 1979).

3. See Walt Wolfram and Erik R. Thomas, *The Development of African American English* (Malden, Mass.: Blackwell, 2002), and Walt Wolfram, "Reexamining the Development of African American English: Evidence from Isolated Communities," *Language* 79, no. 2 (2003): 282–316, for examples of the research contributions from communities in North Carolina.

4. See William Labov, *Dialect Diversity in America: The Politics of Language Change* (Charlottesville: University of Virginia Press, 2012), for a recent version of this position.

5. See North Carolina Language and Life Project, "Fieldsites," http://www.ncsu.edu/linguistics/ncllp/fieldsites.php, for descriptions of these field sites and a listing of publications from this research.

6. See Walt Wolfram, Kirk Hazen, and Jennifer Ruff Tamburro, "Isolation within Isolation: A Solitary Century of African American Vernacular English," *Journal of Sociolinguistics* 1, no. 1 (1997): 7–38.

7. See Maggie Ronkin and Helen E. Karn, "Mock Ebonics: Linguistic Racism in Parodies of Ebonics on the Internet," *Journal of Sociolinguistics* 3, no. 3 (1999): 360–80, for a discussion of these parodies and translators.

8. See Sally Johnson, "Who's Misunderstanding Whom? Sociolinguistics Debate and the Media," *Journal of Sociolinguistics* 5, no. 4 (2001): 606.

9. Books such as John R. Rickford, *African American Vernacular English: Features, Evolution and Educational Implications* (Malden, Mass.: Blackwell, 1999), and Lisa A. Green, *African American English: A Linguistic Introduction* (Cambridge, UK: Cambridge University Press, 2002), give explicit details on many of these patterns.

10. The report of this experiment is found in Walt Wolfram, "African American English and the Public Interest," in *The Languages of Africa and the Diaspora: Educating for Language Awareness*, ed. Jo Anne Kliefgen and George Bond (Clevedon, Bristol, UK: Multilingual Matters, 2009), 249–69. See Walt Wolfram, "Language Knowledge and Other Dialects," *American Speech* 57 (Spring 1982): 3–18, for the initiation of the study of speaker judgments of dialect forms and the results of these experiments.

11. Wolfram, "Language Knowledge and Other Dialects."

12. See Erik R. Thomas and Jeffrey Reaser, "Delimiting Perceptual Cues Used for the Ethnic Labeling of African American and European American Voices," *Journal of Sociolinguistics* 8, no. 1 (2004): 54–87.

13. See Wolfram and Thomas, *The Development of African American English*, for details.

14. Interviews from these studies are archived at http://ncslaap.lib.ncsu.edu/.

15. See Wolfram and Thomas, *The Development of African American English*.

16. See Becky Childs and Christine Mallinson, "African American English in Appalachia: Dialect Accommodation and Substrate Influence," *English World-Wide* 25, no. 1 (2004): 27–50.

17. See David S. Cecelski, *The Waterman's Song: Slavery and Freedom in Maritime North Carolina* (Chapel Hill: University of North Carolina Press, 2001), for details.

18. See David S. Cecelski, "The Shores of Freedom: The Maritime Underground Railroad in North Carolina, 1800–1861," *North Carolina Historical Review* 71 (April 1994): 205–6.

19. See chapter 6, "The Bryants," in Alton Balance, *Ocracokers* (Chapel Hill: University of North Carolina Press, 1989), for more on the Bryant family in the Ocracoke community.

20. See Walt Wolfram, "African Americans by the Sea," in *Life at the Edge of the Sea: Essays on North Carolina's Coastal Culture*, ed. Candy Beal and Carmine Prioli (Raleigh: Coastal Carolina Press, 2002), for more detail.

21. From recording at http://ncslaap.lib.ncsu.edu.

22. Ibid.

23. The social context and the speech of Beech Bottom are described in Christine Mallinson and Walt Wolfram, "Dialect Accommodation in a Bi-Ethnic Mountain Enclave Community: More Evidence on the Development of African American Vernacular English," *Language in Society* 31, no. 5 (2002): 743–75.

24. Sociohistorical details and linguistic analysis is from Childs and Mallinson, "African American English in Appalachia."

25. Recorded oral histories and the accompanying text in Christine Mallinson, Becky Childs, and Zula Cox, comps., *Voices of Texana* (Texana, Tex.: Texana Committee on Community History and Preservation, 2006).

26. From Neal Hutcheson, producer, *Voices of North Carolina* (Raleigh: North Carolina Language and Life Project, 2005).

27. See Raven I. McDavid and Virginia McDavid, "The Relationship of the Speech of American Negroes to the Speech of Whites," *American Speech* 26, no. 1 (1951): 3–17.

28. For the initial explanation of this hypothesis, see William A. Stewart, "Sociolinguistic Factors in the History of American Negro Dialects," *Florida FL Reporter* 5, no. 2 (1967): 11, 22, 24, and 26; and J. L. Dillard, *Black English: Its History and Usage in the United States* (New York: Random House, 1972).

29. For example, in Michel DeGraff, "Linguists' Most Dangerous Myth: The Fallacy of Creole Exceptionalism," *Language in Society* 34, no. 4 (2005): 533–91, some linguists argue convincingly that Creole is a case of linguistic exceptionalism that stems from the ideology related to European colonization of Africa and other

regions. He points out that all languages go through extensive contact situations that strongly influence their language; for example, it is estimated that 65 percent of English words are from French.

30. See John R. Rickford, "Prior Creolization of AAVE? Sociohistorical and Textual Evidence from the 17th and 18th Centuries," *Journal of Sociolinguistics* 1, no. 3 (1997): 315–36, as well as his book, *African American Vernacular English*.

31. A number of different kinds of earlier written and spoken data have now been analyzed, including Edgar W. Schneider, *American Earlier Black English: Morphological and Syntactic Variables* (Tuscaloosa: University of Alabama Press, 1989); Guy Bailey, Natalie Maynor, and Patricia Cukor-Avila, eds. *The Emergence of Black English: Text and Commentary* (Philadelphia: John Benjamins, 1991); and Michael Montgomery, Janet Fuller, and Sharon Demarse, "'The Black Men Has Wives and Sweet Harts and Third-Person Plural –s Jest Like the White Men': Evidence for Verbal -s from Written Documents on Nineteenth-Century African American Speech," *Language Variation and Change* 5, no. 3 (1993): 335–58.

32. The work of Dr. Shana Poplack and her colleagues in Shana Poplack, ed., *The English History of African American English* (Malden, Mass.: Blackwell, 2000), and Shana Poplack and Sali Tagliamonte, *African American English in the Diaspora* (Malden, Mass.: Blackwell, 2001), has been at the forefront of the study of expatriate speech in Samaná and Nova Scotia. Dr. John Singler's work on Liberian English is also noteworthy (for example, see John V. Singler, "Plural Marking in Liberian Settler English, 1820–1980," *American Speech* 64, no. 1 [1989]: 40–64), though his conclusions are quite different from those of Poplack and Tagliamonte. Singler is strongly opposed to the Anglicist Hypothesis.

33. See Poplack, *The English History of African American English*, and Poplack and Tagliamonte, *African American English in the Diaspora*.

34. See Wolfram and Thomas, *The Development of African American English*, for the technical details behind this argument.

35. Ibid.

36. Geneva Smitherman, *Black Talk: Words and Phrases from the Hood to the Amen Corner* (Boston: Houghton Mifflin, 2000), is an example of some of these terms, but terms can change rapidly.

37. At one point, we sent a resident from Hyde County to New York City with our researchers to interview his relatives who had moved there. These observations come from the report of our researchers.

38. See Labov, *Dialect Diversity in America*.

39. "Sistahs University," http://sistahsuniversity.blogspot.com/.

40. See Signithia B. Fordham and John Ogbu, "Black Students' School Success: Coping with the 'Burden of "Acting White,"'" *Urban Review* 18, no. 3 (1986): 176–206.

41. From Hutcheson, *Voices of North Carolina*.

42. See Janneke Van Hofwegen and Walt Wolfram, "Coming of Age in African American English," *Journal of Sociolinguistics* 14, no. 4 (2010): 427–55.

43. See Holly K. Craig and Julia A. Washington, *Malik Goes to School: Examining the Language Skills of African American Students from Preschool–5th Grade* (Mahwah,

N.J.: Lawrence Erlbaum Associates, 2006), for details of how a dialect index is applied.

44. From Hutcheson, *Voices of North Carolina*.

Chapter 8

1. Estimates of the size of the American Indian population at the arrival of European explorers vary greatly; however, even using more-conservative estimates, it is clear that many groups suffered losses of at least 80 percent of their population. See, for example, David E. Stannard, *American Holocaust: The Conquest of the New World* (Oxford and New York: Oxford University Press, 1992), for less-conservative estimates.

2. In Edward Sapir, with Morris Swadesh, "American Indian Grammatical Categories," published posthumously and reprinted in *The Collected Works of Edward Sapir*, vol. 5, *American Indian Languages 1*, ed. Philip Sapir and William Bright (Berlin: de Gruyter & Co., 1989), 133.

3. Ives Goddard and William C. Sturtevant, eds., *Handbook of North American Indians*, vol. 17, *Languages* (Washington, D.C.: Smithsonian Institution, 1997).

4. Ibid.

5. U.S. Census Bureau, "State and County QuickFacts: USA," http://quickfacts .census.gov/qfd/states/00000.html.

6. From "Irish revival movement," quoted in John R. Edwards, *Multilingualism* (London: Routledge, 1994), 118.

7. *Oxford English Dictionary* (online edition), http://www.oed.com.

8. See, for example, Peter Matthiessen, *In the Spirit of Crazy Horse* (New York: Penguin, 1992).

9. David Wilton, *Word Myths: Debunking Linguistic Urban Legends* (Oxford, UK: Oxford University Press, 2008).

10. Stannard, *American Holocaust*.

11. Compare, for example, the previously cited *Handbook of North American Indians* with the *Handbook of South American Indians*, ed. Julian H. Steward, 7 vols. (Washington, D.C.: U.S. Government Printing Office, 1946–59) .

12. See, for example, the response to "Native American" on one prominent American Indian resource at http://www.nativeweb.org/pages/legal/shoshone/ indian.html.

13. *Oxford English Dictionary* (online edition), http://www.oed.com.

14. Table 4 of Clyde Tucker, Brian Kojetin, and Roderick Harrison, "A Statistical Analysis of the CPS Supplement on Race and Ethnic Origins," (Washington, D.C.: U.S. Census Bureau, 1995), 17–18, available online at http://www.census.gov/prod/2/ gen/96arc/ivatuck.pdf.

15. Christina Berry, "What's in a Name? Indians and Political Correctness," http:// www.allthingscherokee.com/articles_culture_events_070101.html.

16. *Oxford English Dictionary* (Online edition). http://www.oed.com; there is one much earlier attestation with the variant spelling "Injin," from 1683, but neither spelling enters popular usage until the nineteenth century.

17. The phrase appears in the correspondence of George Bernard Shaw and Ellen Terry. *Ulysses* was serialized between 1918 and 1920 before being published as a single work in 1922.

18. *Oxford English Dictionary* (online edition), http://www.oed.com.

19. *Harjo, et al. v. Pro Football, Inc.*, filed September 12, 1992.

20. The initial ruling was overturned on the basis of *Laches*, a legal term denoting an unreasonable delay in pursuing a claim, which may be used as a means of dismissing a complaint.

21. September 2004, summary available online at http://sportsillustrated.cnn .com/2004/football/nfl/09/24/bc.fbn.redskins.indians.ap/.

22. Tommy Hawk, the official mascot, and the American Indian imagery can both be seen here: http://blackhawks.nhl.com/club/page.htm?id=58316.

23. See, for example, NCAA president Dr. Myles Brand's statement on the ban, "NCAA Correctly Positioned as a Catalyst for Social Change," *NCAA News*, October 24, 2005.

24. "NCAA: UNCP will keep the Braves," http://www.uncp.edu/news/2005/braves_ nickname.htm.

25. *Florida Flambeau*, November 7, 1947.

26. See, for example, "Victoria's Secret Apologizes for Use of Native American Headdress," http://articles.latimes.com/2012/nov/13/business/ la-fi-victorias-secret-native-american-20121113.

27. While estimates vary widely, three of the most commonly cited estimates include Ubelaker (2.1 million); Thornton (7 million); and Dobyns and Swagerty (18 million). See Douglas H. Ubelaker, "Prehistoric New World Population Size: Historical Review and Current Appraisal of North American Estimates," *American Journal of Physical Anthropology* 45, no. 3 (2005): 661–66; Russell Thornton, *American Indian Holocaust and Survival: A Population History since 1492* (Norman: Oklahoma University Press, 1990); and Henry F. Dobyns and William R. Swagerty, *Their Number Become Thinned: Native American Population Dynamics in Eastern North America* (Knoxville: University of Tennessee Press, 1983).

28. Cody's filmography can be found at http://www.imdb.com/name/ nm0002014/?ref_=fn_al_nm_1.

29. Despite maintaining her American Indian Heritage, Senator Warren declined to be pronounced the first American Indian senator from Massachusetts. See the media report at http://bostonherald.com/news_opinion/local_politics/2013/01/ liz_warren_won%E2%80%99t_beat_drum.

30. Alanna Nash, *Dolly* (Los Angeles: Reed Books, 1978).

31. "FAQ of Dolly Mania," http://www.dollymania.net/faq.html#64.

32. "The American Indian and Alaska Native Population: 2000," http://www .census.gov/prod/cen2010/briefs/c2010br-10.pdf.

33. "Cornell University Genetic Ancestry Project," http://3cpg.cornell.edu/index .cfm/page/AncestryProject.htm.

34. See, for example, William S. McFeely, *Grant: A Biography* (New York: Norton, 2002), 308.

35. Gary E. Moulton, *John Ross: Cherokee Chief* (Athens: University of Georgia Press, 1978).

36. Quoted from Neal Hutcheson, producer, *Voices of North Carolina* (Raleigh: North Carolina Language and Life Project, 2005).

37. "Uniform Indians: Personal Reflections on the Eastern Band of Cherokee Boarding School Experience," *Appalachian Heritage* 37, no. 4 (2009): 49–55.

38. Quoted from Hutcheson, *Voices of North Carolina*.

39. Ibid.

40. Joseph M. Williams, *The Origins of the English Language* (New York: Free Press, 1975), 104.

41. Thomas Harriot, *A Brief and True Report of the New Found Land of Virginia* (1588), 35.

42. *Ethnologue: Languages of the World*, http://www.ethnologue.com.

43. North Carolina Department of Administration, Commission on Indian Affairs, "Tribes and Organizations," http://www.doa.state.nc.us/cia/tribesorg.htm; the Coharie Tribe, http://www.coharietribe.org/.

44. Tuscarora Indian School, http://www.nwcsd.k12.ny.us/tuscarora; *Ethnologue: Languages of the World*, "Tuscarora," http://www.ethnologue.com/show_language. asp?code=tus.

45. William C. Sturtevant and Bruce G. Trigger, eds., *Handbook of North American Indians*, vol. 15, *Northeast* (Washington, D.C.: Smithsonian Institution, 1978), 287–88.

46. Meherrin Nation, http://meherrinnation.org/.

47. Horatio Hale, "The Tutelo Tribe and Language," *Proceedings of the American Philosophical Society* 21 (1883): 1–47.

48. Ives Goddard, "The Identity of Red Thunder Cloud," *Society for the Study of Indigenous Languages of the Americas Newsletter* (April 2000). Available online at http://anthropology.si.edu/goddard1.html.

49. Haliwa-Saponi Tribe, http://haliwa-saponi.com/; Occaneechi Band of the Saponi Nation, http://www.obsn.org/; Sappony, http://www.sappony.org/; Waccamaw Siouan Tribe, http://www.waccamaw-siouan.com/.

50. A good overview of Mississippian history and culture can be found in *The New Georgia Encyclopedia*, "Mississippian Period: Overview," available online at http://www.georgiaencyclopedia.org/nge/Article.jsp?id=h-707.

51. See, for example, Judith A. Bense, *Archaeology of the Southeastern United States: Paleoindian to World War I* (New York: Academic Press, 1994), 256–57, 275–79.

52. North Carolina Historical Sites, "Town Creek Indian Mound," http://www.nchistoricsites.org/town/.

53. Theda Perdue, *Mixed Blood Indians: Racial Construction in the Early South* (Athens: University of Georgia Press, 2003), 51–52.

54. Perhaps the most complete account of Jackson's wars on American Indians is Robert Remini, *Andrew Jackson and His Indian Wars* (New York: Viking, 2001). There are dozens of histories on the Trail of Tears, including such excellent accounts as Anthony Wallace, *The Long, Bitter Trail: Andrew Jackson and the Indians* (New York: Hill and Wang, 1993), and Grant Foreman, *Indian Removal: The Emigration of the Five Civilized Tribes of Indians*, 11th ed. (Norman: University of Oklahoma Press, 1989).

55. The first edition of the *Cherokee Phoenix* newspaper, published on February 21, 1828, uses this form for self-identification, as the masthead reads: "Tsalagi Tsulehisanvhi." For differing accounts of the origin of the name "Cherokee," see http://www.accessgenealogy.com/native/tribes/cherokee/cherohist.htm; Charles Augustus Hanna, *The Wilderness Trail: Or, the Ventures and Adventures of the Pennsylvania Traders on the Allegheny Path, with some New Annals of the Old West, and the Records of Some Strong Men and Some Bad Ones* (New York: G. P. Putnam's Sons, 1911); and William C. Sturtevant and Raymond D. Fogelson, eds., *Handbook of North American Indians*, vol. 14, *Southeast* (Washington, D.C.: Smithsonian Institution, 2004), 349.

56. Compare James Mooney, *Myths of the Cherokee* (Mineola, N.Y.: Dover Publications, 1995), 393, a republished piece of part 2 of Mooney's *The Nineteenth Annual Report of the Bureau of American Ethnology to the Secretary of the Smithsonian Institution, 1897–98: In Two Parts* (Washington, D.C.: Government Printing Office, 1900); and Sturtevant and Fogelson, *Handbook of North American Indians*, vol. 14, *Southeast*, 132.

57. See, for example, Ludovic Grant, "Historical Relation of the Facts," *Journal of Cherokee Studies* 26 (2008): 64.

58. Quoted in Bartholomew Rivers Carroll, ed., *Historical Collections of South Carolina: Embracing Many Rare and Valuable Pamphlets, and Other Documents, Relating to the History of That State from Its First Discovery to Its Independence, in the Year 1776* (New York: Harper Brothers, 1836), 432–33.

59. Willard Walker and James Sarbaugh, "The Early History of the Cherokee Syllabary," *Ethnohistory* 40, no. 1 (1993): 70–94.

60. Terrence G. Wiley, *Literacy and Language Diversity in the United States*, 2nd ed. (Washington, D.C.: Center for Applied Linguistics, 2005), 26.

61. See table 6 of Thomas D. Snyder, ed., *120 Years of American Education: A Statistical Portrait* (Washington, D.C.: U.S. Department of Education, 1993), 21, available online at: http://o-nces.ed.gov.opac.acc.msmc.edu/pubs93/93442.pdf.

62. Litefoot, http://www.litefoot.com/.

63. Cherokee Nation, http://www.cherokee.org/; Eastern Band of Cherokee, http://nc-cherokee.com/.

64. The Cherokee removal began in the winter of 1838 and involved a march of about 1,000 miles. Few Cherokee had extra clothing, and many went barefoot. The government provided blankets for warmth, but the blankets had been previously used in a Tennessee hospital that had just had an outbreak of smallpox. Many Cherokees contracted the disease, resulting in even more deaths and hardship. Because of the outbreak among tribal members, the travelers were forbidden to enter any towns along the route, greatly increasing the distance they were required to walk. Adding to their misery were the abnormally cold winter temperatures. All told, between 2,000 and 8,000 of the roughly 16,000 to 20,000 Cherokees who took the journey died en route. The most commonly cited estimate of 4,000 Cherokee deaths during the forced removal, or about one in four, traces to James Mooney's work at the Smithsonian Institution near the end of the nineteenth century. For slightly different accounts, see, for example, William L. Anderson, ed., *Cherokee*

Removal: Before and After (Athens: University of Georgia Press, 1991); John Ehle, *Trail of Tears: The Rise and Fall of the Cherokee Nation* (New York: Doubleday, 1988); and Samuel Carter, *Cherokee Sunset: A Nation Betrayed* (New York: Doubleday, 1976).

65. For one account of the early history of the Eastern Band of the Cherokee, see John R. Finger, *Cherokee Americans: The Eastern Band of Cherokees in the 20th Century* (Lincoln: University of Nebraska Press, 1993).

66. Sarah Margaret Sneed, "Uniform Indians," *Appalachian Heritage* 37, no. 4 (2009): 49–55.

67. Cherokee Nation, "Immersion School," http://www.cherokee.org/Services/Education/ImmersionSchool.aspx.

68. Cherokee Preservation Foundation, "Cherokee Language Revitalization," http://www.cherokeepreservationfdn.org/cultural-preservation-connect/major-programs-and-initiatives/cherokee-language-revitalization.

69. Quoted from Hutcheson, *Voices of North Carolina*.

70. Eastern Band of Cherokee, "Kituwah Preservation and Education," http://nc-cherokee.com/education/hom/youth-adult-education-services/kituwah-preservation-education/.

71. Quoted from Hutcheson, *Voices of North Carolina*.

72. These and the following quotation are all from Hutcheson, *Voices of North Carolina*.

73. "Consortium Word List," http://www.sandiegocherokeecommunity.com/Consortium_Word_List.pdf.

74. Cherokee Preservation Foundation, "Cherokee Language Revitalization," http://www.cherokeepreservationfdn.org/cultural-preservation-connect/major-programs-and-initiatives/cherokee-language-revitalization.

75. Quoted from Scott McKie, "Seven Years! New Kituwah Academy Celebrates Anniversary," *Cherokee One Feather*, April 19, 2011, available online at http://theonefeather.com/2011/04/seven-years-new-kituwah-academy-celebrates-anniversary/.

Chapter 9

1. Population estimates for 2011 from U.S. Census Bureau, "State and County QuickFacts: Robeson County," http://quickfacts.census.gov/qfd/states/37/37155.html.

2. From Fergus Bordewich, *Killing the White Man's Indian* (New York: Doubleday, 1966), 60.

3. See http://www.uncp.edu/uncp/about/history.htm for the history of the University of North Carolina at Pembroke.

4. See http://www.ncga.state.nc.us/Sessions/2005/Bills/House/HTML/H371v3.html for the act designating the University of North Carolina at Pembroke as North Carolina's historically American Indian University.

5. Archived at http://ncslaap.lib.ncsu.edu.

6. From Bordewich, *Killing the White Man's Indian*, 62–63.

7. See Adolph L. Dial and David K. Eliades, *The Only Land I Know: A History of the*

Lumbee Indians (San Francisco: Indian Historian Press, 1975), for efforts in the earlier 1900s to classify the Lumbee as American Indian.

8. Neal Hutcheson, producer, *Indian by Birth: The Lumbee Dialect* (Raleigh: North Carolina Language and Life Project, 2001).

9. Ibid.

10. Quoted in Stanley Knick, *The Lumbee in Context* (Pembroke, N.C.: Museum of the Native American Resource Center, 2000), 77.

11. See Lumbee Regional Development Association, Inc., "More History," http://www.lumbee.org/history.html, for a chronology of acts requesting recognition.

12. See Senate Report 111-116, "Lumbee Recognition Act," http://www.indian.senate.gov/upload/Report-111–116.pdf.

13. See H.R. 31, "Lumbee Recognition Act," http://beta.congress.gov/bill/111th-congress/house-bill/31.

14. Quotes with emphasis in Walt Wolfram, Clare Dannenberg, Stanley Knick, and Linda Oxendine, *Fine in the World: Lumbee Language in Time and Place* (Raleigh: North Carolina Humanities Extension/Publications, 2002), 3.

15. Hamilton McMillan, *Sir Walter Raleigh's Lost Colony: Historical Sketch of the Attempts Made by Sir Walter Raleigh to Establish a Colony in Virginia with Traditions of an Indian Tribe in North Carolina, Indicating the Fate of the Colony of Englishmen Left on Roanoke Island in 1587* (Raleigh: Edwards and Broughton Printing, 1888; revised edition, 1907), 25. Text available online at http://archive.org/stream/sirwalterraleighoomcmil#page/n1/mode/2up.

16. Personal communication with Blair A. Rudes. Also see Blair A. Rudes, "Cofitachique and Yupaha: The Ethnicity of a Chieftan" (unpublished manuscript, 2000). See http://www.coastalcarolinaindians.com/research/BlairARudes/default.htm for Rudes's word lists and papers.

17. See http://www.accessgenealogy.com/native/tribes/siouan/sugereehist.htm for a history of the Sugaree.

18. McMillan, *Sir Walter Raleigh's Lost Colony*, 25. Text available online at http://archive.org/stream/sirwalterraleighoomcmil#page/n1/mode/2up.

19. See Knick, *The Lumbee in Context*.

20. Dial and Eliades, *The Only Land I Know*, 13.

21. For some of the detailed analysis of vowels, see Erik R. Thomas, *An Acoustic Analysis of Vowel Variation in New World English*, Publication of the American Dialect Society, no. 85 (Durham, N.C.: Duke University Press, 2001), 20, 29, 35, 42, 197–98.

22. All of these interviews are archived at the Sociolinguistic Archive and Analysis Project website, http://ncslaap.lib.ncsu.edu/.

23. See Benjamin Torbert, "Tracing Native American History through Consonant Cluster Reduction: The Case of Lumbee English," *American Speech* 76 (Winter 2001): 361–87.

24. See Walt Wolfram, "Dynamic Dimensions of Language Influence: The Case of American Indian English," in *Language: Social Psychological Perspectives*, ed. Howard A. Giles, Peter Robinson, and Phillip M. Smith (Oxford and New York: Pergammon Press, 1980), 377–88.

25. See Natalie Schilling-Estes, "Investigating Intra-Ethnic Differentiation: /ay/ in Native American Indian English," *Language Variation and Change* 12, no. 2 (2000): 141–74.

26. See Michael Montgomery and Margaret Mishoe, "He Bes Took up with a Yankee Girl and Moved up There to New York: The Verb *Bes* in the Carolinas and Its History," *American Speech* 74 (Fall 1999): 240–81.

27. See Walt Wolfram and Jason Sellers, "Ethnolinguistic Marking of Past Tense *be* in Lumbee Vernacular English," *Journal of English Linguistics* 27, no. 2 (1999): 94–114.

28. From Wolfram, Dannenberg, Knick, and Oxendine, *Fine in the World*, 16. Based on Renee Hammonds, "People's Perceptions of Lumbee Vernacular English" (M.A. thesis, North Carolina Central University, 2000).

29. For summaries and analyses of the patterns described in the following sections, see Clare J. Dannenberg, *Sociolinguistic Constructs of Ethnic Identity: The Syntactic Delineation of an American Indian English*, Publication of the American Dialect Society, no. 87 (Durham, N.C.: Duke University Press, 2002); and Walt Wolfram and Clare Dannenberg, "Dialect Identity in a Tri-Ethnic Context: The Case of Lumbee American Indian English," *English World-Wide* 20, no. 2 (1999): 179–216.

30. Hayes Alan Locklear, Walt Wolfram, Natalie Schilling-Estes, and Clare Dannenberg, *A Dictionary of Lumbee English* (Raleigh: North Carolina Language and Life Project, 1999).

31. Schilling-Estes, "Investigating Intra-Ethnic Differentiation."

32. Ibid.

33. See Natalie Schilling-Estes, "Constructing Ethnicity in Interaction," *Journal of Sociolinguistics* 8, no. 2 (2004): 163–95.

34. See Thomas, *An Acoustic Analysis of Vowel Variation in New World English*, 20, 29, 35, 42, 197–98, for more detail on Lumbee vowels.

35. Archived at http://ncslaap.lib.ncsu.edu.

36. Ibid.

37. See Daniel Schreier, "Terra Incognita in the Anglophone World: Tristan da Cunha, South Atlantic Ocean," *English World-Wide* 23, no. 1 (2002): 1–29.

38. See Montgomery and Mishoe, "He Bes Took up with a Yankee Girl and Moved up There to New York."

39. See Clare Dannenberg and Walt Wolfram, "Ethnic Identity and Grammatical Restructuring: Be(s) in Lumbee English," *American Speech* 73, no. 2 (1998): 139–59.

40. From Hutcheson, *Indian by Birth*.

41. See http://www.schoolmap.org/School/Purnell-Swett-High-Student/.

42. From Hutcheson, *Indian by Birth*.

Chapter 10

1. Archived at http://ncslaap.lib.ncsu.edu.

2. See William S. Powell, *North Carolina through Four Centuries* (Chapel Hill: University of North Carolina Press, 1989). Also see Aleck Loker, *La Florida: Spanish Exploration and Settlement of North America, 1500 to 1600* (Williamsburg, Va.: Solitude Press, 2010).

3. See, for example, Carmine Prioli, *The Wild Horses of Shackleford Banks* (Winston-Salem, N.C.: John F. Blair, 2007); also see "Wild Horses of North Carolina," http://www.ncbeaches.com/Features/Wildlife/WildHorsesNorthCarolina/.

4. Archived at http://ncslaap.lib.ncsu.edu.

5. See, for example, Alan M. Kraut, *The Huddled Masses: The Immigrant in American Society, 1880–1921*, 2nd ed. (Hoboken, N.J.: Wiley, 2001).

6. See Hannah Gill, *The Latino Migration Experience in North Carolina: New Roots in the Old North State* (Chapel Hill: University of North Carolina Press, 2010).

7. Quoted in Andres Viglucci, "Hispanic Wave Forever Alters Small Town in North Carolina," *Miami Herald*, January 2, 2000.

8. See Gill, *The Latino Migration Experience in North Carolina*.

9. Quoted in Chris Burritt and Timothy R. Homan, "Rural North Carolina Absorbing Surge of Hispanics," *Seattle Times*, March 6, 2011.

10. See Connect NCDOT, "North Carolina Demographic Information—Hispanic Population by County," https://connect.ncdot.gov/business/trucking/Trucking%20 Documents/Hispanic_Population_by_County.pdf.

11. See Gabriela Zabala, director of Hispanic/Latino Affairs, Office of the Governor, with Steven Mann, "Demographic Trends of Hispanics/Latinos in North Carolina," http://www.ncdhhs.gov/mhddsas/providers/DWI/hispanic latinodemographicsreport.pdf. Also see U.S. Census Bureau, "The Hispanic Population: 2010," available online at http://www.hacu.net/images/hacu/OPAI/2012_ Virtual_Binder/2010%20census%20brief%20-%20hispanic%20population.pdf.

12. See Hannah Pick, Walt Wolfram, and Jacqueline Lopez, "Indigenous-Language Students from Spanish-Speaking Countries: Educational Approaches," in *Heritage Briefs Collection* (Washington, D.C.: Center for Applied Linguistics, 2011).

13. From Carmen Fought, *Chicano English in Context* (New York: Palgrave Macmillan, 2003), 17.

14. Ibid.

15. Ibid.

16. From Thomas Bonfiglio, *Race and the Rise of Standard American* (Berlin: Mouton de Gruyter, 2002), 62–63.

17. From Phillip M. Carter, "Shared Spaces, Shared Structures: Latino Social Formation and African American English in the U.S.," *Journal of Sociolinguistics* 17, no. 1 (2013): 66–92.

18. Personal communication.

19. There are many references and a variety of theories for explaining code-switching in terms of linguistic and sociolinguistic theory. They range from the classic early descriptive work of Uriel Weinriech in *Languages in Contact: Findings and Problems* (New York: Linguistic Circle of New York, 1953) to Jeff MacSwan, "Code-Switching and Grammatical Theory," in *Handbook of Bilingualism and Multilingualism*, 2nd ed., ed. Tej K. Bhatia and William C. Ritchie (Hoboken, N.J.: Wiley-Blackwell, 2013), 323–50, which discusses current perspectives on code-switching in terms of language theory.

20. From Danica Cullinan, producer, *Spanish Voices: Spanish and English in the Southeastern United States* (Raleigh: North Carolina Language and Life Project, 2010).

21. From Tonya E. Wolford and Phillip M. Carter, "The 'Spanish as Threat' Ideology and Cultural Aspects of Spanish Attrition," in *Spanish in the U.S. Southwest: A Language in Transition*, ed. Susana Rivera-Mills and Daniel Villa (Madrid: Iberoamericana, 2001), 111.

22. See report at http://www.newstaco.com/2011/05/27/north-carolina-diner-no-speak-english-no-service/.

23. See, for example, James Crawford, *At War with Diversity: U.S. Language Policy in an Age of Anxiety* (Clevedon, Bristol, UK: Multilingual Matters, 2000).

24. See the current bill text at http://thomas.loc.gov/cgi-bin/query/z?c110:S.1335.

25. Dr. S. I. Hayakawa's book was originally published as *Language in Action* in 1941, but a larger, unabridged edition was published in 1978 as *Language in Thought and Action* (San Diego: Harcourt Brace Jovanovich).

26. See report in http://www.chiefsplanet.com/BB/archive/index.php/t-160936.html.

27. See General Statutes of North Carolina, 145–12, "State Language," http://www.languagepolicy.net/archives/nc.htm.

28. Quoted from Theodore Roosevelt, *Works*, vol. 24 (New York: Scribner and Sons, 1923–26), 554.

29. See Linguistic Society of America, "Resolution: English Only," http://www.linguisticsociety.org/about/what-we-do/resolutions-statements-guides/lsa-res-english.

30. From Geoff Pullum, "Here Come the Linguistic Fascists," *Natural Language and Linguistic Theory* 5, no. 4 (1987): 604.

31. For the language policy of Latvia, see http://valoda.lv/en/downloadDoc_436/mid_644.

32. See Wolford and Carter, "The 'Spanish as Threat' Ideology and Cultural Aspects of Spanish Attrition," 113.

33. Ibid.

34. It is, of course, difficult to estimate these figures precisely given the self-reported figures in U.S. census data (http://www.census.gov/hhes/socdemo/language/data/acs/ACS-12.pdf), but there is little doubt about the discrepancy between the United States and other countries.

35. See Fergus I. M. Craik, Ellen Bialystok, and Morris Freedman, "Delaying the Onset of Alzheimer Disease: Bilingualism as a Form of Cognitive Reserve," *Neurology* 75, no. 19 (2010): 1726–29.

36. Archived at http://ncslaap.lib.ncsu.edu.

37. See Fought, *Chicano English in Context*, and Walt Wolfram, *Sociolinguistic Aspects of Assimilation: Puerto Rican English in New York City* (Washington, D.C.: Center for Applied Linguistics, 1974).

38. See Fought, *Chicano English in Context*.

39. See Walt Wolfram, Mary E. Kohn, and Erin Callahan-Price, "Southern-Bred Hispanic English: An Emerging Socioethnic Variety," in *Selected Proceedings of the 5th*

Workshop on Spanish Sociolinguistics, ed. James Michnowicz and Robin Dodsworth (Somerville, Mass.: Cascadilla Proceedings Project, 2011).

40. Archived at http://ncslaap.lib.ncsu.edu.

41. See Walt Wolfram, "Variability in Tense Marking: A Case for the Obvious," *Language Learning* 35, no. 2 (1985): 229–53.

42. Beckie Moriello, "'I'm Feeksin' to Move': Hispanic English in Siler City" (M.A. thesis, North Carolina State University, 2003).

43. See Mary E. Kohn and Hannah Askin Franz, "Localized Patterns for Global Variants: The Case of Quotative Systems of African American and Latino/a Speakers," *American Speech* 84, no. 3 (2009): 259–97.

44. Ibid. Recording archived at http://ncslaap.lib.ncsu.edu.

45. Archived at http://ncslaap.lib.ncsu.edu.

46. See Phillip M. Carter, "Phonetic Variation and Speaker Agency: Mexicana Identity in a North Carolina Middle School," *Penn Working Papers in Linguistics* 13 (2007): 1–14.

47. Ibid., 3.

Chapter 11

1. Republican strategist Dr. Frank I. Luntz describes his polling that led to the use of "Death Tax" in the 1994 "Contract with America" in his book *Words That Work: It's Not What You Say, It's What People Hear* (New York: Hyperion, 2007), 164–66.

2. See one account in William L. Shirer, *The Rise and Fall of the Third Reich: A History of Nazi Germany* (New York: Simon and Schuster, 1990), 1092.

3. The U.S. War Department created a seventy-five-page booklet titled *Pocket Guide to China* (1942) that included a comic titled "How to Spot a Jap" (65–75), which was subsequently removed from the 1944 second printing. The panel on page 71 relies on linguistic cues for identification. The comic is reprinted here: http://en.wikipedia.org/wiki/File:US_Army_How_To_Spot_A_Jap.png.

4. Read more about these and other instances of linguistic legislation in Dennis Baron, "Language Legislation and Language Abuse: American Language Policy through the 1990s," in *Language Ideologies: Critical Perspectives on the Official English Movement*, vol. 2, *History, Theory, and Policy*, ed. Roseann Dueñas Gonzalez (Urbana, Ill.: National Council of Teacher of English Press, 2001), 5–29.

5. See story at http://www.cnn.com/2003/ALLPOLITICS/03/11/sprj.irq.fries/.

6. Florence Goodenough, "Racial Differences in the Intelligence of School Children," *Journal of Experimental Psychology* 9, no. 5 (1926): 388–97.

7. Uriel Weinreich, *Languages in Contact: Findings and Problems* (New York: Linguistic Circle of New York, 1953).

8. Sassaure's *Cours de Linguistique Générale* (Course in General Linguistics) was published posthumously in 1916. The quotation cited comes from the Dr. Roy Harris translated and edited version of this seminal linguistics text (Peru, Ill.: Open Court, 1983), 7.

9. "The Socially-Minded Linguist," *Modern Language Journal* 63, no. 8 (1979), 407.

10. *English with an Accent: Language, Ideology, and Discrimination in the United States*, 2nd ed. (New York: Routledge, 2011), 73.

11. Louis Alverez and Andy Kolker, producers, *American Tongues* (New York: Center for New American Media, 1988).

12. Quoted from Neal Hutcheson, producer, *Mountain Talk* (Raleigh: North Carolina Language and Life Project, 2004).

13. Quoted from Alverez and Kolker, *American Tongues*.

14. This quote is widely attributed to mid-twentieth-century poet and author Pearl Strachan Hurd.

15. The most oft-cited definition and discussion of implicit attitudes remains Anthony Greenwald and Mahzarin R. Banaji, "Implicit Social Cognition: Attitudes, Self-Esteem, and Stereotypes," *Psychological Review* 102, no. 1 (1995): 4–27.

16. In 1758 the Catholic Church's *Index of Prohibited Books* removed many works defending the heliocentric model; however, it was not until 1835 that all such works, including Galileo Galilei's *Dialogue Concerning the Two Chief World Systems*, were permitted.

17. See one such report at http://www.nytimes.com/2005/08/30/science/30profile .html.

18. This quotation is widely attributed to Marcus Aurelius; however, it does not appear in his *Meditations*.

19. Albert Einstein, quoted in Eric Temple Bell, *Mathematics, Queen, and Servant of Science* (Washington, D.C.: Mathematics Association of America, 1951), 42.

20. Dr. John Baugh has been the most prominent linguist researching linguistic profiling. His chapter "Linguistic Profiling" in *Black Linguistics: Language, Society, and Politics in Africa and the Americas*, ed. Sinfree Makoni, Geneva Smitherman, Arnetha F. Ball, and Arthur K. Spears (New York: Routledge, 2003), 155–63, remains one of the best-detailed overviews of the issue. His website also contains links to additional information on linguistic profiling: http://www.artsci.wustl.edu/~jbaugh/Site/ Welcome.html.

21. See report at http://news.newamericamedia.org/news/view_article .html?article_id=88d97b82640f6ba16f5e07d9d695a1b3.

22. The acceptance of this fact led researchers in the 1960s to develop programs to help teach code-switching to students who spoke stigmatized dialects. While this approach may seem practical on the surface, it ignores the reality that all language varieties are linguistically equal, leading University of Texas scholar Dr. James Sledd to deem it "The Linguistics of White Supremacy" (*English Journal* 58, no. 9 [1969]: 1307).

23. The "Pygmalion Effect" or "Rosenthal Effect" was first described by Dr. Robert Rosenthal and Lenore Jacobson in their seminal work, *Pygmalion in the Classroom* (New York: Holt, Rinehart, and Winston, 1968). It was expanded and republished under the same title in 1992 (New York: Irvington Press).

24. See Keith Basso, *Portraits of "The Whiteman": Linguistic Play and Cultural Symbols among the Western Apache* (Cambridge, UK: Cambridge University Press, 1979); and

Stephanie Prescott, ed., *The American Indian: Yesterday, Today, and Tomorrow; a Handbook for Educators* (Sacramento, Calif.: California Department of Education, 1991).

25. The full text of Judge Joiner's opinion is included in David J. Ramirez, Terrence G. Wiley, Gerda de Klerk, Enid Lee, and Wayne E. Wright, eds. *Ebonics: The Urban Education Debate*, 2nd ed. (Tonawanda, N.Y.: Multilingual Matters, Ltd., 2005).

26. *The Teaching of English Usage* (Urbana, Ill.: National Council of Teachers of English, 1974), 5.

27. "Principle of debt incurred" from William Labov, "Objectivity and Commitment in Linguistic Science," *Language in Society* 11, no. 2 (1982): 172–73. "Principle of linguistic gratuity" from Walt Wolfram, "Ethical Considerations in Language Awareness Programs," *Issues in Applied Linguistics* 4, no. 2 (1993): 225–55.

28. Wolfram, "Ethical Considerations in Language Awareness Programs," 227.

29. Phyllis Blanton and Karen Waters, producers, *The Ocracoke Brogue* (Raleigh: North Carolina Language and Life Project, 1996); Hutcheson, *Mountain Talk*; Benjamin Torbert, producer, *Hyde Talk* (Raleigh: North Carolina Language and Life Project, 2002); Danica Cullinan, producer, *Spanish Voices: Spanish and English in the Southeastern United States* (Raleigh: North Carolina Language and Life Project, 2010).

30. Neal Hutcheson, producer, *Indian by Birth: The Lumbee Dialect* (Raleigh: North Carolina Language and Life Project, 2001); Akram Khater and Danica Cullinan, producers, *Cedars in the Pines: The Lebanese of North Carolina* (Raleigh: North Carolina Language and Life Project, 2011).

31. Andrew Grimes and Ryan Rowe, producers, *Princeville Remembers the Flood* (Raleigh: North Carolina Language and Life Project, 2004); Ryan Rowe and Andrew Grimes, producers, *This Side of the River* (Raleigh: North Carolina Language and Life Project, 2007). Neal Hutcheson, producer, *The Queen Family: Appalachian Tradition and Back Porch Music* (Raleigh: North Carolina Language and Life Project, 2006); Neal Hutcheson, producer, *Core Sounders* (Raleigh: North Carolina Language and Life Project, 2013).

32. Andrew Grimes, producer, *Celebrating Muzel Bryant* (Raleigh: North Carolina Language and Life Project, 2004).

33. The tribute to Roy Parsons is included on an extra to Hutcheson's *The Carolina Brogue*. Neal Hutcheson, producer, *The Last One* (Raleigh: Sucker Punch Productions, 2008).

34. Helen Marie Cloud, Becky Childs, and Walt Wolfram, comps., *Ocracoke Speaks: The Distinct Sounds of the Hoi Toide* (Raleigh: North Carolina Language and Life Project, 2001); *Ocracoke Still Speaks: Reflections Past and Present*, compiled by Jeffrey Reaser, Paula Dickerson Boddie, and Walt Wolfram (North Carolina Language and Life Project) and DeAnna Locke, Chester Lynn, Phillip Howard (Ocracoke Preservation Society) (Raleigh: North Carolina Language and Life Project, 2011); Christine Mallinson, Becky Childs, and Zula Cox, comps., *Voices of Texana* (Texana, Tex.: Texana Committee on Community History and Preservation, 2006); Neal Hutcheson, producer, *An Unclouded Day* (Raleigh: North Carolina Language and Life Project, 2008); Hutcheson, *The Queen Family*.

35. The *Voices of North Carolina: Language and Life from the Atlantic to the Appalachians*

dialect awareness curriculum is available online at http://ncsu.edu/linguistics/
dialectcurriculum.php.

36. Preface to Johnson's dictionary, full text available online at http://www.bl.uk/
learning/images/texts/dict/transcript1387.html.

Index of Dialect Words and Phrases

Carry (accompany, take), 74, 86, 235

Catched (caught; Mountain Talk), 147

Catterwampus (crooked, not straight or square), 10. See also Antigoglin; Cattywampus; Sigogglin; Whopperjawed

Cattywampus (crooked, not straight or square; Coastal Plain), 10, 71, 84, 86, 116. See also Antigoglin; Catterwampus; Sigogglin; Whopperjawed

Chimbly (chimney), 90

Chunk (throw), 84, 86, 116, 117

Clift (cliff; Mountain Talk, Outer Banks Brogue), 145

Coke (any carbonated beverage [also Co-cola]; rural), 83

Cornpone (cornmeal bread), 86

Cove (gap between ridges of a mountain; Mountain Talk), 135, 136, 142, 150

Creek (inlet between ocean and sound; Outer Banks Brogue), 64, 70, 116, 117

Crowd (group of two people or more; Outer Banks Brogue), 117, 120–121

'Cue (barbecue), 74

Cut on/off (turn on/off), 72, 84, 86

Cuz (good friend; Lumbee), 11, 141, 233

Daddy (good friend; Lumbee), 11, 33

Devil's shoestring (hobblebush, branches spread among the ground; Mountain Talk), 9

Dingbatter (outsider or nonnative; Outer Banks Brogue), 10, 64, 100, 111, 114, 115, 141

Directly (in a little while; Outer Banks Brogue), 117

Ditch (mouth of the harbor; Outer Banks Brogue), 115

Dit-dot (outsider or nonnative [also dit-dotter]; Outer Banks Brogue), 10, 64, 115, 117, 141

Doast (a cold or influenza; Outer Banks Brogue), 116

Done (completely, as in, "I done finished the house"), 92

Dope (soda; Mountain Talk), 69, 145

Drain (small stream; Mountain Talk), 142

Drime/droim (interjection for calling someone's bluff; Outer Banks Brogue), 117

Ellick (coffee, usually with sugar; Lumbee), 234

Extree (extra; Outer Banks Brogue, Mountain Talk), 11

Fatback (fatty part of the hog similar to bacon), 72, 115, 234

Fatback (menhaden [fish]; Outer Banks Brogue), 64, 115

Favor (resemble), 84, 86

Feller (fellow, guy; Mountain Talk, Lumbee, Outer Banks Brogue), 144, 237

Fine in the world (doing well; Lumbee), 234

Fixin' to (plan to, intend), 50, 53, 72, 86

Flat(-out) (completely), 84. See also Plumb; Right

Floridee (Florida; Mountain Talk, Outer Banks Brogue), 145

Foreigner (outsider or nonnative), 11, 64, 107, 115, 131

Gaum (sticky or dirty mess [also gaumed up]; Mountain Talk), 143, 243

Getting above your raisin' (putting on airs), 95–96

Goaty (foul smelling; Outer Banks Brogue), 116

Good ole boy (humble and respected person, or someone who engages in cronyism), 95–96

Grilling (cooking outside), 64, 98

Guano (fertilizer from fowl or coastal birds; Outer Banks Brogue), 64

Hain't (ain't; Outer Banks Brogue, Mountain Talk), 113, 145, 237

Halfback (a northern transplant to Florida who vacations in the mountains during the summer; Mountain Talk), 64, 131, 142

Hammock (grove of trees; Outer Banks Brogue), 27, 64, 70

Hard blow (strong wind; Outer Banks Brogue), 64

Head'nes (overwhelming, very bad; Coastal Plain), 234

Heared (heard; Mountain Talk), 133, 147

Hey (friendly greeting), 98, 264

Hit (it; Outer Banks Brogue, Mountain Talk), 113, 137, 145, 237

Hoi Toider (a person from the Outer Banks, so called because of the traditional pronunciation of the letter i in the words "high tide"; Outer Banks Brogue), 2, 104, 112, 126, 163, 166

Holler (gap between ridges of a mountain; Mountain Talk), 64, 118, 142, 144, 167

Hoover Days (period of the Great Depression), 234

Hushpuppies (fried bits of cornmeal, typically accompanying barbecue or seafood), 83

Idn't (isn't), 90

Jack tale (a traditional story involving trickster characters; Mountain Talk), 3, 143

Jarfly (cicada; Mountain Talk), 143

Jasper (a contemptible person; Mountain Talk), 64, 131, 142

Juvember (slingshot; Lumbee, Coastal Plain), 10, 61, 72, 234

Kelvinator (refrigerator), 234

Kin(folk) (relatives), 84, 86

Knowed (knew; Mountain Talk), 147

Laurel (rhododendron; Mountain Talk), 143. See also Lettuce

Laurel bed (thicket of rhododendron or mountain laurel [also laurel hell, laurel rough, laurel slick]; Mountain Talk), 143. See also Lettuce bed; Rough

Law, the (law-enforcement officers), 56

Leaf-lookers (tourists who go to the mountains to see the fall foliage; Mountain Talk), 136

Leeward (with the wind; Outer Banks Brogue), 115

Lettuce (rhododendron; Mountain Talk), 143

Lettuce bed (thicket of rhododendron or mountain laurel; Mountain Talk), 143

Lightering (removing cargo to make a boat lighter; Outer Banks Brogue), 64, 110, 116

Liketa (nearly, as in, "He liketa froze to death"), 50, 91–92, 149

Lum (an insider term for a fellow Lumbee Indian; Lumbee), 11, 141, 222, 230, 233

Manteo to Murphy (the entire state of North Carolina), 1, 2, 47, 48, 57, 58, 254. See also Murphy to Manteo

Mash (push), 72, 74, 84, 116, 117, 235

Mater (tomato [also tomater]; Mountain Talk, Outer Banks Brogue), 144

Meddlin' (interfering), 84

Meehonkey (a game that is a cross between hide-and-seek and Marco Polo; Outer Banks Brogue), 10, 61, 68, 82, 114–11

Might could (may be able to, but noncommittal [also might should, useta could, might oughta]), 50, 93, 98, 149

Mommuck (harass, bother; Outer Banks Brogue), 70, 100, 115

Mommuck (mess up; Lumbee, Appalachian), 70, 143, 234

Mouf (mouth; African American English), 90

Sodee (soda; Outer Banks Brogue, Mountain Talk), 113, 145

Sorry in the world (doing badly, not feeling well; Lumbee), 234

Spell (a period of time or weather; Mountain Talk), 143

Squall (a violent gust of wind with rain; Outer Banks Brogue), 116

Swamp Indian (lower-class Lumbee; Lumbee), 233

Swanny (swear), 84, 86, 235

Sweet tea (tea sweetened with sugar), 83, 86, 98

Tar Heel (North Carolina native), 3, 5, 6, 11, 13, 18, 42, 80, 98

Tarpin (turtle or terrapin; Mountain Talk), 143

Taters (potatoes), 74, 144

Throwed (threw; Mountain Talk), 147

Till (to, as in, "It's quarter till five"; Mountain Talk), 38

To (at, as in, "She's to the house"; Outer Banks Brogue, Lumbee), 63, 71, 119

Toboggan (knitted hat; Mountain Talk), 27, 64, 70

Token (a sign or presage of death; Outer Banks Brogue, Lumbee), 82, 115, 235. See also Toten

Tomater (tomato [also mater]; Mountain Talk, Outer Banks Brogue), 144

Toten (spirit or ghost; Lumbee), 234, 235

Touron (an outsider or nonnative; a derogatory term for tourists [combination of the words "moron" and "tourist"]; Outer Banks Brogue), 11, 64, 115

Twicet (twice; Outer Banks Brogue, Mountain Talk), 113, 145, 237

Up the beach (off the island to another island; Outer Banks Brogue), 64, 115, 116

Varmint (objectionable creature, mischief maker [also varment]; Mountain Talk), 143

Vittles (food for a meal; Mountain Talk), 38, 64, 143

Wadn't (wasn't), 90

Water fire (light that occurs in water [on the sound] from decaying plant matter; Outer Banks Brogue), 64

Ways (track for pulling a boat out of water; Outer Banks Brogue), 64

Weren't (wasn't, used for past-tense singular; Outer Banks Brogue, Lumbee), 3, 63, 65, 69, 71, 118, 149, 163, 175, 177, 229, 230, 239, 240, 285

Whenever (at that time; Mountain Talk), 2, 71

Whistle pig (groundhog; Mountain Talk), 143

Whoop and holler (hide-and-seek; Outer Banks Brogue), 115

Whopperjawed (crooked, not straight or square), 10, 71, 84, 86, 117. See also Antigoglin; Catterwampus; Cattywampus; Sigogglin

Winard (into the wind; Outer Banks Brogue), 115

Winder (window; Outer Banks Brogue, Mountain Talk), 113, 144

Woodser (outsider or nonnative; Outer Banks Brogue), 10, 64, 115

Woodses (woods; Lumbee, Appalachian English, Outer Banks Brogue), 237

Y'all (plural form of "you"), 14, 81–83, 86, 98, 146, 264

Yander. See Yonder

Yankee (person not from the South), 64, 79, 80, 81–82, 94

Yerker (mischievous child; Lumbee), 234

Yonder (over there, more distant; arrive, here, as in, "Yonder comes Billy" [also yander]; Mountain Talk), 74, 144

Index of Subjects

Page numbers in italic type indicate illustrations or audio/video enhancements.

A-prefixing, 38, 92–93, 119, 120, 128, 137, 146–47, 229, 237

Accent, 19, 20, 53, 80, 124, 217, 230, 244, 248, 262, 264, 274, 276, 281. *See also* Dialect

Accommodation, linguistic, 76, 98, 126, 175, 211, 248, 282, 284

African American English: attitudes toward, 152–53, 154–56, 278; development of, 153, 159–60, 170–73, 173–76, 176–79, ; grammatical features of, 156–57, 169–70, 173, 175; influence of African languages on, 3, 171, 172, 173, 175; influence of integration/contact with whites on, 168, 174, 175–76; influence of slavery on, 34, 43–44, 87, 171–73; influence upon Latino English (*see* Latino English); influence upon Lumbee English (*see* Lumbee English); myths about, 156; pronunciation features of, 168, 169, 170, 175, 235, 236; the term, 154; vocabulary of, 172–73, 177–78

African Americans: arrival of, 29, 30, 31, 40–44, 87, 160, 167; on the coast, 153, 158, 158–59, 160–63, 163–66, 287; culture of, 52, 152, 179; emancipation of, 44, 48–49, 161–62; identity of, 179–82, 194; migration of, 45; in the mountains, 43–44, 55, 56–57, 153, 159, 166–68; urban/rural distinction among, 158–60, 168–69, 177–78

African diaspora, 87, 172, 173

Ahoskie, N.C., 11–12

Albemarle, N.C., 11, 74

Albemarle Sound, 3, 49

Algonquian Indians, 25, 197, 199–200

Algonquian language family, 25, 27, 108, 109, 197–98, 198, 199, 200, 202, 204, 225, 226

Alleghany County, N.C., 26, 247

Allegheny Mountains, 132. *See also* Appalachia

Amadas, Philip, 26

American Indian English, viii. *See also* Lumbee English

American Indian languages, viii, 3, 19, 27, 183–84, 197–204, 198, 206–9, 211–12; endangered, 184, 195, 199, 200, 212; place names from, 12, 26–27, 108–9, 183, 210; preservation of, 184, 201 (*see also* Cherokee language: revitalization of); words from, 27, 197, 204; culture of, 27, 197; demographics of, 192, 193–94

American Indians: and European contact, 25–27, 27–28, 36, 131, 183, 199, 200, 201, 203–4, 204–6, 210, 214; federal and tribal recognition of, 193–94, 202, 222–23, 241–42; identity of, 193–94, 185–88; outsider perceptions of, 192–95, 196–97, 208; removals of, 192, 194, 204, 206, 208, 209, 210–12, 214 (*see also* Cherokee Removal Act; In-

Huguenots. *See* French Huguenots
Hurricane Floyd, 51–52
Hyde, Edward, 30
Hyde County, N.C., 65, 158–59, 159, 160, 162, 163, 170, 174–75, 176–79, 244, 262

Idiolect, 278
Indentured servants, 32, 35–36, 43, 171
Indian (term). *See* American Indian
Indian Normal School. *See* Pembroke, University of North Carolina at
Indian Removal Act, 204
Inflectional *be*, 67, 69, 71, 72, 230, 239, 240
Injun (term), 185, 189–90
Intensification model of language shift, 123, 177, 230
Iroquoian Indians, 25, 197, 200, 201, 204–5
Iroquoian language family, 25, 197–98, 200, 202, 204
Isogloss, 8, 65, 72

Jackson, Andrew, 203–4, 210
Jack tale, 143
Jacobs, Harriet, 49, 50
Jacobson, Lenore, 282
James I (king of England), 29
Jamestown, Va., 28–29, 29, 43, 109
Johnston, Gabriel, 31, 32, 37, 42

Kitty Hawk, N.C., 101, 106
Knick, Dr. Stanley, 240
Kudzu, 14, 59–60, 60

Language: attitudes toward, 13–18, 91, 98, 155–56, 278, 285; change in, 14, 39–40, 96, 100, 106, 108, 114, 121–27, 135, 175, 176, 288–90; contact, 42, 43, 44, 66, 76, 176, 226–27; as culture, 13, 15, 17, 18, 19, 20, 73, 124, 126, 152, 197, 212, 215, 240, 242, 260; diversity of, 18, 25, 66, 277; endangered, 111, 123–26, 184, 195, 199, 200, 212; fami-

lies, 197–98; importance of, 272–76; as means of control, 33–34; preservation of, 19, 150–51, 184, 258, 286; recession of, 248; shift, 171, 259, 260; symbolic value of, 11, 14, 19, 121, 123, 126, 134, 146, 181, 241, 242, 267–69. *See also* Dialect
Latino (ethnic label), 249–52, 252–53
Latino English: development of, 259–60, 261–62, 264–66, 268, 269–70; grammatical features of, 261, 263–65; influence of African American English on, 265, 266; influence of southern English on, 264, 266; language variety in, viii, 260–70, 270; pronunciation features of, 261, 265; rhythm/timing of, 261, 265–67
Latinos in North Carolina, 83; immigration of, 2, 45, 243–48; population of, 52–53, 214, 216, 245, 246, 247, 252, 254; in Raleigh, 247, 262, 268
Leatherman, Dr. Stephen, 102
Lee, Robert E., 5
Lexical geography, 63
Linguistic discrimination, 271–76, 281–82, 255, 273–74, 284–85
Linguistic equality, 281–85
Linguistic gratuity, principle of, 285
Linguistic profiling, 275, 281–82. *See also* Linguistic discrimination
Linguistic subordination, principle of, 14–15
Linking verb *be* absence, 166, 169, 170, 173, 175, 177
Linn Cove Viaduct, 135–36, 136
Litefoot (rapper), 208
Little Washington. *See* Washington, N.C.
Locational *to*, 63, 71, 119
Locklear, Heather, 220, 222, 233
Lost Colony: celebration of, 48; history of, 20, 27–29, 48, 49, 101, 226, 229
Lumbee English: grammatical features of, 63, 69, 149, 229, 230, 237–40, 240; history of, 227–30, 241–42; influence

of African American English on, 227, 230, 239–40; language variety in, viii, 18, 126, 232, 241, 241–42, 231–32; preservation/celebration of, 240–42, 271, 286; pronunciation features of, 228, 235–37; vocabulary of, 10, 11, 141, 230, 233–35, 235

Lumbee Indians: history of, 222–23, 225–27; Homecoming celebration, 220; identity of, 221–22, 222, 233; the term, 223–24; tribe, 191, 216–18, 220

Lumber River, 217, 218, 221, 224

Lumberton, N.C., 224

Maggie Valley, N.C., 139, 287

Manteo (person), 26, 27, 199

Manteo, N.C., 1, 11, 47–49, 56–57, 101, 107, 110, 254, 286

"Manteo to Murphy," viii, 1, 2, 47, 48, 49, 57, 58, 254

Maritime Underground Railroad. *See* Underground Railroad

McCreery, Scotty, 89

McCrory, Pat, 89

Means, Russell, 187, 188

Mergers, vowel, 59, 60, 90, 98, 113, 267, 276

Mexican (ethnic label), 249. 250, 251, 252, 268. *See also* Latino (ethnic label)

Mill Bridge, 36

Mississippian Indians, 25, 26, 197, 202–3

Montgomery, Dr. Michael, 34, 35, 69, 137

Moonshine, 128, 129–30, 287

Moravians, 36, 39–40, 45

Mountains. *See* Appalachia

Mountain Talk: grammatical features of, 3, 63, 71, 128, 137, 146–50, 229; influences/development of, 3, 37, 39, 128, 134–35; the label, 130, 134; preservation of, 131, 136–37, 150–51, 277, 286, 287; pronunciation features of, 61–63, 69, 85–87, 90, 113, 128, 134, 137, 144–46, 189; vocabulary of, 9, 10, 64, 69–72, 82, 85, 115, 128, 131, 137, 140–46, 175

Mount Airy, N.C., 16, 92

Mount Mitchell, 131

Multiple negation, 170

Munster, Sebastian, 24

Murphy, N.C., 1–2, 47–48, 55–57, 168, 254

"Murphy to Manteo." *See* "Manteo to Murphy"

Muscogee Indians, 197, 203–4, 205, 206, 210

Muskogean language family, 202–4

Nags Head, N.C., 106, 108

Native American (label), 186–88. *See also* American Indians

Neuse River, 27, 32, 183

New Bern, N.C., 32, 33, 44, 45

Newport, Christopher, 29

North Carolina Language and Life Project (NCLLP), 2, 10, vii–viii

North Carolina State Fair, viii, 8, 10, 12, 271, 272, 279–80, 280

Oakland controversy. *See* Ebonics

O'Cocker, 117. *See also* Hoi Toider

Ocracoke, N.C., 3, 11, 100, 101–2, 104, 106, 118, 123, 127, 155; celebration/preservation of, 286, 287; demographics of, 111, 114; history of, 110, 160, 161–62, 164, 244; immigration to, 243–46; isolation of, 106–7, 107–8; language shift on, 123, 124, 240; local words of, 10–11, 61, 68–69, 82, 115, 116–18; the name, 27, 108–9

Ocracoke brogue. *See* Outer Banks Brogue

Old English, 82, 101, 129, 133, 140–41, 227. *See also* Elizabethan English

Old North State, 4, 6, 11, 46

Old Salem, 40, 41

O'Neal, Rex, 104–5, 107

Onslow Bay, 101

Orange County, N.C., 39

Outer Banks: celebration of, viii, 286, 287, 290; dialect region of, 3, 8, 18, 23,

43, 50, 65, 69, 100, 102, 141, 177, 233, 237, 249; history of, 24, 31–32, 101–3, 106, 111, 109–11, 141, 160–62, 163–64, 226, 229; the name, 103–4, 109

Outer Banks Brogue: grammatical features of, 3, 18, 63, 65, 71, 72, 118–19, 149, 175, 229, 237, 239; history of, 105–7, 107–11; language use conventions in, 119; performance of, 104–5, 105; preservation of, 104, 106–7, 111, 121–26, 126–28, 131, 177, 290; pronunciation features of, 13, 61, 62–63, 65, 66, 70, 72, 85–87, 89, 105, 106, 111–14, 121, 145, 166, 175, 229, 235; the term, 103–4; vocabulary of, 10, 64, 68, 70–71, 72, 100, 110, 115, 114–18, 141, 234, 235

"Over the left talk," 121. *See also* Talking backwards

Overt prestige, 17

Oxendine, Linda, 240

Palatines. *See* German Palatines

Paleo-Indians, 25

Pamlico County, N.C., 26, 65

Pamlico Sound, 24, 27, 37, 50, 116, 183

Parsons, Roy, 287

Parton, Dolly, 193

Pasquotank, N.C., 11–12, 26, 41

Pea Island, N.C., 101, 161

Pee Dee Indians, 203

Pee Dee River, 27, 224

Pembroke, N.C., 217, 218, 220, 230, 241

Pembroke, University of North Carolina at, 191, 219, 240, 286

Pidgin, 30, 173–73. *See also* Creole

Piedmont: as dialect region, 2, 9, 31, 52, 53–54, 65, 68, 72, 132, 155, 201, 229, 232, 233; history of dialect in, 31, 32, 33, 37, 45, 53, 87; the name, 54; pronunciation features of, 61, 63, 70, 87, 90, 145; settlement of, 32, 36, 39, 45, 135; vocabulary of, 64, 70–71

Piedmont Triad, 78–79

Pin-pen merger. *See* Mergers, vowel

Plantation South, 35, 41–42, 50, 63, 85, 87, 171, 173, 236

Plural -s absence, 63, 71, 167

Pocahontas, 29

Polish language and settlers, 21, 29, 45, 257, 259, 284

Political Linguistic Slumming, 89

Pory, John, 29

Possessive -s absence, 170, 173, 175

Princeville, N.C., 44, 51, 51–52, 153, 154, 170, 286

Qualla Boundary. *See* Cherokee Indians: reservation/land of

Queen, Mary Jane, 128, 129, 130

Queen's English. *See* Elizabethan English

Quotative *be like*, 85, 146, 265

R-loss, 50, 62–63, 70, 85, 87–88, 97, 170, 236

Raleigh, N.C., 12, 19, 29, 52, 54, 74, 79, 88, 80, 89; dialect of, 76, 87, 90, 153, 170, 177; urbanization of, 52, 78. *See also* Research Triangle

Raleigh, Sir Walter, 26, 27, 187, 199

Raleigh-Durham area. *See* Research Triangle

Raleigh News and Observer, 1, 18, 89, 123, 208

Redskin (term), 189, 190

Red Thunder Cloud, 201–2

Remote time *been*, 170, 173

Research Triangle, 78–80, 132

Revolutionary War, American, 4, 31, 38, 40, 42, 183

Rhodhiss, N.C., 11, 54, 54–55

Roanoke Indians, 26, 199

Roanoke Island, 1, 26, 48–49, 101, 104, 107, 110, 162, 225

Roanoke Marshes Lighthouse, 48

Roanoke River, 49

Robeson County, N.C., 12, 61, 201, 216–27, 230–32, 234–36, 239, 241, 284

Made in United States
Orlando, FL
07 September 2022

22122793R00207